OUTDOOR RECREATION SAFETY

Neil J. Dougherty IV

The State University of New Jersey

Editor

a publication for the
School and Community Safety Society of America

Human Kinetics

This text is dedicated to the past, present, and future professionals and volunteers who enrich our lives through the provision of safe and exciting outdoor recreational activities.

Library of Congress Cataloging-in-Publication Data

Outdoor Recreation Safety / Neil J. Dougherty IV, editor.
     p. cm.
    "A publication for the School and Community Safety Society of America."
    Includes bibliographical references and index.
    ISBN 0-87322-944-4
    1. Outdoor recreation--United States--Safety measures.
I.   Dougherty, Neil J.   II. School and Community Safety Society of America.
GV191.625.098   1998
790'.028'9--dc21
                                 97-38948
                                  CIP

ISBN: 0-87322-944-4

Acquisitions Editor: Scott Wikgren **Developmental Editor:** Andrew Smith **Assistant Editors:** John Wentworth, Phil Natividad **Editorial Assistants:** Jennifer Hemphill, Laura Seversen **Copyeditor:** Denelle Eknes **Proofreader:** Sue Fetters **Indexer:** Prottsman Indexing **Graphic Designer:** Robert Reuther **Graphic Artist:** Tom Roberts **Photo Editor:** Boyd LaFoon **Cover Designer:** Chuck Nivens **Photographer (cover):** © New England Stock/Peter Cole **LineArt Illustrator:** Keith Blomberg **MacArt Illustrator:** Jennifer Delmotte **Printer:** Braun-Brumfield

Human Kinetics books are available at special discounts for bulk purchase. Special editions or book excerpts can also be created to specification. For details, contact the Special Sales Manager at Human Kinetics.

Printed in the United States of America

10 9 8 7 6 5 4 3 2 1

Human Kinetics
Web site: http://www.humankinetics.com/

United States: Human Kinetics
P.O. Box 5076
Champaign, IL 61825-5076
1-800-747-4457
e-mail: humank@hkusa.com

Canada: Human Kinetics, Box 24040
Windsor, ON N8Y 4Y9
1-800-465-7301 (in Canada only)
e-mail: humank@hkcanada.com

Europe: Human Kinetics, P.O. Box IW14
Leeds LS16 6TR, United Kingdom
(44) 1132 781708
e-mail: humank@hkeurope.com

Australia: Human Kinetics
57A Price Avenue
Lower Mitcham, South Australia 5062
(088) 277 1555
e-mail: humank@hkaustralia.com

New Zealand: Human Kinetics
P.O. Box 105-231, Auckland 1
(09) 523 3462
e-mail: humank@hknewz.com

Contents

Preface

During the last decade we have observed an increasing demand for outdoor recreational activities. As a result, our programs have grown in number and breadth. Interest in adventure activities that have the perception of risk is particularly high and has resulted in developing such activities as white-water rafting, rappelling, and wall climbing within traditional recreational delivery systems. Sometimes professionals, in their zeal to capitalize on the growing interest in an activity, will overlook fundamental safety measures. Such omissions often result in needless injuries. Moreover, ours is a litigious society. The increases in the level and perception of risk in recreational activities have, therefore, resulted in many lawsuits and great demands for appropriate and effective safety practices.

In the past, there were individual sources with safety guidelines for some activities and instructional resources that included general safety guidelines. However, there was no single source providing practical safety guidelines for the broad range of activities that the recreation professional must address. The School and Community Safety Society of America has developed this text to fill that void. It provides, in a single volume, the essential information a program manager must have to safely implement the array of activities in outdoor recreational settings. In addition to its direct reference application for current practitioners, the text fulfills an essential requirement in training recreational managers. Whether the material is in a course on risk management or out-

door recreational programming, understanding and applying the content is essential to the preparation and job performance of professionals of the following types: outdoor recreation specialists, sport management specialists, camp directors, and college and university recreational services personnel.

Part I of the text addresses the principles essential to injury prevention and risk management in all recreational activities. Here you will find the legal principles necessary to sound program management and defensibility. We also include guidelines for dealing with medical emergencies, which are unwanted but foreseeable byproducts of any physical activity. Each chapter in part II focuses on the specific safety procedures applicable to a particular recreational activity. We will address four areas of concern in each chapter: A section on environmental conditions details the requirements for providing safe facilities and equipment. A section on supervision outlines procedures to effectively observe and control the individual participants. We also discuss selection and conduct of the activity, and this section provides techniques for reducing risk by controlling the nature of the activity itself. Finally, a section on administration presents details of planning, staff training, organizing, and paperwork that impact the safety of the activity. Because the purpose of this text is to facilitate delivering safer activity programs, we frequently provide practical checklists and outlines. Each chapter, therefore, will assist you in developing safe programs and formulating effective preactivity safety checks.

There is no doubt that most outdoor recreational activities entail a variety of physical dangers and it is not my claim that this book provides you with all the tools you need to be safe in the outdoors. Outdoor activities are, however, valuable endeavors that we can and should make available to as many people as possible. Although we cannot eliminate all hazards or injuries from these activities, neither can we accept unnecessarily or improperly dangerous situations.

We must take appropriate moral and legal responsibility for the well-being of the participants entrusted to our care. We must carefully calculate those risks that participants undertake to minimize the likelihood of injury and to enhance the recreational experience. Routinely applying the principles in *Outdoor Recreation Safety*—as well as continuing to expand your knowledge of safe practices through safety courses and other publications—will help you reduce participant injuries and will diminish the fear of litigation as a result of injuries that do occur.

ACKNOWLEDGMENTS

I would like to extend my deepest appreciation to the individual authors who collaborated on this project. Chosen because of their knowledge and prominence in their fields of expertise, they are without exception very busy people. Thankfully, they also share a level of professional dedication which led them to accept yet another major task, not for some sort of tangible gain but because they truly value and take satisfaction from their efforts to promote safe and enjoyable recreational activities. Without them, this project would still be a good idea under discussion in our board meetings.

I am also very grateful to Andy Smith and the entire Human Kinetics family. Andy blended a great deal of support and cooperation with an unyielding demand for excellence, which has resulted in a book of which we are all very proud.

Finally, I would like to thank Jan Houtman for retyping, reorganizing, and handling correspondence, all of which were very necessary to bring together nineteen separate chapters into a single coherent text. Her efficiency and most especially her patience are greatly appreciated.

Neil J. Dougherty
Editor
President, School and Community Safety Society of America

PART I

Principles of Safety in the Outdoor Environment

Safety in the Outdoor Environment

Kenneth S. Clarke

According to estimates prepared by the National Safety Council (National Safety Council 1996), there were nearly 5,000 reported injuries resulting from approximately 8,700 boating accidents in 1995. Personal watercraft accounted for 79 of the 836 reported boating deaths. There were, in addition, an estimated 130,300 swimming injuries and 1,700 fatalities, with 107 hunting fatalities among the 1,200 reported injurious accidents. Based on the estimated numbers of participants and injuries in 1995, about 1 in every 180 ice-skaters suffered injuries requiring emergency care. For roller and in-line skaters the odds were 1 in 204 participants, and about 1 in every 457 water-skiers ended up in the emergency room.

These figures represent estimates based on a variety of reporting sources. They cannot, therefore, be taken as accurate predictors of relative injury rates, nor can they tell us how many reported injuries could have been prevented using proper safety principles. They do, however, clearly illustrate the potential for serious injury in outdoor recreation and, thus, the critical need for each of us to eliminate needless hazards.

DEFINING THE TERMS

When looking at the title of this book, *Outdoor Recreation Safety,* there are two terms that stand out—safety and outdoor recreation. Although subsequent chapters deal with specific safety issues in depth, let's examine how we define the two terms that provide a basis for the discussions to come.

Outdoor Recreation

Outdoor recreation consists of activities undertaken outdoors in open environments, with little to no control imposed on the environment. As opposed to outdoor activities like miniature golf, riding a roller coaster, or bungee jumping, the outdoor recreation we discuss in this book deals with activities in which the participants must apply their own controls (insofar as this is possible) without changing the

In outdoor recreation, participants must apply their own controls without changing the environment.

environment. Because the participants apply the controls, our need for strong knowledge of safety is all the more important.

Safety

Obviously, there is no way to completely avoid risk in outdoor recreation. The outdoor environment has many natural hazards that we must respect. Often these hazards are beyond the participants' control in outdoor recreational activities. However, along with natural hazards come the more controllable hazards associated with flawed judgment, physical and mental inability to perform the activity, inadequate skills of the participant and provider, poor planning, poor equipment, and so on.

This book prepares the recreational leader and the potential participant for the dangers in the natural environment, but we gear it specifically toward recognizing and controlling preventable hazards. As such, for the purposes of this text, we define safety as a conscious and intelligent attempt to minimize hazards we must face to gain the enjoyment, satisfaction, and physical and mental fulfillment of participating in the outdoor recreational activity. There are no guarantees that injuries will not occur, but there are ways to reduce the likelihood of injury and to minimize the impact of those injuries we cannot avoid.

PARTICIPANT CONTROLS

Above all, safety in outdoor recreation activities rests with the participants. We cannot entirely control the outdoor environment, and although professionals who provide the activity or the equipment bear a legal obligation to meet reasonable standards, barring cases of negligence (see chapter 2), it is the participants who must adapt to the equipment and environment to meet their goals. The responsible participant has four general categories of safety controls to consider (see table 1.1).

None of these four controls is subservient to the others, but the last, adapting, primarily determines the outcome of an outdoor recreation venture. One appealing aspect of entering an outdoor environment is expecting something new but not knowing specifically what it will be. Using your new experience as you continue to gain experience keeps the old pro as excited about outdoor recreation as the new rookie—if you see it as a control as well as a benefit. Those who seek to eliminate unnecessary hazards in the

Table 1.1
FOUR GENERAL CATEGORIES OF SAFETY CONTROLS

CATEGORY	DEFINITION
Planning	Envisioning the tasks you intend to pursue outdoors, the hazards of those tasks, and the measures to best control those hazards.
Training	The effort you take to ready your body for the environment and the activity required to meet the tasks while you participate in that environment.
Practicing	The effort you take to gain skill to perform those tasks effectively.
Adapting	Envisioning "what if," considering backup planning, then using the experience you have gained.

Table 1.2
SPECIALIZED CATEGORIES OF SAFETY CONTROLS

CATEGORY	DEFINITION
Good equipment	Selecting, fitting, practice in using, and maintaining the equipment recommended for the tasks of your outdoor recreation experience.
Good teaching	The exposure to and demonstrated compliance with the advice of an expert in the tasks you select. Sincerity is not enough.
Good facility	Selecting the outdoor environment where you can perform the intended tasks with reasonable understanding and confidence.
Good medical care	A functional awareness of resources for first aid, emergency evacuation, and medical care of injuries and illness experienced while outdoors.
Good teamwork	Relying on and coordinating with all others who share your intentions to gain the benefits and control the hazards of participating outdoors.

outdoor recreation experience have five specialized control categories to consider (see table 1.2).

By adhering to the general controls and the controls specific to outdoor recreation activities, participants can understand how to responsibly perform such activities. Gaining specific knowledge of their chosen activity and its particular controls, reasonably safe participation will become possible. This does not necessarily mean that the participant's safety depends totally on individual initiative. As stated previously, providers of recreational equipment, activities, and so on can be held accountable for the product or service they provide. To properly meet their professional obligations, providers too must adhere to reasonable safety controls.

PROVIDER CONTROLS

Few can enjoy recreating outdoors without relying on the courtesies, products, and investments of providers. From your hiking boots, to the air in a scuba tank, to the trail master's supervision, the odds would favor the participant who knows the quality and

appropriateness of what the providers are offering.

The concept of calculated risk includes the presence of, or reliance on, what the provider offers so the participant can pursue the activity. Is my horse appropriate for my skill? What happens if the sea-kayaking guide's first aid kit is not equal to the need or is lost after capsizing? As much as our discussion of outdoor recreation safety hinges heavily on the participant, the provider must assume a certain responsibility as well. Typically, provider controls fall under the headings of equipment and services, both of which, when used properly, enable the participant to undertake the recreational activity as intended.

Provider equipment (e.g., clothing, tools, transportation) consists of the materials that participants use to aid them to perform the activity. Provider services (e.g., guides, transportation, food, supervision within the accessible environment) consist of the provider's oversight that helps individuals participate in the recreational activities. Individuals primarily employ equipment and services to enable their participation, but

SPECIAL CONSIDERATIONS

We expect that a backpack producer understands the needs of backpacking in the wilderness and a scuba instructor understands the physiology of respiration. It is now becoming expected that providers of outdoor recreational opportunities understand the nuances of psychological and sociological influences on the person performing the outdoor recreational activity. Three important types of people to consider are individuals with disabilities, individuals who are HIV positive, and victims of sexual abuse. Provider sensitivity (and adaptation) to the specialized concerns of such individuals has become as important a safety concern as good ropes for a rappeller and thorough planning for a week-long hiking expedition.

The Americans With Disabilities Act (ADA)

The ADA has brought significant responsibility upon those providing opportunities for public participation in recreational programs. Unlike concurrent expectations for employment and accessibility, the regulations governing required availability of recreational programs for persons with a disability are not yet clear in detail, and challenges continue to be argued at the local level. Until these regulations become more clear, the provider can work with the following principles:

1. Show individuals with special needs the same respect and courtesy you show to all participants.

2. The provider is expected to accommodate those who are qualified to participate in the promoted activity. Consequently, in defining the personal characteristics necessary for the challenges, it is best to have valid criteria for determining qualification or disqualification. Many high-risk outdoor recreational programs already have much of this in place through testing and training. However, the provider should formally document it.

3. The provider can only judge a person according to a formal, individualized test. By performing such a test, the provider avoids bias and discrimination based on the disability alone.

4. The provider must help the person with special needs become qualified if reasonable accommodation will make participation in the activity possible. This is not meant to incur financial hardship on the providers or to change substantively the programs they offer, but this principle will be examined if the provider judges the applicant unqualified.

Human Immunodeficiency Virus (HIV)

Because of the possibility of being infected with HIV, although the risks may be minimal, another important concern for providers and participants of recreational pursuits is individuals contacting the blood of others. Procedures for handling exposed blood are well defined in the controlled workplace, and athletic programs now have formalized policies for handling bleeding athletes and the blood on floors, uniforms, and so on. Although injuries in which blood is shed are not uncommon in outdoor recreational activities, formalized policies do not often exist for these activities. To determine the best protection for those performing first aid, start with the principles and processes required by OSHA for those exposed to blood in the workplace. You can then adapt these principles to the activities you are providing or performing.

continued ☞

Sexual Abuse

Awareness of sexual abuse has become widespread in recent years. From the workplace, to public areas, to private homes, our society has become sensitive to sexual misconduct and its effects on the victims. There is no reason to believe that outdoor recreational pursuits are immune from these problems. Providers of such services must include formal hiring, training, and supervisory practices that make every reasonable attempt to keep abusive persons from participating in or overseeing their programs. Providers must undertake visible formal policies and practices with periodic evaluations. Local law enforcement and social service agencies can provide guidelines and resources for evaluating potential employees and participants.

they must always evaluate them for safety. If an accident occurs, the safety of the equipment or services provided will frequently be called into question, and liability issues may arise.

INSURANCE

We advise participants and providers to select a competent agent or broker in their community and listen to their counsel about risk of exposure to costs, with and without available insurance. The critical principle of insurance is that, for a price, the insurance company accepts a transfer of financial responsibility for selected risks. You should regard it as any other form of safety control: a mechanism to improve the odds against having a negative experience for which you are financially accountable. Although you can purchase many forms of insurance, two types are relevant to outdoor recreation safety—medical and liability.

Medical Insurance

The purpose of medical insurance is to pay, on a no-fault basis, costs of treatment and professional care for injuries incurred as a participant or employee. The service provider may require the participant to assume all medical costs of any injury experienced while participating in the activity being provided, or the provider may furnish coverage for the medical costs the participant's personal, employment, or family medical insurance doesn't cover. It is in the participant's

and provider's interest that some medical insurance is in place that would bear most of the costs of an injury experienced while performing a recreational activity. The participant's calculated risk for undertaking the activity increases if subsequent medical costs would produce hardship. Particularly relevant to the provider is the fact that many negligence claims arise when the medical bills exceed the provisions of existing medical insurance. This underlines the need for effective medical coverage and introduces the need for liability insurance.

Liability Insurance

The purpose of liability insurance is to prevent the insured from assuming the financial responsibility of a claim of wrongful injury and to pay costs on its behalf if necessary. All insurance payments are subject to the provisions of the policy that was purchased. In choosing a company from which to purchase liability insurance, an A rating means that the risk of company default of payments to the injured participant is minimal. Purchasing insurance from a company with less than an A rating is a risk that you should not take. Do your homework before taking out a policy. By paying attention to the details now, you may avoid problems later.

CONCLUSION

There is little doubt that participants in outdoor recreational activities will encounter a variety of hazards. In spite of their best efforts

You can purchase many forms of insurance, but medical and liability are particularly necessary for outdoor recreation.

and those of the professionals who provide goods and services, some risks will remain. We cannot, however, be too blase in accepting these risks. We must accept full moral and legal responsibility for our actions. We must carefully calculate those risks that we undertake to minimize the likelihood of injury and must justify them in light of the legitimate goals of the activity. We must take a proactive approach to eliminate *unnecessary* risks.

The chapters that follow will assist the provider and the participant in recognizing potential hazards in the outdoor recreational setting and in developing effective procedures for risk management.

BIBLIOGRAPHY

National Safety Council. 1996. *Accident facts*. Itasca, IL: National Safety Council.

Chapter 2

Legal Responsibility for Recreational Safety

Betty van der Smissen

Many individuals restrict offerings or participation in outdoor recreation because of their perception of risk and fear of liability. Thus, the ogre of liability in our litigious society prevents them from having the exhilaration of participation and a possible peak experience. This fear of liability is based in ignorance regarding legal concepts of liability and responsibilities for safety. It is not the activity that brings liability, but the leaders, participants, and the manner of conducting the activity. We might say, "not activity hazards, but people hazards!"

This chapter presents some legal concepts to determine the conduct of these sports and define the operational practices that will guide you should injury occur and a lawsuit be filed.

LEGAL CONCEPTS OF NEGLIGENCE

Most injury-related lawsuits are based in negligence. Negligence is an unintentional *tort*, an act or wrong by one person against another, whereby that person is injured. The one injured usually brings the lawsuit against not only the person who was the *tortfeasor* or wrongdoer, but also the corporate entity, that is the agency, organization, institution, association, or private enterprise sponsoring the activity, the provider of the service, program, or opportunity. The corporate entity is held liable under the *doctrine of respondeat superior*, "let the superior respond." If the person, whether employee, intern, or volunteer, conducting the activity is acting within the scope of authority and responsibility, then the negligence or wrongdoing is *imputed* to the corporate entity. This sometimes is referred to as vicarious liability. If not, then the individual stands alone and is solely liable for the injury. For example, a coach used the school's driver education car to take some athletes to a clubhouse for a social activity. This was against school policy, which was consistently enforced, hence outside the scope of the coach's authority. The coach had an accident, injuring one of the athletes severely—he stood alone for liability for the injury; the school was not liable. Thus, it behooves every employee,

intern, and volunteer to act within the guidelines of the entity providing the activity, and the entity should set forth such guidelines. So, the first responsibility for recreational safety is to provide operational guidelines for specific sports and activities offered, such as those we discuss in subsequent chapters.

Components of Negligence

There are four components of negligence, all of which must occur (or be proven) for an injured party to recover compensation for injury. These components are

1. a duty is owed to protect the injured from unreasonable risk of harm;
2. the act breaches the standard of care required to protect the participants;
3. this breach is the proximate cause of the injury; and
4. damage does, in fact, occur.

Whether there is a duty owed depends on whether there is a special relationship between the provider and the injured person such that there is a responsibility to protect. Usually there is no question, as the relationship is obvious, such as leader-participant, instructor-student, supervisor-user, and so on. Similarly, there usually is no issue as to proximate cause or actual damage. Most lawsuits focus on the act, specifically, the standard of care with which the activity was conducted—hence, the importance of this book.

Standard of Care

When you accept a responsibility, the expectation is that you will perform the task according to the standards or practices of the profession. The standard is not determined by the background of the person in charge, such as experience, skill, credentials held, maturity, or knowledge. There is not one standard for beginners and inexperienced persons and another for persons of some years of experience. The participant is owed a duty to be protected from unreasonable risk of harm, regardless of who is in charge. The standard is situational and has three determinants. They include the desirable professional practices for (a) the environmental conditions, for example, heat and humidity, a class V river, lightning, a muddy field, and snow conditions. The leader must be able to read the environment, know how to protect the participants, and provide safe facilities and equipment; (b) the nature of the activity, whether simple or complex, and the supervision it requires; and (c) the type of participants, whether exuberant youngsters, persons with physical or mental disabilities, and so on. The person in charge must understand the clientele and know how to work with them in relation to their participation, including prerequisite skills, instructions, warnings, and safety rules. It is appropriate for every professional to keep up on the best, and latest, practices of the profession. See later section on operational practices and procedures as a source of risk reduction (page 21) for further detail on each determinant.

DEFENSES AGAINST CLAIMS OF NEGLIGENCE

If you are sued for negligence, what are the defenses? There are three types—immunity, contract, and elements of negligence.

Immunity

Some individuals, agencies, and associations by statute may be immune from liability in certain situations and for certain types of acts. There are three types of immunity statutes, related to volunteers, specific activities, and governmental entities.

Volunteers

About two-thirds of the states have immunity statutes for volunteers servicing nonprofit organizations, and in 1997 Congress passed similar legislation. These statutes encompass recreation and sport, with about one-third of these states having laws specific to sport volunteers. Although the volunteer is immune from liability for ordinary negligence, the corporate entity (nonprofit organization) remains liable. However, the volunteer retains personal liability for gross negligence, that is, acts that exhibit considerable lack of care or are aggravated, manifesting disregard for the duty owed, but falling short of willful conduct to injure.

What about the Good Samaritan laws? Do they protect employees or volunteers? In all but a couple of states, the laws do not protect because the leadership owes a duty to not expose participants to unreasonable risk. The Good Samaritan laws apply to citizens who see an injured person and the need to render aid, and do so out of the goodness of their heart and not because they have a duty toward the person in need. Such Good Samaritans are immune from ordinary negligence, but not gross negligence.

Both the volunteer and the Good Samaritan statutes, in essence, reduce the standard of care that must be provided. However, this is sometimes questioned, particularly when volunteers have direct leadership responsibilities, even though the sponsoring entity does retain liability for ordinary negligence. The volunteer statutes have been enacted to encourage citizens to help with community activities and not be afraid of being held liable for any small miscue.

Specific Activities

In some states there is legislation directed toward specific activities, for example, the Ski Responsibility Acts, which provide that managers (corporate entity) retain the liability for injuries as a result of operations' negligence, such as ski lift malfunction, but places responsibility on skiers for knowing how to ski and skiing within their ability. Nearly all states with downhill skiing have such laws. Several states also have a law relating to equestrian activities. These statutes provide for a shared responsibility, but there is no reduction in the standard of care.

Many private landowners have been reluctant to let individuals use their property for recreation. To open private lands to outdoor recreation, nearly all states have enacted Recreational User Statutes. These statutes provide that landowners permitting use of their property for outdoor recreation gratuitously owe a duty to such users the same as toward a trespasser, that is, they must only warn of

Nearly all states with downhill skiing have laws placing responsibility on skiers for knowing how to ski and skiing within their ability.

ultrahazardous conditions. This is a reduced standard of care from that owed by a landowner to either an invitee or licensee. Many state statutes now are applicable to public lands as well. Of course, if an agency or association sponsors an outing on such lands, although the landowner has limited legal responsibility, the sponsoring entity retains full legal responsibility for conducting the outing.

Governmental Immunity

Depending on the state, there may be governmental immunity for public agencies (e.g., schools, municipalities, state institutions) under Tort Claim Statutes or Hazardous Recreation Statutes. Even in those states that provide immunity from negligent acts related to the conduct of activity, there usually is liability for dangerous conditions of facilities and areas. However, many Tort Claims Statutes do provide for either authorization of insurance coverage or indemnification of employees acting

within the scope of their responsibility, that is, the reimbursement for any damages award levied against them.

Contract

Liability may be shifted to another corporate entity or individual by contract, that is, the defense that the liability has been contracted to another. There are three types of contracts useful as a defense: independent contractor, user rental agreement or lease, and participant waiver.

Independent Contractor

An independent contractor is a person or company that contracts to provide a particular service and assumes the risks incurred in providing the service. For example, a school or an agency camp may hire a private enterprise to conduct a spelunking experience. The private enterprise, then, assumes the legal responsibility for proper conduct (i.e., the equipment, the leadership, the instruction, et al., for the experience). Similarly, a school or YMCA may employ as an independent contractor a scuba instructor to teach a class. The school gives that instructor full autonomy about how to teach the class, and in return, the instructor assumes the legal responsibility for any injury that may occur during instruction.

Lease or Rental Agreement

When you have a facility or equipment others would like to use, the lease or rental agreement should require an insurance certificate or include an indemnification clause wherein the user contracts to assume the risks of use. Also, it is well to specify (a) that the users (sponsors of activity) are responsible for properly conducting any activities for which they use a facility; (b) that the equipment users know how to use the equipment; and (c) for both facilities and equipment, that the sponsors or users are responsible for participant behavior. If a person rents skis or an ATV, assuming the skis or ATV are in good condition, then the rental agreement should indicate that the person renting is responsible for knowing how to use the equipment and for any injury caused by misuse, particularly injuries to another. The person at the rental desk should be careful not to assess an individual's ability to use the equipment, particularly skiing a particular slope or traversing a specific trail. To assess capability puts you in a different relationship and increases the legal responsibility—a responsibility ill assumed, for it requires knowledge of the individual's skill and the state of the natural environment. Equipment rental shops should restrict their role to just renting equipment, unless they have qualified instructional staff. Many equipment shops do offer qualified instruction and expeditions. Facilities must be in good condition, without dangerous situations. If a club rents an ice-skating rink or other facility, the agreement should provide that the club is responsible for the conduct of the activity and the behavior (discipline) of the participants.

Exculpatory Clause or Waiver

An effective defense with adults is an exculpatory agreement, commonly referred to as a waiver or release. It is a contract between the provider and the participant not to hold the provider liable for injuries during participation due to the ordinary negligence of the provider. Most states hold waivers valid, if properly written. The participant must be of majority age and must sign voluntarily. Two principles for valid waivers are (a) explicit, clear language that covers all aspects of activity participation and injury from whatever cause, including negligence; and (b) the format provides conspicuous exculpatory language in a print size that is easily readable. Usually waivers are not held valid for minors because they cannot contract, although they may ratify a waiver (contract) upon reaching age of majority. For minors, see the section on Warnings and Participation Forms.

Challenging the Elements of Negligence

The defense most commonly used relates to the elements of negligence. The defendants try to prove that one or more elements were not present and, thus, there would be no liability. Because there seldom is an issue about whether there was a duty owed or whether the act was the proximate cause of damage, most defenses focus on the second element of negligence, the act. However, there are two considerations. One is whether the act met the prerequisite standard of care. We discuss this in greater detail in the Operational Practices for Risk Reduction section, which sets forth legal responsibilities regarding the determinants of the standard care—the environmental conditions, the nature of the activity and its supervision, and the participants and conduct of activity. The other consideration relates to (a) foreseeability of an unreasonable risk and (b) the plaintiff or injured person, specifically, whether the injured assumed the inherent risks of participation (primary assumption of risk) and whether the injured's conduct contributed to the occurrence of the injury (contributory fault).

Foreseeability

Foreseeability is essential to liability. Under the circumstances that existed (the situation), could a reasonable and prudent professional have foreseen, expected, or anticipated that the participants (the injured) would be exposed to an unreasonable risk of injury? If no, then that is a defense, as there is no need to perform an affirmative act to protect the participants if there is no foreseeable risk. If yes, then there is a responsibility to act to protect the participants, and the standard of care test applies regarding negligence. For example, if there is lightning, a reasonable and prudent professional at an aquatic activity would foresee potential injury to participants and would act to get them out of the water. We must emphasize that the standard is foreseeability by a professional, not the ordinary person.

Primary Assumption of Risk

Primary assumption of risk, as a defense, is based on *consent* of the injured party and is a bar to recovery. There are three essential components of this consent.

First, the participation must be free and voluntary; the individual must not be coerced into participating.

Second, the individual consents only to those risks that are inherent in the activity, that is, integral to the activity and without which the activity would lose its character. For example, if a person were injured on the pool deck while doing flip-flops, such activity would not be considered inherent in swimming, but extraneous. Also, the participant does not assume any risks the provider's negligence causes, such as defective equipment or improper instruction.

The third component for valid consent has three aspects—the participants' knowledge of the activity, understanding of their own condition and skill, and appreciation for potential injuries. Under ordinary circumstances, the participants do not assume any risk for either activity or condition of which they are ignorant, and thus, the leadership must make every effort to properly inform and instruct. Knowledge of the activity relates to the nature of the activity and the basics for participating. The understanding aspect is more difficult for leaders, as the participants need to apply their knowledge about an activity and its conditions to their capabilities. They must assess their skill, competence, physical and emotional condition, and understand the prerequisite safety precautions. Appreciation extends to awareness of possible accidents and resultant injuries, minimal and catastrophic.

In 1994 the consent concept was extended to include open and obvious field conditions played upon voluntarily. The courts have been pretty tough on leadership requirements regarding these three aspects. Providers can communicate with participants using methods other than oral instructions, such as information on the application form or the agreement to participate; videos; and printed information on brochures, handouts, and signs. If participants are experienced and highly skilled, they should know the risks when they consent to participate. On the other hand, if participants are beginners, it is important that the provider give appropriate instructions and supervision as the participants are learning. Some providers feel that they should offer only beginning activities to reduce liability. The opposite is true! Because experienced persons participate in advanced activities, they have a greater knowledge about, understanding of, and appreciation for the activity, thus assuming the inherent risks to a greater extent than would a beginner.

Primary assumption of risk can be either *implied*, knowing the risks you will encounter you participate anyway, or *express*, usually a written or oral statement saying specifically that the inherent risks are assumed. In some literature and in a few jurisdictions, the term *express assumption of risk* may be used synonymously with waiver; however, as described previously, a waiver is a contract not to hold the provider liable for ordinary negligence and has nothing to do with inherent risks. The term *informed consent* is often used synonymously with primary assumption of risk, for the participant must be informed, then consent. However, informed consent originally came from the medical and research fields in which the clients or subjects are informed of the treatment to be done and what results they can expect.

The concept of consent includes open and obvious field conditions played upon voluntarily.

Secondary Assumption of Risk or Contributory Fault

Secondary assumption of risk is contributory negligence or fault. It is not acceptance of the inherent risk of the activity, but addresses the *conduct* of the participants, that is, the participants' behavior that contributes to their own injury. Such behaviors could include, for example, failure to obey rules, follow directed skill progression, heed warnings, properly use safety devices, or follow the sequence of instructions the leader gives. Previously, in most states, any amount (even one percent) of contributory negligence or fault by the injured would bar their recovery of any award. However, in the '90s less than half a dozen states still adhere to this point of view, and most states have merged contributory fault into the concept of comparative fault (see next paragraph). If the provider (defendant) expects to use contributory fault as a defense, two practices are essential. First, the provider must set forth appropriate rules, give proper warnings, and instruct as to desirable practices. The participant must be informed orally or in writing about the expected behaviors. Second, the provider must document what was informed, their practices in conducting the activities or services, and the participants' behavior (see phase 4 of the Risk-Management Plan on page 21).

Concept of Comparative Negligence or Fault

Comparative negligence is not a defense, but a method of apportioning a damages award—how much should the plaintiff receive? The jury determines the percentage of contributing fault accorded to the plaintiff and the percentage of fault for all defendants aggregated; then they make the award according to the ratio of fault. There are two methods provided in the statutes. About a dozen states have what is called the pure form, that is, the plaintiff can receive whatever percentage the defendant is at fault. For example, if the plaintiff was 10 percent at fault and the defendant 90 percent, the plaintiff would receive 90 percent of the award. If the plaintiff was 80 percent at fault, he or she would receive only 20 percent of the award.

The other method is the 50/50 approach. Some states say if the plaintiff's fault is not greater than the defendant's fault, then the plaintiff may receive the proportionate amount of the award, otherwise no award. Other states will say the plaintiff's fault must be not as great as or less than the defendant's to receive any pro rata share (plaintiff does not receive an award if fault equal to that of defendant). Whichever the statutory language, the basic holding is that when the plaintiff contributes more than 50 percent of the fault toward the injury, there is no award. For example, if the plaintiff is 60 percent at fault, there is no award. However, if the plaintiff is 40 percent at fault and aggregate defendant fault is 60 percent, the plaintiff receives 60 percent of whatever the jury awards. Thus, the defendant seeks to establish as much contributory fault on the part of the plaintiff as possible, making a documentation system essential.

Warnings and Participation Forms

The foregoing defenses are based on the participant having enough information to make an informed decision when agreeing to participate and assume the inherent risks (consent) or to engage in the activity in a certain manner, notwithstanding the circumstances (conduct). Integral to providing this information are warnings and participation forms.

The essence of warnings is communicating to the participant about how to engage in the activity; what is required not to have unreasonable risk of injury; or the condition of the physical environment, including equipment, and the modifications to prevent injury. For effective communication there are four criteria for a warning:

1. Obvious and direct, cannot be subtle

2. Specific to the risk, cannot be generalized but must indicate the risk

3. Comprehensible, in language understandable by the one being warned

4. Location, at the point of hazard or when such warning is appropriate

Warnings can come in various forms—oral instruction, video, pictures, posters, literature, signs, and so on—and it is often desirable to use more than one form for emphasis and reinforcement. Warnings are essential in all aspects of programs and services, for example in skill instruction, appropriate use of safety equipment, and condition of the snow or river. Chapters on individual sports and activities provide further guidance regarding specific warnings. Because warnings about how to participate to reduce the likelihood of injury are so pervasive, it is understandable that they have become one of the most important risk-management tools. However, to use warnings for showing contributory fault, the agency must keep complete records of the warnings and the related conduct of the participant, specifically when the participant ignores or violates the warning.

You can use agreement to participate forms both to provide information about the nature of the activity and possible injury, which provides a basis for assumption of risk defense, and to present expectations for the participant, an element in contributory fault. Usually an agreement to participate has three sections. The first provides a description of the activity so participants have some knowledge of it and understand what capabilities they must have to appropriately participate. It also sets forth in a positive way the possible consequences of participation in terms of injury. The second section presents the expectations placed on the participants. This includes behavioral policies, such as those related to drugs, drinking, and smoking; discipline; and group responsibilities. The third section has special requirements, such as any skill level or physical condition, equipment and clothing, physical disability or health concerns (e.g., food allergies, bee stings, recent injuries not healed yet, or stamina not at full strength), and insurance. Although agreement to participate forms are not contracts and should not be confused with waivers (exculpatory clauses), they do give some documentary evidence of an effort to inform and educate the participant.

Even though participants may be minors, they should sign the form, because they must understand the activity and the expectations about activity performance and general behaviors. To have parents also sign serves as an excellent public relations device. You can include these forms as part of a regular application or registration form. Legal information does not need to be on a separate sheet, as waivers often are.

How do the liabilities for negligence and understanding legal concepts translate into operational practices? Although we provide the specifics of each sport or activity in subsequent chapters, there are some general guidelines for meeting our legal responsibilities.

THE RISK-MANAGEMENT PLAN

It is imperative that each agency, organization, business enterprise, or other corporate entity have a risk-management plan, up-to-date and implemented (for more information, see van der Smissen 1990). There are many operational policies and practices that can ameliorate the liability or exposures. There are two types of risks—the risk of financial loss and the risk of personal injury. Of course, in addition to personal injury causing individuals pain and suffering, they often lose the ability to perform work-related tasks and personal enjoyment tasks, all of which usually translates into damages or financial loss.

However, a risk-management plan is more than safety checklists. It is systematically analyzing your operations for potential risks or risk exposures, then establishing a plan to reduce such exposures. It is an integrating opportunity, integrating many operational elements. It is not only a diagnostic process of preventive actions that forestall problems, but also a tool to encourage professional practices; to increase employee and volunteer pride, loyalty, productivity, and confidence; and to foster good stewardship of human, financial, and physical resources. A risk-management plan has four phases:

1. Analyzing risks and determining approaches to control

2. Obtaining policy statements from the policy makers

3. Establishing the desirable operational practices identified and formatting them into a plan

4. Implementing the plan

Phase 1. Analysis and Control Approaches

There are three steps in this phase: (a) identifying risks, (b) estimating the frequency and severity of each risk, and (c) determining alternative approaches to controlling the risks. Initially, do this phase extensively; then review and update it annually as circumstances change, that is, changes in activities or services, financial circumstances, personnel, and so on. You can do the first two steps together. Identify all the actual and potential risks in the operation of activities and services. Then, as you identify the risks, assess the frequency of exposure and potential severity of injury. Characterize frequency and degrees of severity with descriptive words, such as high or often, medium or infrequent, low or seldom for frequency; and vital or high, significant or medium, insignificant or low for severity. In addition to supervisors and administrators, involve maintenance and program staff because they will have direct contact with the clientele; keep up the facilities, areas, and equipment; and conduct activity.

Once you have identified the risks and determined frequency and severity, examine the alternative control approaches. There are four basic approaches: avoidance, transference, retention, and reduction.

Avoidance

Avoidance is choosing not to offer or to discontinue an activity or service because of the perceived liability. Avoidance is often used when someone does not want to offer an activity or service, claiming the liability risk is too great. This is an improper use of avoidance! You should use it when you cannot provide the appropriate standard of care for leadership, facilities, and equipment, causing the activity to have an undesirable risk exposure. It is not the activity that is hazardous, but the way it is conducted. If you cannot provide the appro-

priate standard of care, but you want to make the activity available, you can hire an independent contractor, thus transferring liability.

Transference

Transference shifts the liability to another. The most common way is by purchasing insurance. You pay a premium and the insurance company accepts financial responsibility for the insured potential risk that you may incur. Insurance usually is carried on risks of high severity, but low frequency, such as catastrophic injury. For transference by other contracts, see Contract under the previous section, Defenses Against Claims of Negligence (page 13).

Retention

Retention is accepting the risk within the budget and financial structure of the agency, organization, or business enterprise. This method is used primarily for risks of low severity but high frequency and could include losses such as for minor physical injuries by providing emergency first aid treatment.

Reduction

The previous three approaches relate primarily to potential financial risks or losses, and you may use all three at the same time for a specific risk, depending on its nature. The fourth approach, reduction, addresses reducing exposure through operational management. You should approach all risks from both financial and operational management perspectives. We address this approach in detail in a later section, Operational Practices for Risk Reduction.

Phase 2. Policy Statements

Along with reviewing alternative approaches to managing risks, the corporate entity's governing body will need to establish policies on which to base the operating procedures (phase 3). For example, what is the policy regarding medical insurance for injuries—is the family's insurance to be used first? Will the organization cover minor treatment expenses (e.g., ambulance, emergency room, or emergency first aid)? Should the agency carry only catastrophic insurance or should a participant (or parents) be required to carry such? What is the policy relating to travel? Will no personal participant cars be used, no staff cars be used, only school or agency vehicles be used, all transportation be hired through independent contractors, or will the organization get insurance to cover staff and volunteer cars? There will not be many, but there are some important policy decisions if there are alternative choices.

Phase 3. Operational Practices and Procedures

In this phase, the operational practices and procedures are established for reducing risk exposure. These must be detailed and specific to all aspects of operations. Because this is the focus of this book, we discuss it more fully in the next section.

Phase 4. Implementing the Risk-Management Plan

A risk-management plan encompassing risk analysis, policy statements, and operational procedures is of little value unless you implement it. Every organization should have a person designated as the risk manager. This would be a specific position in larger organizations or an assigned responsibility in smaller organizations. To say all personnel are responsible for risk management is inadequate because "everybody's business is nobody's business!" A specific person must be responsible for overseeing risk management. The director may want to take this responsibility. It is this person's job to see that a risk-management manual (which for many of our outdoor sports and activities is "the manual") is prepared and regularly updated. Personnel must not only receive in-service training in risk-management practices and procedures, but also implement them. The interaction between employees, administrators, and supervisors should assure this implementation.

The risk manager also is in charge of the information and documentation system, which is an integral part of all risk management. Specifically, it should have available data for risk management, such as participant forms, health

and accident forms, operations information, program documents, and so on. There also should be a public relations program directed toward risk-management concerns. It is well known that an irritated, unsatisfied customer or participant is prone to bring legal action more quickly than a person for whom you show concern and take care of minor expenses. The risk manager must also monitor the plan, including systematically evaluating and adjusting the effectiveness and cost efficiency of risk-management practices, as appropriate. Neither implementing the plan nor assessing its effectiveness just happens.

OPERATIONAL PRACTICES FOR RISK REDUCTION

Legal responsibilities for recreational safety are implemented as part of a systematic effort to reduce liability risks. Because it is the standard of care that usually is at issue in a lawsuit, give special consideration to the determinants of that standard of care, as described in the first part of this chapter. They are (1) the environmental conditions, (2) the nature of the activity and its supervision, and (3) the type of participants and the fitting (selection, conduct) of the sport or activity to them. Again, the chapters on individual sports and activities will provide great detail for these three determinants.

Environmental Conditions

There are three dimensions to environmental conditions. The obvious one for outdoor recreation is the natural environment. The leadership must know about the elements of the natural environment essential to a particular sport, not only to protect participants from exposure to unreasonable risks but also to heighten the quality of their experience. The natural environment may be the primary challenge in a sport, and it is important that the participants understand the environment for their comfort and to enable them to better care for their own safety. Participants must have enough knowledge about the outdoors to make informed decisions.

When the natural environment provides the challenge in a sport, safety depends on understanding what might happen and knowing how to deal with it.

A second dimension is equipment, and all outdoor recreation has specialized equipment, whether it is personal clothing and equipment or group equipment. Equipment must be appropriate to the activity and to the participant's size. There must be adequate protective devices and instructions on how to fit or use them.

Areas and facilities is the third dimension. Many sports and activities have specialized areas or facilities. Give special attention to the design of rest rooms and shower areas, architectural barriers for the physically disabled, and the layout of activity areas for safety and supervision. Also, diagram and assess vehicular and pedestrian traffic flow for ease of supervision and control (e.g., entry control and personal safety problems, such as hidden or dark areas). As to maintaining areas and facilities, remember, pre-

mises-related injuries are the responsibility of both the premises owner and the activity sponsor! A maintenance inspection system with records is necessary, including the following four aspects:

1. Ongoing, daily inspection as part of the job description
2. Formal, detailed checklist periodically used, dated, and signed
3. Critical parts inspection, needing a specialist to check condition
4. External evaluation—a pair of eyes not so familiar with the operation; may be paid consultant or exchange of services with another provider

How much time do you have to repair noted deficiencies? It depends on the density of use, the likelihood of an injury, and severity of injury, if one might occur.

© Mary Langenfeld

Supervision

Supervision is one of the most important legal responsibilities in conducting an activity. There are two types of supervision, general and specific. General supervision is that provided to oversee an activity or area, whereas specific supervision is that directly related to individual participant instruction. We address the latter in the chapters specific to a sport or activity. This section deals with general supervision. The focus is supervision of participants and areas or facilities, not other staff. There are seven functions of general supervision.

1. Supervisory plan
2. Behavior management
3. Rules and regulations
4. Identifying dangerous situations and conditions
5. Security
6. Care of injured and accident reports
7. Emergency plans

Formulating a supervisory plan is a critical function of supervision. You should write it and communicate it to the staff. Provide an in-service education program about responsibilities and personnel assignment, according to competence in the activity or function and suitability in handling participants. Designate the location and number of staff by areas of responsibility and pattern of circulation. Behavior management is a second important function. It includes discipline policy and procedures and crowd control for large events. However, policies and procedures also must address drug abuse, child abuse, intoxication, and antisocial behaviors. Establish a minimum of rules and regulations for the participants' safety. Communicate these to participants by various media, and enforce them consistently and fairly.

It is essential that the leadership receive the authority to add rules and regulations for specific situations that may arise, and the participants must be aware of this authority. Leaders must identify dangerous conditions and establish procedures for remedying them. There must be inspections to determine hazardous physical conditions. Also, the leaders must watch for participants engaged in activities in a dangerous manner. Another function of supervision is security (protection against criminal acts). Implement a security plan for the premises and for excursions, and consider the participants' safety from rape, kidnapping, robbery, shootings, and so on.

The care of the injured and emergency procedures are a sixth function, which we address in detail in chapter 3, Managing Medical Emergencies in the Outdoors. However, as part of a risk-management plan, the emergency procedure plan should include rendering first aid, emergency procedures following aid (e.g., emergency equipment; hierarchy of care; transportation arrangements; knowing location of emergency treatment permissions for minors; checking vehicles, routes, and insurance policies, if using participant's, etc.), disposition and follow-up, and media contact. Accident reporting forms and procedures also are integral to any risk-management plan. Distinguish accident forms, treatment forms, statistical reporting forms, and insurance forms and know the role of each. Table 2.1 includes information necessary for an accident form to be useful if you get involved in a lawsuit. Maintain accident records in the documentation system for a period equal to the state statute of limitations, plus two or three years after reaching age of majority. There also should be emergency plans, as appropriate, for disasters (tornadoes, fire, flood); runaway children; and external violence, riots, and demonstrations.

Participants and the Conduct of Activity

It is the legal responsibility of the leadership to understand the nature of the participants and to conduct the activity or sport in accord with this knowledge. One essential aspect of conducting the activity relates to the maturity and condition of participants, that is, their age, developmental stage, and size; physical, emotional, and social maturity; skill and experience; and mental and physical capability. Also, do they have a temporary condition, physical or emotional, or any permanent disabilities that relate to the specific activity? Consider the adequacy of instruction and learning progress,

Table 2.1
INFORMATION NECESSARY ON AN ACCIDENT FORM

CATEGORY	DESCRIPTION
Identification information	Full ID information on injured, person in charge, date and time of accident, event, witnesses and addresses, insurance.
Location of accident	Specific diagram.
Action of injured	What was the injured doing?
Sequence of activity	Relates to contributory fault — had injured done this activity before, had there been instruction, and so on.
Preventive measures by injured	What could injured have done to prevent injury? (Do not include what the provider could have done or it might be construed as an admission of negligence.)
Procedures followed in rendering aid	Keep good records of all procedures that were performed, as well as timing.
Disposition	What happened to the individual following the injury?

including skill with progression, safety instruction, courtesies, rules, and regulations of the sport or activity, and protective devices and equipment. The specific chapters give details regarding proper conduct of activity.

LEGAL RESPONSIBILITIES REQUIRE PROFESSIONALISM

After reading this chapter, you may say, "Oh, why bother? I can never fulfill all the legal responsibilities. It's just not worth the hassle!" Wait! Go back and review the responsibilities. Aren't you already doing most of the operational practices? The legal responsibilities are nothing more and nothing less than current professional practices, which all should be doing anyway. You can use this chapter as a self-assessment of your present practices checklist. Where do you excel? What needs more attention?

You should *not* fear the ogre of liability, but be confident in the quality of your operational practices so you can move forward positively and with enthusiasm. Be the best professional you can be and serve with pride! Do not deny youth or adults the opportunity to engage in challenging and exhilarating outdoor recreation because of your fear of liability.

BIBLIOGRAPHY

Dougherty, N., D. Auxter, A. Goldberger, and G. Heinzmann. 1993. *Sport, physical activity, and the law*. Champaign, IL: Human Kinetics.

Hanna, G. 1991. *Outdoor pursuits programming—Legal liability and risk management*. Edmonton, AB: University of Alberta Press.

van der Smissen, B. 1990. *Legal liability and risk management for public and private entities—Sports and physical education, leisure services, recreation and parks, camping and adventure activities*, 3 vols. Cincinnati: Anderson.

chapter 3

Managing Medical Emergencies in the Outdoors

Susan Skaros

Participation in outdoor activities is increasing by leaps and bounds. Most people participate for pleasure and relaxation, but others do so to live life on the edge. Organizations are being created to expedite and consolidate interest groups, develop training programs, and provide safety guidelines for outdoor activities. In spite of these efforts, people can and will become injured or ill while participating outdoors.

Insult of trauma or illness can be challenging at any time. Adding to it the impact of adverse weather conditions, remote locations, altitude while climbing or depth under water, difficult accessibility, and medical inexperience only makes the problem more complex. Even minor illnesses or injuries can become serious and possibly fatal when they occur under challenging conditions. For activity leaders this, as well as the risk of litigation, should be cause to reflect on their roles and responsibilities.

This chapter is not intended to provide a how-to course in treating medical emergencies. Its purpose is to provide program personnel with procedures that can help minimize risk, prepare for adverse situations, and cope with a medical emergency, so everyone can be better assured of having a safe and pleasurable outdoor experience.

All activity leaders should enroll in formal first aid training programs and maintain current training and certification. There are many programs available for that purpose. In addition, there are several good, basic resource books such as *Medicine for the Outdoors* by Paul S. Auerbach, MD (1986). It covers a variety of medical problems and is small enough to fit into a pack or duffel. It also lists several activity-specific resources.

PREVENTION

The *FIRST* first aid for every activity is *prevention*. Most accidents, no matter what the setting, are preventable. If all participants make a concentrated effort to ensure adequate training and supervision, dependable equipment, and appropriate surveillance, the number of medical emergencies can significantly diminish. Then we can direct further efforts toward dealing with the potential mishaps and unexpected situations that do occur. The outcome of this preparation is a fun and safe experience. Steps that help activity leaders and participants prevent medical emergencies include the following:

• Obtain first aid and cardiopulmonary resuscitation (CPR) training, as well as specialty safety and emergency training geared toward the specific activity. Maintaining a current certification and conducting ongoing training and emergency drills under controlled circumstances better prepares participants for dealing with emergencies.

• Continually do scheduled equipment maintenance and repair, assuring a safer activity. Check all equipment before use, and have broken items repaired or missing ones replaced. Following use, make the same check for repairs or replacement before storing.

• Maintain surveillance throughout the activity by experienced and well-trained leaders. This involves, first, continuous and consistent observation of all participants while they are engaged in the activity and, second, active intervention to maintain safe standards of involvement. Depending on the activity, this may range from one individual for an advanced group to a one-on-one system for beginners or participants with special needs.

• Maintain ongoing supervision by experienced, qualified, currently certified individuals. They are responsible for ensuring a continuous process and implementation of safety guidelines, communication, and emergency procedures.

TRAINING

Activity leaders and supervisory personnel should have at least current general first aid and CPR certifications. Ideally, all participants should receive this training. It is imperative that no activities occur without at least one person in the group being certified in this training. Several organizations offer first responder (Emergency Medical Technician level) courses geared toward handling emergencies in the

© Cheyenne Rouse

Ongoing equipment maintenance and repair can help avoid injuries.

outdoor environment. This level of training is necessary for activities occurring in remote areas or those areas far from professional emergency responders, such as local emergency medical services (EMS) assistance. Agencies such as the American Red Cross and the National Safety Council offer basic first aid courses. The Red Cross offers an advanced course (Responding to Emergencies), which addresses outdoor activities, and their When Help Is Delayed course trains participants in what to do in case of delayed professional rescue response. First responder courses are offered by the Red Cross (Emergency Response), National Safety Council (First Responder), and many community colleges. The American Heart Association, National Safety Council, and the Red Cross provide multilevel CPR courses. Many groups encourage their members to become trained as instructors in these courses to better facilitate training other members.

Activity-specific training, such as cave extrication for spelunkers, ski patrol for downhill skiers, hunter safety courses for hunters, and lifeguarding for aquatic personnel, should also be undertaken. Often, nationally recognized organizations such as the U.S. Coast Guard, National Rifle Association, Professional Association of Diving Instructors (PADI), and the Wilderness Medicine Society offer activity-specific programs and materials. You can find addresses for these organizations in many outdoor and wilderness medicine books and by contacting activity-specific organizations.

Managing outdoor medical emergencies may mean doing no more than stabilizing and keeping the victim comfortable, calling for appropriate help, and preventing further injury to the victim or to the rest of the participants. The purpose of having individuals with advanced training is not to extricate or carry out a rescue. It is to recognize that a medical emergency does exist and be able to act appropriately to minimize the severity of that emergency. Activity leaders who have specialty extrication and rescue training may be able to expedite getting the ill or injured person to medical care. However, individuals should never attempt extrication and rescue if it will further endanger the victim or other group members.

Require activity leaders and supervisory personnel to participate in regularly scheduled in-service training sessions about safety and dealing with medical emergencies. Monthly programs are ideal. Also, encourage activity participants to use these opportunities. In-service programs should contain both didactic and experiential training. In-services can include activity-specific training techniques, practice, and emergency procedures.

PREPARATION

In addition to first aid, emergency response, and CPR training, the most important mechanism outdoor activity leaders and participants can have is a plan for handling emergencies. An *emergency action plan (EAP)*, a term used by the American Red Cross in its health and safety courses, describes the steps for responding to an emergency in a given area and activity. It designates the responsibilities each team member has. A good example of an EAP is found in chapter 9, Waterfront Safety, the chapter by Sue Grosse. Practicing this plan using various emergency presentations, with members alternating their roles, should be a regular, ongoing part of in-service training. In addition, include copies of the EAP format in all first aid and emergency response kits, and distribute them to all activity participants. It is essential that everyone have a working knowledge of the plan and of their responsibilities during an emergency.

All activities, whether entry level or advanced, need an EAP, leaders with first aid training, a defined chain of command, and activity structure. The following steps will help accomplish this:

• Establish safety guidelines for the activity, and ensure all participants are willing to accept and adhere to them before engaging in the activity.

• Determine who is in charge for medical problems and emergencies. Many outdoor activity participants have a strong denial of personal illness or injury. They may be unwilling or unable to realistically determine their level of impairment. At no time should the ill or injured person determine whether medical care, evacuation, or removal from the activity should occur, even if he or she has the most advanced level of medical training. The person in charge would also function as a safety observer. This role includes monitoring other group members for potential problems (e.g., the need for rest or additional fluids, time to put on more sun protection, or time to stop the activity because of fatigue). Designate a backup person in case the in-charge person becomes ill or injured.

• Have a trip or activity plan, including where, when, how, and with whom the activity is going to occur.

• Have a contact person who is not participating in the activity but who knows names, phone numbers, vehicle license plate numbers, and emergency contact persons for all participants. This person should have a copy of the activity plan, routes to and from the activity site, emergency rescue phone numbers, and anticipated date and time of return. Call any changes in the trip plan to this person, who serves as the liaison between activity members and their families. It is also prudent on extended trips to periodically keep in contact with this person.

• Require all participants to carry a copy of their health history, name and phone number of their personal physician, medication list, and a list of allergies with them in a waterproof, sealed bag. The activity leader should also keep a copy.

• Be sure the charge person is aware of individual medical problems. He or she should not only know what the problems are, but also know what to do to assist individuals in caring for themselves. This may mean being trained in how to administer emergency epinephrine shots to people allergic to bee stings, how to give nitroglycerin tablets under the tongue for people with heart disease, or when to give sugar or insulin to a diabetic. These skills are not taught in routine first aid courses and may entail specialized training from the individuals or from their health care providers.

• Gear the intensity and complexity of the activity to the skill level of the participants. Everyone should be physically prepared through prior conditioning and mentally prepared through training before engaging in activities. Organizations offering these activities to the public should explain and practice basic skills. They should then keep the activity at an appropriate level.

• Know the emergency rescue resources (EMS, U.S. Coast Guard, National Park Service, Sheriff's Department, Ski Patrol, etc.) for the areas in which the activities will be occurring. Also give this information to the trip or activity contact person.

• Know how to access the emergency rescue system. Not all areas use a 911 emergency program.

• Have the appropriate equipment for accessing the emergency rescue system, be it marine radio, citizen's band radio, cellular phone, and so on. Just taking the precaution of including emergency phone numbers and several quarters and dimes in each first aid and emergency response kit could be life saving. Be sure to replace any used coins at the end of each trip.

• Require participants to bring an extra set of medication to give to the group leader or keep in a pack separate from their own in case something happens to their pack.

• Have a backup plan should an emergency result in loss of equipment and personal gear. Activity leaders need to have a good knowledge of emergency care and survival procedures. First aid training or resource books don't cover every circumstance, and books can easily be at the bottom of a river or chasm. This includes first aid as well as wilderness survival (i.e., identifying edible and hazardous plants and foods). The more remote the activity area, the more skilled activity leaders must be in

survival skills. Rescue may easily be days off and miles away.

• Have personal and group first aid equipment and rescue gear, including backup signaling devices such as whistles, mirrors, flashlights, aluminum foil, and flares. Smoke flares are effective for helping rescue aircraft determine wind direction. This will facilitate landing and extrication attempts. Each person should carry their own medications, including sunblock, bee sting kits, and so on. Each group should also have one or more first aid kits. If there is a risk of losing a kit, such as in a canoe capsize, include several kits in the group gear and disperse them throughout the group.

• Have skills in survival training when going into remote areas. Activity leaders for extended, remote trips need to know how to build emergency shelters, such as snow caves or branch shelters. They should be able to start a fire without matches and know how to build a smudge fire for emergency signaling. More and more amateur groups, many of which have a minimum of preparation, are engaging in outdoor activities. Personal gear can easily be lost or destroyed. Having training in survival skills can mean the difference between life or death.

• Preview the activity area to anticipate any problems or areas to avoid. Do this even if the area is familiar, because things change with seasons, weather, and natural growth and attrition.

• Know where to find the nearest emergency department or hospital for minor injuries and illnesses. A health care provider should evaluate any injury or illness that is not improving within 24 hours of onset.

• Know the location of special needs facilities, such as hyperbaric chambers.

• Contact, in advance, the appropriate authorities responsible for the activity area to alert them to what is happening and how many persons are involved. Give them a copy of the trip plan, including anticipated date and time of return. You might also ask them for recommendations about special equipment needs, special training, areas to avoid, and so on. Be sure to notify these authorities when the group has returned from the activity or is leaving the area.

Additional recommendations may be included based on the activity, intensity level, and location.

Staffing

One question that comes to mind is "How many trained people should be on an activity, and what emergency management skill level should they possess?" An axiom that you can apply is the more remote the activity and the farther from professional help, the more skilled emergency training is needed. Table 3.1 can assist activity leaders in decisions regarding trained personnel. It is a guide for determining the ratio of first aid trained individuals to number of participants and the level of first aid training needed according to intensity of the activity. There is a hierarchy of first aid training and experience. A more advanced activity requires individuals with more sophisticated training in addition to those with basic training.

Include a first responder trained person any time individuals with special needs (e.g., individuals with a physical impairment) or with specific medical needs (e.g., possible injections or administration of medications such as nitroglycerin or asthma inhalers) are participating. When groups are going into remote areas and when conducting advanced activities, the ratio of first responder trained individuals to participants should be closer to 1:5. Seriously consider including a physician, physician assistant, or nurse practitioner with wilderness emergency medicine training on these more challenging trips. We should emphasize, however, that even though some or all participants may have advanced first aid training, it is usually best, when possible, to leave rescue and extrication attempts to the professionals.

First Aid Kits

First aid kits and equipment are a standard part of all activity equipment. They can vary in size and composition depending on the background of activity leaders and the type of activity. Individuals or groups can make up the kits, or you can purchase them. Professionally made kits range from those containing only the bare basics to those including sophisticated drugs, suture kits, and surgical supplies. All kits should have personal protective equipment such as disposable gloves (vinyl preferable to latex because it is less likely to cause an allergic reaction), a pocket mask with dispos-

Table 3.1

RATIO OF LEADERS TRAINED IN EMERGENCY CARE TO NUMBER OF PARTICIPANTS

EMERGENCY ACTIVITY	BEGINNER ACTIVITY	INTERMEDIATE ACTIVITY	ADVANCED ACTIVITY
Basic first aid (BFA)	1 BFA:10 participants (at least 2 for each event)	1 BFA: 5 participants in addition to	all particpants BFA in addition to
Advanced first aid (AFA)		1 AFA:10 participants (at least 2 for each event)	1 AFA:5 participants in addition to
First responder (FR)			1 FR: 10 participants (at least 2 for each event)

able one-way valve, and a high-efficiency particulate air (HEPA) filter. They should also include a communication device such as a whistle.

Activity leaders, lifeguards, and personnel with first aid responsibilities should carry gloves, a pocket mask and valve, a whistle, some four-by-four gauze pads, and a roll of tape in a fanny pack. Individuals can wear this during activities without encumbering movement. They can then initiate resuscitative efforts and bleeding control immediately and safely without waiting for the group kit to arrive. Items in a group kit are presented in table 3.2. We use specific brand names in this table only as examples and do not intend to imply an endorsement. Modify kits based on the activity, group size, duration of the trip, and training level of emergency medical personnel. You

can obtain additional suggestions from specialty organizations and wilderness medicine resource books.

Spare blankets (wool or thermal), splints, and emergency flares should be available, although not necessarily in the kit. You can add equipment such as snakebite kits or oxygen according to the activity and training of supervisory personnel. You should probably not include resuscitative equipment (resuscitators, automatic defibrillators, and cardiac medications, for example) in wilderness activities. A person having a heart attack five days from medical help by canoe will either live or die. Having resuscitative gear along is unlikely to alter the outcome. First aid supplies are, at best, clean, not sterile. Therefore, first aid does not preclude the need for medical evaluation and treatment.

Table 3.2
ITEMS TO BE INCLUDED IN A GROUP KIT

☐ copy of the Emergency Action Plan	☐ tweezers
☐ Emergency phone numbers and change for pay phone	☐ triangular bandages
☐ pocket mask with disposable one-way valves and HEPA filter	☐ sealable plastic bags for disposing of contaminated materials
☐ whistle or other communication device	☐ matches—waterproof
☐ roller bandages of various widths	☐ elastic bandage
☐ gauze pads—2x2 inch and 4x4 inch	☐ sterile eye patches
☐ large bandages or trauma dressings	☐ adhesive bandages
☐ "butterfly" bandages	☐ moleskin
☐ sterile eyewash (saline)	☐ sterile eyewash (saline)
☐ non-allergenic soap	☐ film bandages like Op-Site
☐ aspirin, ibuprofen, acetaminophen, anti-fungal cream (Tinactin, Micatin)	☐ triple antibiotic ointment
☐ over the counter antihistamine	☐ topical anti-itch medicine
☐ alcohol and Betadine swabs	☐ tape—paper and plastic
☐ insulating blanket ("space blanket")	☐ anti-diarrheal medicine
☐ incident report forms, notebook, and pen or pencil	☐ antacid tablets
☐ safety pins	☐ scissors
☐ disposable vinyl gloves	☐ chemical cold packs
	☐ airways of several sizes
	☐ waterproof flashlight with fresh batteries

DEALING WITH MEDICAL EMERGENCIES

Everyone is at risk of developing illness or injury in any activity. People with preexisting medical problems, such as angina, diabetes, asthma, and epilepsy, even if they are well controlled, can become symptomatic with the stress of the activity. Conditions such as diabetes and circulation problems cause individuals to be much more prone to injury and infection from even minor wounds. Diabetics and people taking diuretics (water pills) are susceptible to dehydration. Seizure-prone individuals may have more severe injuries should they seize in the water or on rough terrain, such as while climbing or spelunking. Make additional efforts to protect these people. This is not to suggest people with chronic illnesses should not participate in outdoor activities, only that affected participants and activity leaders must be aware of potential problems and performance limitations.

Figure 3.1 is a chart listing medical problems commonly associated with each category of activity. Some activities may also have some specifically related problems. This chart is not, in any way, all-inclusive. Activity-specific organizations are a good resource for additional illnesses and injuries you should consider.

The more intense the activity, the greater the likelihood for serious injury. However, you can take measures to decrease the possibility of adverse events. You need to consider four areas: health, equipment, environment, and nutrition. Some recommendations include the following.

Health

Having to deal with health problems and injuries can turn a great outdoor experience into a nightmare. By being prepared for the worst, you can often avoid major problems. Require

Under the physical or mental stress of an activity, people with preexisting medical problems might become symptomatic.

a current health certificate annually on file for all participants. Also, prohibit all alcohol and mind-altering substances while engaging in any aspect of the activity. Individuals wishing to use these substances should save them for their return home or be prevented from participating. People requiring strong pain medication and medicines that can make them drowsy or impair thinking (narcotic pain medication, some allergy and cold medications) should not be allowed to participate until they can do so without being under the effects of the medication. In warm temperatures, alcohol and many medications can mask the signs of impending dehydration. In addition, they play a significant role in causing dehydration as well as impairing judgment and compromising physical abilities.

Prohibit ill or injured people from participating until they have completely recovered. They are not only more prone to reinjury, dehydration, and exhaustion, but also less able to do their part should an emergency occur. People who develop nausea, vomiting, or diarrhea are susceptible to dehydration and are unable to consume adequate fluids while in an outdoor environment.

Use PABA-free sunblocks with a high sun protection factor (SPF) and sunglasses with UVA and UVB protection to prevent sunburn. Try sunblocks before going on remote or extended activity trips to be sure there is no sensitivity to them. Avoid perfumes and bright clothes when climbing, camping, hiking, and fishing. These attract stinging insects which, at the least, leave an uncomfortable reminder of their presence and may cause death. Perfumes are found in soaps, deodorants, and skin lotions.

Allow sufficient time for acclimatization when engaging in high-altitude or hot-weather activities. Allot and enforce adequate decompression time when scuba diving. Ensure that all participants are conditioned appropriately before the activity, and schedule and take frequent, regular breaks for rest and fluids. In warm weather and during strenuous activity, participants should drink even if they don't feel thirsty. Intervals between breaks depends on the intensity of the activity, environmental conditions, and condition of participants.

Be sure to clean wounds thoroughly. No matter how small a wound may be, it is always susceptible to infection. Being outdoors means getting dirty, so clean wounds with soap and water and protect them from further contamination. Be sure all participants have current immunizations, especially tetanus. When going into foreign or remote areas, activity leaders should contact health authorities for immunization and prophylaxis recommendations (e.g., malaria) well before their departure date.

Equipment

Equipment is often essential to outdoor activity participation. Having equipment that is in good condition and fits correctly will make the activity safer and more enjoyable. Activity leaders must insist on appropriate protective clothing and equipment for all participants. For example, hunters should wear blaze orange and fishermen should wear hats and personal flotation devices (PFDs). Climbers, kayakers, white-water canoers, roller bladers, spelunkers, and cyclists should wear helmets. Every activity has its basic clothing and equipment needs that you must adhere to. Also consider proper protection from the elements, including long-sleeved shirts and wide-brimmed hats in sunny areas or down, Hollofil, and Polartec layers for cold-weather activities. Do not allow individuals without the proper equipment or clothing to participate. Activity leaders should be sure participants are familiar and comfortable with their equipment. Leaders should teach emergency procedures (clearing a water-filled mask, emergency releases, controlled falls) under controlled, well-supervised circumstances. Allow only trained and experienced individuals to carry firearms and large hunting knives. Keep all firearms with the safety in the on position. Do not load shells should into firing position until the weapon is readied for use. When walking with a firearm, it should have its breech open and shells removed. Keep knives sheathed or closed, and keep them in a pack rather than worn to avoid injury during slipping or falling.

TYPES OF MEDICAL PROBLEMS PER PHYSICAL ACTIVITY

Types of Medical Problems

Activities	Musculoskeletal — Extremity sprains, strains, fractures, dislocations	Neck injury	Back injuries	Facial injuries	Wounds — Contusions and abrasions	Lacerations	Punctures	Eye injuries	Blisters	Cold — Hypothermia	Frostbite	Heat and Sun — Sunburn	Heat exhaustion and heatstroke	Dehydration	Thermal burns and friction burns	Respiratory — Asthma	Inhalation injuries
Cold weather activities																	
Ice skating	•	•	•		•	•			•	•	•	•		•		•	
Downhill skiing	•	•	•	•	•	•		•		•	•	•		•		•	
Cross-country skiing	•	•	•		•	•		•	•	•	•	•		•		•	
Climbing activities																	
Rock and wall climbing and rappelling	•	•	•	•	•	•		•	•	•	•	•	•	•	•	•	
Mountaineering	•	•	•	•	•	•		•	•	•	•	•	•	•			
Spelunking	•	•	•	•	•	•	•	•	•		•	•			•	•	•
Wheeled activities																	
In-line and roller-skating	•	•	•	•	•	•		•	•			•	•	•		•	
Cycling	•	•	•	•	•	•		•	•			•	•	•			
ATVs	•	•	•	•	•			•		•	•	•	•	•			
Mountain biking	•	•	•	•	•	•	•	•	•			•	•	•		•	
Survival activities																	
Hunting and shooting	•	•	•	•	•	•	•	•		•	•	•	•	•	•		
Fishing	•			•	•	•	•	•		•	•	•		•	•		
Hiking	•			•	•			•	•	•	•	•	•	•	•	•	
Camping	•				•	•				•	•	•	•	•	•	•	•
Aquatic activities																	
Waterfront					•	•				•	•	•	•	•			
Sailing and small craft	•	•	•	•	•	•	•	•	•	•	•	•	•	•			
White water	•	•	•	•	•	•	•	•		•	•	•	•	•			
Towed water	•	•	•	•	•			•		•	•	•	•	•			
Personal watercraft	•	•	•	•	•			•		•	•	•	•	•			
Skin and SCUBA diving		•		•	•	•	•	•		•	•	•		•		•	•
Surfing and body boarding	•	•	•	•	•	•		•		•	•	•	•	•			

Figure 3.1   Medical problems arising from various activities.

Carbon monoxide

Hypoxia

Trauma

Abdominal and pelvis injuries

Chest wall injuries

Head injury

Crush injuries

Propeller injuries

Clothesline injuries

Motor vehicle accidents

Gunshot and arrow wounds

Animal bites

Psychological

Claustrophobia

Vertigo (dizziness)

Disorientation

Infections

Water borne

Athlete's foot

Swimmer's ear

Eye infections

Gastrointestinal

Aquatic

Drowning

Swimmer's itch

Stings and bites

Poisons

Plant

Insects

Snakes

Depth and altitude

Decompression illness

Nitrogen narcosis and oxygen toxicity

Ruptured lungs (pneumothorax and hemothorax)

Nosebleeds

HAPE and HACE

Environment

Changes in the environment can be sudden and drastic. What is initially a low-key, beginner activity can quickly become high risk. Activity leaders need to closely watch the weather and abort the activity or seek shelter at the first sign of deteriorating conditions. They should also avoid areas where animal attacks are likely. Some places, whether in the wilderness or underwater, may seem ideal for an activity, but if animal attacks have been reported in the area, postponement or changing location may be the wisest course. If someone gets bitten by a warm-blooded animal, consider the risk of rabies transmission. Obtain medical attention as soon as possible, even if the bite is minimal. Use caution in activities where the risk of poisonous snakes exists. Participants should be aware of the risk of snakebite and always look carefully before placing their hands or feet into a tent or sleeping bag, or putting on boots and shoes.

Nutrition

Activity participants are seldom aware of how much energy and fluids they are using. Activity leaders should provide plenty of high-energy, nutritious food with a high calorie content. Outdoor activities are strenuous. Participants should not be concerned about weight loss while they are engaging in them. Everyone should have a personal supply of high-carbohydrate foods, such as trail mix or Power Bars, and powdered fluid supplements, such as Gatorade, in addition to the group food stock. In some activities, such as high-altitude mountaineering, it can be difficult for participants to take in enough calories. Even though it may be tempting, activity leaders must ensure that participants avoid eating wild plants and mushrooms unless a knowledgeable individual has unquestionably identified them as safe for consumption.

The most important nutritional responsibility an activity leader has is to ensure a constant and sufficient supply of safe, potable water. Outdoor activity participants are at risk of developing dehydration, and leaders should ensure an adequate water supply. Waterborne bacterial, viral, and parasitic infections (traveler's diarrhea, hepatitis, Giardia, cryptosporidium) are always possible, especially in remote areas. Use water from government-inspected sites or sterilize water for the group.

This is by no means an all-inclusive listing. Rather, its purpose is to provide some general recommendations and encourage critical thinking and preparation. Specific brand names are not intended as an endorsement, but rather a familiar example.

The Occurrence of Medical Emergencies

In spite of the most arduous prevention, training, preparation, surveillance, and supervision, illnesses occur and injuries happen. When they do happen, the objectives are to stabilize and support the ill or injured person, get help, and keep the situation from worsening. First aid training emphasizes the following:

- Survey the area to be sure there are no hidden dangers and no one else can be injured while rendering aid.

- Perform an initial (primary) survey. Assess the victim's airway, breathing, and circulation (ABCs). Perform indicated life support.

- Stop, reassess the situation, and reassess emotions. Wilderness areas can be unforgiving when it comes to illness and injuries. Take time to reevaluate what has happened, how severe it is, and what the options are. There may not be a second chance.

- Perform a more in-depth (secondary) survey. Determine if there is other, less obvious bleeding that you need to control or possible fractures you need to immobilize. Perform indicated first aid.

- Treat for shock, even if it is not apparent. Participants in outdoor activities are usually healthy, vigorous individuals, so the symptoms of shock may not appear until the ill or injured person has deteriorated significantly. Reassess the victim periodically as shock can develop at any time.

- Assess for head, neck, and spinal injury. If the injury is one that carries this potential, stabilize the victim as if the injury does

DON'T PANIC

Outdoor activities are physically and emotionally challenging. That is what makes them so much fun. However, even the most healthy and stable adult can suddenly be faced with over-whelming *fear*. A gentle, downhill slope can appear as a sheer mountainside to a novice cross-country skier, or a canoer caught on a rock in the middle of a rapids may suddenly *panic*. Nothing may be physically wrong, but if these people are not quickly helped to regain control, a serious and probably injurious situation can develop. Checking out the course ahead, practicing skills such as clearing a mask underwater, and rappelling from progressively greater heights can help prevent these psychological emergencies, but they might still occur. When this does happen, clearheadedness and patience must prevail. Trying to push the frightened person or hurry through the situation will only make matters worse. Most important, minimize the external stimuli, instructions, and commands. Frightened people are already overstimulated and unable to sort out productive, helpful suggestions and actions.

exist, even if he or she seems all right.

- Immobilize known or suspected extremity fractures.
- Document what happened, where it happened, and what care you are giving. Pass this information on to the professional rescue personnel at the time of the call. Continue to document the victim's status, vital signs, level of consciousness, change in condition, and change of care until you turn him or her over to rescue personnel or medical care.
- Call for professional rescue and transportation if there is any risk of making the victim worse or having others injured while transporting the individual.
- Move the victim only if staying put will cause him or her further danger. This would include fire, prolonged immersion, severe heat or cold, or unstable surroundings, such as mud slides or avalanches.
- Identify or describe snakes and insects that have inflicted venomous bites.
- Refrain from giving anything by mouth unless the injured or ill person is fully conscious and rescue is not imminent.

Abiding by these basic steps increases the likelihood the ill or injured person will have a positive outcome. Bear in mind, however, some injuries and illnesses are so severe, even the most sophisticated care will not alter an ad-

verse result, permanent disability, or even death. Fortunately, this seldom occurs when you take proper precautions and give appropriate support.

Transporting Victims

Another problem activity leaders may have taking groups into remote areas concerns transporting an injured or ill person. Ideally, professional rescue assistance will be available, but sometimes this is not possible. The leader may have to choose between sending part of the group for help or transporting the injured or ill person out. This decision becomes even more complex when there are only two people in the group, one of whom is ill or injured.

Some considerations include the following:

- Ambient temperature—extremes of heat and cold will make even minor injuries and illnesses worse.
- Available resources—are first aid kits intact and do they have items appropriate for caring for the victim? Can you keep the victim protected from the elements, and is there adequate food, water, and fuel?
- Skill level of other group members—novice members may be unable to safely find their way to help. They also may be unable to stay behind to care for the victim due to lack of first aid training and skills. Is the group able to move the person to safety without jeopardizing the safety of others?

- Likelihood of other people in the area who can go for help—this may be possible in some areas and unlikely in others.
- Condition of the ill or injured persons—are they stable? Are they in shock? Are they having difficulty breathing? Is their pulse weak or strong? Are they conscious? How severe are their injuries? Moving ill or injured individuals can make them worse, but leaving them behind may result in their death before help arrives.

Unfortunately, there is no easy way to quantify these factors. All group members, and certainly the victim, if able, can have input, but ultimately, it is the person in charge of managing medical emergencies who must make the decision. This person needs to periodically reevaluate all aspects of the situation before deciding. It should never be made in the heat of emotions or the rush of stabilizing a victim. Once the situation is under control, the ill or injured person is stabilized, and everyone is calm, the leader can make decisions about seeking professional rescue assistance or attempting transport. Should the leader decide to leave the victim behind, take steps to provide shelter from animals as well as the elements, food and water, adequate clothing and blankets, firewood, first aid supplies, and a signaling device.

ENVIRONMENTAL CONCERNS

Wind, weather, air and water temperature, humidity and aridity, terrain, altitude, and cloud cover all affect individual tolerances. Proper clothing, adequate fluids, and sun protection are essential for all outdoor activities. Some additional concerns, although not exhaustive, include the following.

Weather

Changes can occur rapidly and drastically, even with the most diligent forecasting sources. Abort or postpone outdoor activities when threatening weather develops. If the activity is in a remote area, establish a secure shelter. Caves and river-beds flood quickly; mud and rock slides occur even after short periods of rain; river speeds change dramatically. The pressure from moving water is massive and overwhelming. Get off the water or under nonconductive protection at the *first* sign of lightning or thunder. Don't wait until it's just a little closer.

Wind

Wind potentiates the cooling effect of water. It can carry foreign objects that irritate eyes and skin. Wind can easily cause fires to be out of control quickly in dry situations.

Ambient Temperature

Cold predisposes to hypothermia and frostbite, especially when coupled with wind and moisture. It is important to emphasize that any victim who appears dead (no pulse and not breathing) when they are hypothermic may not, in fact, be dead. No one is dead until they are warm and dead. Heat predisposes to fluid loss, dehydration, heat exhaustion, and heatstroke. Changes in temperature may be drastic, abrupt, and difficult to anticipate. Cyclists may be warm and perspiring during the day, yet rapidly chill after the sun goes down and the air cools.

Wildlife

Any time you plan activities in areas that may have aggressive wildlife (e.g., bears, sharks), participants should have special training addressing avoidance procedures and defensive measures. Review common wildlife precautions, such as garbage or food protection, avoiding skunks, and removing porcupine quills, before departure.

Plants

Noxious and poisonous plants are everywhere. Protective clothing and the ability to recognize which plants can be troublesome are important. People should be aware of the type of problems these plants may cause. Take care when selecting camp and latrine sites because poison ivy, nettles, or cacti do not make good intimate companions. Should someone have actual skin contact with a poisonous plant, washing the exposed area vigorously with soap (brown soap like Fels Naphtha is best) can diminish the toxic effects of the plant; however, be careful to avoid further contamination of either the exposed person or their caregiver. Use caution before ingesting any wild plants. Nature has many mimics, and what appear to be luscious blueberries, may in fact be poisonous bear berries.

Insects and Spiders

Insects and spiders are everywhere! Stinging insects, mosquitoes, biting flies, ticks, and chiggers (mites) are part of the outdoors and will get everyone at some time or another. Some insects and ticks carry diseases (encephalitis, Lyme disease, Rocky Mountain spotted fever), so keep track of even insignificant-appearing bites. Disease symptoms may not appear until long after the activity is over. Limiting the amount of bite exposure, wearing protective clothing, and using insect repellents containing DEET are the most effective methods in preventing bites. Children are vulnerable to toxic absorption of DEET. If you must use it on them, apply only small amounts. Less toxic substances are preferable but may not be as effective. Bright clothes and perfumes attract insects, so avoiding these is helpful. Some areas and activities may require head and face nets for adequate protection. Spiders are usually harmless, although they can leave an annoying bite. Environments indigenous to poisonous species, such as the brown recluse, black widow, or scorpion, should heighten participants' diligence and level of observation.

Aquatic Life

Animals (sea urchins, catfish, leeches, and jellyfish, for example) and plants (coral) found in aquatic environments can cause abrasions, lacerations, bites, and stings, some of which can be serious. Many aquatic-borne parasites cause skin irritations (swimmer's itch) and disease (Giardia, cryptosporidium).

Altitude

Altitude can cause problems for asthmatics and people with respiratory and cardiac problems. It enhances effects of the sun, especially when reflected off snow or water. Bleeding is much more difficult to control at high altitudes because of the atmosphere's lower oxygen content. Even small lacerations can become problematic. High altitudes offer little shelter from severe weather. Coordination and judgment can be severely hampered at high elevations. The effects of diminished oxygen supply can compromise neurological functioning, behavior, and thought processes. High-altitude cerebral edema (HACE) and high-altitude pulmonary edema (HAPE) are more likely to occur at elevations higher than 8,000 feet (Auerbach 1986).

Water

Water enhances the effects of sun and wind. It intensifies heat loss and predisposes people to hypothermia. Impact with the water such as occurs in waterskiing, personal watercraft falls, and white-water activities can cause extremity fractures and head, neck, and spinal injuries. It hides submerged objects such as rocks, stumps, and propellers, which can cause significant injury. It can cause dehydration if individuals fail to drink enough fluids, even though they are surrounded by water. Rapid ascents when diving or repeating descents too close together can lead to decompression problems. The deeper one dives, the more water pressure alters the state of gases in the body, such as oxygen and nitrogen. This makes their use by the body more difficult, if not impossible. An injury or illness becomes doubly complicated in the water because submerged or facedown victims cannot breathe.

Ground Temperature

Hot tarmac, sand, rocks, and unshaded areas all increase the effects of ambient heat. Hot feet in hot shoes are more prone to blister formation and fungal infections. These same components hold the cold and increase the risk of frostbite.

Sun

Sun causes burning of unprotected skin in all races. Its effects are potentiated by altitude and reflection off water, sand, snow, and metal. Be aware, sunburn can occur even on cloudy days. The eyes are especially susceptible to burning. Wear sunglasses with both UVA and UVB protection when activities occur in sunny areas. Add side protectors to the glasses on particularly bright days or during activities with a potential for prolonged exposure (open water or snowfields).

Terrain

Whether on a populated lake, a country highway, a city skating park, or a remote climbing site, the terrain carries its own risks. Anticipating potential problems and wearing appropriate protective equipment can help keep injuries minimal. Caves and many climbing areas have loose rock, which can fall and strike activity participants in the head. Asphalt and tarmac get hot and sticky, and snow makes keeping warm more challenging. Populated areas require greater vigilance and slower speeds.

Caves

Caves have a consistent temperature but are usually damp. There is a risk of head trauma from overhead and falling objects. Abrasions and lacerations are common. Dust, molds, and dried animal residue can cause breathing problems for asthmatics. Noxious gases can collect and make breathing difficult or impossible. They can even potentiate an explosion. Bats often inhabit caves and are known to carry rabies. Assume infection should someone get bitten, and seek medical treatment as soon as possible. Rabies vaccines may not be as effective when more than several days have passed since the bite occurred.

Fire

Any time conditions are dry, the risk of fire is present. Careless use of campfires and smoking materials are usual causes, but lightning is also a factor. Always abide by local regulatory agency restrictions on fire starting. Keep a bucket of sand or water next to every fire for emergency use. Don't leave campfires unattended, and be sure they are completely out and cool to the touch before leaving. Thoroughly extinguish and fieldstrip all smoking materials and pocket the filters. Avoid wearing flammable clothing (e.g., nylon windbreaker) when tending a fire. You can identify additional, more specific, environmental concerns according to the activity and location.

POPULATION CONCERNS

Age, physical impairment, cognitive impairment, and emotional impairment all impact the safety of an activity. Activity leaders need to be aware of and comfortable with the needs of special populations.

Age Considerations

Age considerations include the following:

- Lower tolerance for dehydration in children and geriatric populations.
- Greater likelihood for chronic diseases, heart and respiratory problems, and musculoskeletal injuries in older populations.
- Greater likelihood that older people are taking medications that may reduce their tolerance to environmental and physical stresses.
- Lower tolerance for respiratory compromise or failure in children.
- Higher risk of sudden cardiac problems in older adults.
- Less likelihood of fractures in children than adults. When fractures do occur in children, they are likely to be more complex and serious.
- Greater potential for sunburn in children and geriatric age groups.

Special Populations

Special populations provide additional considerations, among which include the following:

- Need for one-on-one guiding.
- Need for special or adapted equipment.

- Presence of sign language interpreters.
- Coexistence of other medical and physical problems (spastic movements, impaired balance, loss of limb function).
- Need for care of specialized health equipment (urinary catheters, ostomy bags, hearing aids, respirators).
- Concomitant learning and emotional impairment.
- Dyscoordinated breathing attempts in water.
- Need for additional assistance in performing self-cares.
- Difficulty in relating the presence of illness or injury.
- Greater susceptibility to overstimulation and hyperactivity.
- Less overall experience in the activity and the outdoors.
- Need for assistance when taking medications.

CONCLUSION

Outdoor activities are exciting and fun, with increasingly more people participating in them. Prevention is essential to minimizing risk of injury and illness associated with these activities. Activity leaders need training to recognize and respond to medical emergencies. Knowing when to act, what action to take, and when to seek professional assistance will be one of the most important decisions an activity leader may have to make. Having well-trained people and a well-prepared activity will increase the likelihood all participants will have a safe and enjoyable experience, even if a medical emergency should occur.

Addendum

In May 1997, the American Red Cross released a new course directed specifically at safety in sports. Sports Safety Training not only discusses first aid with sport-specific references, but also presents conditioning, nutrition, injury prevention, and staff responsibilities. It includes both injury and illness first aid as well as adult and child CPR. You can easily adapt the multiple components to the composition of activity groups, whether adult, child, or both. It is directed at coaches and program leaders, participants, and support staff. Sport-specific resource lists are provided and an easy-to-carry handbook is included in the materials. Encourage activity groups to include this program in their training schedules.

RESOURCES

Following is a partial list of resource agencies for basic training courses in first aid and CPR. You can also contact local community colleges and EMS services about related programs and activity-specific organizations for more in-depth training. Many of these organizations are listed in outdoor and wilderness medicine resource books.

American Heart Association, National Center
7272 Greenville Ave.
Dallas, TX 75231
(You can find local chapters in most major metropolitan areas.)

American Red Cross, National Headquarters
8111 Gatehouse Rd.
Falls Church, VA 22042
(You can find service delivery units in most metropolitan areas and some rural areas.)

National Safety Council
First Aid Institute
1121 Spring Lake Dr.
Itasca, IL 60143-3201
708-285-1121, 800-621-7619 for orders

Wilderness Medical Society
P.O. Box 397
Point Reyes Station, CA 94966

BIBLIOGRAPHY

Alberron-Sotelo, R., L. Flint, and K. Kelly, eds. 1994. *Basic life support.* Dallas: American Heart Association.

American Red Cross. 1993a. *CPR for the professional rescuer.* St. Louis: Mosby Lifeline.

———. 1993b. *Emergency response.* St. Louis: Mosby Lifeline.

————. 1993c. *Standard first aid*. St. Louis: Mosby Lifeline.

————. 1996a. *Responding to emergencies*. St. Louis: Mosby Lifeline.

————. 1996b. *When help is delayed*. St. Louis: Mosby Lifeline.

Auerbach, P. S. 1986. *Medicine for the outdoors: A guide to emergency medical procedures and first aid*. Boston: Little, Brown.

————. 1993. *Management of wilderness and environmental emergencies*. St. Louis: Mosby Yearbook.

National Safety Council. 1992. *First aid and CPR*. 2nd ed. Boston: Jones and Bartlett.

————. 1993. *Bloodborne pathogens*. Boston: Jones and Bartlett.

————. 1995a. *First responder*. Boston: Jones and Bartlett.

————. 1995b. *SCUBA diving first aid and accident management*. Boston: Jones and Bartlett.

PART II

Safety Guidelines for Outdoor Recreational Activities

Hiking and Camping

Norman L. Gilchrest

John Muir was ecstatic about wilderness and enthusiastically proclaimed the benefits he believed would accrue to wilderness users: "Climb the mountains and get their good tidings. Nature's peace will flow into you as sunshine flows into trees. The winds will blow their freshness into you, and the storms their energy, while cares will drop off like autumn leaves." In a gentle and elegant way, George Santayana stated what every hiker feels, "I like to walk about amidst the beautiful things that adorn the world."

Millions of Americans are agreeing with these sentiments and are hiking and camping in record numbers. In the *1994 Sports Participation Survey,* camping, with 42.9 million participants, ranked as the sixth most popular sports activity in the United States.

Although hiking and camping have admirable safety records, any activity that involves millions of people going into wilderness areas possesses the potential for injury. This chapter will present, as fully as space limitations permit, the major safety considerations in hiking and camping.

ENVIRONMENTAL CONDITIONS

One tenet of wilderness safety is that the hiker must be prepared, not for the ideal or what probably will happen, but for the worst that can happen. The purpose of this section is to outline those topics you must consider to fully prepare hikers and campers for the varied safety challenges in wilderness. It would be normal to read this information and vow never to take anyone hiking if all these circumstances could happen to you. Hiking is a safe activity. Keep in mind that most people experience few or none of these occurrences. Several safety challenges we discuss in this chapter can occur in various places, not just while hiking. With that in mind, be prepared, venture into wilderness, and profit from the benefits and magic such experiences will bring to people's lives. Environmental safety considerations relating to hiking and camping are presented alphabetically.

Altitude Sickness

Altitude sickness will occur to all hikers who venture to high altitudes. As you go higher, the air gets progressively thinner, and significantly less oxygen is available to the body. The severity differs among hikers and may vary in the same person when exposed to the same altitude on different occasions. The higher you hike and the faster you ascend, the greater the safety risk. The three types of altitude sickness often overlap and are considered a continuum. The symptoms progress insidiously. Altitude sickness rarely occurs below 6,500 feet and usually becomes noticeable at altitudes between 8,000 and 10,000 feet.

Acute Mountain Sickness (AMS)

The symptoms of acute mountain sickness are headache, nausea, fatigue, shortness of breath, sleep disturbance, loss of appetite, and a general feeling of unwellness. Acute mountain sickness is more miserable than serious, but it can lead to more severe altitude sickness.

High-Altitude Pulmonary Edema (HAPE)

HAPE, a potentially fatal illness, is caused by accumulating fluid in the lungs. Early symptoms include shortness of breath, irritating cough, weakness, rapid heart rate, and headache. Later symptoms are cough with bloody sputum, low-grade fever, increasing chest congestion, crackling sound (rales) in chest, and labored breathing. If untreated, the victim will lapse into coma. Death usually occurs within 6 to 12 hours after onset of coma.

High-Altitude Cerebral Edema (HACE)

Less common than AMS or HAPE, HACE is more dangerous and potentially fatal. Caused by accumulating fluid in the brain, symptoms are severe headache, loss of dexterity, impaired judgment, hallucinations, confusion, disorganized thinking, disorientation, impaired vision, vomiting, restless sleep, and progressive loss of consciousness.

Other High-Altitude Problems

Hikers going to high altitudes may experience other forms of altitude sickness. *Retinal hemorrhage (HARH)* is bleeding and swelling in the

STARTING OFF ON THE RIGHT FOOT

The following concepts are important in providing a philosophical basis for wilderness safety.

Attitude

Attitude sets the tone for your wilderness experience and determines the degree of enjoyment, success, and safety. Unwise, competitive, or thoughtless behavior can lead to danger for yourself and others.

Responsibility

Our actions in wilderness have consequences, both for ourselves and for others. Each hiker is responsible for his or her well-being. In addition, each hiker is responsible for avoiding behaviors that diminish the safety and enjoyment of others.

Risk

The acceptable degree of risk varies from person to person. In deciding what is an acceptable risk, you should determine the odds of success and the consequences of failure. Wilderness activities will never be risk free, but each hiker and camper can choose the level of risk that is personally appropriate. A good rule is, "If in doubt, don't." No goal in hiking and camping is worth serious injury or death.

Respect for Nature

It is easy to be lulled by the beauty of wilderness, then suddenly encounter the fierceness and power of nature. Realize that nature does not care, and always be prepared for whatever circumstances you might encounter in wilderness.

Prevention

Injury prevention must be foremost in your planning and actions. Think through to the end the results of any action you are contemplating. It is much easier to prevent a tragedy than to deal with its aftermath.

membranes lining the back of the eyes. Common in hikers going higher than 15,000 feet, HARH is thought to cause no serious or lasting problems. *Peripheral edema* is swelling of hands, face, and feet. Though not serious in itself, it can signal body changes at altitude. *High-altitude flatulent expulsion (HAFE)* is more embarrassing than serious, and you can reduce it by avoiding foods that cause gas at low altitude.

Preventing Altitude Sickness

You can prevent altitude sickness by slow ascent to permit the body to acclimatize gradually to altitude. Observe the rule "travel high, camp low." Beginning at 9,000 feet, the hiker can travel high during the day but should not sleep more than 1,000 vertical feet higher than

the previous night. Other preventive measures include remaining well hydrated, eating a high-carbohydrate diet, reducing fat intake, and exercising moderately.

Treating Altitude Sickness

Because of the seriousness of HAPE and HACE, altitude sickness must receive careful consideration. The basic treatment for altitude sickness is to descend immediately at least 2,000 feet and preferably to 6,500 feet altitude. The longer a person with altitude sickness remains at high altitude, the greater the danger of health deterioration and need for assistance in traveling. Some drugs have shown promise for combating or treating altitude sickness, but the average hiker will not have the drugs nor the expertise to use them properly. For groups

Wilderness explorers should always prepare for the worst case scenario—as unlikely as it is that this may occur.

going to very high altitudes, a Gamow Bag (portable hyperbaric bag) can help victims by simulating lower altitudes. Supplemental oxygen is useful prevention and treatment at extremely high altitudes.

Coping With Animals

Observing wild animals can bring pleasure and knowledge. Hikers must keep in mind that animals in wilderness are wild and unpredictable, and many animals can cause people serious harm. All animals have some means of protection, which they will use when they feel threatened. By observing a few commonsense rules, hikers can greatly enhance their safety (see table 4.1).

Small Animals

Small animals, like mice, armadillos, porcupines, chipmunks, possums, raccoons, squirrels, skunks, foxes, and bats, are cute, appealing, and interesting. The major dangers they pose to humans are risk of infection, soft tissue injury, and rabies. Observe and enjoy animals from a distance.

Large Animals

Unless they have become accustomed to the presence of people, large animals usually want nothing to do with humans. Few consider humans as a source of food. Most problems come from mothers protecting their young, males protecting territory, and deviant animals (old, physical problems, and mentally aberrant). Teach hikers about the animals that live in your hiking area, know their habits and characteristics, and abide by the rules that pertain to each animal and situation, particularly those most capable of causing harm to a hiker. Of course, avoidance is the surest safety strategy of all. A bear cannot harm you unless you are in bear territory.

Snakes

Snakes are beneficial members of the animal community. They usually shun people, yet, a snake will bite if it is startled or pressured. The four types of poisonous snakes in the United States—rattlesnake (accounts for most snakebites and nearly all deaths from snakebites in this country), water moccasin, copperhead, and coral snake—inspire fear far out of proportion to the number of fatalities they cause. Approximately 8,000 people are bitten by snakes in the United States each year, but the average number of deaths from snakebite is less than 12. It is estimated that 20 percent of rattlesnake bites and 30 percent of cottonmouth water moccasin and copperhead bites do not involve envenomization.

To prevent snakebite, watch where you step and put your hands. Wearing protective clothing such as high boots and long pants will help protect hikers in snake territory.

Treating snakebite is controversial. Few areas of medical treatment have evoked more disagreement. The American Red Cross instructs the first aid provider to wash the wound, immobilize the affected part, keep the affected area lower than the heart, and get the victim to a doctor. If you cannot reach advanced medical care within 30 minutes, you may place a loose constricting band between the wound and the heart and use a commercial kit to suction the wound. Do not apply ice, cut the wound, apply a tourniquet, or use electrical shock.

Insects and Arachnids

Two types of arthropods commonly cause problems in wilderness—insects (mosquitoes, ants, bees, wasps, hornets, blackflies, no-see-ums, flies) and arachnids (spiders, scorpions, ticks). Many varieties exist, and some pose safety considerations for hikers. Few insect and arachnid bites are fatal. The danger is that some people are sensitive to the venom and can have immediate anaphylactic shock.

Two types of spiders in the United States are poisonous, the black widow (hourglass on underside) and ... brown recluse (violin-shaped marking on top of body). Bites can be fatal. Avoid placing unprotected body parts in dark, secluded places. Get medical assistance if symptoms are present. Symptoms include difficulty breathing or swallowing, sweating and salivating profusely, irregular heart rhythms that can lead to cardiac arrest, severe pain in the sting or bite area, a

Table 4.1
RULES FOR DEALING WITH ANIMALS IN THE WILD

RULE	EXPLANATION
Do not touch, get too close to, pressure, or feed animals.	This is for the safety of animals as well as hikers. If you treat them with dignity and do not make them feel threatened, they usually will not present a threat to individual safety.
Do not touch dead animals.	Touching dead animals serves no purpose and exposes hikers to diseases. If large predators are near, they may view you as a competitor for their food supply.
Separate sleeping areas from areas for food storage, preparation, and consumption.	Store food and items containing food smells safely, choosing a place away from the sleeping area. Use an animal-proof container sufficient to the threat, or suspend your food container above the ground by tying a rope horizontally between two objects and attaching the container to the rope tied to the horizontal rope.
Most animals want nothing to do with hikers.	Let them know of your presence, and they usually will go elsewhere. Do not surprise large animals, especially mothers.
Know the symptoms of an animal with rabies.	They include the following: ☐ active in daytime when the animal should be nocturnal ☐ may not run when it should ☐ salivation ☐ partial paralysis ☐ irritability ☐ aggressiveness ☐ strangely quiet Currently, wildlife rabies is at an all-time high in the United States. If bitten by an animal suspected of rabies, seek medical attention immediately.
Do not feed any wild animals.	Regardless of how appealing, follow this rule. To feed them will make them a nuisance to everyone, may endanger your life, and will diminish the quality and quantity of the animals' lives in many ways.

mark indicating a possible bite or sting, and swelling at the site. Within 36 hours, a brown recluse bite causes a necrotic ulcer, which gradually enlarges.

Scorpions, which live in dry regions of the United States, can inflict a painful sting. Although only a few species are fatally poisonous, bites can cause localized pain, slight swelling, and numbness. Most active at night, scorpions like to stay under rocks and logs. Always check the inside of your shoes and other articles of clothing before dressing.

Mosquitoes are a nuisance, but rarely cause serious illness in this country. Worldwide, mosquitoes are responsible for the deaths of more humans annually than any other creature. To avoid no-see-ums and biting gnats, use a tent with netting small enough to keep these fierce biters away.

Ticks are small bloodsucking parasitic arachnids that can cause serious illnesses (see figure 4.1). Two major dangers of tick bites are Rocky Mountain spotted fever, which can be fatal, and Lyme disease, which can cause serious heart, joint, and nervous system abnormalities. Lyme disease is the most commonly reported vector-borne disease in the United States. Transmitted primarily, but not exclusively, by the deer tick, Lyme disease is characterized by sudden onset of lameness with feverish, swollen joints. Prevention includes tucking pants into socks or boots; using DEET, which is effective against ticks; and spraying clothing with permethrin .5 percent spray. It is wise to check hairlines, ears, armpits, groin areas, and behind the knees at least once a day.

Prevention for insect and arachnid bites includes the following: avoid geographical areas of contact, minimize the target area by wearing adequate clothing (including gloves and head net), use living quarters (such as tents) that repel insects, check for insects in all clothing before dressing, and use repellents. To repel most insects and arachnids, formulas containing DEET work best. To kill chiggers and mosquitoes on contact, permethrin, a chemical that is put on protective clothing, not on the skin, is frequently used. Used in combination, DEET and permethrin present a formidable barrier to insects.

Take care in using repelling chemicals, because they can cause allergic and toxic problems. Children have greater risks from chemicals than adults. Keep chemicals out of eyes and mouth, remove from hands before handling food, and avoid prolonged use. Repellents can cause damage to many materials, so check the label before application.

Treatment for bites from different insects and arachnids may vary, but general guidelines are the following:

1. If stung by a bee, remove the stinger if still attached. Scrape it away with a fingernail or an object like a credit card.

2. Wash the wound with soap and water.

3. Apply cold to reduce pain and swelling.

4. Observe the victim. Seek medical care if needed.

Treatment for tick bites involves the following:

1. Remove ticks promptly (see figure 4.2). According to Forgey (1994), hard ticks (which transmit both Rocky Mountain spotted fever and Lyme disease) cannot transmit diseases if they are removed within 24 hours. Grasp the tick as close to the skin as possible with sharp-tipped tweezers, and pull steadily and firmly. Avoid squeezing the body of the tick. If tweezers are not available, protect fingers with a cover such as a glove, plastic wrap, paper, or leaf. Do not use some techniques that have been suggested for tick removal—burning the tick, coating the tick with oil, or painting with nail polish.

2. Wash hands, the bite area, and tweezers with soap and water.

3. Apply antiseptic or antibiotic ointment to prevent infection.

4. Obtain medical care if flulike symptoms develop.

Figure 4.1 A bite from the deer tick can cause Lyme disease; make sure you are adequately protected.

Coping With Poisonous Plants

In most cases, plants are a source of pleasure to hikers. Some, however, can create safety problems by causing internal poisoning, external poisoning, and puncture wounds.

Ingesting Poisonous Plants

Some people enjoy eating natural foods found in wilderness. In such cases, indisputable identification is an important safety procedure. It is not necessary to eat wilderness plants for survival, so the only reasons a hiker would eat wilderness plants are for curiosity or pleasure. The surest way to avoid internal poisoning from wilderness plants is to eat only safe food taken into wilderness by the hiker.

Touching Poisonous Plants

Hikers should be aware of three plants that are poisonous to touch—poison ivy, poison oak, and poison sumac. The plants produce an oil, urushiol, which causes reactions in approximately 85 percent of people. Direct contact with the plants is not necessary for contamination. The oil can last for months and be transmitted by clothing, animals, and other objects. Symptoms of reaction include reddening skin, swelling, itching, and sometimes blisters. If you don't already know what poison ivy looks like, see the photo on the following page and make a mental note.

To prevent contact poisoning from plants, first learn to recognize them. Poison ivy and poison oak have beautiful compound leaves in clumps of three and small, round, grayish-green or white berries at appropriate times. Poison sumac has leaves in groups of 7 to 13, arranged in two rows of leaflets opposite each other and a leaflet at the tip. The plants vary in size, with poison ivy tending to be either a shrub or vine, poison oak tending to be more a shrub than a vine, and poison sumac tending to be a larger shrub. Avoid the plants and things that may have touched them.

Treatment calls for washing promptly (speed is important) with soap and water, applying calamine or other suitable lotion, using commercial products made specifically to combat urushiol, and seeking medical help if conditions warrant.

Plants That Can Cause Puncture Wounds

Many plants have thorns or sharp leaves. Some are capable of producing nasty wounds if the body slams into the sharp object with enough force. Some plants produce frustration by leaving small thorns in the skin after impact. Preventing puncture wounds from plants involves watching where the hiker is stepping, sitting, or grasping; avoiding situations where the hiker might fall or slide into a dangerous plant; and being careful not to handle objects (shoes, shoelaces, socks, pants, ropes, packs, and so forth) imbedded with thorns.

Harmful Microorganisms

You can't always see things that may hurt you. Wise hikers realize that some potentially harmful life forms are invisible with normal vision and give no warnings before invading humans. You can acquire germs, microorganisms that can infect people and cause disease, from food, water, dirt, air, or other things. They can enter the human body through any opening—breaks in the skin, nose, eye, mouth, urethra, and rectal openings. To avoid microscopic pathogens, hikers don't have to be microbiologists; they simply need to acquire and use basic knowledge, good judgment, and good sanitation practices. Careful selection, storage, treatment, and consumption of food and water are important.

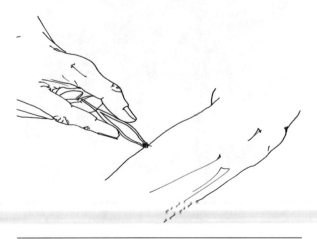

Figure 4.2   To remove the tick, grasp it with the tweezers as close as possible to the point of attachment; pull it off and avoid squeezing its body.

Anyone hiking through or near woods should be able to recognize the pointy-tipped leaves of poison ivy.

© Norman Gilchrest

Microorganisms in Food

Be careful about the safety of foods. Factors leading to spoilage include light, oxygen, and microorganisms. Many foods are naturally safe for long periods. You can keep foods that are dried, freeze dried, powdered, or canned safe for extended periods. If in doubt about the safety of food, do not eat it.

Microorganisms in Water

In spite of the clarity, coldness, and good taste of most wilderness water, there is no untreated water a backpacker can know is safe to drink except that which comes from an approved source. Many water sources are contaminated with organisms originating in the feces of native animals, domesticated animals, or humans. Treat *all* water you don't obtain from an approved source.

The most common harmful microscopic organisms in wilderness water are viruses (for example, hepatitis), bacteria (for example, E.

coli), and protozoans (for example, Giardia lamblia and cryptosporidia). The common symptoms of most of these illnesses are varying degrees of nausea, vomiting, and diarrhea. Persons suspecting contamination should consult a doctor. Because humans are the greatest source of pathogens in wilderness, all hikers have a responsibility to protect themselves, others, and the wilderness environment.

Obtaining Water in the Wilderness

Sources of water in most wilderness areas are streams, lakes, snowfields, and springs. In desert areas, look for water where shown on maps, where there are signs of vegetation, at the bottom of a canyon, at the base of a hill, at the end of game trails, where birds fly in morning and evening, and in dry streambeds at the lowest point on the outside of a bend. In emergencies, a solar still or moisture stored in some plants may provide small amounts of water.

Take the clearest, cleanest, fastest moving water possible, well away from the shoreline and upstream from animal waste. Avoid areas that are breeding places for microorganisms, such as backwaters, stagnant areas, and eddies. Water with critters and plant life growing in it will be good to drink when purified. If they can live in it, you can live on it. Never get water near beaver dams or beaver lodges. Turn the mouth of the container downstream while filling, and if the water in the container has too much solid matter to suit you, empty it and begin again. If the water needs straining, do so through a cloth. If the water contains silt, let the silt settle and pour off the cleaner upper levels.

Weather-Related Problems

Weather has much to do with a hiker's safety, success, and enjoyment. Extreme weather can add to the complexity of situations; affect morale; obscure landmarks; make travel hazardous; bring lightning, hail, snow, wind, and water; and lead to the many health problems related to heat and cold. Although hikers cannot change the weather, we can use our knowledge of current and probable weather situations for safer and more enjoyable adventures. Know the norms for the geographical area and the season, and be prepared for the worst weather you might encounter. Avoid being surprised. Any time the weather threatens safety, it is wise to change plans and hike another day. A hiker can learn the professionals' weather prediction in the target area from newspapers, TV, radio, backcountry rangers, and telephone weather forecasts.

Predicting the Weather

Trying to predict the weather is a challenging task, as evidenced by the many chagrined professional weather forecasters who make errors such as telling the audience that today will be sunny, while it is raining at the very moment. Armed with common sense, accumulated knowledge and wisdom about weather, observation, and perhaps an altimeter, a hiker can do a pretty good job of weather forecasting.

• Storms center around areas of low pressure. High pressure moves into areas of low pressure, causing turbulence. Air tends to rise and may move in a circular direction. If you observe clouds moving in different directions, there is probably a low, and a storm is possible. When clouds move in one direction, expect no change. You can measure barometric pressure on an altimeter, an instrument that measures pressure and gives an altitude reading in feet or meters. Falling barometric pressure signals a likelihood for stormy weather. When the altimeter tells hikers that they have gained altitude, even though they have stayed in the same place, the pressure has dropped.

• Signs that a bad storm is near may be a sudden rush of cold air, huge snowflakes, large hailstones, a cloudburst of enormous raindrops, and the calm before the storm (if the wind dies, head for cover).

• You can use wind to predict the weather. Slogans include the following: Wind from the south brings rain in its mouth. Wind from the east brings weather that's a beast. Wind from the west suits everybody best.

• Red sky at night, sailor's delight. Red sky in morning, sailors take warning.

• If smoke hangs low to the ground (indicating low pressure), rain is on the way. If it rises high in a vertical column (high pressure), expect good weather.

• Frogs increase vocalization several hours before a storm arrives.

• Springs flow at a higher rate and the air in caves rushes outward as storms approach, due to lower pressure.

• A halo, often called a sun dog, around the sun or moon indicates a change in weather, most often rain. This is caused by light showing through ice particles of high clouds.

• Rain before seven, dry by eleven.

• Heavy frost or dew indicates up to 12 hours of continued good weather.

Cold-Related Safety Considerations

Hiking during cold weather can be exciting, beautiful, and rewarding; however, hikers should realize that their skills and equipment must be good enough to deal with the realities of a cold environment. Hiking in cold is covered in detail in the Winter Hiking and Camping chapter.

Hypothermia. Hypothermia, the lowering of a person's core temperature resulting in the inability of the body to function properly, is the leading medical problem in wilderness. The major environmental factors that contribute to hypothermia are cool or cold weather, wind, and moisture. Symptoms of hypothermia are shivering, loss of coordination, slurred speech, and stupor. As the body gets progressively colder, the victim descends into unconsciousness and death. One of the most challenging things about hypothermia is that victims do not recognize that they are in trouble. It is important for hikers to observe each other and give assistance when someone becomes hypothermic.

Preventing hypothermia includes staying warm, dry, hydrated, sufficiently fed, and avoiding fatigue. Treatment calls for warming the victim as soon as possible with dry clothing, additional insulation, warm liquids and food, a warm environment, and activity as appropriate. If serious symptoms exist, seek prompt medical attention.

WATER PURIFICATION METHODS

You can make water safe for drinking by boiling or using a combination of chemicals and filtration. Here are several methods for purifying water.

Boiling

Boiling kills all microorganisms in water. Boil water for approximately 10 minutes. The drawbacks to boiling for sterilization are the amount of time and fuel you need to boil enough water.

Iodine Tablets (Pills)

One tablet provides eight parts per million iodine concentration per quart. You need more than three to five parts per million iodine concentration to kill amoebae and their cysts, algae, bacteria and their spores, and enterovirus. Take care to follow the instructions on the bottle. If water is cold or dirty, increase time or dosage. Be mindful of the shelf life, which is one year for opened bottles and four years for unopened bottles. Store iodine tablets in the refrigerator between hiking trips. People with thyroid problems, iodine allergies, and pregnant women should contact their doctors before using iodine to treat water.

Two-Percent Tincture of Iodine

Tincture of iodine is found in pharmacies around the world and is probably the most available chemical disinfectant. Apply the drops by eye dropper, 5 drops per quart to clear water and 10 drops if the water is cloudy. Mix iodine and water, rinse container threads with the iodine and water solution, and wait 30 minutes before drinking if using clear water and 60 minutes if using cloudy water.

Iodine Crystals

Iodine crystal purification kits take some preparation time but are easy to use, have good dosage consistency, and can purify up to 500 gallons of water for less than two cents per gallon.

Chlorine-Releasing Agents

Although municipal water supply systems have used chlorine-based systems for years, chlorine agents are thought to be less effective than iodine in wilderness. *Entamoeba histolytica* and *Giardia lamblia* tend to resist chlorine. Halazone tablets release chlorine, requiring five tablets per quart of clear water. Halazone tablets have a limited shelf life, so you should use a new bottle for each hiking trip. You can use household bleach to treat water. Read the label on the bleach to learn the percentage of chlorine in the solution. Liquid laundry chlorine bleach usually has four to six percent available chlorine. At that strength, use two drops per quart of clear water or four drops per quart of cold or cloudy water. If you do not detect a chlorine smell, repeat. Wait 30 minutes before drinking.

continued ☞

Filtration

Filters strain water through a matrix containing many small pores that are large enough to let the water pass through but small enough to trap bacteria and protozoans. Currently available backpacking filters vary in the size of the pores in the screening device, ranging from .2 microns to 1 micron. A micron is a millionth of a meter. A human hair is about 90 microns thick. By comparison, tapeworm eggs are 25 microns, protozoans are 5 to 15 microns, bacteria are .2 to 10 microns, and viruses are .004 to .1 microns. Filtration with .2-micron filters takes out all microorganisms except viruses, which are too small to be trapped in a filter.

The filtering agent varies in water filters, with ceramic and charcoal being used frequently. You need to change the filtering element in some filters periodically to prevent contamination, whereas others you can clean easily and are safe to use indefinitely. Be aware that some filters may cease to be effective after you have used them for some time, without the loss of protection being apparent.

Combination Approaches to Water Treatment

If you want to be sure that water is free of all microorganisms, the solution is to either boil the water or use a combination of filtration and chemical treatment, which will eliminate both large and small microorganisms. Figure 4.3 shows several water purification methods and the organisms they kill.

Methods of Purification	CONTAMINATING ORGANISMS		
	Protozoans (5 to 15 microns)	Bacteria (0.2 to 10 microns)	Viruses (0.004 to 0.1 microns)
Filters	Eliminates	Eliminates if pores are small enough	Not eliminated
Iodine	Some not killed	Kills	Kills
Chlorine	Not effective on larger microorganisms	Kills	Kills
Boiling	Kills	Kills	Kills

Figure 4.3   Water purification methods and the organisms they kill.

Frostbite. We discuss frostbite in the Winter Hiking and Camping chapter.

Heat-Related Safety Considerations

The ability to hike in hot climates can permit you to safely experience beautiful places, such as the Grand Canyon and the Okefenokee Swamp. However, hot environments can be harsh with hikers who are unwise, unskilled, or unprepared. Before venturing into hot environments, you should be aware of important medical considerations and their effect on your safety.

Heat Cramps. Heat cramps are caused by overexposure to heat. According to the American Red Cross, the exact cause is not known, although it is thought to be a combination of fluid loss and salt loss caused by heavy sweating. Symptoms are painful spasms of skeletal muscles, usually in legs and abdomen, dilation of the pupils of the eyes, and cold and clammy skin. Treatment calls for the victim to rest comfortably in a cool place, consume generous amounts of cool water, and stretch and massage the muscles.

Heat Exhaustion. The causes of heat exhaustion are similar to those for heat cramps. Symptoms include headache; excessive sweating; weakness; dizziness; cramps; pale, moist, cool, and clammy skin; rapid heart rate; and nausea. Treatment for heat exhaustion involves drinking fluids containing a pinch of salt, cooling the body (shade, moisture, fanning), and prone body position with feet elevated. Recovery is usually rapid. If conditions persist, see a doctor, because heat exhaustion may advance to heatstroke.

Heatstroke. Heatstroke occurs when the heat-control process of the body completely breaks down. Sweating stops because body fluid levels are low. This is a true emergency that will result in death if not treated aggressively. Symptoms are hot, dry, red skin; rapid, weak pulse; rapid, shallow breathing; nausea and vomiting; and mental confusion leading to unconsciousness. The core temperature rises higher than 105 degrees Fahrenheit, resulting in a progressive state of shock. Treatment calls for immediate cooling (dip in water, place in shade, soak clothes, fan the victim), consumption of all the water the victim will drink, and medical assistance as soon as possible.

The National Weather Service has created a heat index, similar to the windchill index, which combines actual temperature with the amount of humidity to produce an apparent temperature, indicating how the weather really feels. Figure 4.4, a heat index table, will be useful to people backpacking in hot weather.

Sun Damage

The sun emits ultraviolet rays that damage the skin and lips. For every 1,000-foot increase in altitude, the intensity of sunburn-producing ultraviolet light increases by four percent. Snow, clouds, water, and sand increase exposure by reflecting light to unprotected areas. You must protect skin and lips to prevent burning, accelerated aging of the skin, and increase in the likelihood of skin cancer. There has been a 13-fold increase in skin cancer since the 1970s. About 600,000 cases are diagnosed in the United States each year, and approximately one of every six Americans will develop skin cancer in his or her lifetime. To prevent sun damage to skin and lips follow these suggestions:

• Spend less time in the sun and be selective about the time of day. Between 10 A.M. and 2 P.M. (11 A.M. and 3 P.M. daylight savings time) a hiker gets the most exposure.

• Wear protective clothing—a hat with a wide brim (each inch of brim on your sun hat reduces your chance of skin cancer by 10 percent), long sleeves, long pants.

• Use sunblock with high SPF (sun protection factor). The SPF number indicates the number of hours a person can be exposed to the sun equivalent to one hour with no sunblock. Most people need at least SPF 15. People with extreme exposure or sensitive skin need at least SPF 29. Sunblock should be waterproof and screen both ultraviolet A and ultraviolet B rays.

Extreme exposure to sunlight can result in snow blindness. To prevent snow blindness,

HEAT INDEX

APPARENT TEMPERATURE
A measure of the effect of high temperature and humidity on the body

Temperature in °F	Relative Humidity														Heat Stress Index**
	10%	20%	30%	35%	40%	45%	50%	55%	60%	65%	70%	75%	80%	90%	
70	65	66	67	67	68	68	69	69	70	70	70	70	71	71	
75	70	72	73	73	74	74	75	75	76	76	77	77	78	79	I
80	75	77	78	79	79	80	81	81	82	83	85	86	86	88	
85	80	82	84	85	86	87	88	89	90	91	93	95	97	102	II
90	85	87	90	91	93	95	96	98	100	102	106	109	113	122	III
95	90	93	96	98	101	104	107	110	114	119	124	130	136	*	
100	95	99	104	107	110	115	120	126	132	138	144	*	*	*	
105	100	105	113	118	123	129	135	142	149	*	*	*	*	*	
110	105	112	123	130	137	143	150	*	*	*	*	*	*	*	IV
115	111	120	135	143	151	*	*	*	*	*	*	*	*	*	
120	116	130	148	*	*	*	*	*	*	*	*	*	*	*	
125	123	141	*	*	*	*	*	*	*	*	*	*	*	*	
130	131	*	*	*	*	*	*	*	*	*	*	*	*	*	
135	*	*	*	*	*	*	*	*	*	*	*	*	*	*	
140	*	*	*	*	*	*	*	*	*	*	*	*	*	*	

* beyond the capacity of earth's atmosphere to hold water

** HEAT STRESS INDEX

Danger Category	Heat Index	Heat Syndrome
I. Caution	80°-89°	fatigue possible with prolonged exposure and/or physical activity
II. Extreme	90°-104°	heat cramps and heat exhaustion possible with prolonged exposure and/or physical activity
III. Danger	105°-129°	heat exhaution, heat cramps likely. Heatstroke possible with prolonged exposure and/or physical activity
IV. Extreme danger	greater than 130°	heatstroke highly likely with continued exposure

Figure 4.4   Heat Stress Index. A person's reaction to heat can vary with age, health, and body characteristics.

Data from *Heat Stress, Environmental Information Summaries C-19*. Asheville, NC: National Oceanic and Atmospheric Administration 1-6.

wear good sunglasses. If sunglasses are not available, cover the eyes with anything available and create a slit through which to look. Symptoms are redness of eyes, swelling, burning or a filled-with-sand feeling, watery or inflamed eyes, headaches, and poor vision. Treatment is to protect the eyes from additional light with a lightproof bandage or dark environment and to bathe the eyes frequently with cold, wet compresses. Usually, within 24 hours, the victim will recover sufficiently to travel with sunglasses. In severe cases, recovery may take several days.

Eyes are damaged by ultraviolet light. Because this damage is cumulative, avoid it at all costs. Protect the eyes by wearing sunglasses that block ultraviolet light. ANSI-approved sunglasses block 99.8 percent of the ultraviolet B wavelength.

Lightning

Lightning is one of nature's most remarkable and beautiful displays. Caused by particles of water, ice, and air losing electrons as they move within storm clouds, lightning is a sudden release of electrical charges that have been stored in the clouds. Around the world, there are approximately 2,000 active thunderstorms at any time, with 100 lightning bolts striking the ground in any second. There are about 40,000,000 strikes to ground in the United States every year, resulting in approximately 4,000 people being struck. Lightning is extremely dangerous, causing approximately 100 to 300 deaths annually in this country. Lightning kills more people than hurricanes and tornadoes combined. It is the second most dangerous threat to hikers, following hypothermia.

Hikers must be concerned about direct strikes and the subsequent ground currents. Lightning seeks the path of least resistance between clouds and the earth. It tends to hit the highest point in an area and travels through the best conductor it can find. Good conductors in the hiking environment are ionized air, trees, rocks, earth, the human body, and metals. All conductors transmit lightning better when wet.

There are 100 billion billion electrons in an average lightning bolt, which may be longer

then five miles. The usual width is from as wide as a pencil to one inch. Traveling at speeds up to one-half the speed of light, lightning may deliver 100 million volts, 300,000 amps of current, and may reach 50,000 degrees Celsius, five times hotter than the surface of the sun. The bolt reaches its target almost the instant it is produced. Shock waves can be heard up to 15 miles away. An average thunderstorm produces about 250,000,000 watts of electricity. If we could harness all the energy in one flash of lightning, it could provide electrical power to several homes for a month.

We cannot stop lightning, but we can take precautions. The warning signs of lightning danger are that the approaching storm is visible and audible (most thunderstorms move from west to east), hair may stand on end, the air smells of ozone, and you may hear a sizzling sound. Most storms in mountainous areas occur from early afternoon until dusk. You can determine a storm's distance by counting the number of seconds between the lightning and the thunder and dividing by five. Preventive actions to avoid lightning are the following:

• Go to a place that lightning is not likely to strike. Avoid being the tallest thing in the vicinity. Descend from mountain summits and ridges. Stay away from pinnacles and solitary trees. If you are higher than the timberline, get between and below the tops of two flat boulders. In open areas, seek a ravine or valley. Get off open water, and avoid standing in water. Disperse party members several yards apart. Seek safety in the shorter trees of a forest, in a house or large building (but stay away from openings such as doors or windows), or in a car. Avoid small buildings in open areas, anything metal, walls, fences, and plumbing.

• Avoid likely paths of diffusion, such as cracks and recesses in cliffs, small streams, grassy areas, debris at the base of cliffs (get 50-80 feet from the face of a cliff), moist areas, crevices in rocks, overhangs, and the mouths of small caves.

• Assume a body position that is as short as possible (to prevent being struck) and spans as small an area as possible (to prevent currents entering through one foot and going out the other foot after traversing the body). Keep feet close together and hands off the ground. We recommend a sitting position or a low crouch, preferably on insulating material such as a sleeping pad, sleeping bag, or coiled rope. Sitting on a small rock is preferable to sitting on the ground. Do not lie down. Keep the mouth open during times of great danger to reduce barotrauma to the ears. In a tent, sit or kneel on the sleeping pad and avoid touching wet things and metal.

A direct hit by lightning is usually fatal. Otherwise, the victim is unlikely to die unless cardiopulmonary arrest occurs. Victims of a lightning strike carry no electrical charge and can be handled safely. Seventy-two percent will suffer loss of consciousness. When needed, administer CPR as long as physically possible. All lightning victims require prompt medical attention. Most will need evacuation assistance. Monitor respiration and pulse until help arrives.

Foreign Travel

Hiking and camping in foreign lands offer adventure, beauty, knowledge, variety, and challenge. Plan ahead to eliminate or mitigate illness and misfortune, for these can put a damper on a dream adventure. Do enough research during the planning stage to ensure that you fulfill all medical and legal requirements. Require proper immunizations, learn about the safety of various foods and beverages (types and preparation methods) and instruct your party accordingly, carry enough first aid supplies, and be able to sterilize drinking water. If needed supplies are not available at your destination, take them with you. It is also important to plan for the personal safety of the hikers.

SUPERVISION

Leaders of hiking and camping groups should possess the following knowledge and skills:

- Knowledge of the wilderness environment, safety considerations, equipment, and the particular wilderness experience at hand
- Good judgment

- Good interpersonal skills
- Personal wilderness skills and physical fitness appropriate to the task
- Experience in group and wilderness leadership
- First aid certification

Everyone should understand the game plan for the activity. Take new leaders on training hikes and provide them growth and leadership opportunities with skilled staff. Leaders should be skilled at listening to their bodies for danger signals and should be adept at observing group members for indicators of potential problems.

The number of leaders needed with a group varies with the difficulty of the activity and the size, age, and skill of the group. It is important to place a leader at the front of the group to set a good pace; navigate successfully; and be alert for dangers such as animals, poison ivy, and drop-offs. A leader at the back of the group serves as the sweeper and keeps the group together, observing and evaluating hikers' behavior, retrieving dropped equipment, and so forth. No one hikes behind the sweeper. Other staff members are interspersed among the group as appropriate.

We encourage personal interaction between the staff and other group members, to enable the staff to appraise group safety and enhance hikers' knowledge and skills. In addition, staff and hiker interaction in wilderness frequently affords teaching opportunities for hikers to learn truths much more important than getting from point A to point B. The goals of optimum leadership include enabling the group to be safe, facilitating the success of each participant, leading without the members of the group feeling they are being led, and helping individuals enjoy the activity and feel good about themselves.

SELECTION AND CONDUCT OF THE ACTIVITY

The skill of the participants and the difficulty of the hike should be compatible. Evaluate participants concerning what they can safely and enjoyably accomplish. Almost everyone can participate in a hike of some kind, and, as wilderness areas become more accessible to handicapped persons, hiking and camping will become an increasingly appealing and wise choice for more people. The challenge of group planners and leaders is to match the activity with the participants, considering physical fitness, knowledge, experience, equipment, duration, distance, difficulty, and current conditions. The more remote the activity, the better your skills must be, because help and rescue become less likely.

Provide participants with written instructions, explanations, and rules. All participants should know the purpose and objectives of the activity. Teaching sessions are important, both before the trip and en route. If participants are not of legal age, it is a good idea to provide parents with the written materials and involve them in their hiker's learning and understanding. Deal with violation of safety rules gently, firmly, and with certainty. Never permit hikers to endanger their lives or the lives of others.

Campsite Safety

Because hikers spend many significant hours in camp, it is important that they choose campsites wisely, for their safety and the well-being of the environment.

Campsite Location

When selecting a campsite location, consider the following: valleys tend to be colder and damper than higher locations; ridges tend to be windy and likely targets of lightning; solitary trees attract lightning; avoid avalanche chutes; stay out of natural drainages and back from the banks of streams that are likely to rise; avoid falling rocks by not camping beneath cliffs; avoid dead trees or trees with large, dead limbs; and camp at least 200 feet from water sources. Camping ethics include avoiding camping in beauty spots or places with delicate plant life and providing privacy and quiet for others.

Campfires and Wilderness Fires

Hikers can endanger themselves, others, and the environment through careless use of fires.

Use open fires only where permitted, safe, and environmentally acceptable. Avoid building a fire under a tree that might catch fire or be damaged, in a site near flammable material, or on top of the forest floor. Be sure to dig through to the soil. Do not put wet rocks in the fire ring. Exercise extreme caution in windy settings, and be sure a fire is totally extinguished before leaving the fire or going to sleep. Sparks can start wildfires and burn holes in clothing and tents. Keep a shovel or container of water handy to extinguish the fire in an emergency.

Stove Safety

Most people do wilderness cooking on camping stoves. There is simply not enough firewood to sustain the current number of hikers. Camp stoves are engineering marvels that weigh little and produce abundant heat. Hikers should follow these safety rules when using camp stoves:

- Only use a stove inside a tent in emergencies. Tent materials may melt or burn, and air in a closed tent with a burning stove becomes dangerous from oxygen depletion and the presence of carbon monoxide. Cook outside or in the vestibule, or forego hot food and beverage.

- Guard against spilling hot liquids.

- Do not attempt to refuel a hot stove.

- Do not enclose a stove in a windscreen unless the fuel is stored separate from the burner and the stove is intended to be used in that configuration.

Sanitation

Proper disposal of human waste is important for health and aesthetic reasons. Use public toilets where available. Otherwise, urinate in places not frequented by others, and defecate no less than 200 feet (preferably up to 300 feet) from the nearest waterway or lake. Dig a cathole six to eight inches deep for the feces. Cover the cathole with the dirt you removed in digging it. You can burn the toilet paper if fire-safety conditions permit. The safest (in terms of preventing fire and disease) disposal of toilet paper is to seal it in a plastic bag, store it in your garbage bag, and carry it out of wil-

Hikers spend many significant hours in camp.

derness. Some wilderness areas now require this method.

Wash dishes and hands with biodegradable soap at least 100 feet from water sources. Do not bury garbage. You packed it in. You pack it out.

Special Concerns

In conducting hiking and camping activities, leaders should possess the skills and judgment to deal with the following factors.

Fatigue

In addition to reducing your enjoyment of hiking and camping, fatigue is also a safety hazard. Most injuries occur when a person is fatigued. Fatigue contributes to impaired judgment and makes you susceptible to many other wilderness illnesses and safety problems. You can diminish fatigue by adequate physical conditioning before the adventure. Recommended training activities include running, walking, climbing stairs, carrying a loaded pack, and physical activity that produces aerobic fitness.

A wise pace will help prevent fatigue. The story of the rabbit and the turtle is true when applied to hiking. Set the pace to the slowest person, for struggling to keep up with the group creates a tired, careless, easily lost, discouraged, and miserable person. A 5-to-10-minute rest stop each hour is wise. When going uphill, use the rest step (momentarily taking weight off the foot as you place it forward at the beginning of each new step) and power breathing (forcefully exhaling each breath, often synchronized with steps).

Navigation

Navigational skills are necessary to understand where you are, where you want to go, and how best to get there. You can enhance safety, success, and enjoyment through acquiring and wisely using navigation skills. All hikers should carry essential navigation tools (map and compass are necessary and an altimeter is helpful) and be trained to use them effectively. Space limitations prevent explaining navigation in this chapter.

Dehydration

Preventing dehydration is one of the most important considerations for backpackers. Water is essential to life and is important in body functions relating to energy, metabolism, controlling body temperature, and eliminating metabolic wastes. Various environmental conditions (cold, dry air or hot temperatures) and personal conditions (heavy breathing, perspiration) add to fluid loss during hiking. A person of average size needs at least 2 quarts of fluid per day at rest, approximately 4 quarts per day when exerting heavily, and 8 to 12 quarts per day in desert climates. The motivation for consuming water should be need, not thirst. If hikers wait until thirsty to drink, they are already fluid deficient. Consume fluids in generous amounts before, during, and after strenuous hiking. Sport drinks and juices work best when diluted by half with water. Because water is heavy (two pounds per quart), it is impossible to carry enough for a multiday outing. Hikers can usually find water to treat and drink in most wilderness areas. Adding your favorite ingredients (tea, coffee, chocolate, lemonade, and powdered drinks) can increase palatability.

Many wilderness problems are caused or exacerbated by insufficient water consumption. In addition to thirst, a good way to determine if you are consuming enough fluid is to check the color of urine. Dark yellow urine indicates insufficient water intake. As you go up in altitude, hydration becomes a greater challenge because the mountain air is dry, and backpackers lose much more water than they realize from breathing and sweating. To stay healthy in wilderness, it is essential to drink enough water consistently.

Falls

You can reduce the number and severity of falls by being in good physical condition, avoiding places where dangerous falls are likely to occur, wearing shoes with good traction and support, concentrating in situations involving exposure, and using proper rope techniques when needed.

Stream Crossing

Take care when crossing wilderness streams, which can present the challenges of cold water, slick stream bottoms, holes, waterfalls, and fast currents. Safety principles for stream crossing include the following:

- Search up and downstream for the best place to cross.
- Be careful when crossing on rocks or logs, which are slick when wet. In early morning, rocks or logs may be covered with a coat of clear ice.
- Cross at a wide spot, where the water is shallow and slow. Do not cross above a waterfall.
- Water levels are higher at the end of the day than in the morning.
- Unbuckle the waist belt on the backpack. If you fall, jettison the pack, turn onto your back with feet downstream, fend off objects with your feet, and work toward shore.
- Stabilize by using a stick to make a tripod, using three people to make a human tripod, or using proper rope techniques to provide a belay.
- If too dangerous, do not cross.

Foot Care

Feet are a hiker's wheels, and, like a car with a flat tire, bad feet can bring to a halt the strongest or most motivated hikers. Prevention is better than cure. Measures to ensure happy feet include the following:

- Boots—proper fitting, broken in, appropriate for the activity.
- Socks—thin inner liner sock with thick outer sock, or one thick sock. Fitted socks are better than tube socks. Avoid socks with prominent seams and cotton socks, which absorb water and create friction. Change socks periodically. Smooth wrinkles when they occur.
- Remove all foreign objects from boot immediately.
- At the first sign of a hot spot, treat the tender area with a product like tape, moleskin,

molefoam, or moist gel pads made specifically for treating blisters.

Harmful People

Regretfully, this is not a perfect world, and we sometimes need to ensure our safety against our own kind. Hikers are safer from criminal acts in wilderness than in most other areas of our society. In this country, crimes against hikers are rare. Exert caution in parts of the world where hikers are sometimes attacked in wilderness for the valuables they are carrying. In some countries, guides help make hikers safer, and armed guards are sometimes used.

Survival

Although space limitations do not permit a thorough discussion of survival situations, we should discuss some basic considerations.

- Keep the party together. In adverse situations, the combined knowledge and resources of all members are an advantage. Later, two or more strong members may want to walk for help, if appropriate.

- Keep calm, sit down, breathe deeply, relax, keep warm and dry, and think. Your brain is your best survival tool.

- Assess the situation and take care of emergencies.

- Most survival situations consist of staying alive until rescued. If people outside of wilderness know where you are, they will find you. Effective ways of signaling for help include three of anything, blazing fires at night, smoking fires during the day, reflected sunlight, whistles, flares, electronic devices, bright colors, and spelling out SOS with available objects (tree branches, rocks, etc.). The ten *essential* items hikers should always carry are shown in the photo on the next page.

- The most important things hikers need to stay alive are shelter and water. Food is not a major consideration, because a person can go more than three weeks without food. Water will become critical in approximately three days. If water is limited, do not gulp it, avoid unnecessary activity that causes sweating, and limit food and salt intake. If no water is available, do not eat. Never drink urine or seawater, as the high solute content will cause increased dehydration.

- The big decision is whether to walk out or stay put and be found. Contrary to human ego and adventure needs, the safest option is to stay put and be rescued.

- Do whatever is necessary to survive. Survival largely depends on human will. Survive!

Hikers should create a list of personal essential items that they will always want to keep handy. The list might include such items as water (bottles and means of treatment), two garbage bags, whistle, glasses, skin and lip protection, insect repellent, personal items, medicine, lubricating cream, toilet paper, money, repair kit, and so forth. Group leaders should always carry a survival kit appropriate to the situation.

ADMINISTRATION

Trip planning must ensure that the group will carry and be able to use equipment appropriate to the locale and current conditions. In addition to the equipment and safety principles we have noted throughout the chapter, leaders should keep in mind the following leadership practices and principles.

Study routes for possible danger areas, and plan emergency removal routes. If circumstances warrant, it is wise to carry a cell phone (with appropriate numbers to call) or radio you can use to call for help. If you need help to remove an injured hiker and you can't get it by telephone or radio, devise a plan in which some members of the party stay with the injured hiker and others go for help. Leave adequate supplies and trained personnel with the victim. The persons going for help should be skilled in navigation and should carry a map noting the exact location of the person, the nature of the injury and condition of the hiker, money and telephone numbers of rangers and local law enforcement, and any other items (such as car keys, etc.) necessary to carry out the rescue.

Ten essential supplies for outdoor safety.

Be sure the rescue plan is understood before the party splits.

Provide a written schedule of events to all staff, participants, parents of minors, and a specified responsible person who can initiate search and rescue procedures if the group does not return in a reasonable time. The trip leader should notify the responsible person when the group returns. Keep records in accordance with policies of the sponsoring entity and other regulatory agencies.

Train staff to retreat from an objective, regardless how desired, if it is too difficult or risky. Safety comes before pleasing others, trying to keep a schedule, or achieving an objective.

BIBLIOGRAPHY

American Red Cross. 1993. *Emergency response.* St. Louis: Mosby Lifeline.

Brown, R.E. 1990. *Emergency/survival handbook.* 5th ed. Bellevue, WA: American Outdoor Safety League.

Darvill, F.T., Jr. 1994. *Mountaineering medicine: A wilderness medical guide.* 13th ed. Berkeley, CA: Wilderness Press.

Exercise walking still number one activity. 1995. *The Journal of Physical Education, Recreation & Dance.* 66 (5): 12.

Forgey, W.W. 1994. *Wilderness medicine.* 4th ed. Merrillville, IN: ICS Books.

Ganci, D. 1991. *Desert survival.* Merrillville, IN: ICS Books.

Graydon, D., ed. 1992. *Mountaineering, the freedom of the hills.* 5th ed. Seattle: Mountaineers Books.

Powers, P. 1993. *NOLS wilderness mountaineering.* Mechanicsburg, PA: Stackpole Books.

Tilton, B. 1994. Talking dirty. *Backpacker* 22 (132): 48-53.

chapter 6

Winter Hiking and Camping

Norman L. Gilchrest

Winter turns the wilderness world into a beautiful, majestic, challenging, and unique place. Camping in winter can be a wonderful experience. The purpose of this chapter is to provide information and ideas that will help you conduct a safe and enjoyable winter adventure in wilderness.

Winter camping experiences vary greatly, depending on the geographical area of the country and current weather conditions. For example, hiking in central Texas in January during warm weather may require only equipment and techniques appropriate in spring. In contrast, hiking in Wyoming at the same time during a winter storm may involve near-survival conditions, during which safe and enjoyable camping will depend on specialized equipment and wise and effective behavior. This chapter will focus on how to safely enjoy cold winter wilderness conditions. Most people enjoy winter camping when done safely and at a level appro-priate for their skills. Give winter hiking and camping a try. You will be rewarded beyond your wildest dreams.

ENVIRONMENTAL CONDITIONS

We will discuss topics relating to environmental conditions in alphabetical order. Please remember that this chapter supplements, and will not duplicate, the information in the Hiking and Camping chapter.

Avalanches

Few things in nature are as gentle as a single snowflake. Wind blows it off course. A touch melts it. However, snowflakes do not fall alone. Snowflakes fall with billions of other snowflakes. As snowflakes settle on the ground, they immediately attach to their neighbors and become part of an interconnected mass of snow.

UNIQUE ASPECTS OF HIKING AND CAMPING IN WINTER

Winter campers must understand that the realities are different for winter. Some are fascinating, such as the effects of shorter days and longer nights, which means less travel time and longer sleep time than most folks want. Some experiences require a learning curve, such as how to use the toilet in snow at midnight when there is a 20-mile-per-hour wind and the temperature is minus 25 degrees Fahrenheit.

The big difference is the cold and the effect it has on all aspects of the camping experience. All activities carry additional risks and require additional care, better equipment, superior skills, and increased fitness. The penalty for mistakes is greater, and the chance for rescue is reduced. Keep in mind that there is no ski patrol out there. A mishap that might be a mere inconvenience in summer can be serious in winter. You must be aware of the realities of the environment and make adjustments. Winter is not forgiving of carelessness or foolishness.

However, winter is rewarding for those who go into it using good skills and judgment. For those who have experienced wilderness in winter, no explanation is needed. For those who have not, you owe it to yourself to go. Persons venturing into wilderness in winter must keep in mind the possible severity of situations that may develop. Winter hikers must acquire knowledge from experience and a number of sources; develop skills in a safe, progressive manner; use safe and effective equipment; and use good judgment at all times. Ways of gaining experience include hiking with capable winter travellers and attending courses availiable from professional groups.

When the tug of gravity on snow exceeds the cohesiveness in the snowpack, the snow slides downhill, causing a snow avalanche.

Avalanches can travel at speeds of 279 miles per hour, weigh up to 2 billion pounds, hit objects with a force of more than 200,000 pounds per square meter, and carry people long distances before burying them under tons of snow. It is estimated that in this country 10,000 avalanches are seen and approximately 100,000 avalanches occur each year. We must avoid such potentially destructive power.

There are two types of avalanche, slab and loose snow. Most serious avalanche injuries are caused by slab avalanches, which are characterized by large cohesive areas of snow beginning to slide at once at a fracture line. In contrast, loose snow avalanches start at one point and move as a formless mass with little internal cohesion.

Conditions Contributing to Avalanches

Although it is important to be able to predict when snow will slide, even experts cannot predict avalanches with certainty. However, learning about avalanches and paying attention to environmental conditions can make winter travel safer. Consider three main variables—snowpack, weather, and terrain. The following are contributing conditions to avalanches and clues to avalanche danger:

• Most slab avalanches start on slopes with angles between 30 and 45 degrees. Slopes steeper than 45 degrees tend to slide so frequently that snow buildup is less, and slopes less than 30 degrees have less sheer stress. However, there are exceptions, and all slopes between 25 and 60 degrees merit careful scrutiny. No slopes are guaranteed safe. You can measure the incline of a slope by an inclinometer. A less accurate method of measuring slope steepness is to contrast the angle of the slope with a person's hand held with the index finger pointing straight up and the thumb pointing 90 degrees to the side (see figure 5.1).

• Convex sections of slopes, which are the high-stress points, are more likely to avalanche.

• Rapid snowfall (one foot total or one inch per hour) increases the danger of avalanche. Be alert to dangerous conditions of six inches or more of new snow. Eighty to ninety percent of all avalanches occur during and shortly after storms, so be careful for at least a day or two after a storm.

• Lack of cohesiveness between snow layers leads to avalanche. Dig a pit to examine the snow layers and determine the degree of

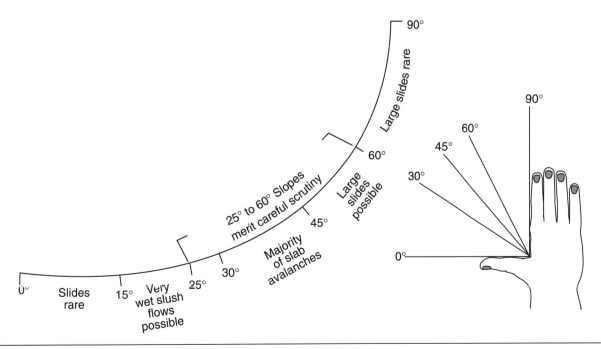

Figure 5.1   Effect of slope angle on avalanche probability.

© Norman Gilchrest

When hiking in the snow, ridges are much safer than slopes, where avalanches can occur.

cohesion. Kits are available to facilitate this procedure.

• Temperature affects the stability of snow. Long, hot spells, followed by heavy snow, create an unstable layer. Cold temperatures can maintain instability in the snowpack, whereas warm temperatures allow snow settlement and increasing stability.

• Wind greater than 15 miles per hour, even during clear weather, can lead to instability. The windward side of a slope or ridge is safer than the leeward side. Snow plumes from ridges and peaks indicate that snow is being moved to leeward slopes.

• Different types of snow crystals have diverse effects on its stability. Small crystals (pellets and needles) may result in more dangerous conditions than the classic star-shaped crystals.

• A cornice is consolidated snow that extends to the leeward side of a ridge top. When traveling atop a ridge, the cornice may not be apparent, so be careful not to walk atop a cornice and cause it to break. Because cornices sometimes break off without any help from hikers, it is also wise to avoid traveling under a cornice.

• Avalanche dangers increase with elevation. Most large avalanches start higher than timberline. Trees add a degree of stability to a slope but are no guarantee.

Avoiding and Dealing With Avalanches

Rule number one of avalanche safety is *avoid*. Determine present conditions and future weather possibilities by using your knowledge and reports by appropriate government agencies (National Park Service, National Forest Service, Bureau of Land Management), local authorities, local ski areas, outdoor shops, newspapers, radio, and TV. Look for signs of avalanche—snowballs rolling down the slope, cracks (particularly those running for some distance), and sounds like a collapse "whumpf." To study the cohesiveness between layers of snow, dig a pit, study the snow layers, and determine their stability. If unacceptable avalanche danger exists, do not go. The mountain will exist tomorrow. Be sure you exist tomorrow.

Avoid apparent avalanche slopes. These are obvious, with a lack of trees being a good clue. Generally, avalanches occur repeatedly in the same areas. Be mindful that solo travel in avalanche country carries quite a risk.

If caught in a rare situation that necessitates traveling in areas of avalanche danger, cross possible avalanche areas at the coldest time of day; avoid the center of a slope by going straight up or down the edge; do not traverse back and forth across the slope (skiers turning start many avalanches); cross higher than the avalanche zone or in the valley beyond the runout zone, rather than in midslope; and avoid steep, open gullies and slopes that funnel into a gully or over a cliff.

Generally, the two safest areas to travel are ridges (but watch for cornices on the leeward side) and valleys, far from the steep sides of mountains and beyond the runout area. Realize that sometimes there is no safe route. Turn back.

If you absolutely must cross an avalanche slope, expose only one person at a time. Loosen things attached to you, such as ski attachments, pole straps, pack straps. Get as warm as possible. Close all clothing openings, and put on hat and gloves. Be sure your transceiver is turned on and set to TRANSMIT.

If you get caught in an avalanche call out to the party to watch you. Discard your skis, poles, and pack. Swim to stay on top—thrash about. This may result in your being spit out or bringing an arm or a leg to the surface when the avalanche stops. Put your hands over your face if swimming does not help. Keep your mouth closed during the avalanche. Try to get to the side and out of an avalanche. Before the snow halts, take a deep breath, clear out space in front of your face, and put up a hand. Most victims are found because something is visible above the snow. If trapped, conserve oxygen. Exercise self control. If one hard push does not get you out, do not struggle. If you are buried

Table 5.1
AVALANCHE RESCUE EQUIPMENT FOR EVERY GROUP MEMBER

EQUIPMENT	DESCRIPTION
Transceiver	This electronic device transmits and receives signals. Put in new batteries at the beginning of the trip, turn the transceiver on, set it to TRANSMIT mode, place it around your neck, and leave it there the entire trip. After an avalanche, all rescuers change their transceiver mode from TRANSMIT to RECEIVE and initiate search patterns. It is important that all transceivers operate on the same frequency (the new international standard is 457 kHz, replacing the old American standard frequency of 2.275 kHz) and that you perfect search techniques through practice before an emergency. The transceiver is far superior to the old practice of attaching a 50-foot red avalanche cord to winter hikers in the hope the cord would be visible on the surface after an avalanche.
Shovel	Each hiker is responsible for being able to dig out victims. Hands or other objects are ineffective.
Ski poles	Poles that join to form a probe are useful.

more than two feet deep, you probably cannot free yourself. If you hear voices, yell once or twice loudly. Do not go to sleep. Expect it to be black if you are buried more than one foot deep.

Avalanche Rescue Principles and Techniques

Table 5.1 describes the essential equipment for performing avalanche rescue. If you are called on to rescue someone from an avalanche, keep the following in mind.

- Time is critical. You are working against the clock. Do not go for help, unless help can get there almost immediately. You are a buried victim's only hope for rescue. Survival rates for length of time buried under an avalanche are: 30 minutes—50 percent, 1 hour—30 percent, 2 hours—20 percent, 3 hours—10 percent. Search for 24 hours, in hopes that there will be an air pocket.

- Avoid being caught in another avalanche.

- Mark the point you last saw the victim. Do a quick search in the avalanche path.

- Rescuers set their transceivers to RECEIVE mode and conduct a search. Rescuers who do not have transceivers search with probes.

- Dig the victim out if found. Only one in three completely buried victims survive. Suffocation is the greatest killer, due to lack of oxygen and the fact that buried victims have difficulty expanding their chests. Hypothermia is also a serious problem. The survival rate for buried victims is 85 percent if visible on the surface or buried no deeper than nine inches, 20 percent if buried six feet, and statistically zero if buried lower than seven feet.

- If found alive, treat the victim for hypothermia and shock. In addition, treatment may be needed for suffocation, cardiac arrest, bleeding, and fractures. Evacuation should take place as soon as possible.

Medical Problems Related to Cold

Hypothermia is the most common and dangerous hiking-related health problem, but frostbite is also a major concern for winter hikers.

Use the following guidelines to protect yourself from the effects of cold weather.

Hypothermia

Resulting from loss of heat from the body's core, hypothermia occurs when body temperature drops lower than approximately 95 degrees Fahrenheit and the body loses heat more rapidly than it can produce it. Conditions need not be extreme for hypothermia to develop. Death can occur in a surprisingly short time (a few hours), even in temperatures higher than freezing. Major factors leading to hypothermia are cool or cold weather, wind, and wet clothing. Other contributing elements include physical exhaustion, improper clothing, and insufficient nourishment. To prevent hypothermia, do everything you can to stay warm. Keep the trunk and head warm to keep blood flowing to extremities. Carry, and use when needed, good insulation and a shell garment that can deal effectively with wind and moisture. Keep dry, and replace wet clothes with dry clothes when appropriate. Eat and drink frequently, consuming hot food and beverages. Build a fire. Check all members of the party. Hikers with hypothermia usually cannot identify their problem and will maintain that they are all right, but stay alert for the symptoms of hypothermia (see table 5.2). Rest before exhaustion occurs.

Treatment of Hypothermia

Prompt treatment for hypothermia is important. Warm the victim gradually. Provide warm clothing and additional insulation, such as sleeping bag, blankets, jackets, hats, gloves, and insulating pads. Use shared body heat inside sleeping bags if necessary, and move the victim to a warm environment, one that provides shelter out of the wind and moisture. Aid circulation by loosening boots, belts, and other constrictive clothing. Give warm, sweetened liquids, sweets, and carbohydrates if the victim is alert. Do not give alcohol. Increase exercise level as appropriate. Vigorous exercise can increase heat production by 1,000 percent.

If medical help is near, seek it immediately. Keep working to save the victim. Very cold patients may appear dead but might revive when normal temperatures are restored.

Table 5.2
SYMPTOMS OF HYPOTHERMIA

LEVEL OF SEVERITY	SYMPTOMS
Early-stage hypothermia	☐ Shivering. ☐ Feel cold. ☐ Loss of coordination and increasing clumsiness. ☐ Slow, irregular pulse. ☐ Numbness, fatigue, sleepiness. ☐ Questionable judgement, irresponsibility. ☐ Hallucinations. ☐ Irritability. ☐ Slurred, thick speech. ☐ Stupor, glassy stare. ☐ Lethargy, apathy, and decreased levels of consciousness.
Severe hypothermia	☐ Shivering will cease. ☐ Breathing will slow or stop. ☐ The pulse will be slow and irregular. ☐ The body will feel stiff. ☐ Person descends into unconsciousness. Death may result in a few hours if body temperture is not raised. ☐ Few individuals survive body temperatures lower than 75 degrees Fahrenheit.

Frostbite

Frostbite occurs when the fluid in body tissues freezes. The body parts most often affected are the face, hands, and feet. Although it can be painful and may result in permanent damage, frostbite is seldom directly responsible for death.

Preventing Frostbite

You can prevent frostbite by keeping the body warm and protected. The temperature of the skin must be 24 degrees Fahrenheit to freeze. The degree of frostbite damage is determined by the temperature, the length of exposure, and the wind. Other contributing factors are fatigue, dehydration, and lack of food. The principles of hypothermia prevention discussed previously also apply to frostbite. Key considerations are to use adequate insulation and to avoid exposing skin to extreme cold or windchill. Watch each other for symptoms of frostbite (see table 5.3).

Treating Frostbite

Handle frostbitten areas gently. Do not rub the area, especially with snow. To do so can cause tissue damage and result in gangrene. In emergency situations, a person can walk on frostbitten feet, but it is best for victims not to use frostbitten areas.

Table 5.3
SYMPTOMS OF FROSTBITE

SYMPTOMS
☐   At first a cold feeling that is painful
☐   Later a loss of sensation
☐   Skin appears waxy, white, grey, or purple tinged
☐   Skin cold to touch
☐   Stiffness

Warm the affected area. In less serious cases, place the area against the warm skin of the victim or a companion. Warm serious cases by gently soaking the frostbitten area in water no warmer than 100 to105 degrees Fahrenheit. Do not hold the injury close to a fire or stove. Once a part is warmed, don't allow it refreeze. If you cannot keep it warm, do not thaw it. A delay of up to one day in thawing makes relatively little difference. Seek medical attention.

Keeping Warm

People who dislike winter or wilderness recreational activities usually do so because they get cold. No one enjoys being cold. It is just plain miserable at best and dangerous at worst. The good news is that most people can be warm, comfortable, and safe in even the coldest conditions. All you need to do is to observe the principles of warmth. People who get cold are usually violating one or more of these principles. So, if you get cold in wilderness in winter, changing your behavior will probably solve your problem. Following are the basic principles of warmth.

Humans are warm-blooded animals and must maintain a temperature near 98.6 degrees. Body reactions to cold are the following:

- Shivering begins. Shivering increases heat production fivefold (Gill 1991).

- Vasoconstriction (constriction of blood vessels in all extremities except the head) occurs, reducing heat loss through skin, muscles, and fat. This ensures a flow of warm blood to vital organs such as the brain, heart, lungs, and digestive organs.
- The heart beats harder and faster.
- The metabolic rate increases up to sixfold. As much as our bodies try to maintain a temperature of 98.6 degrees, it cannot be done without proper behavior on our part. We can stay warm in two ways—acquiring heat and preventing heat loss.

How We Lose Body Heat

Understanding how the body loses heat and preventing heat loss is of utmost importance

If well prepared, you can be warm, comfortable, and safe in even the coldest conditions.

© Cheyenne Rouse

in staying warm. The body loses heat in four ways.

1. *Radiation* of heat from the body is the most important method of heat loss, normally accounting for more than one-half of the body's heat loss. The body constantly emits heat waves into the surrounding environment. Much radiant heat loss is through the head and the thighs. The head has a large amount of blood flow, and an unprotected head can account for 50 percent of the body's total heat loss at 40 degrees Fahrenheit and up to 75 percent at 5 degrees Fahrenheit. The head is the thermostat of the body. If you are cold, put on a hat; if you are hot, take off your hat. Putting on a hat can warm the entire body because of vasodilatation. It works like this: putting on a hat prevents heat loss through the head. When the body gets warm enough, the blood vessels to the extremities dilate, permitting a flow of warming blood throughout the body. The extremities become warm; hence the truth in the statement, "To warm your feet, put on a hat."

2. *Conduction* is heat transfer to a colder object through direct contact. Heat loss through conduction is usually small, but when it happens, it occurs rapidly.

3. *Convection* is transferring heat from the body by the motion of air. Convective action is constant and, unless counteracted, can have a large effect, as data in the accompanying wind-chill chart illustrates (see figure 5.2).

4. *Evaporation* is nature's way of cooling the body. Evaporating fluid generates a cooling effect, causing a heat loss of 580 calories for each gram of water evaporated from the skin. There are three types of evaporative heat loss:

- *Sensible perspiration (sweat)* occurs when we get too hot. In cold weather, avoid perspiring. In addition to cooling the body, the moisture will get into the insulation and inhibit the insulating properties. To avoid sweating, ventilate by opening cuffs and the neck of garments, and taking off layers of clothing.
- *Insensible perspiration* is the constant production of moisture by the body. We cannot stop this type of fluid loss, but we must be aware of it and deal with the result.
- *Breathing (respiration)* expels warm, moist air with every breath. As with insensible perspiration, we cannot stop this type of cooling, but we must deal with it. In extreme cold, the air we inhale is cold unless we prewarm it by breathing through a mask or scarf covering the mouth and nose.

Acquiring Heat

We acquire heat in two ways. First, we create heat by taking in fuel (food, whose heat-producing potential is measured in calories) and burning that fuel through exercise. Body movement, whether involuntary (shivering) or voluntary, produces heat. Vigorous exercise can increase heat production by 1,000 percent.

Also, remember seeking warmth by standing near a stove or standing in sunlight rather than shade? Remember how good hot chocolate or coffee tastes and feels on a cold day? In each case, you were getting warmer by acquiring heat through absorption.

Insulation

The way to stop heat loss is to lessen the difference between the temperature of the body and the air surrounding it. Unlike most other animals, humans have little natural protection against the cold. We have no feathers, no down, and insufficient hair to stay warm, but we can use insulation to achieve the same result. Insulation does not produce heat, but it can stop heat loss. The quality of an insulator is determined by its ability to trap spaces of nonmoving air. The more nonmoving air an insulator can trap, the better the insulator and the warmer the wearer. In most cases, warmth is directly related to the thickness of insulation. Three factors work against insulation—pressure, wind, and moisture. A hiker must ensure that nothing interferes with the insulation's ability to trap spaces of nonmoving air.

Pressure. Layers of clothing should fit loosely, allowing insulation to be as thick as possible. Any compression of insulation will inhibit its ability to insulate.

WIND CHILL									
Wind speed in MPH	Air Temperature in °F								
	40	30	20	10	0	-10	-20	-30	-40
	Comparable windchill temperature								
0 - 4	40	30	20	10	0	-10	-20	-30	-40
5	37	27	16	6	-5	-15	-26	-36	-47
10	28	16	4	-9	-21	-33	-46	-58	-70
15	22	9	-5	-18	-36	-45	-58	-72	-85
20	18	4	-10	-25	-39	-53	-67	-82	-96
25	16	0	-15	-29	-44	-59	-74	-88	-104
30	13	-2	-18	-33	-48	-63	-79	-94	-109
35	11	-4	-20	-35	-49	-67	-83	-98	-113
40	10	-6	-21	-37	-53	-69	-85	-100	-116
over 40	little effect on windchill								
	Little danger of frostbite			Increasing danger of frostbite			Great danger of frostbite		

Figure 5.2 Windchill chart. Other factors (such as moisture, age, health, and body characteristics) can affect how the human body responds to temperature extremes. This chart is an estimation for dry, properly clothed, healthy adults.

Data from *Wind Chill* (National Oceanic and Atmospheric Administration one page mailout) 1997 and *Winter Recreation Guide* (U.S. Department of Agriculture, Forest Service, Rocky Mountain Region pamphlet) 1987.

Wind. Wind can destroy the properties of insulating materials by driving out the nonmoving air and replacing it with colder air. Wear a shell (outside) garment that prevents wind from entering the insulation.

Moisture. Moisture destroys the insulating qualities of several types of insulators and, in all insulators, creates problems when it freezes in the outer part of the insulation during cold weather. Hikers must be conscious of moisture and choose a method of dealing with both internal moisture (produced by the body) and external moisture (produced by the external environment).

A hiker can use a clothing system that permits moisture to pass from the body through all layers of clothing to the air. This is called the vapor pass approach to moisture. In dressing using the vapor pass approach to moisture, wear three types of clothing: (1) an inner *wicking layer* to wick the moisture from the skin and pass it outward, (2) one or more *insulating layers* (as much insulation as needed), and (3) an *outer shell garment* to keep wind and external moisture out of the insulation while permitting the escaping moisture to pass to the outside. The challenge to the vapor pass approach is twofold: the shell must be capable of letting internal moisture pass while prohibiting external moisture from entering, and in extreme cold, the escaping moisture will freeze on the outer portions of the insulating system.

With the second method, a hiker puts a vapor barrier, usually coated nylon or plastic, on both sides of the insulation to keep internal and external moisture out of the insulation altogether. A hiker using this approach to moisture would dress as follows: (1) a thin *internal layer* next to the skin, (2) a *vapor barrier layer*, (3) one or more *insulating layers* (as much insulation as needed), and (4) an *outer shell* to keep wind and moisture out of the insulation. The body's moisture sensors retard moisture production when the skin reaches an appropriate dampness, preventing hikers from sloshing around in their own portable sauna. This system works well only in extreme cold (below zero degrees Fahrenheit). The vapor barrier approach works best when the hiker is sleeping or inactive. During periods of hard work, the body may not sufficiently reduce sweat production. The two strong points of the vapor barrier approach are that it reduces the body's fluid loss and it keeps insulation dry.

Insulating and Shell Materials

We can classify fabrics used in hiking as natural or synthetic. Each fabric has its positive and negative qualities. Major considerations in choosing insulating and shell materials are weight, compressibility, insulating quality (ability to trap spaces of nonmoving air), ability to continue insulating when wet, feel, and cost.

Natural Insulators. Cotton is a favorite fabric, but its ability to attract and hold water makes it a terrible insulator. In winter, avoid wearing any cotton garments. Cotton kills!

Wool is a good insulator and warms even when wet. Negatives are that it is heavy, does not compress well, and makes some people itch.

Down is the fine, soft, fluffy feathers next to the skin of ducks and geese. Advantages are lightness, compressibility, great feel, longevity, and low long-term cost. Down is the lightest insulator known, providing twice as much warmth for the weight as the next best insulator. Negatives of down include inability to insulate when wet and high initial cost.

Silk is used for wicking layers such as socks, underwear, and long underwear.

Synthetic Insulators. Synthetic insulators have several positive attributes as wicking layers and insulators, tending to have lower initial cost, ability to insulate when wet, and ability to wick water from the body. Negatives include being heavier, less compressible, and shorter-lived than down.

Shell Garments. The ideal shell garments let body vapor pass and keep external moisture and wind out. Fabrics such as Gore-Tex accomplish this well. Impermeable shell garments are good for the vapor barrier approach only. In other uses, the wearer gets wet from internal moisture.

Additional Pointers

Here are some additional recommendations for winter hikers.

- Dress in layers to facilitate adjusting to changing temperature needs.
- Securely attach critical items to prevent loss. Carry spare items of critical clothing such as socks, mittens, and hat. Spare shoes are a good idea for many winter wilderness situations.
- Mittens are warmer than gloves.
- Sun protection in the form of sunblock, lip protection, good sunglasses, and sun hat are critical in winter.

SUPERVISION

Supervision of winter hiking and camping includes all the concepts discussed in the Hiking and Camping chapter, plus the knowledge and skills needed to provide good supervision in the harsher winter environment. The duties and skills of a leader should include planning, understanding environmental conditions, navigation, breaking trail, setting the pace, and gathering the group's opinions before making major decisions.

Anticipate needs—eat before you are hungry, drink before you are thirsty, take off clothing before you sweat, put it back on before you are chilly, and rest before you are tired. Good leadership and supervision can make the difference between pleasure and misery, between safety and danger.

Do not exceed the limits of the group. There are plenty of challenges without creating unwanted ones. It is a poor leader who gets pleasure out of showing his speed and strength in ways that diminish the safety and enjoyment of other group members. Nobody sets out to experience a difficult and painful ordeal. Good supervision will help to ensure that the adventure will be safe and enjoyable for all.

SELECTION AND CONDUCT OF THE ACTIVITY

Consult and apply the principles discussed in the Hiking and Camping chapter. In addition, selection criteria for participants are more stringent for winter hiking and camping. Be sure participants are capable of safely engaging in the planned activity. Do not permit people to participate who might endanger their health or the safety of others. Before ambitious activities, it is wise to screen the participants by review of written vitae and, if possible, by personal observation. Hikers should gradually increase the difficulties of their activities, ensuring that they are not exceeding their capabilities at each step. Each participant should be properly skilled, conditioned, motivated, and equipped. Safety is enhanced by having at least four people in the group.

The Campsite

A good campsite is important to safe and enjoyable winter camping. Select the site in daylight, and set up camp before dark. Seek a flat area at least 200 feet from water. Avoid camping in avalanche areas, in windy areas, and under trees. Keep in mind that cold settles. Establish separate cooking and toilet areas, and make trails to each.

Shelter

The need for adequate shelter in winter camping is obvious. Favorable comments are frequently written about using natural shelters (see figure 5.3, a and b) in winter; however, most people who have spent much time in a natural shelter in winter feel that a tent is a far better choice. Natural shelters have these advantages: you do not have to carry a tent, they may be a place of refuge in an emergency, warmer, and quieter. Disadvantages of natural shelters are the following: time and effort needed to build them, and moisture. Types of natural shelters include a snow cave, a pit at the base of a tree covered by branches, a snow ditch covered with branches or other objects, a lean-to, fallen trees, rocks, and a shallow cave. If nothing better is available, use a plastic bag to cover your body to protect it from the wind. Whatever shelter you use, insulate the floor as deeply as possible with any personal and natural materials that are available. What is beneath your body is as important as what is covering it.

Winter tents are marvels of design. Features usually include strong materials (cloth, poles, and stitching), tunnel entrances, more than one door, and streamlined design.

Sleeping

The long winter nights, which are about 14 hours long at the winter solstice, provide ample, even too much, time for sleeping. If you go to sleep at 6 P.M., you will have your 8 hours completed at 2 A.M.. There are other hindrances to a sunset-to-dawn sleeping experience. Seldom will you make it through the night without answering the call of nature, and, on snowy nights, someone needs to go out to shovel the snow away from the ventilation areas of the tent. The consolation is that the star-spangled sky that greets your grudging trips out of the sleeping bag will be some of the most spectacular you will ever see. Awesome!

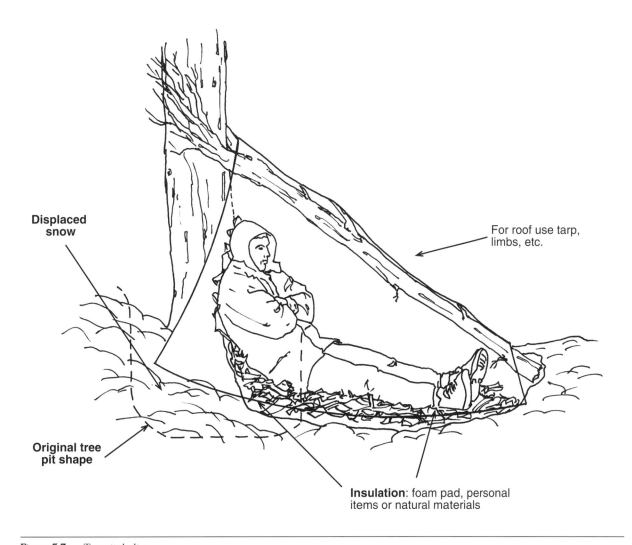

Displaced snow

For roof use tarp, limbs, etc.

Original tree pit shape

Insulation: foam pad, personal items or natural materials

Figure 5.3a   Tree pit shelter.

Several items are important to safe and comfortable sleeping in winter. One or more sleeping pads are essential for warmth and comfort. The cold will seep up from the snow and ice you are sleeping on, providing you with a textbook example of conductive heat loss. Several combinations of pads are capable of protecting you from the snow:

- Closed-cell foam pads, half inch (use minimum of one) or quarter inch (use minimum of two).

- Inflatable, foam-filled air mattress, full thickness (use one).

- Both closed-cell pad (use one) and inflatable, foam-filled air mattress (use one). This is preferred.

A good four-season sleeping bag is necessary. Features to look for are thick insulation (the thicker the insulation, the warmer the bag), draft collar (a flap to keep warmth from escaping from around the shoulder area), hood, baffle covering zipper, mummy shape, large enough for you to feel comfortable, differential cut construction (the inner wall of the bag is smaller than the outer wall), the type of insulation appropriate to your situation, and long enough to provide warm storage for items you do not want to freeze. You can extend the temperature comfort range of a sleeping bag by adding a Gore-Tex cover, wearing additional clothing inside the bag, laying clothing over the outside of the bag (taking care not to reduce the loft of the bag's insulation), putting one sleeping bag inside another, putting a

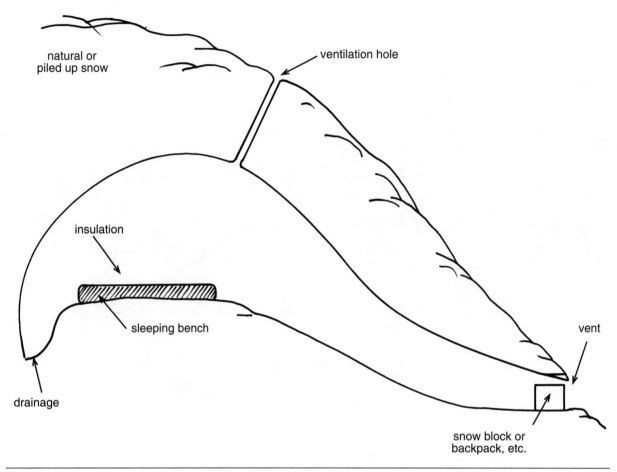

natural or
piled up snow

ventilation hole

insulation

sleeping bench

drainage

vent

snow block or
backpack, etc.

Figure 5.3b   Snow shelter.

container of warm liquid inside the bag, doing isometric contractions inside the bag (serves the same function as shivering or exercises), and sharing body heat (put one rectangular bag over two people or zip two bags together).

Do not sleep with your head inside the bag, for you will add much moisture to the insulation of the bag. When extremely cold, you will want to prewarm the air you inhale by placing a garment over your head. Dry the sleeping bag and all wet clothing at every opportunity.

Fire

Heat is always important and sometimes critical in winter camping. Uses include melting snow for water and cooking. Because wood fires are difficult to build and use in winter, you should use them only in emergencies. Dry wood is hard to find, and you must clear snow to the ground to provide a solid base for the fire. When built on snow, the fire simply melts the snow beneath it and stops burning as it disappears into the snow.

Backpacking stoves are ideal for winter camping. Select a brand and model noted for good performance in winter. If the temperature is below zero degrees Fahrenheit, store the stove and fuel in the sleeping bag at night to keep ingredients in the fuel from consolidating. Carry spare stove parts, and know how to use them. If the stove is critical to your survival, carry two stoves, as well as several ways of starting a fire. To keep the hot stove and cooking utensils from melting the snow and sinking, it is a good idea to use an insulator between the stove and the snow or to clear the snow all the way to the ground.

Sanitation

Personal cleanliness is always important in wilderness and need not be abandoned in winter. Clean the body as needed with warm water, alcohol, or baby wipes (keep them from freezing). It is best to do these minibathing sessions in a warm sleeping bag, but you may accomplish them in the open on a warm day, depending on your hardiness. As always, be sure to wash hands after using the toilet and before eating.

Sanitary defecation and urination practices are necessary for your immediate and long-term health and for the safety of those who follow. Procedures and precautions are the same as for the other seasons of the year. Choose areas that will not be traveled frequently when the snow melts. Do not just bury the feces beneath the snow; instead, clear the snow and dig a cathole in the ground if possible.

Miscellaneous Equipment

Every winter camper has favorite equipment. Some frequently used equipment not mentioned elsewhere in this chapter or in the Hiking and Camping chapter are the following: ice ax (used as a brake to arrest falls on steep slopes, for chopping steps, and as an anchor); candle (produces light, cheer, and some warmth inside a shelter); thermos (keeps drinks warm); and wands (highly visible material on a lightweight shaft to place along the route as navigational markers).

Special Concerns

Here are some additional issues to consider before you head out on your winter hiking expedition.

Food

Proper diet is important to winter hikers, who need about 1,000 more calories per day than in summer. The winter diet is different in quantity and type, because winter hikers work harder, carry more equipment, and deal with the effects of cold weather. Plan menus to ensure approximately 5,000 calories or more per day, consuming more fats than at other seasons of the year. Breakfast and dinner should include hot food and beverage, but you will usually eat lunch on the move. Frequent snacking on high-energy

food aids in providing body warmth and vigor. We encourage vitamin and mineral supplements.

Water Consumption

Hikers frequently neglect fluid needs in winter. Keep in mind that the body needs fluid for such important functions as energy, metabolism, controlling body temperature, and eliminating metabolic wastes. In addition, adequate hydration is important in dealing with frostbite and altitude sickness.

There are several reasons hikers tend to drink less water in winter: (1) psychologically, being surrounded by all that frozen water, we tend to be less mindful of our fluid needs; (2) water is harder to obtain and keep handy; and (3) we sometimes are not prompted by thirst to drink. Force liquids in winter. Keep fluids handy, and make them more appealing by making your favorite beverages. A thermos of your favorite hot drink can provide a psychological and physical lift. Avoid alcoholic beverages, because alcohol makes the body colder by dilating the surface blood vessels and depressing body functions when optimum function is essential.

You can obtain water from unfrozen streams and lakes and by melting snow. As in other seasons, you must purify *all* water from wilderness, regardless the source, by appropriate methods. Regretfully, our concept, "as pure as the driven snow," does not apply.

In melting snow, begin with clean snow, and put some water in the bottom of the pot. Defeat the flat taste by pouring the water back and forth between containers or adding your favorite flavors. If weather and time permit, you can reduce fuel consumption for melting snow by placing a thin layer of snow on a dark plastic bag and an open container at the lower end of the plastic. The sun will cause the snow to melt and run into the container.

When getting water from streams, be careful not to fall in. Rather than get too close to a dangerous situation at water's edge, extend your reach by dipping water with an open container tied to a ski pole.

Locomotion

Frozen precipitation as snow or ice presents locomotion challenges for winter hikers. Snow, unless well compacted, permits the feet to sink below its surface because it cannot support the body weight concentrated on the small surface area of the foot. You will find firmer snow, which provides faster and safer travel, early in the day, in shade, on south and west slopes, and in dirty snow (because it absorbs more heat and therefore consolidates more quickly).

Hikers have several options for footwear in winter. If the snow is shallow or compacted, normal winter hiking boots or other insulated footwear will be best. If the snow is deep or not compacted, snowshoes or skis will distribute the body weight over a larger area and prevent or reduce sinking into the snow. When traveling on ice, crampons (strong metal spikes attached to footwear) are necessary to provide traction. Strong, adjustable ski poles are necessary for skiing and useful (for stability and getting up after a fall) with other modes of winter locomotion.

Winter hikers should learn to use these important transportation tools safely, not only to prevent injury during use, but also to provide the skills necessary to deal successfully with many winter wilderness challenges. Skillful locomotion enhances wilderness safety.

Pace

Pace is important in any wilderness activity, and it is critical in winter hiking. Our bodies are not totally predictable machines, and we must take care to avoid perspiration and fatigue. Set the pace to the slowest person in the group.

Navigation

The consequences of getting lost in winter are more severe than in summer. In addition, navigation in winter is more challenging because snow can erase or change the looks of

Careful planning and preparation can maximize the safety, comfort, and enjoyment of the winter camping experience.

familiar landmarks. For these reasons, good navigational skills are necessary to winter hiking safety.

Snow Bridges

At times hikers will walk on snow that spans cavities beneath it, sometimes knowingly and sometimes not. When hikers can see the cavity, know of the cavity, or suspect the cavity, they can make a decision about the strength and trustworthiness of the snow. Sometimes there is no way of knowing such a cavity exists, in which case various body parts, ranging from a foot to the entire body, may fall through the snow into the void, resulting in slowed progress, broken bones, wet body parts, or serious injuries. Preventing injury due to breaking through the surface of the snow includes being on the lookout for cavities under the snow; testing known snow bridges; traveling when snow is strongest (early morning); being aware that hidden holes exist next to logs, trees, and rocks; testing with a ski pole or ice ax, rather than a foot; and never crossing a snow bridge over a known stream just above a waterfall.

Water Crossing

Crossing water in winter can be harder or easier than in summer. Certainly, it carries graver risks. Falling through ice into a moving stream is one of the most dangerous situations. The survival rate is depressingly low. Dangers include drowning, becoming numb, and being swept under the ice by the current.

The most important precaution is to avoid venturing onto ice that is not strong enough to hold the load. The number of vehicles parked on frozen lakes in winter is testimony to the ability of ice to hold considerable loads, but the number of vehicles partially submerged on frozen lakes shows people's tendency to push their luck and exercise bad judgment concerning whether the ice will support them. There is no universal rule relating to acceptable ice thickness for bearing human weight, but a conservative yardstick is at least 4 inches for ponds and lakes (Mohney 1976) and at least 8 to 10 inches for streams. Ice covering flowing water is thicker at the edge than in the middle. In crossing as well as in rescue, spreading the weight over a larger area will increase the likelihood that the ice will bear the load. Other precautions include loosening pack and snowshoe bindings; crossing streams one person at a time; spreading the party to a minimum distance of 20 feet on lakes, farther if the ice is suspect; and carrying ropes or long sticks to facilitate rescue efforts.

If a hiker should fall into water in winter, treatment involves rescuing the victim from the water, removing wet clothing, drying the body, putting on dry clothing, warming the body in the best way possible (open fire if possible), and feeding the victim warm food and beverage. Abandon the trip immediately.

Transportation Into Wilderness

As with hiking in other seasons, the most dangerous part of winter camping is the trip to and from wilderness. Winter roads are capable of being slick, and it is easy to skid into objects on or off the road. Drive at speeds appropriate to the situation. Take care to winterize the car to prevent, or be able to deal with, survival situations that arise en route. Carry adequate equipment and supplies, such as chains or four-wheel drive capability, extra food and water, extra clothing and blankets, and a means of signaling.

ADMINISTRATION

Please refer to the Hiking and Camping chapter. All principles discussed there also apply in winter. Be ever mindful that the potential for danger is greater than in other seasons. You can maintain safety by good judgment, skill, equipment, and planning.

Be prepared for unexpected contingencies. Give careful attention to the route and timetable (provide all party members with a copy), equipment needed, personal gear, group gear, menus, health considerations, and safety strategies. Provide a packing list to all participants. To ensure inclusion and proper functioning of all gear, an equipment check should precede the trip and a repair kit should accompany the group.

BIBLIOGRAPHY

Avalanche awareness. 1988. Montreal, QC: Alliance Communications. Video.

Forgey, W.W. 1985. *Death by exposure: Hypothermia.* Merrillville, IN: ICS Books.

Gill, P.G., Jr. 1991. *Pocket guide to wilderness medicine.* New York: Fireside Books.

Graydon, D., ed. 1992. *Mountaineering, the freedom of the hills.* 5th ed. Seattle: Mountaineers Books.

March, B. 1983. *Modern snow and ice techniques.* Cumbria, England: Cicerone Press.

McClung, D., and P. Schairer. 1993. *The avalanche handbook.* Seattle: Mountaineers Books.

Mohney, R. 1976. *Wintering: The outdoor book for cold weather ventures.* Harrisburg, PA: Stackpole Books.

Prater, G. 1988. *Snowshoeing.* Seattle: Mountaineers Books.

Tilton, B. 1992. *Avalanche safety.* Merrillville, IN: ICS Books.

Weiss, H.E. 1992. *Secrets of warmth.* Seattle: Cloudcap.

Wilkinson, E. 1986. *Snow caves for fun and survival.* Denver: Windsong Press.

Mountaineering Safety

Joel M. Stager · David A. Tanner

It should come as no surprise that mountaineering is the recreational pursuit associated with the highest risk of personal injury and death. Although exact values do not exist, the associated risk is clearly situational and location dependent. Short day hikes on maintained state and national park trails can be relatively risk free if you are properly prepared. Hazards include twisted ankles, fatigue, dehydration, and an occasional bee sting. In contrast, mountaineering in remote backcountry locations usually holds substantial risk from the unanticipated and uncontrollable aspects of the weather, terrain, and high-altitude illness. It is estimated that the number of fatalities per summit attempts ranges from 1 death in 100 summit attempts on Denali (20,320 feet) in Alaska, to 1 death in 2,000 summit attempts on Mt. Rainier (14,410 feet) in Washington state. Certainly, higher estimates exist for the extremely remote and high 8,000-meter peaks in the Himalayas. For instance, it has been reported that for every three climbers who reach the summit of Mt. Everest, one climber dies during an attempt. Lower values exist for less demanding and more accessible peaks, such as those located within the Cascades, Rockies, Appalachians, and Alps. Are these high risks and high-fatality rates necessary and inherent to the activity, or can we reduce the injuries and deaths through improved knowledge, adequate preparation, and education?

The following discussion will focus on the safety issues associated with mountaineering per se, the leisure pursuit that incorporates moderate and high-altitude exposure. It will not include wilderness camping or backcountry camping, fishing, or hunting. These activities have been extensively detailed in other chapters. We describe technical rock and ice climbing such as that which requires specific protection and safety equipment in the next chapter and will only briefly discuss it here. Mountaineering safety knowledge is essential and can substantially reduce the degree of risk associated with this rewarding leisure pursuit.

ENVIRONMENTAL CONDITIONS

The environmental conditions experienced by mountaineers are extreme, to say the least. From altitude to severe weather to avalanches, you must take significant precautions to avoid injury or even death.

Altitude Illnesses

One category of safety problems specific to mountaineering relates to the consequences of the high altitude itself. With the increase in altitude comes the decline in oxygen availability (hypoxia). As climbers ascend, the density of the atmosphere becomes less, because the total number of air molecules per unit volume is less. Thus, the total number of oxygen molecules is less, and the decline in oxygen is roughly proportional to the decrease in barometric pressure and increase in altitude. At 18,000 feet, the barometric pressure is about half that at sea level, and the number of oxygen molecules per liter of air is halved as well. This decline in the amount of oxygen has several physiological effects. Some will be life threatening. You can find a detailed description of the physiological consequences of hypoxia in *High Altitude Medicine and Physiology*, (Ward, Milledge, and West 1995).

Acute Mountain Sickness (AMS)

Over time, most people adapt to the lack of oxygen at moderate altitudes and experience few prolonged adverse symptoms. Other individuals do not fare so well and display a variety of symptoms collectively known as acute mountain sickness (AMS). One important safety rule on the mountain concerns ascending slowly enough that altitude acclimation can occur. Schedule rest days on arrival at significantly high elevations. For moderate altitudes higher than 10,000 to 12,000 feet, it is inadvisable to ascend more than 1,000 feet per day if unacclimated.

AMS is not necessarily life threatening, and you can prevent it by slow ascents and/ or ameliorate it by several well-known thera-

Exhilarating and rewarding, mountaineering is also the recreational pursuit associated with the highest risk of personal injury and death.

MOUNTAINEERING PARTICIPANT CHARACTERISTICS

By no small measure, the makeup of the mountaineering population is young (18 to 30 years) and primarily male. Although it is difficult to obtain exact values, it is possible that this cohort represents more than 75 percent of the mountaineering population. Thus the mind-set of the mountaineer may be one that is prone to accepting relaxed standards of safety compared with the general population. In other words, the mountaineering cohort is not overtly responsive to sound advice from anyone, at any time, under any circumstance. As a result, more than a few members of this group will become statistics of mountaineering accidents.

Although mountaineering is becoming more popular in the United States and Canada, many climbers in North America are from Europe and Asia. This is due to the low cost of travel to the United States and the accessibility of our summits. Thus, in addition to the communication problems associated with youth, there may be true language barriers as well. To go along with these problems are cultural differences that may alter the expected responses to the inherent hazards associated with mountaineering. Between 1986 and 1992, for example, all but 2 of the 24 climbers who died on McKinley were foreigners, and 75 percent of the rescues made on Denali by the National Park Service during this time involved foreign nationals (Meyer 1992).

Perhaps the factor that plays the most important role in terms of its contribution to mountaineering injury and death is poor judgment. According to the American Alpine Club, more accidents occur involving the inexperienced or moderately experienced mountaineer than the experienced mountaineer by a factor of two to one. This appears true despite the fact that experienced mountaineers are more likely to attempt more technically difficult or physically demanding routes. The difference in incident frequency appears to be primarily related to judgment or lack thereof.

Lack of judgment can be expressed in many forms. Its most frequent display occurs before individuals take a single step toward the summit. They can display poor judgment in preparing for an expedition in terms of team organization and member selection, choosing equipment, physical preparation, nutritional planning, assessing the weather, and estimating the mountaineering skills necessary for the chosen route. The preparatory phase may be the most important phase in reducing risks associated with mountaineering and enhancing mountaineering safety.

peutic agents. There are wide variations in an individual's expression of symptoms (see table 6.1). AMS may occur at moderate altitudes in some individuals or not until much higher altitudes in others. One of the best sources of information pertaining to AMS and other high-altitude diseases is *High Altitude: Illness and Wellness* (Houston 1993). A copy of this text may be important to managers, administrators, and supervisors. We strongly recommend it as essential reading for all members of an expedition during the preparation phase, because it may be crucial to saving lives later on.

Acute mountain sickness is one of several illnesses that occur with altitude. The best therapy for AMS is descent. AMS is usually a short-term problem that you can eliminate by rest and acclimation.

High-Altitude Pulmonary Edema (HAPE)

Pulmonary and cerebral edema also result from hypoxia and represent a much more significant threat to life. High-altitude pulmonary edema,

Table 6.1

SYMPTOMS OF ACUTE MOUNTAIN SICKNESS (AMS)

☐ Headache	☐ Dizziness
☐ Insomnia	☐ Mental confusion
☐ Anorexia	
☐ Nausea	☐ Uncoordination
☐ Breathlessness	☐ Loss of visual fields
☐ Muscular fatigue	☐ Giddiness
☐ Lassitude	☐ Vomiting
☐ Tachycardia	☐ Mild fever
☐ Loss of concentration	☐ Decreased urinary output

Adapted from Singh, I., P.K. Khanna, M.C. Srivastava, M. Lal, S.B. Roy, and C.S. Subramanyam. 1969. Acute mountain sickness. *New England Journal of Medicine* 280: 175. Hackett, P.H., D. Rennie, and H.D. Levine. 1976. The incidence, importance, and prophylaxis of acute mountain sickness. *Lancet* 2: 1149.

or HAPE, is less common than AMS but more serious. The primary symptoms of HAPE are

- shortness of breath, even while resting;
- a cough that may eventually produce a rusty-colored sputum;
- the individual may be uncomfortable or anxious and exhibit a rapid pulse rate in excess of 100, even lying down;
- extreme fatigue, mental confusion, and coma may follow; and
- possibility of a fever.

Because of the possibility of a slight fever, HAPE is sometimes confused with chest colds or the flu. The danger here is that some symptoms are subtle and slow to progress. Other symptoms can develop rapidly and can be fatal. Climbers left to rest, recover, or see how things go tomorrow may become comatose before you can evacuate them. If bad weather develops and climbers are forced to wait it out, it may be too late; HAPE may progress and become fatal. Supervisors must be aware of the symptoms and be conservative in their judg-

ment. The best treatment for an individual suspected of developing HAPE is to descend immediately. Sometimes as little as 1,000 feet of descent is enough to reduce and eliminate HAPE completely (Houston 1993).

High-Altitude Cerebral Edema (HACE)

HACE is the third malady associated with hypoxia. It is the least common of the three and probably the most deadly. The initial symptoms may be similar to AMS and HAPE and include

- nausea,
- sleeplessness,
- headache, and
- confusion.

More specific symptoms include problems with fine motor function such as fingers and hands. Climbers with HACE become ataxic, meaning they may stumble and walk only with great difficulty. Symptoms can include hallucinations. In any event, in the case of suspected HACE, rapid descent is crucial. The symptoms of HACE may be quick, and death may be imminent after only a few hours. Supervisors must be in constant contact with climbers to continually assess changes in behavior or physical coordination associated with illness that normal fatigue may mask (Houston 1993).

Hypothermia

Although not an altitude illness per se, hypothermia may be the most common problem for the unprepared mountaineer. When exposed to the cold, the first line of defense against a lower body temperature is our behavior. We put on more clothes (gloves, hats, long pants, etc.). If the cold and wind don't allow clothing to meet the heat loss, we must increase heat production physiologically. We accomplish this through shivering. Unfortunately, shivering will only provide five times more added heat. When heat loss continues to exceed heat gain, our body temperature will fall and hypothermia will ensue. Symptoms of hypothermia begin with peripheral vascular shutdown or skin vasoconstriction and progress from there (see table 5.2 on p. 73 for more information).

- The skin becomes pale and cold.
- We lose our sense of touch and pain.
- Coordination diminishes and fine motor skills become difficult.
- Shivering becomes uncontrollable and exhausting.
- Judgment and mental processes become impaired.
- Behavior may change. Climbers may become withdrawn and apathetic.
- Walking may become difficult and stiff.
- Shivering may cease and the heart rate slows.
- As body temperature declines to less than 80 degrees Fahrenheit, individuals may lose consciousness, and the heart and respiration may stop.

The symptoms of hypothermia may vary from individual to individual. Thus, it is difficult to gauge exactly the severity of the decline in body temperature. The best index is core temperature, and the best treatment is to end exposure. Consider core temperatures lower than 95 degrees Fahrenheit valid evidence of hypothermia. Regardless of what the victim may claim, attempts at rewarming should be immediate and aggressive (Lentz, Macdonald, and Carline 1990).

In areas where many climbers begin day hikes at modest altitudes readily accessible by car and can reach remote sites significantly higher than the tree line in a few hours, hypothermia can be a significant threat. Hikers may not appreciate the sudden changes in weather and may not be prepared for the rapid drops in temperature. Shorts and a T-shirt are never appropriate as the only clothing when higher than the tree line.

High-Altitude Nutrition

Proper nutrition is an essential ingredient in the success and safety of any high-altitude mountaineering expedition. Climbers spend thousands of dollars on the latest lightweight equipment but have not devoted similar effort toward solving the problems of fueling their bodies to survive the high-altitude environment. Nutrition may be the last big frontier for mountaineers.

Supervisors and team leaders need to decide early in the preparatory phase of the expedition who will be responsible for nutrition. In short, moderately difficult trips, it may be easier for individuals to be responsible for their own food. On longer expeditions, food falls under the group gear category. In either case, make available pertinent information concerning nutrition to ensure the safety and enjoyment of the sojourn.

The biggest challenge facing the high-altitude climber is maintaining energy balance (i.e., consuming enough calories to meet the body's energy requirements). Few mountaineers have been successful at preventing high-altitude cachexia (HAC), a general physical wasting and malnutrition, resulting in severe weight loss and performance decreases (Potera 1986). As much as three-fourths of this weight loss has been reported as lean body mass, specifically muscle tissue.

Several reasons for the occurrence of HAC have been proposed. The results of Operation Everest II, a simulated climb of Mt. Everest in a hypobaric chamber (Rose et al. 1988) indicated that hypoxia (low oxygen) alone could have been sufficient cause for the 43-percent decrease in food consumption and the 9-percent weight loss observed in the study. Another factor in HAC is dehydration, which can occur rapidly at altitude. Climbers typically experience decreased fluid intake, increased urinary water loss, and increased water vapor loss from the lungs hyperventilating the cold, dry mountain air. Dehydration can intensify the severity of AMS symptoms, impair temperature regulation, slow altitude acclimatization, and increase the chances of frostbite. Suggested fluid requirements range from three to five liters per day.

Another factor in HAC is anorexia, the inability to eat or drink due to nausea, which reduces appetite, thereby decreasing energy intake. Appetite fails to maintain the energy content of the body, especially higher than 6,000 meters, where fatigue, cold, hypoxia, and glycogen depletion combine to impair mental and physical ability so much that preparing a meal is a major chore. Caloric intake has been reported to fall as low as 1,500 calories per day at higher than 7,000 meters. Fortunately, energy expenditure at these altitudes is much lower, as climbers lead a semisedentary lifestyle awaiting the proper conditions for a summit attempt.

Energy requirements at rest and during exercise increase as much as 10 percent for every 1,000-meter increase in altitude. The proposed caloric requirements at altitude range from 3,200 calories per day to 6,000 calories per day. The most widely recommended composition is 10- to 12-percent protein, 20- to 35-percent fat, and 55- to 70-percent carbohydrate. The benefits of carbohydrate as a fuel source are similar to those for the endurance athlete at sea level. Although fat contains nine calories per gram, compared with four calories per gram for carbohydrate, fats are not well tolerated at altitude due to nausea and inefficient fat metabolism. It is well documented that climbers prefer a carbohydrate-rich diet because it is readily available and easy to prepare.

Carbohydrate supplementation improves performance during strenuous exercise at altitude, possibly due to increased oxygen in the blood, an increase in respirator quotient (RQ), or an increase in the diffusion capacity of the lungs. Because carbohydrate ingestion improves performance, it has been suggested that climbers eat a higher percentage of simple carbohydrates on hard climbing days and increase fat and protein consumption on rest days, when they will be more tolerated. Also, a light carbohydrate snack just before bedtime may help the resting body stay warmer during the night. Although the protein-sparing benefits of carbohydrate have been demonstrated, at higher than 5,400 meters it appears that muscle protein catalysis will occur despite a high-carbohydrate diet.

There is evidence to support the benefits of carbohydrate supplementation in reducing the symptoms of AMS, among which include decreased nausea, decreased headaches, decreased shortness of breath and syncope, increased mental efficiency and happiness, and increased cold tolerance. Carbohydrate supplementation before rapid ascent to altitude also reduces AMS symptoms.

There is no evidence that altitude increases the body's need for extra vitamins or minerals; however, Vitamin E and iron supplements have been suggested to increase oxygen delivery and physical performance at high altitude. Individuals who have low iron stores may not be able to acclimate to the high altitude by synthesizing new red blood cells. This discussion clarifies the desired characteristics of the appropriate high-altitude nutrition plan. Keeping in mind a target diet of 10- to 12-percent protein, 20- to 35-percent fat, and 55- to 70-percent carbohydrates, evaluate each potential food relative to the desirability factors presented in table 6.2.

Carefully select provisions for an expedition based on these 12 factors. Do not consider foods that are difficult to prepare, do not preserve or travel well, or have excessive packaging. You can grubstake an expedition adequately from the local supermarket, but specially designed freeze-dried foods are more convenient to prepare. However, the need to minimize weight, volume, and cost should not override the nutritional factors important for the health of the climbers.

In summary, the importance of proper nutrition is often overlooked by high-altitude mountaineers. The problems associated with inadequate energy and fluid intake have been well documented. They include loss of appetite, weight loss, decreased physical and mental performance capacity, acute mountain sickness, dehydration, and hypothermia. You can reduce these problems by selecting an appropriate diet consisting of 55- to 70-percent carbohydrates. However, an altitude of 6,000 meters appears to be a critical level, above which physiological deterioration occurs no matter what type of diet you consume. Climbers should attempt to spend as little time as possible higher than 6,000 meters. Take great care, when selecting the provisions for an expedition, to provide the energy the mountaineer needs in situations where enough energy supply may mean the difference between life and death.

Table 6.2
DESIRABLE FACTORS FOR HIGH-ALTITUDE NUTRITION

FACTOR	EXPLANATION
High nutritional quality	The Index of Nutritional Quality (INQ) is a convenient way to compare the quality of food differences.
High-nutrient density	Foods high in calories per gram will provide more energy relative to the effort it takes to carry them. Quick alpine ascents require nutrient-dense, ready-to-eat foods.
High-carbohydrate content	We have already discussed the importance of a high-carbohydrate diet.
Low bulk and weight	Heavy foods that occupy too much space are difficult to pack and carry. It is estimated that each person needs 2 pounds of food by dry weight per day to sustain moderate climbing effort. The density should be high to facilitate transport.
Easy to prepare	The best strategy for a steady supply of energy and improved digestion is to eat small, carbohydrate-rich meals frequently throughout the day. Each climber should have a personal grab bag of simple, ready-to-eat, carbohydrate-rich foods. The main meals should be easy to prepare. No-cook and one-pot dehydrated meals are especially convenient, requiring only the addition of boiling water. It takes approximately 15 to 20 minutes to melt snow to water and another 10 to 15 minutes to bring to a boil, so consider the cost of the fuel for the stoves and the effort needed to transport it when you select these meals.
Durability during transport	Do not choose fragile foods that will be destroyed when packed tightly.
Preservability	Eliminate perishable foods that cannot withstand temperature extremes. Select foods with a significant water content only if you can eat them frozen.
Low-fiber content	Avoid gas-forming foods and foods high in dietary fiber, not only as a courtesy to your tent mates, but also to reduce the discomforts of frequent elimination in subzero temperatures and minimize the amount of waste left on the mountain.
Limited packaging	Eliminate foods with excess packaging, such as canned goods. Courtesy requires that you carry all trash off the mountain, so you can consider the weight of food packaging a fixed energy cost for the entire expedition. You can repackage most foods in lightweight Ziploc plastic bags to minimize this cost.
Good taste	Although the sense of taste is dulled at altitude, select appetizing foods that are well liked to offset the expected appetite loss at the higher elevations. Taste test all foods before the expedition.
Avoid alcohol	Alcohol and certain spices, such as red pepper and MSG, trigger peripheral vasodilation and give a false sense of warmth. Avoid alcohol because of its increased effect on the nervous system at altitude.
Low cost	It is the rare expedition that has an unlimited budget. Therefore, select foods that supply the most energy and convenience for the money.

Weather

It is frequently stated that the only thing you can count on about mountain weather is that you cannot count on it. Weather conditions on mountains change quickly and dramatically. Preparing for all types of weather is the only safe approach, regardless of the length of the trip. Climbers can experience excessive heat with intense solar radiation one moment and strong winds, sleet, and snow the next. Weather-related safety concerns exist regardless of the severity of weather conditions.

For several reasons, the air at higher altitudes is dryer than at low altitudes. Thus, as stated earlier, climbers need to pay attention to rehydration under all weather conditions. When the weather is warm and climbers are working hard, they may lose additional water because of the evaporation of sweat. Climbers may need as much as five or six liters of water a day for these reasons. In terms of appropriate dress, layering is essential so you can rapidly take off or add clothing. It is important that the clothes do not absorb the sweat and thus alter the insulative characteristics of the fabrics. This aspect will become important during rest stops or changes in the weather conditions.

Clear skies also mean a high amount of solar radiation. At high altitude, the atmosphere filters less light because of the fewer air molecules. This radiation can be further intensified by reflected solar radiation from snow, ice, and smooth rock surfaces. Skin can be quickly damaged as a result. Warn climbers to minimize exposure. Under these conditions, severe burns can occur in less than 30 minutes. Climbers should wear lightweight, long-sleeved shirts, gloves, and pants despite the warm temperatures. Wear sunblock and lotions rated in excess of SPF 30 at all times. Lip balms containing zinc oxide may be advisable. Also, consider hats with brims and sunglasses with noseguards and side shields mandatory. You can use bandannas and Sahara hats to protect ears and necks. Climbers may be just as susceptible to sun poisoning at high altitude as they would be on the beaches of the Riviera.

An additional safety issue on snowfields and glaciers with warm weather is difficult and dangerous surfaces due to daytime melting. Snow bridges may become fragile, icefall may increase, and surfaces may become slushy. When the trail conditions become difficult, energy expenditure increases dramatically and fatigue occurs more quickly. You need more food, travel time is reduced, and the hazards much greater. The only option here is to be prepared to travel at night, after surfaces freeze and glacier movement is minimized.

Mountaineers, particularly team leaders or supervisors, should understand meteorology. Inexpensive altimeters are available that you can use as barometers to forecast changing weather conditions. We also recommend lightweight AM/FM radios that can pick up NOAA and NWS bulletins. In many locales, cellular telephones may be able to reach local information sources. National parks may require communication equipment whereby you can receive weather reports and dangerous wind and avalanche conditions continuously. Instruct climbers to always exercise good judgment by paying attention to these reports (i.e., don't go higher if bad weather is predicted).

Teach climbers local weather trends and information that will allow interpretation of such things as cloud formations and snow conditions. In certain locales, it is important to know what prevailing weather patterns represent significant risks. For instance, in the Rockies in central Colorado during the summer months, it is well known that storms develop in the early afternoon. These storms represent substantial danger from frequent lightning strikes.

Lightning

In certain mountainous areas, lightning represents one of the principal risks. Although not always lethal, it nevertheless can result in serious injury. Clearly, the first defense against lightning strikes is to stay away from objects that might be hit. In contrast to what is usually preached, we suggest that a location offering an object higher than your head may be safer than the wide-open spaces. Projections taller than the climber offer some limited protection above tree line.

- Avoid moist areas such as crevices and gullies.
- Keep feet together and hands off the ground.
- Use insulative material to sit or stand on.
- Avoid depressions.
- Avoid small caves and overhangs.
- The outer edges of ledges are better than being directly on the rock face.
- Rappelling is inadvisable during lightning storms.
- Set aside metal objects and keep them from direct contact (Graydon 1992).

Perhaps the best advice is to go up and back down the mountain early to avoid these high-risk situations.

Windchill

In addition to other factors, wind represents a significant hazard at high altitude. Convective heat transfer increases with increasing wind velocity. Frostbite can occur almost instantaneously with exposed skin under high-wind conditions (see figure 5.2 on p. 76 in chapter 5).

Wind can create ground blizzards and whiteouts leading to fatal falls. You can predict certain windy conditions by observing cloud formations referred to as lenticular clouds. These give the summits the appearance of having stocking caps.

Avalanches and Crevasses

Experience and prudence are the keys when traveling in mountainous areas with avalanche tendencies and hidden crevasses. Crevasses are restricted to areas with active glaciers, so you are less likely to encounter them than slopes prone to avalanches. In either case, it is important for supervisors and team leaders to know the inherent dangers and appropriate rescue gear and techniques. Expose participants to self-rescue practices and alert them to appro-

Experienced hikers can predict windy conditions by looking at lenticular clouds.

priate dos and don'ts. An opportunity for team members to practice techniques is valuable. Minimize travel in these areas and perform it only when roped together in teams of three or four. A good source of information on crevasse rescue and expedition skills is *Glacier Travel and Crevasse Rescue* by A. Selters (1990). We also suggest mountaineering courses that stress these skills for team leaders and supervisors. Another helpful source is *Avalanche Safety* by E. LaChapelle (1985).

Essential Equipment

You can limit a mountaineering equipment list to a few items or make it truly exhaustive, depending on the nature and duration of the sojourn. There are several rules to govern equipment decisions, however. The first rule is that you should not cut corners on the quality of mountaineering gear. This is the equipment that climbers rely on to keep them warm and dry, safe and sound, and alive. Items designed for heavy, extreme use are expensive. Costs for a several-week expedition can require several thousand dollars of personal gear and clothing. Yet, putting a price on fingers and toes lost to severe frostbite is difficult. Do not compromise on gear quality and condition. A sleeping bag rated to 20 degrees Fahrenheit will not keep anyone warm at minus 30 degrees Fahrenheit.

You can usually divide gear into group gear and personal gear. Inspect and replace both types if damaged or worn. Inadequate or inappropriate gear of one climber can place the trip and the lives of other climbers at risk. It is the responsibility of the supervisor or team leader to be familiar with the group gear and each team member's gear. Provide a list to all members many months in advance to ensure that they can acquire gear before departure. An abbreviated list for personal and group gear appears in table 6.3.

An added word of caution here might be appropriate. Some items may not be available locally or may only be available seasonally. Manufacturers may build equipment only for which they have orders. Initiate plans early to accommodate for this.

We provide these lists as a preliminary guide. Equipment may vary according to the destination and terrain. Clearly, day trips require much less gear than do extended expeditions. Areas without snowfields or glaciers do not require many items in table 6.3. You can find more extensive equipment descriptions in books such as *Mountaineering, the Freedom of the Hills*, D. Graydon, ed. (1992) or *Mt. McKinley Climber's Handbook*, G. Randall and H. Johnson (1987). Local book shops, outdoor shops, and nature clubs can also be sources of invaluable information.

Today's mountaineering clothing and equipment is highly refined and much lighter than what has been available recently. Nevertheless, there are several schools of thought about what equipment every climber should have. Some experts believe that climbers should pack light. Make it clear to each individual that whatever is packed will have to be carried. "Don't pack two when one will do" is an often-repeated phrase that holds a lot of truth. A four-pound telephoto lens might be nice, but not essential. A long day on the trail becomes even longer with every pound that you must lift, step by step toward the summit.

The alternative view is to pack for every possible need, attempting to maintain a lifestyle similar to home. Clearly, there are certain limits here. To start on an expedition with gear or clothing that would substantially increase the risks of the individual or team in an emergency makes no sense. Planning and research is essential. Supervisors can improve the safety of all by ensuring that team members bring appropriate gear.

First Aid

It should be obvious by now that knowledgeable personnel acting as leaders or supervisors for mountaineering sojourns are necessary. To reinforce this, however, a brief discussion about first aid procedures may be appropriate.

The mountains are remote and hazards are ever present. Thus, trained medical assistance is commonly needed and often unavailable. Once more, pretrip preparation and knowledge of specific first aid skills relevant to mountaineering are essential to improve the success of any visit to the mountains. The problems of providing aid, should an emergency situation

Table 6.3

GEAR FOR A MULTIDAY SOJOURN TO MOUNTAINOUS AREAS WITH SNOW OR ICE FIELDS

PERSONAL GEAR

- ☐ Ax, ice 70 to 80 cm
- ☐ Bandannas, cotton (x2)
- ☐ Boots, stiff shank, lug sole, crampon tabs (insulated, plastic double boots)
- ☐ Bottles, polycarbonate, 1 quart, with lids (x4)
- ☐ Bottle holders, insulated (x2)
- ☐ Bowl with lid, cup, and plastic utensils
- ☐ Cap, ski, wool or polypropylene
- ☐ Carabiners (x6), plus 2 locking
- ☐ Compression stuff sacs, several assorted sizes
- ☐ Crampons, rapid fix
- ☐ Gators, Gore-Tex
- ☐ Gloves, polypropylene glove liner (x2)
- ☐ Gloves, midglove, wool or polypropylene fleece, mitten
- ☐ Gloves, outer shell, windbreak, Gore-Tex, mitten
- ☐ Harness, sit
- ☐ Jacket, pile polypropylene fleece
- ☐ Jacket, parka, wind shell, breathable
- ☐ Overboots, full coverage, insulated (for extreme conditions)
- ☐ Pack, professionally fitted, lightweight 6-8,000 cc
- ☐ Pads, insulated, closed cell, 20 x 72 x 1/2 inch (1 or 2)

- ☐ Pants, underwear, polypropylene, expedition weight and lightweight
- ☐ Pants, windbreaker, Gore-Tex, full-side zip
- ☐ Pants, pile or fleece, polypropylene, full-side zip
- ☐ Picket, snow, 18- or 24-inch aluminum (x2)
- ☐ Poles, ski, telescopic
- ☐ Screw, ice (x2)
- ☐ Shirts, light and expedition weight capalene, wicking
- ☐ Sleeping bag, synthetic insulation, Gore-Tex shell
- ☐ Snowshoes, lightweight
- ☐ Socks, polypropylene liners, expedition weight (x2)
- ☐ Socks, polypropylene, expedition weight or heavy wool (x2)
- ☐ Sunscreen, SPF 30 to 50+, lip balm
- ☐ Sunglasses, with noseguard and side shades, full UV protection
- ☐ Hat, baseball with long bill
- ☐ Urine bottle, 1 liter
- ☐ Other essential gear — map, compass, flashlight, personal, first aid supplies, pocket knife, lighter or matches, toilet paper, insect repellent, watch, camera, goggles, notebook with pen

GROUP GEAR

- ☐ Beacon, avalanche (optional)
- ☐ Food
- ☐ Fuel for stove, 1-liter bottles
- ☐ First aid kit, group
- ☐ Ice hammer
- ☐ Rescue pulley, belay device (8, ATC)
- ☐ Ropes, 9.5mm, dry, 150-foot
- ☐ Slings and runners, assorted

- ☐ Snow saw
- ☐ Snow shovel
- ☐ Stove, lightweight, collapsible, multigas
- ☐ Tent, 3 or 4 season, lightweight, ripstop-treated nylon
- ☐ Wands (50)
- ☐ Water purification system

A general rule for packing your pack: Don't pack two when one will do!

occur, are numerous. Rather than a quick fix or stopgap measure until trained professionals show up, first aid performed in the mountains may necessitate hours or even days of close care. We recommend that all team leaders, if not all participants, of extended expeditions enroll in a first aid course such as offered by the Mountaineers in the Pacific Northwest. Texts derived from such courses are available but are poor substitutions for supervised practice (Lentz, Macdonald, and Carline 1990). Other courses such as those offered by the American Red Cross are not as specific but are a good background for all mountaineering participants and outdoor enthusiasts.

Preparation for an expedition should include developing a first aid kit. We offer a simple guide here. Consider this kit group gear and make its location known to all team members. We recommend a physician's help, as some items may be available through prescription only. Each team member may wish to prepare

a miniature version of this, containing items of personal preference or need (see table 6.4).

SUPERVISION

Supervisors of mountaineering activities must have clear and extensive credentials and qualifications. Knowledge of the first aid techniques specific to mountaineering is important. You can obtain this through courses offered by organizations such as the American Alpine Institute (AAI), Outward Bound, the National Outdoor Leadership School (NOLS), or the Mountaineers. We recommend Red Cross certification in first aid, personal safety, and cardiopulmonary resuscitation. If food and nutrition is a responsibility of the supervisor or sponsoring organization, knowledge of dietetics and nutrition for high-level performance is also valuable. Leadership skills are essential, and experience in similar field settings as a participant or second in command is

Table 6.4
CONTENTS OF A BASIC FIRST AID KIT

BASIC ITEMS

☐ Aspirin or acetaminophen (Tylenol or equivalent)

☐ Strong pain killer (consult prescribing physician)

☐ Prescription-strength antibiotic (for sore throat)

☐ Myoflex (or equivalent)

☐ Antibiotic cream (Neosporin)

☐ Zinc oxide for sunburn

☐ Canker sore medication (Herphlex)

☐ Diamox, nefedepene, and so on

☐ Large Band-Aids

☐ Sterile gauze pads (4-inch square)

☐ Thick, absorbent dressing for lacerations

☐ Adhesive tape (2 inches wide)

☐ Elastic bandage

☐ Triangular bandage

☐ Roller gauze

☐ Antifungal foot powder

☐ Paper and pencil (to record for physician's review)

☐ Manual of medical care

☐ Moleskin

OTHER ITEMS TO CONSIDER

☐ Antibiotic soap (hexoderm)

☐ Hydrogen peroxide

☐ Phenergan or Compazine suppositories (for nausea)

☐ Eye ointment or drops containing cortisone (for snow blindness)

☐ Adhesive foam (for padding boot pressure points)

☐ Antiacid (for sour stomachs)

☐ Antihistamine (for colds)

☐ Tweezers

☐ Razor

☐ Safety pins, needle, and thread

☐ Bandage scissors (with rounded tips)

☐ Lomotil (for diarrhea)

☐ Throat lozenges (for dry-air cough)

☐ Thermometer reading down to 70° F (for hypothermia victims)

☐ Baby wipes

Data from Lentz, M.J., S.C. MacDonald, and J.D. Carline. 1990. *Mountaineering first aid, A guide to accident response and first aid care.* 3rd ed., rev. Seattle: Mountaineers Books.

important. Team leaders and supervisors must be physically fit and be versed in orienteering and map reading. They should be experienced decision makers and practiced communicators. Experience in group dynamics is also essential.

Ratio of Supervisors to Participants

How many supervisors or leaders do you need? Under certain circumstances, such as short trips or those in which all members are equally experienced, an officially designated team leader may not be necessary. A mature group can handle problems democratically. It is often practical and advisable to identify a tie breaker. During a dilemma, the final decision will be his or hers. Otherwise, one team leader is enough, with a second individual assuming these responsibilities in the event of an accident or injury.

How many individuals constitute a team? It is not wise to travel in mountainous areas with fewer than three individuals. If for no other reason, when an injury or illness occurs, with a party of two, you must abandon the injured or ill member if the situation demands assistance. When traveling on glaciers or avalanche-prone slopes, two rope teams of three each is a safe lower limit.

How should you position team leaders or supervisors? This relates to the circumstances and the number of qualified or experienced climbers. Often it is recommended that a qualified leader head the first team to select the route. Position additional experienced members at the rear of the following rope teams.

Is there an upper limit for team size? The complications of organization and planning increase exponentially with the number of team members. More food, more tents, more stoves, more fuel, and more time are required as parties gain members. Under most circumstances a group of six to nine individuals appears most workable. In the case of illness or accidents with numbers in this range, the expedition can continue without all members being required for support. On highly technical climbs six to nine climbers are probably too many. A team of three to four members is safer and more appropriate.

Surveillance

The issue here is primarily one of communication. Leave a trip schedule and route with supervisory or other responsible individuals. Electronic communication equipment is realistic in most parts of the world today, and you should consider it mandatory. Amateur radio equipment, citizens band radios, powerful walkie-talkies, and cellular phones provide contact worldwide. When routes are difficult and/or extensive, you may want to establish a base camp that is constantly staffed and in daily contact with local authorities. It is the responsibility of the supervisor or team leader to establish a communication schedule and make timely contact if extreme situations develop.

SELECTION AND CONDUCT OF THE ACTIVITY

With enjoyment and safety being the primary objectives, it is clear that you must consider

issues relevant to safety on the mountain from the start. Team selection is critical, and you should communicate conduct expectations early in trip planning.

Screening Participants

This is a troublesome issue in discussing mountaineering. Some issues, such as those related to health and personal perspectives, we have already reviewed. Other issues may be important as well. Groups planning mountaineering trips lasting for a week or more need to consider temperament and personality in addition to the health and physical characteristics of the potential climbers. Trips with a poor mix of personalities can seemingly last much longer than the calendar suggests. Individual

Electronic communication equipment is realistic in most parts of the world today. Consider it mandatory to bring a CB radio, walkie-talkie, or cellular phone along for all long excursions.

objectives and goals must be consistent within the group for members to work as an effective team. Develop a plan for screening applicants and a means to review qualifications of the team members at the onset.

Preparation

The necessary steps in preparing for a mountaineering experience are described below:

1. Team development and team organization; identification of a team leader and acceptance of a decision-making hierarchy by the team.

2. Identifying or developing specific expertise; shared or dispersed responsibility for equipment selection and acquisition; first aid knowledge and developing a team first aid kit; nutrition and meal planning and food acquisition; physical-training plan; lodging, transportation, and so on; weather forecasting and specific skills associated with glaciers and avalanches; and knowledge and licensing for communication equipment.

3. The mental attitudes of the team members may primarily determine the success or failure of the expedition. Consider success an adventure into the mountains in which all team members return home safely and without injury. Climbers who return with 10 fingers, 10 toes, and no broken bones are successful climbers. Goals, team or personal, that are singularly associated with "baggin' a summit" can lead to summit fever and result in team division and unnecessary risk. Team members must be positive and enthusiastic without being unrealistic and ego driven. It is the experience of the climb and the knowledge gained from the experience that makes the adventure—not the destination itself. It is essential that team members recognize and appreciate the inherent risks involved. Individuals must accept responsibility for the health and welfare of themselves and their team members.

4. Few of us would run a marathon or attempt a triathlon without being in good physical condition. Only after a prolonged training regime designed specifically for these events

would we participate in them. Individuals who compete in these events are considered by most to be athletes. Surprisingly, a high percentage of failed expeditions or negative experiences associated with mountaineering is related to inadequate physical preparation. Every group member must be physically prepared to carry the gear and food necessary for a trip. Also, after a short rest, team members need to be prepared to do it again tomorrow, and possibly tomorrow, then tomorrow once more. Few of us consider mountaineers to be athletes or consider an expedition an athletic event. Perhaps we should. It is not unusual for members of a two-week mountaineering expedition to carry food and gear nearly equal to their body weight!

Participants must therefore be screened for health and physical fitness. Certainly, you should not consider individuals with back problems or a history of heart disease for an extended expedition. Knees, ankles, and hips are also put under extreme forces during the uphill and the downhill phase. Advise individuals with chronic joint problems or reconstructions of these hazards. Consider individuals with pulmonary diseases such as emphysema and severe asthma unlikely candidates. Consider at significant risk those with endocrine or peripheral vascular diseases, particularly during cold exposure. It is inappropriate for preadolescent children, pregnant women, the obese, and the elderly to participate in prolonged, moderate- or high-altitude expeditions.

Training for mountaineering should include prolonged, repetitive, moderately intense exercise. A generalized training program is appropriate, including jogging, stair climbing, swimming, and cycling. Guidelines for fitness programs are available from many sources. A good source of information is *Being Fit, a Personal Guide*, by B. Getchell (1982). However, in addition to these programs, we also recommend that participants break in packs, boots, and so on before their first mountaineering event by planning several day hikes or backpacking weekends. These serve as specific, prolonged physical training bouts and excellent opportunities to evaluate food choices and clothing comfort. Once again, inform potential mountaineering participants of the importance of physical fitness months before the event. This will improve the enjoyment of the trip and the overall team safety. Many mountaineering accidents happen because of excess fatigue or unequal fitness levels of the participants. It has been reported that accidents occur when descending more often than when ascending. Fatigue, mental and physical, may be the cause. Ankles are twisted, climbers stumble and fall, all aspects of risks are intensified due to fatigue. Climbers are pushed beyond their limits or push themselves to exhaustion, and when dangerous situations occur, they are unable to adequately respond or assist in emergency procedures. Thus, physical training in the preparation phase is paramount to reducing inherent risks and enhancing safety on the mountain.

Safety Rules to Enforce

Consider the following list of mountain safety rules primary, and always enforce and adhere to them:

1. Never climb unroped on exposed slopes, glaciers, snowfields, and areas prone to avalanche.

2. Rope teams should consist of at least three team members unless dire emergencies exist.

3. On glaciers, team members should remain roped and at a distance (30-50 feet) from one another, with no slack in the rope until they make a thorough safety check of the camping area. Mark boundaries and consider them sacred on all crevasse fields.

4. Make every effort to treat equipment as if it may save your life. Never stand on

Be prepared physically—many mountaineering accidents are a result of excess fatigue.

ropes, keep stoves and tents in good repair, and so on.

5. Teams should always remain together. Never leave climbers alone or travel alone regardless of the circumstances. Teams should always remain teams.

6. All climbers should carry clothing, emergency food, and personal equipment at all times.

7. Choose routes that do not exceed the physical ability of the weakest team member.

8. Leave a trip schedule and accessible-route map with a responsible, informed individual.

9. Communicate significant deviations from the schedule to the appropriate authority.

10. When traveling at moderate or high altitude, continually evaluate mental and physical traits of team members. Enforce a conservative attitude toward proceeding if AMS symptoms develop.

Stress that all members are responsible for the health and well-being of each other. Saving the life of a team member may place other team members at significant risk. Failure to observe these rules can result in tragedy. For a better appreciation of what can occur, you can review the primary causes of mountaineering accidents in *Accidents in North American Mountaineering*, published yearly by the American Alpine Club (Safety Committees 1994).

ADMINISTRATION

Dealing with administrative and logistical issues of a mountaineering trip can sometimes seem like a daunting task. However, by planning the trip well in advance and making sure that each team member is well prepared and well informed, the trip has a much higher probability of being a great experience.

Team Organization

At the onset, make it clear to all potential expedition or hike participants that each individual represents a member of a *team*. Hold a discussion concerning leadership and team responsibilities. It is important for team members to recognize that failure to be adequately prepared, foolhardy activity, or simple ignorance may place other members of the team at risk as well as themselves. Each team member needs to accept responsibility for their own safety and that of the team.

Developing the team concept is important. All members must accept a process to solve dilemmas that will surely occur, and the team must establish some form of organizational structure. Identify team members with extensive experience in certain areas. Most important are those individuals with expertise in areas such as first aid or gear and clothing. These team members must be willing to provide others with needed assistance in the preparatory phase. However, if the team is lacking experience in crucial areas, members should enroll in courses or schools to ensure the safety and success of the expedition. Planning must take place early, and each member must recognize the risks associated with mountaineering as substantial and real.

Facility-Management Perspective

From the facility-management perspective, much recreational activity classified as mountaineering takes place on public rather than private land. Access to national parks and similar public lands generally cannot be denied, and as such these areas are open to all. The debate that is becoming more pressing is, thus, who is responsible for evacuating and rescuing injured or stranded climbers? If participants are screened, do the managers assume legal liability? These questions have financial as well as moral aspects.

Perhaps the most important practical consideration of administering mountaineering activities is developing a system to contact or track teams. Impose communication requirements that will allow contact if it is necessary. Aside from this, develop an emergency action plan in which you can alert all individuals involved in rescue operations on short notice. Acquire emergency medical equipment, and disperse knowledge of its use. Establish an emergency network, and widely advertise a plan of action. Determine how restrictive the activity should be and who is going to make the decisions. Evaluate teams on such things as mountaineering experience, first aid knowledge, rescue equipment, adequate food supplies, and physical and mental preparation.

There is a growing perception that those who administer the area are responsible for the welfare of those who recreate within it. The contrasting view, from the perspective of many young mountaineers, is what can be described as the Disneyland mentality. If a problem arises, many climbers expect the authorities to step in, provide a rescue, shake hands, and disappear. In today's legal and financial climate, this expectation is no longer realistic. Climbers in the United States' high-risk areas may now be required to pay an access fee, allowing the costs of rescue efforts to at least be partially reimbursed. We cannot settle problems associated with these topics here. Nevertheless, give these issues careful administrative consideration.

BIBLIOGRAPHY

Bezruchka, S. 1994. *Altitude illness, prevention & treatment*. Seattle: Mountaineers Books.

Fredston, J.A., and D. Fesler. 1988. *Snow sense, A guide to evaluating snow avalanche hazard*. 3d ed., rev. Anchorage, AK: Alaska Mountain Safety Center.

Getchell, B. 1982. *Being fit, A personal guide*. New York: Wiley.

Graydon, D., ed. 1992. *Mountaineering, The freedom of the hills*. 5th ed. Seattle: Mountaineers Books.

Hackett, P.H., D. Rennie, and H.D. Levine. 1976. The incidence, importance, and prophylaxis of acute mountain sickness. *Lancet* 2: 1149.

Houston, C.S. 1987. *Going higher, The story of man and altitude*. 3d ed., rev. Boston: Little, Brown.

———. 1993. *High altitude: Illness and wellness*. Merrillville, IN: ICS Books.

La Chapelle, E. 1985. *ABC of Avalanche Safety*. 2d ed. Seattle: Mountaineers Books.

Lentz, M.J., S.C. Macdonald, and J.D. Carline. 1990. *Mountaineering first aid, A guide to accident response and first aid care*. 3d ed., rev. Seattle: Mountaineers Books.

Meyer, M. 1992. Deathwatch on Mount McKinley—It's more dangerous than it looks. *Newsweek*, 8 June.

Potera, C. 1986. Mountain nutrition: Common sense may prevent cachexia. *The Physician and Sports Medicine* 14 (3): 33-237.

Randall, G., and H. Johnson III. 1987. *Mt. McKinley climber's handbook*. Talkeetna, AK: Genet Expeditions.

Rose, M.S., C.S. Houston, C.S. Fulco, G. Coates, J.R. Sutton, and A. Cymerman. 1988. Operation Everest II: Nutrition and body composition. *Journal of Applied Physiology* 65 (6): 2545-2551.

Safety Committees 1993, American Alpine Club & Alpine Club of Canada. 1994. *Accidents in North American Mountaineering*, vol. 6, no. 5, issue 46.

Selters, A. 1990. *Glacier travel and crevasse rescue*. Seattle: Mountaineers Books.

Singh, I., P.K. Khanna, M.C. Srivastava, M. Lal, S.B. Roy, and C.S. Subramanyam. 1969. Acute mountain sickness. *New England Journal of Medicine* 280: 175.

Ward, M.P., J.S. Milledge, and J.B. West. 1995. *High altitude medicine and physiology*. 2d ed. London: Chapman & Hall.

Rock and Wall Climbing and Rappelling

Jeff Steffen · Jim Stiehl

Technical rock and wall climbing are international pastimes with a growing number of devotees. Both types of climbing employ a rope, specialized techniques, and equipment that safeguards a climber. Although one occurs on a rock face and the other on a wall that simulates rock, each is exhilarating, challenging, healthy, and fun—an activity unlike any other. When undertaken with caution and the proper instruction, they are far less dangerous than they appear. "Statistically, rock climbing is the safest of all the so-called thrill sports because it employs over a century's worth of refined technique and solid technology to the normal end of having fun" (Long 1989). Nonetheless, we must stress that the information presented in this chapter is no substitute for qualified instruction and years of climbing experience, and that it is impossible to describe and avoid all circumstances that climbers may encounter.

It is important to understand the differences among rock climbing, wall climbing, and rappelling, none of which are synonymous with mountaineering (see chapter 6, Mountaineering Safety). Wall climbing occurs in a relatively closed environment (i.e., gym). Rock climbing is far more complex. The environment is open and affords much less consistency, thereby demanding more attention and judgment. Weather, loose rocks, snakes, and the like require specialized knowledge. Whereas wall and rock climbing primarily involve *ascending* a real or simulated rock face, rappelling involves controlled movement down the rope for a speedy *descent* of the rock face.

Mountaineering—of which rock climbing is an important part—involves movement not only on rock, but also on snow and ice, glaciers, steep grass, scree, and more. Although many climbers are keen mountaineers, a growing number of rock and wall gymnasts concern themselves exclusively with rock and wall climbing. Consequently, they might not require as much familiarity with many prerequisites of safe mountaineering (e.g., backcountry travel and navigation; negotiating glaciers, and avoiding mountain hazards, such as swift water, sudden storms, lightning, avalanches, and physiological disorders from altitude and cold). Nonetheless, because rock climbing occurs outdoors, we will mention common environmental hazards and concerns specific to this activity.

Finally, in this chapter we will emphasize top roping, which involves rigging an anchor above the desired climb before climbing. We will not discuss single-pitch and multipitch climbing, which involve placing protection during the climb and require specialized techniques and equipment beyond the scope of this chapter. A strong reminder—climbing can be a potentially dangerous activity. Thus, instruction by qualified climbing instructors is essential to safe climbing and rappelling. There is no substitute for professional instruction!

ENVIRONMENTAL CONDITIONS

Several factors contribute to good rock and wall climbing and rappelling, but chief among them is the condition of the face you are climbing and the equipment you are using. Indeed, as in few other sports, these two factors can mean the difference between life and death.

Facilities

Whether indoors or outdoors, the most critical features of any facility are the climbing medium and access to that medium. Moreover, any climbs you select should be appropriate for the level of participant skills. There is no such thing as a typical artificial climbing wall, yet construction of a wall must meet the latest industry standards for safety, high-quality materials, and construction practices. The wall itself should have four to six inches of pea gravel or chipped rubber at the base, extending eight feet from the farthest overhanging section. You may substitute gymnastic matting, or any soft cushioning, if it provides equivalent protection (AEE 1993). As with walls, there now exists an incredible variety of artificial holds. Though it has become impossible to describe a normal bolt-on hold, there are many that meet basic requirements of durability, versatility, and ease of installation at relatively low cost.

© Dan Levinson

Rock climbing primarily involves *ascending* a rock face.

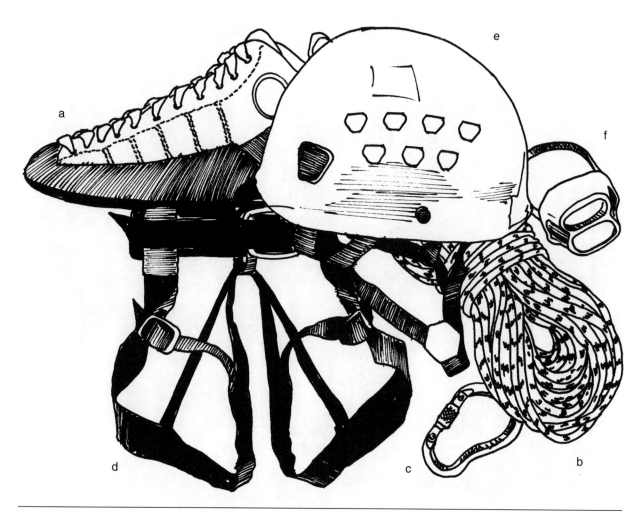

Figure 7.1   Rock climbing and rappelling equipment includes (a) climbing shoes, (b) rope, (c) carabiner, (d) a harness, (e) a helmet, and (f) a belay and rappel device.

At rock climbing and rappelling sites, most injuries occur while approaching or leaving the climb. Needless to say, appropriate staff should be familiar with the site and have inspected the routes before participants' climb on the rock face. Environmental conditions to consider include new rock fall; loose rocks; nesting birds and bees (AEE 1993); snakes; and unsafe ground cover, such as exposed roots, stumps, dead branches, and litter.

Regarding the latter, as the community of climbers has increased, so too has the amount of trash left behind by a few irresponsible climbers. Although this chapter is about reducing personal risk in climbing activities, if we are to reap maximum enjoyment from this rewarding sport, then we also must reduce our impact on and, hence, the risk to our fragile surroundings. A few unofficial guidelines are

worth bearing in mind: remove trash when you find it, whether or not you brought it; stick to established trails; and avoid disturbing nesting birds and other wildlife. We are the guests of the crags and their inhabitants.

For both wall climbing and rock climbing, the program should maintain a usage and conditions log and should follow an established inspection schedule (AEE 1993). Most programs rely on outside experts for scheduled, regular inspections of artificial walls. These inspections typically include examining the strength of materials and extensively checking fastenings. Program leaders, on the other hand, must assure that in-house inspections are conducted before each use of the facility, primarily to determine that holds are secure, that the climbing surface is not damaged, to discover any tampering,

Table 7.1

GUIDELINES FOR PROPER USE AND CARE OF ROPES

- ☐ Never step on a rope (debris can enter through the sheath and cut the core).
- ☐ Always store in a cool, dry, shady place (hence, do not store in direct sunlight or sources of heat such as a car trunk).
- ☐ Keep battery acid and other corrosives away from ropes.
- ☐ Do not allow a rope to run over sharp edges, especially under a heavy load.
- ☐ Keep the rope reasonably dry, if possible; dry before storing.
- ☐ Do not leave a rope stretched or under tension for an extended time.
- ☐ Remove all knots after using and before storing.
- ☐ Completely examine a rope before each use (for frays and soft spots), and immediately after it has held a severe fall.
- ☐ Examine the rope at regular intervals.
- ☐ Maintain a rope log to include age (date into service), days in use, average number of participants per day.
- ☐ Retire a rope after 3 years (even if used occasionally); after 2 years (for normal, weekend use); after 1 year (for an indoor or outdoor program with almost daily use). All rope life will depend on variables such as amount of ultraviolet light, moisture, dirt, abrasion, and hours of use.

and to provide a backup to the periodic outside inspections.

Equipment

An inevitable risk in climbing is falling. When climbing outside, there is also the risk of being struck by falling debris. To minimize these risks, climbers require a solid, dependable protection system. An acceptable protection system combines reliable anchors, ropes, and connecting links with alert, trustworthy partners. When you see someone climbing, all the odd-looking gadgets and knots may seem complicated. Actually, the basic system for top-rope climbing is quite simple. In a nutshell, a climber and companion (belayer) are tied to their respective ends of a rope. The rope runs from the climber up through a carabiner (aluminum alloy link) that is attached to a fixed anchor, then down to the belayer. The climber ascends a route on the wall or rock while the belayer pays out and takes in enough rope to arrest a fall should it occur. Personal safety in wall and rock climbing, therefore, requires close attention to the following equipment: ropes, harnesses,

anchors, carabiners, belay devices, descenders, and helmets (see figure 7.1).

Ropes. Your climbing rope is the most important piece of safety equipment. Modern climbing ropes are extremely reliable, but must always be respected and treated correctly. Such ropes are dynamic (they stretch slightly under load), and this helps them to absorb the shock of a fall. Kernmantle rope consists of a core (kern) of many small cords held together by a sheath (mantle). It is this structure that makes kernmantle so strong, yet extremely flexible, easy to handle, and able to hold a knot well.

The UIAA (Union Internationale des Associations d'Alpinisme) is an international organization that sets minimum standards that commercially available ropes should meet. Most programs use only 11-millimeter (1/2-inch) kernmantle ropes that pass UIAA certification and are so labeled. Though extremely strong, climbing ropes are made of supple nylon, which is easily damaged when even slightly abused. We present guidelines for proper use and care of your lifeline in table 7.1.

Harnesses. A climber can be connected to a rope by simply tying the rope around the climber's waist. However, the security of the rope is safer and more comfortable when attached to a harness. Two common types are seat harnesses (which are self-tied) and sewn harnesses (which are commercially made). Seat harnesses frequently consist of several turns of nine-millimeter kernmantle rope or wide tubular nylon webbing around the waist secured with specific knots. They are favored in some programs that emphasize students assuming responsibility for their own safety system. Before climbing, belaying, or rappelling, participants should be proficient at tying all necessary primary and safety knots. They also should be able to inspect the rope or webbing for unraveling and other weaknesses. Lastly, they should be aware that seat harnesses will develop slack as the result of a fall or controlled lowering so they will need to retie afterward.

A popular alternative to seat harnesses are sewn harnesses, which, despite the higher cost, are easier to use and more comfortable. There are many harnesses on the market, but it is hard to go wrong from a safety standpoint. Generally, any harness that is sold commercially and has an established trade name will provide comfort and safety. Be aware, however, that things can go wrong. Many harnesses require special buckling procedures, which, if neglected, render the harness potentially dangerous. Read instructions carefully and follow them to the letter. If a manufacturer does not provide specific information about using their harness, it might be wise not to buy that harness. Regardless of using seat harnesses or sewn harnesses, keep each as clean and dry as possible, and maintain a usage log.

Although methods and gear seem endlessly varied, tying in correctly to a harness is critical to avoid equipment failure and human error. Although there are probably a dozen knots suitable for connecting the rope to the climber's harness, a standard tie-in procedure is absolutely crucial to ensure that the climber and belayer are in the system safely (Powers 1993). A harness (along with the rope and the tie-in

knot) does not have a backup, so it deserves exceptional care and attention.

Anchors. The anchor is the fail-safe point of protection that secures a climber to a wall or rock. On a climbing wall, these may consist of using either locking carabiners or pulleys on belay cables. You can purchase each in several places. Ensure, however, that they meet proper specifications. Do not step on pulleys or drop them from heights. Inspect pulleys regularly for signs of wear. As with all climbing equipment, keep careful and consistent records.

Outdoors, the anchors become more varied. Anchors provided by the terrain are *natural* anchors, be they a tree, a large rock, a stone securely wedged in a crack, or whatever. *Artificial* anchors are mechanical devices that exploit pockets, grooves, and cracks in the rock. Nowadays, you can buy many types of artificial anchors (e.g., nuts, friction devices, passive and active camming devices, opposing wedge devices, expandable tubes) that work in an amazing variety of cracks and pockets. Part of their popularity is that they are removable and require no hammering or drilling to place. Consequently, they cause little or no rock damage. A third type of anchor, *permanent* anchors, may cause rock damage. When the rock is bereft of natural anchors and cracks, a climber may drill a hole in the rock and place a bolt.

A sloppy approach to locating and placing anchors can result in serious injury or death. Thus, once again, there is no substitute for professional instruction. Nonetheless, climbers should adhere to the rules in table 7.2.

Carabiners, Belay Devices, and Descenders. Biners, tubers, ATCs—all part of the jargon of rock climbing. In the event of a fall, it is technical equipment such as this that may prevent injury. It is imperative, therefore, that climbers understand exactly what each piece of equipment is designed to do.

Carabiners, often called biners (pronounced beeners), are metal snap links, with a spring-loaded gate. They are used as connections between a range of climbing equipment and allow climbers to clip their ropes directly into protection without having to

Table 7.2
GUIDELINES FOR LOCATING AND PLACING ANCHORS

☐ Use only strong placements. Natural anchors must be strong and well anchored to the terrain. Artificial protection is only as strong as the rock it contacts and the amount of surface area in contact with the rock.

☐ Always inspect the placement (give a tug when using artificial anchors).

☐ Keep the system simple so it is quick to set, easy to double-check — and safe.

☐ Make sure the system is redundant or backed up (generally 3 to 4 solid anchors). No rock-climbing anchor is 100% reliable (remember, the harness, rope, and tie-in knot are not redundant, thus each requires special consideration and frequent, thorough inspection).

☐ Consider all possible directions of loading and equalize (distribute) the load between the anchors.

☐ Reduce shock load. If one anchor fails, the system should not suddenly have slack and drop the climber a short distance, impacting the remaining anchors.

☐ Extend anchors over the edge at the top to prevent rope drag and abrasion. Pad any sharp edges.

☐ Belay top-rope climbers safely from the ground when possible. If the belayer weighs significantly less than the climber or might get pulled away from a stable or safe position, he or she should be anchored. An anchor belayer is a sitting duck for loose rocks or dropped gear; if possible, don't belay directly underneath any climber.

☐ Inspect your gear frequently for loosened knots or defects. Lubricate moving parts. Retire slings at the sight of abrasion or ultraviolet damage (or after 2 or 3 years, whichever comes first). Retire hardware if you observe cracks or other defects in the metal, or if the cable becomes oxidized, frayed, or kinked.

☐ Become proficient at partner rescue techniques.

untie and thread the rope through that protection. Snap carabiners, which have no threaded sleeve on the gate, are used mainly for connecting the climbing rope to a piece of protection. Locking-D carabiners have a threaded sleeve that stops the gate from accidentally opening. They are always used when attaching belay devices and descenders to your harness. Carabiners are designed to be weighted along the major axis. Used in this manner they are exceptionally strong. Used inappropriately, they can become a major liability. To prevent unwanted opening, use either a locking carabiner, or use two carabiners that are turned so the gates are opposing (i.e., can only open in opposite directions).

Belay devices are friction brakes used to stop the rope from moving during a fall. Their main value is that they require little strength to hold a fall, and there is little chance of it failing, or of the belayer suffering rope burns, provided the entire system is set up correctly. Moreover, the devices perform only as well as the user knows how to employ them. Common devices include the Low tuber, the Sticht plate, and a figure eight.

Descenders are made from strong but lightweight alloy. They are variable friction devices used to control the speed of a rappel. The figure eight is the most common form of descender and must be connected to the main attachment point on the front of the harness with a locking-D carabiner. Though adequate, many belay devices, when used for rappelling, can bind the rope and overheat. Consequently, the figure eight descender remains the device most recommended for use in rappelling situations (Long 1989). None of these devices should be dropped from heights. To do so is to guarantee their immediate retirement.

Helmets. Helmets are not designed to protect climbers from falling directly onto their heads. Rather, they protect by deflecting falling rock and debris or by preventing hitting your head against rock or other terrain features in a fall. Buy only UIAA-approved helmets that are designed specifically for climbing. Standard climbing helmets have strong shells with shock-absorbent linings. The chin strap is attached to the internal cradle in a manner that ensures the helmet will stay firmly on the head despite blows from any direction. Most climbing helmets are adjustable over a range of head sizes. We cannot overstate their utility and importance.

SUPERVISION

Do not attempt wall and rock climbing activities without proper training or without supervision by trained and properly qualified leaders. Failure to do so may result in serious injury. Although some organizations have established certification processes for outdoor guides and leaders, there has been no nationally recognized accreditation process focusing on adventure programming until recently, with the establishment of the Association for Experiential Education's (AEE) Program Accreditation Services (Gass and Williamson 1995).

At present, the most comprehensive material covering basic, safe operating procedures for climbing and rappelling is AEE's *Manual of Accreditation Standards for Adventure Programs* (1993). The Accreditation Program "provides

Never try rock climbing activities without supervision or proper training.

Table 7.3
POINTS OF FOCUS IN THE AEE ACCREDITATION PROGRAM

POINT OF FOCUS	EXPLANATION
Enviromental understanding	Do the appropriate staff have a working knowledge of the accepted standards for the construction and conduct of an artifical wall?
Human understanding	Do the students have the physical and psychological readiness to participate?
Conducting the activity	Are there written guidelines for conducting the activity, and is there adequate instruction in basic skills such as spotting, belay techniques, tying in to the system, belay signals, and lowering techniques?
Emergency procedures	Do supervisors have appropriate evacuation equipment and skills?
Clothing and equipment	Are belay ropes, harnesses, and carabiners cared for and properly stored?
Nourishment	Because participants can become dehydrated while climbing, is adequate liquid available?

Association for Experiential Education (AEE). 1993. *Manual of accreditation standards for adventure programs.* Boulder, CO: Association for Experiential Education.

guidelines of desirable practices to those who administer ongoing programs (or are planning programs)" (AEE 1993).

The Accreditation Program focuses on both the objective (technical risk management) and subjective (teaching approaches) aspects of a program. We discuss activities such as artificial wall climbing, top-rope rock climbing, and rappelling in table 7.3.

The following suggestions are largely derived from the AEE accreditation manual. Regardless of whether you are climbing artificial walls, top-roping, or rappelling, there are basic safety considerations common to supervising all of them, as well as considerations specific to each.

Use the following guidelines to ensure safe climbing and rappelling.

- Frequently inspect all gear.
- Provide proper instruction on warm-up exercises designed to reduce injuries and postactivity soreness.
- Ensure appropriate staff-to-participant ratios (i.e., 1:5 rock, 1:10 artificial wall). The experience and skill of the staff and participants will determine acceptable ratios.
- Give proper instruction on clothing and protective gear (e.g., wear helmets, remove jewelry and watches).
- Double-check harness buckles to ensure they are double-passed, the climber is tied to the harness correctly, and the knot is properly tied.
- Ensure a solid, dependable (absolutely fail-safe, bomb-proof) protection system (e.g., anchors, ropes, connecting links, and alert partners).
- Provide instruction on communication signals that are concise and understood by all partners.

Belayer Supervision

Belayer supervision is important to have at all times. Here is a list of guidelines that the belayer should always follow.

- Belayer's hand is on the brake and uses belay device correctly.
- Belayers stay alert, focused on the climber, and try to anticipate falls.
- Belayers maintain a secure stance (and be anchored or otherwise safely on the ground).
- Belayers must manage the rope adequately (e.g., stack properly, keep any kinks ahead of the belay device, avoid snags).
- Novice belayers should be adequately backed up by experienced belayers.

Climber Supervision

The climber must be responsible for his or her safety.

- Evaluate the potential trajectory of a fall and try to "plan a safe trip" (e.g., alert the belayer, avoid entangling your legs in the belay rope, picture the direction and force of the fall, interpose hands and feet between your head and the wall or rock, soak up impact by spreading it over as many appendages as possible).
- Always climb with the rope on the correct side of your leg.

Rappeller Supervision

Use the following guidelines when rappelling.
- Plan the descent with rappellers before going up on the climb.
- Before backing off the edge, ensure both ends of the rappel rope reach the ground.
- Never allow rappeller to let go of brake hand.
- Give instruction on using good form (e.g., shoulder-width stance, knees slightly flexed, legs nearly perpendicular to the rock or wall face, upright upper body, leaning back, walking smoothly down the wall).
- Provide instruction on using rappel devices.

- Keep loose clothing and long hair tucked away from the rappel device.
- Depending on experience, belay rappeller with another rope as they rappel.

SELECTION AND CONDUCT OF THE ACTIVITY

Individuals participating in rock and wall climbing programs should meet specific written criteria to ensure a safe and enjoyable experience. Standards for the criteria may vary from program to program, depending on goals and philosophy of institution and the difficulty of climbs.

All participants must fill out a health questionnaire, as in figure 7.2, and perform skills tests to determine if they are able to (a) tie and recognize proper knots, (b) perform the command sequence, and (c) successfully complete a belay test. If participants are using their own equipment, do an equipment test and inspection.

Before instruction, inform the participants on the nature of the environment where instruction will take place. On climbing walls, this might include an orientation to the difficulty of routes available and policies concerning the use of chalk. Rock climbing preparation for instruction becomes much more elaborate. Participants will need detailed information about the environment and human impact. Commonly covered information unique to rock climbing and rappelling include the following:

- Care of vegetation
- Stability of rock
- Identification of areas where helmets are required
- Care of ropes
- Awareness of animals

AEE recommends you meet the following criteria before the activity: providing adequate instruction and supervision, establishing participant climbs and rappels at appropriate levels of control and speed, sequencing experiences appropriately to experience, and

Health History Questionnaire

Date: _____

1. Name _____
   Last   First   Middle initial

2. Company/department _____

3. Position _____

4. Sex _____Male _____ Female

5. Age _____

6. Birthdate _____/_____/_____

7. Height _____

8. Weight _____

   Weight at age 21 _____

9. Has a doctor ever told you that you have one of the following?

   _____ Coronary heart disease   _____ Heart attack
   _____ Rheumatic heart disease _____ Stroke
   _____ Congenital heart disease _____ Epilepsy
   _____ Irregular heartbeats   _____ Diabetes
   _____ Heart valve problems   _____ Hypertension
   _____ Heart murmurs   _____ Cancer
   _____ Angina

   Please explain: _____
   _____

10. Do you have any of the following?
    _____ Back pain
    _____ Joint, tendon, or muscular pain
    _____ Lung disease (asthma, emphysema, other)

    Please explain: _____
    _____

11. Please list any medication you are taking (name and reason).

    _____ _____

    _____ _____

    _____ _____

(continued)

Figure 7.2 Health history questionnaire.

Reprinted by permission from Fitcorp. 1990. *Fitcorp Program Manual*. Waltham, MA: Fitcorp Healthcare Centers, Inc.

12.   Has anyone in your immediate family (father, mother, brother, or sister) had a heart attack or other heart-related problems before the age of 50?

      _____ No   _____ Yes

      Please explain: _____

      _____

13.   Do you have any medical conditions for which a physician has ever recommended some restrictions on activity (including surgery)?

      _____ No   _____ Yes

      Please explain: _____

      _____

14.   Are you pregnant?

      _____ No   _____ Yes

15.   Do you smoke?

      _____ No   _____ Yes

           _____ Cigarettes per day   _____ Cigars per day
           _____ Pipes per day

16.   Do you drink alcoholic beverages at all?

      _____ No   _____ Yes
      _____ 0-2 drinks per week
      _____ 3-14 drinks per week
      _____ More than 14 drinks per week

Note: One drink equals 1 ounce of hard liquor, 6 ounces of wine, or 12 ounces of beer.

17.   Are you presently exercising a minimum of 2 times per week for at least 20 minutes at a time?

      _____ No   _____ Yes

      A.   If yes, please specify:

      _____ Running/jogging   _____ Racket sports

      _____ Brisk walking   _____ Cross-country skiing

      _____ Biking   _____ Weight training

      _____ Aerobic dance   _____ Other (please specify) _____

      _____ Swimming

      B.   Total minutes engaged in aerobic activity per week:

      _____ 40 - 60 minutes/week
      _____ 61 - 80 minutes/week
      _____ 81 - 100 minutes/week
      _____ 100 + minutes/week

Figure 7.2   *(continued)*

18. Have you had your cholesterol measured within the past year?

_____ No
_____ Yes — above 200
_____ Yes — below 200
_____ Yes — do not know value

19. Do you eat from the four major food groups (meats or meat substitutes, vegetables, grain, and milk or milk by-products)?

_____ No _____ Yes

20. Is your diet high in saturated fat (milk products, cheese, meats, fried foods, and desserts)?

_____ No _____ Yes

21. Since 21 years of age, what is the most and least you have weighed?

_____ Most _____ Least _____ No change

22. Check the description that best represents the amount of stress you experience on a daily basis.

_____ No stress _____ Occasional mild stress _____ Frequent moderate stress

_____ Frequent high stress _____ Constant high stress

23. What are your goals for joining this activity? (Please indicate all that apply.)

_____ To lose weight
_____ To improve cardiovascular fitness
_____ To improve flexibility
_____ To improve muscle conditioning
_____ To reduce low back pain
_____ To reduce stress
_____ To stop cigarette smoking
_____ To lower cholesterol
_____ To improve nutrition
_____ To feel better overall
_____ Other (please specify) _____

_____

Figure 7.2 *(continued)*

engaging participants in proper warm-up and exercises before activity.

The instructional strategies for wall and rock climbing are similar. Participants who are exposed to properly sequenced skills and safety procedures will experience greater success and be less likely to be in an accident. Instructors should be prepared or accredited by recognized experts in the field. This might include the following:

- American Mountaineering Association
- Institutions of higher education
- National Outdoor Leadership School
- Outward Bound
- Reputable private guiding programs

Specific safety considerations for on-site instruction must include the following: an established sequence of activities or curriculum to assure participant readiness and coverage of all important information; an instructor-student ratio appropriate to level of difficulty and climber and rappeller experience; and hands-on, low-level bouldering and belay experience to assure competency and check for ability levels. Also, make sure that equipment (such as each harness and helmet) is customized for proper fit. Establish and review emergency rescue and evacuation procedures.

Charge a lead facilitator with overseeing the group. This will assure the entire group is following safety procedures while participants experience the different routes available. Indoor climbing walls should display policies and procedures relative to safety in locations where participants can review them. Outdoor programs often provide this information in a handout.

ADMINISTRATION

Commonly accepted safety practices in adventure programming should include documented safety concepts unique to rock and wall climbing and rappelling. These concepts include the following:

- Explaining accidents, danger, peril, and hazards
- Human dangers and environmental concerns

- Primary safety procedures
- Secondary safety procedures
- Tertiary safety procedures

The program's safety policy should address the following topics:

- Program guidelines
- Safety management plan
- Accident response kit
- Emergency communications
- Transportation
- Equipment
- Litigation protection
- Insurance
- Health care
- Participant selection
- Site selection
- Land use permits
- Safety committee

Safety reviews by outside peers are accepted protocol for checking the programs' safety procedures. A peer review will often consist of several experts visiting a site, watching programs, and reviewing documentation to identify unsafe practices.

BIBLIOGRAPHY

Association for Experiential Education (AEE). 1993. *Manual of accreditation standards for adventure programs*. Boulder, CO: Association for Experiential Education.

Gass, M. 1995. Accreditation for adventure programs. *Journal of Health, Physical Education, and Recreation*, January, 22-27.

Long, J. 1989. *How to rock climb*. Evergreen, CO: Chockstone Press.

Loughman, M. 1981. *Learning to rock climb*. San Francisco: Sierra Club Books.

Powers, P. 1993. *NOLS wilderness mountaineering*. Mechanicsburg, PA: Stackpole Books.

Wall, J., and C. Tait. 1994. *Ropes course manual*. Dubuque, IA: Kendall/Hunt.

Webster, S. 1989. *Ropes course safety manual*. Dubuque, IA: Kendall/Hunt.

Off-Highway Vehicle Safety

Raymond J. Ochs

T he purpose of this chapter is to address safety considerations when conducting off-highway vehicle (OHV) recreational activities. Included is information related to safe rider operation, appropriate environmental conditions, supervisory concerns, and administrative guidelines.

Recreational use of off-highway vehicles has gained widespread popularity during the past several years. According to the Motorcycle Industry Council, Inc. (1996), an estimated 3.2 million off-highway vehicles were used for recreational purposes in 1995. Although surveys reveal that the primary motivation of riders is to sightsee, OHV users can range from novice riders learning to ride or improving their skills, to enthusiasts looking for physical activity or social involvement.

Off-highway vehicles, for the purpose of this chapter, include the *off-highway motorcycle* and the *all-terrain vehicle*. The off-highway motorcycle, often referred to as a trail bike, consists of three types: (1) the dual-purpose model, (2) the enduro model, and (3) the motocross model. Dual-purpose motorcycles come equipped with highway-approved lighting and turn signals, Department of Transportation (DOT)-approved tires, a U.S. Forest Service approved-spark arrester, and conform to Environmental Protection Agency (EPA) noise and exhaust emission standards. These motorcycles are designed for use on paved roads as well as off highway. The enduro motorcycles usually have less lighting, knobby tires, and meet EPA spark arrester requirements. These machines are for off-highway use only. The motocross models have no lighting equipment, do not meet EPA noise or emission standards, and do not come equipped with a U.S. Forest Service-approved spark arrester. They are high-performance motorcycles designed for use by skilled riders in closed-course competition. Unmodified, they cannot be legally ridden on public land.

The all-terrain vehicle (or ATV) is a single-operator, three- or four-wheeled vehicle equipped with low-pressure tires. Most ATVs are 50 inches or less in width, have a dry weight

It is important that the riding area be matched to the ability of the rider and the capabilities of the vehicle.

ATVs handle differently than other vehicles. Care and training is necessary to prevent rollovers.

of 600 pounds or less, have a seat that is straddled, and have a handlebar for steering control.

Off-highway vehicles, as with all motorized transportation, possess an inherent risk of harm that must be minimized. As the number of ATV riders grew, so did the number of accidents. This prompted the Consumer Product Safety Commission (CPSC) to issue the following ATV safety alert.

The Consumer Product Safety Commission has concluded that all-terrain vehicles (ATVs) may present a risk of death or severe injury in certain circumstances. Accidents occur for several reasons:

- *Over 1,104 people, including many children, have died in accidents associated with ATVs since 1987.*
- *Many people have become severely paralyzed or suffered severe internal injuries as a result of accidents associated with ATVs.*
- *Every month thousands of people are treated in hospital emergency rooms for injuries received while riding an ATV.*

You should be aware that an ATV is not a toy and can be hazardous to operate. An ATV handles differently from other vehicles, including motorcycles and cars. A collision or rollover can occur quickly, even during routine maneuvers such as turning and driving on hills and over obstacles, if you fail to take proper precautions.

Off-highway motorcycles are used in similar environments and for similar purposes but have not been as scrutinized as ATVs.

ENVIRONMENTAL CONDITIONS

Using off-highway vehicles requires special considerations regarding the environment. Because ATVs and off-highway motorcycles are capable of affecting the landscape, choosing an appropriate riding area is important. The area must be not only safe and manageable, but also undamaged by riding activities.

Providing Safe Facilities

Off-highway vehicles in a recreational setting usually travel in open fields consisting of a few acres, or trails consisting of several miles. Motorcycle and all-terrain vehicle dealerships or local trail bike and ATV clubs are good sources to check when looking for suitable land. The U.S. Forest Service can also help identify appropriate off-road riding areas. In selecting an open-field area or a trail to ride, consider the criteria in table 8.1.

Essential Safety Equipment

Assuring that the off-highway vehicles are in sound mechanical condition and that all con-

trols and parts are functioning properly is only part of providing a safe and enjoyable recreational experience. Personal protective gear is mandatory for off-highway vehicle operation. Having proper riding gear not only provides comfort and control, but also provides protection from a spill.

The Helmet

The helmet protects the head and brain from injury should a spill occur. Although helmets vary in styles, they must be designed for off-highway vehicle use and should meet minimum state safety standards, that is, be labeled as Department of Transportation (DOT) approved, American National Standards (ANSI)

Table 8.1
CRITERIA FOR SELECTING AN OPEN-FIELD AREA OR TRAIL

AREA	CRITERIA
Open field	☐ The area should be free of large obstacles, ruts, and bumps.
	☐ Surface should be nonpaved, but relatively smooth.
	☐ The surface should support OHV travel and not become environmentally or cosmetically altered.
	☐ The area should be large enough to accommodate routine maneuvering by operators, but not so large as to affect surveillance and supervision.
	☐ The area should be away from vehicular and pedestrian traffic.
	☐ The area should be accessible by roads to allow transport of off-highway vehicles from highways.
	☐ The area should not be near fences, posts, ledges, drop-offs, or any hazardous condition.
Trail	☐ If you choose public land, check with local authorities for regulations regarding trail use.
	☐ If you use private land, gain permission from the landowner.
	☐ Make sure the riding terrain and trail difficulty do not exceed any rider's capability. Avoid water crossings and mud or loose surfaces.
	☐ Check for clear signage
	☐ Obtain a map of the trail system.
	☐ Use a trail loop to avoid backtracking.

TREAD LIGHTLY

Off-highway vehicle riding requires that you give attention to preserving the environment. The U.S. Forest Service has established a way to promote proper care of the land. It's called TREAD Lightly, and it is a slogan to communicate an awareness for the care of wildlands.

To TREAD Lightly is to do the following:

Travel only where allowed.

Respect the rights of others, including hikers, campers, and horseback riders.

Educate yourself by obtaining travel maps and regulations from public agencies.

Avoid streams, lakeshores, meadows, muddy roads and trails, steep hillsides, wildlife, and livestock.

Drive (ride) responsibly to protect the environment and preserve opportunities to enjoy your vehicle on wildlands.

approved, or Snell Memorial Foundation approved. Helmets can be an open-face style, but we recommend a full-face design. A properly fitted helmet is snug and will not wiggle excessively when shaking the head from side to side. Some off-highway riders add a visor to their helmet as additional protection from branches or to serve as a sunblock.

Eye Protection

Eye protection can consist of either a face shield or goggles. Eye protection is essential because it protects the eyes from dust and debris. It also helps a rider see the path of travel and environment factors. Face shields and goggles should be scratch free and fit securely.

Gloves

Gloves provide comfortable use of the off-highway vehicle controls. Additionally, they can provide warmth in colder conditions. Off-highway vehicle gloves typically have extra padding to protect the knuckles from objects such as tree limbs or branches.

Boots

The minimum protective footwear is a pair of strong, over-the-ankle boots. They should have low heels. We recommend over-the-calf boots as they provide better protection.

Clothing

Minimal clothing includes a long-sleeved shirt or jacket and a pair of sturdy pants. Serious off-highway riders often choose specialized apparel such as knee and shin protectors, shoulder pads, chest protectors, a full-face helmet, elbow guards, a kidney belt, off-road gloves and boots, and riding pants.

Tool Kit

Also important is a tool kit. Besides being necessary for adjusting vehicles during a preride inspection, a tool kit can prevent a minor breakdown from becoming an emergency. Off-highway vehicles come equipped with a basic tool kit, but additional items can provide extra security and safety. These include the following:

- An assortment of tools necessary for off highway vehicle repair (check with a local shop for a list of what to carry)
- Electrical and duct tape
- Knife
- Tire pump
- Tire patch kit
- Extra parts such as spark plugs, levers, bulbs

Ensuring Equipment Safety

Off-highway vehicles require complete inspection before any riding activity. A malfunction

All-terrain vehicle		Off-highway motorcycle
• Check the air pressure • Condition • Wheels, axle and lug nuts	**T** Tires and wheels	• Check the air pressure • Condition • Wheels, axle nuts
• Controls • Throttle and other cables • Brakes • Foot shifter	**C** Controls and cables	• Controls • Throttle and other cables • Brakes • Foot shifter
• Ignition switch • Engine stop switch • Headlight and taillight	**L** Lights and electrical	• Ignition switch • Engine stop switch • Headlight and taillight
• Check fuel level • Check oil level and condition	**O** Oil and fuel	• Check fuel level • Check oil level and condition
• Chain • Drive shaft • Nuts and bolts	**C** Chain/chassis and driveshaft	• Chain • Suspension • Nuts and bolts
• Motorcycle only	**K** Kickstand	• Fastened sturdy • Remains up for riding

Figure 8.1 T-CLOCK method for a preride inspection of off-highway vehicles.

Adapted from Specialty Vehicle Institute of America, 1990, A guide to off-highway riding: OHV classroom curriculum. Irvine, CA: SVIA.

could lead to breakdowns or possibly an accident. It's important to have the owner's manual for reference, particularly for specific models that you use. The most common checks for off-highway vehicles, easily remembered as T-CLOCK, are included in figure 8.1.

Tires and Wheels

It is important before any ride to check the tires and wheels to assure they are in good condition and ready for use.

Air Pressure. Use the recommended pressure for the type of terrain. Underinflated or over-inflated tires can cause the vehicle to handle less than optimally. The owner's manual will provide the correct amount of inflation. For trail bikes use a standard tire pressure gauge; ATVs require a special low-pressure tire gauge.

Condition. Tires should be free from cracks, cuts, or gouges. Check the tread for missing knobs or excessive wear.

Wheels. Secure axle nuts on trail bikes and lug nuts on ATVs. Check bearings by rocking the tires on the axle. On trail bikes, the spokes should not be loose or broken; on trail bikes and ATVs, the wheel rims should not be bent or cracked.

Controls

A quick check of each vehicle's operational controls assures trouble-free riding.

Throttle and Other Cables. The throttle should move smoothly and snap back to its original position. Check it with the handlebars in various positions. Cables should not be pinched or restrained when you turn the handlebars.

Brakes and Clutch. Both front and rear brakes should operate effectively. The hand and foot controls should move smoothly without excessive play.

Gear Shift Lever. The lever must be secure on its shaft and not bent, making it difficult to operate.

Lights and Switches

Check the lights and switches on ATVs and off-highway motorcycles for proper operation.

Ignition Switch. If the off-highway vehicle is electric start, the ignition switch should be secure and operate smoothly.

Engine Stop Switch. Check this switch to assure that it will shut the engine off.

Lights. Check the lights on off-highway vehicles equipped with them, including headlight, tail and stop lamp, and turn signals. Instrument cluster lights should illuminate as specified in the owner's manual.

Oil and Fuel

Fluids are critical to the safety and operation of off-highway vehicles. Check the oil level before each ride, and top off the gasoline tank.

Oil. Check engine oil for proper level (when the engine is off). Additionally, check the engine area for oil leaks.

Fuel. Gasoline (or the oil-and-gasoline mixture for some OHVs) must be adequate for the type of riding you are doing. It is wise to begin a ride with the fuel tank full.

Chain and Chassis

Vehicle integrity is important for safe and efficient operation. The chain and chassis components must perform properly to avoid breakdowns and prevent poor handling.

Chain. For those vehicles that are chain driven, adequately lubricate and properly adjust the chain to owner's manual recommendations.

Nuts and Bolts. Tighten all nuts and bolts to assure that they do not vibrate loose. It is wise to periodically check these during any breaks from riding.

Frame and Suspension. Vehicle frames should not show signs of bending or cracking. Suspension components should move smoothly.

SUPERVISION

Off-highway vehicle recreational riding usually occurs in one of two forms, open-field riding or trail riding. For open-field riding, supervision requires diligent observation and surveillance, whereas trail riding additionally requires riding with the group (see table 8.2).

Personnel that manage off-highway vehicle recreational activities should be experienced in trail bike or ATV operation. In addition to being qualified in first aid, CPR, and emergency preparedness procedures, we recommend

Table 8.2
GUIDELINES FOR SUPERVISING OPEN-FIELD AND TRAIL RIDES

TYPE OF ACTIVITY	GUIDELINES
Open-field ride	☐ Assure that the environment is safe and appropriate for the kind of activity conducted. ☐ Limit the riding area to assure sight distances allow observation and surveillance. ☐ Limit participation to a manageable number. ☐ Provide a general traffic-flow pattern that does not create path-of-travel conflicts. ☐ Establish rules of conduct, with appropriate sanctions for violations.
Trail system ride	☐ Keep the group small — 3 to 6 participants is manageable. ☐ The lead rider should not ride at a pace beyond that of the least proficient rider in the group. ☐ Be sure all vehicles pass inspection. ☐ Carry along safety and emergency equipment. ☐ Choose trails within the abilities of the least experienced rider in the group. ☐ Check the riding trails before the group ride. ☐ Have an experienced, skilled rider as the last rider. ☐ Plan frequent stops to assess fatigue and check progress. ☐ At turns and intersections, have a rider verify that the person behind knows the correct path. ☐ Have riders use hand signals. ☐ Consider speed and distance within the constraints of difficulty of terrain, weather, and rider experience.

completing an OHV educational program designed specifically for off-highway riding. One such program is A Guide to Off-Highway Riding conducted by the Specialty Vehicle Institute of America. This program conveys the importance of preparing for a safe and rewarding riding experience. Program topics include factors related to trail bike and ATV operation, maintaining the environment, and proper riding techniques for various terrains and conditions. Graduates of the four-hour program are able to

- describe risks that can occur with OHV riding,

- state preride safety procedures,

- apply riding strategies to be a more responsible rider,

- distinguish between safe and unsafe actions and behaviors,

- demonstrate the value of sharing an OHV trail, and

- state the riding rules for an OHV area.

For developing riding skills and acquiring greater awareness of off-highway vehicle use, hands-on training programs are available from the Specialty Vehicle Institute of America (SVIA), the ATV Safety Institute (ASI), and the Motorcycle Industry Council, Inc. (MIC). The SVIA has developed the Off-Highway Motorcycle RiderCourse. Its purpose is to teach fundamental operational skills for riding trail bikes. Trained facilitators conduct the program, and it is available throughout the country. The course consists of first learning straight-line riding, turning, shifting, braking, then supplementing basic skills with off-road trail bike riding experiences.

The ATV Safety Institute offers the ATV RiderCourse at locations throughout the country. Taught by licensed instructors, the half-day program teaches participants the safe and responsible use of all-terrain vehicles. Lessons are conducted outdoors and include group discussions and several riding exercises for skill development.

Many publications and materials, including audiovisuals, are available from the Specialty Vehicle Institute of America. Their address is 2 Jenner Street, Suite 150, Irvine, CA 92718, 714-727-3727.

SELECTION AND CONDUCT OF THE ACTIVITY

Give careful attention to assure participants conduct off-highway riding safely and responsibly. The riding skills and attitude of participants are important considerations.

Screening Participants

Off-highway vehicle operation requires skills and techniques that must be developed. Not all riders possess the same mental and physical skills to ride a trail bike or ATV. When screening participants, be sure to check that each rider fits his or her vehicle. Here are some guidelines to follow:

© Cheyenne Rouse

Because ATVs and off-highway motorcycles are capable of affecting the landscape, choosing and preserving the riding area are important considerations.

- There should be a minimum of three inches of clearance between the seat and inseam while standing on the foot pegs or footrests, allowing enough room for the legs to absorb shock while riding on bumpy surfaces. Three inches is a recommended minimum.

- Legs and feet should allow for maneuverability and comfort. Upper legs should be approximately horizontal while the rider is seated. The feet must be able to reach the foot pegs and must be able to reach and operate the brake and shifter controls.

- For the grip reach, in a normal, seated position, the elbows should have distinct angle to allow for maneuvering the handlebars. The hands must be able to reach and operate the brake and throttle controls for both straight-line riding and turning.

For those who ride ATVs, here are additional considerations. Young people under the age of 16 should not operate an adult-size ATV. (An adult-size ATV is one that has an engine larger than 90 cubic centimeters (cc) displacement.) Youngsters should be under the direct supervision of an adult. Table 8.3 contains age and size recommendations for ATV use.

Do not allow individuals to participate if they show signs of mental or physical conditions that could affect safety or performance. Riders taking medication or recovering from an injury may not be able to operate their vehicle with optimum performance.

All off-highway vehicle users participating in a recreational setting should first complete

Table 8.3

ENGINE SIZE FOR VARIOUS AGE GROUPS

ENGINE SIZE	AGE
Under 70 cc	6 and older
70 90 cc	12 and older
Over 90 cc	16 and older

Reprinted from ATV Safety Institute. 1992a. *ATV RiderCourse handbook.* Irvine, CA: SVIA.

a training course. Formal instruction is available through programs developed by the Specialty Vehicle Institute of America and the ATV Safety Institute.

Preparation, Instruction, and Warnings

Preparation for off-highway vehicle recreational activity includes checking the site, assuring the availability of equipment, qualifying riders, and inspecting the vehicles.

The site should be adequate for the intended activities. It should not be so large as to make surveillance difficult, nor should it be so small as to create unsafe riding space. Identify and avoid potential hazards. Obstacles, ledges, and drop-offs are particularly hazardous to off-road riders.

Most riding areas are likely to be several miles away from permanent buildings. It may be necessary to acquire portable shelters and restrooms. Equipment necessary for the safety and operation of the recreational experience must be available at the riding site. Tools, first aid kit, emergency items, and communications equipment are important. Medical facilities may be miles away, so identify an action plan should an accident or injury occur.

Riders and their vehicles must show evidence of preparedness. Riders should have all necessary personal protective gear, including an approved helmet, suitable eye protection, long-sleeved shirt or jacket, sturdy pants, gloves, and over-the-ankle boots. The trail bike or ATV should not show signs of damage or abuse and must pass a safety inspection before use.

Provide printed instructions that delineate the participation requirements. These may include state laws or local ordinances, rules for riding in a particular area, a code of conduct, and guidelines important to the safety and comfort of participants.

Communicate warnings to participants. Remind riders of the potential risk in off-highway vehicle operation and of hazardous circumstances related to the riding area. A common method to assure that riders are warned is to incorporate statements regarding potential risk in a waiver form that participants read and sign.

Figure 8.2 is an operational checklist that can serve as a basis for program development. It is

Off-Highway Vehicle Operations Checklist

Pre-event

_____ Permission acquired for use of riding area
_____ Riding area inspected
_____ Parking area identified
_____ Maps to riding area and of the riding area available
_____ Itinerary established
_____ Safety equipment checked and available
_____ Paperwork (registration, waiver, accident/incident reports) and pens available
_____ Emergency care plan established
_____ Rules for conduct identified
_____ Maintenance items including extra tools available
_____ Trash bags available for litter and cleanup
_____ Supplementary gasoline and oil available
_____ Tire pump or air tank and tire gauges available
_____ Trail marked for route of travel and stop points
_____ Timelines for riding have been determined and communicated to participants
_____ Copy of state and local laws available
_____ Participant registration completed
_____ Weather conditions checked

Event

_____ Procedure for unloading and grouping riders established
_____ All vehicles inspected
_____ Each rider uses an appropriately sized vehicle
_____ Communication signals established
_____ Penalties for rules violation established
_____ Emergency procedures provided to participants
_____ Vehicles exhibit registration, if state-required

Post-event

_____ Area cleared of litter and left in original condition
_____ OHVs loaded and secured by participants
_____ Paperwork filed and followed up as needed
_____ Equipment utilized restored to original condition

Figure 8.2   Off-highway vehicle operations checklist.

not intended to be all-inclusive, but instead will provide the fundamentals to consider when managing off-highway vehicle recreational activity. It is divided into pre-event, event, and post-event items.

Safety Rules

There are many dos and don'ts when operating an off-highway vehicle. The safe and responsible rider knows most safe riding practices, but it is a good idea to post and enforce rules for safe riding. Table 8.4 contains rules for participation.

ADMINISTRATION

Consider several administrative and supervisory components to assure efficient off-highway vehicle programming. Attention and follow-up on these matters not only benefits the riders, but helps program planning and development.

Organizational and Administrative Issues

Inspect and ride open fields and off-road trails before you use them for recreational riding. An area may look safe for riding, but often a closer inspection reveals hazardous conditions. Do not use areas if ledges or drop-offs are part of the terrain, potholes or sinkholes are present, excessive vegetation or dense foliage makes reading the terrain difficult, or streams or wetlands will be damaged by use. Off-highway vehicle activities should not take place where there is potential for vehicular traffic such as trucks or four-by-fours, the terrain is a pavementlike surface or too soft for traction, there is insufficient personnel for surveillance, or the land is private and you have not obtained permission. Be aware at all times of threatening weather conditions.

Another concern is transporting the off-highway vehicles to the riding area. Because most off-highway vehicles are not street legal, you must transport them by truck or trailer. An administrator should assure that there is a safe unloading and loading area. Ample parking should be available to allow maneuvering space for those with trailers.

Table 8.4
SAFETY RULES FOR OFF-HIGHWAY VEHICLE ACTIVITES

- ☐ Always wear protective gear when on the vehicle.
- ☐ Carry the vehicle's owner's manual and tool kit.
- ☐ Be sure the vehicle is in safe operating condition by inspecting it before riding.
- ☐ Ride only a vehicle that is appropriate for your size and skill level.
- ☐ Practice courtesy and cooperation.
- ☐ Ride only in designated areas.
- ☐ Keep a safe distance all around.
- ☐ Think how to reduce injury with each riding decision.
- ☐ TREAD lightly.
- ☐ Respect wildlife; turn the engine off if animals are in the same area.
- ☐ Follow state and local laws and ordinances.
- ☐ Ride at a speed appropriate for conditions.
- ☐ Do not perform stunts or be a show-off.
- ☐ Do not operate the vehicle while injured or tired, or while under the influence of medication or other drugs.
- ☐ Do not ride alone; choose a buddy and look after each other.
- ☐ Check areas to the side before making a lateral or turning maneuver.
- ☐ Do not ride on terrain or on hills beyond your capabilities.
- ☐ Do not carry passengers.
- ☐ Avoid wet and muddy terrain.

A potential for injury exists in the unloading and loading process. Take care that riders do not unload or load their vehicle hastily or unsafely. Often fellow riders can lend assistance.

An administrator must assure that appropriate safety equipment is available and working properly. Plan emergency procedures to minimize delays if someone requires medical attention. It is also wise to have a printed schedule or itinerary.

Here is a list of items that should be near the riding area or carried on a trail ride:

- First aid kit
- Fire extinguisher
- Electrical and duct tape
- Extra tools
- Tow strap or rope
- Air tank or tire pump
- Water
- Map and schedule

Record Keeping

Minimum records that you should complete and file include a registration form, a waiver form, and an accident or incident report form. The registration form serves as documentation of attendance and provides a roster to track participation. It also can state the rules of conduct. Completing a waiver form is a normal practice in formal off-highway vehicle activities. It provides notice that there is an element of risk in the riding activity. It also is helpful in a legal situation when an incident occurs that results in personal injury or vehicle damage.

You need to use the accident or incident report only if an occurrence results in injury or damage. We recommend that you document the slightest incidents. Such a report provides a record that you can use to assess quality control.

BIBLIOGRAPHY

ATV Safety Institute. 1992a. *ATV RiderCourse handbook*. Irvine, CA: Specialty Vehicle Institute of America.

———. 1992b. *Tips and practice guide for the ATV rider*. Irvine, CA: Specialty Vehicle Institute of America.

Motorcycle Industry Council. 1996. *Motorcycle statistical annual*. Irvine, CA: Motorcycle Industry Council.

Specialty Vehicle Institute of America. 1988. *Tips and practice guide for the off-highway motorcyclist*. Irvine, CA: Specialty Vehicle Institute of America.

———. 1993. *A guide to off-highway riding*. Irvine, CA: Specialty Vehicle Institute of America.

Wernex, J. 1993. *Off-highway motorcycle on ATV trails: Guidelines for design, construction, maintenance and user satisfaction*. 2d ed. Westerville, OH: American Motorcyclist Association.

Waterfront Safety

Susan J. Grosse

The area of shoreline and its adjacent land and water that people use for open-water aquatics is commonly referred to as the *waterfront*.

Specific open-water activities within a waterfront might include

- canoeing,
- fishing,
- jet skiing,
- powerboating,
- rowing,
- sailing,
- skin and scuba diving,
- springboard diving,
- swimming, and
- waterskiing.

Other chapters of this text provide specific information regarding participant safety in these activities. This chapter focuses on waterfront operation as a whole, describing safe participation in the listed activities. Although most individuals participate safely in waterfront activities, injury and death can occur on any waterfront.

Attention to detail is a key factor in managing risks on the waterfront. It takes only one loose bolt on a diving board to cause a diving injury, one frayed rope on a sailing rig to allow a boom to strike someone's head, one missing marker buoy to send a powerboat into a dangerous area. Before you make any waterfront area available for use, whether it be an organized waterfront at a camp beach or city park, or an improvised waterfront on the side of the river during a canoe trip, you must account for all safety and risk-management factors.

ENVIRONMENTAL CONDITIONS

A waterfront could be a rock ledge for lunch during a canoe trip or a pull-off stop during a raft trip. It could be the lakeshore of a picnic ground, a boat launch, or a park pond. Although the specific characteristics of a site may vary, safe sites have many factors in common.

Site Selection

In selecting a waterfront site be sure that the area is free from underwater hazards, clean (free from pollution, biologically safe, litter free), and large enough to accommodate all anticipated participants. It should be accessible to all individuals who might wish to participate, including individuals with disabilities. Proximity to human waste facilities (toilet, pit toilet, or designated trench) is important, but don't be close enough to contaminate the site. Lastly, the site should be appropriate to the activity you will use it for.

Swimming areas should have the following:

1. A gently sloping bottom, free of sinkholes and drop-offs.
2. A bottom free of sharp objects.
3. Still water rather than moving current.
4. Marked limits beyond which swimmers should not go.
5. Marked areas for swimmers of different ability.
6. A separate area for diving if diving is allowed. If participants are diving from water level, a minimum water depth of nine feet both under and in front of the diving area is necessary. If participants are diving from a height, additional water depth is mandatory.
7. Separate areas for other aquatic activities.
8. Rescue equipment and craft appropriate to the size of the area and conditions of use.

Small craft areas should have the following:

1. Designated landing, dock, or anchor areas.
2. Designated travel patterns to and from shore.
3. Separate areas for other aquatic activity.
4. Separate marked areas for different types of small craft.
5. Rescue equipment and craft appropriate to the particular small craft in use, size of area patrolled, and conditions of use.

Maintaining Facilities

Inspect waterfronts daily, before participants arrive, to ensure safe conditions. In addition, make inspections during operation hours in case conditions change by use. The natural environment is subject to change without notice. Moving water can alter bottom configurations, move hazardous material such as submerged logs, and wash material such as dead fish onto shore. Remove or mark any hazard found so it becomes off-limits to participants.

Although the outdoors is, by nature, more rustic than indoor aquatic facilities, make every effort to keep a waterfront clean. Natural or human litter can be dangerous as well as unsanitary. Regular maintenance should include removing litter; dead fish; decaying weeds; and other natural substances that wash ashore, decompose, and become a health hazard. Keep human waste facilities clean. Check docks, rafts, anchorages, and storage facilities for safety and security.

Maintenance also includes a daily check of all rescue equipment and rescue craft. Each item should be in good repair, in its correct location, and ready to use.

Equipment Maintenance and Management

Equipment management is important in any waterfront operation. Selection, storage, maintenance, and use all contribute to user safety. When selecting waterfront equipment consider the following:

- What activities can you accommodate in the amount of waterfront available for use? A small shoreline may only accommodate swimming and canoeing; a large shoreline can accommodate canoeing, swimming, sailing, and waterskiing.
- What instruction will be available to equipment users?
- What staffing for supervision and surveillance does each equipped activity require?

To ensure safe conditions, waterfronts should be inspected daily before participants arrive.

- How many individuals can you safely allow to participate in an activity at one time? Ten canoes can accommodate 20 paddlers; 20 canoes can accommodate 40 paddlers.

- What is participants' skill level in each activity needing equipment? Sailboards or sunfish are craft for beginning sailors; Flying Jrs. require a higher skill level.

- What support equipment do you need for each selected activity? Sailboards need land storage; powerboats need docking space.

- What are the maintenance requirements of selected equipment? Aluminum canoes require little maintenance; fiberglass craft need upkeep.

- What are the storage requirements for total amount of waterfront equipment available? Equipment not stored properly can be damaged, and damaged equipment is a safety hazard.

You can find specific guidelines for various activity equipment in subsequent chapters. In general, remember that inappropriate or insufficient equipment can result in misuse by participants and needless problems. Carelessly selected equipment may require skills that participants do not possess, cost too much money to maintain or repair, and take space that you could use for more appropriate participation.

Once you obtain equipment you must store or secure it during hours of waterfront closure. When supervision and surveillance are not available, no equipment should be available. Proper storage is closely linked to participant usage. Accidents often occur when equipment is inappropriately available for unsupervised use. For safe storage a system must be devised to do the following:

- Secure all small craft so they cannot be used during hours the waterfront is closed.

- Secure all small craft so they cannot be randomly used during hours of operation.

- Design and implement a sign-out (on-water use) and sign-in (off-water secure) system for all small craft participants to use during hours of waterfront operation so you can always account for all craft.

- Secure all support equipment (life jackets, paddles, oars, motors, sails and rigging, etc.) so it is inaccessible during closed hours.

- Secure all support equipment so it cannot be randomly used during hours of operation.

- Design a system to sign out support equipment during hours of use and sign it in when activity is completed so you can always account for all equipment.

- Design a system for swimmer control so only those logged into the water have access to the dock or pier, and you can always account for every swimmer in the area.

- Design a system of securing all docks and piers so no one has access to them if supervision and surveillance are not available.

- Store all flammable materials securely, locked from random access.

You should always be able to tell what equipment is in use and by whom and know what equipment is in storage, where, and in what condition.

Part of any storage plan includes checks for maintenance needs. Mark damaged or worn equipment; set it aside and secure it from use until you can make repairs. Taking care of those repairs at the end of the day ensures equipment ready for use during the next period of operation. Handling repairs before end-of-season storage ensures equipment ready for next year. Also, in both scenarios, prompt repair reduces the chance that participants inadvertently will use damaged equipment.

SUPERVISION

Risk management relies heavily on participant involvement. Individuals must take responsibility for their actions and make decisions that result in safe aquatic participation. However, many aquatic accidents directly result from inappropriate activity or behavior based on lack of information.

Communication is the foundation of waterfront supervision. People must be informed before they participate. *Supervision* refers to the ongoing communication process that results in safe participation. *Surveillance* refers to continually viewing all individuals once they are participating. The purpose of surveillance is to recognize hazardous actions before accidents or injuries result and to provide active rescue involvement if an accident or injury occurs.

The Task of Supervision

Supervision begins with establishing rules and procedures regarding participation (see table 9.1). All staff must be committed to communicating these rules to each participant. This should take place *before* any activity begins. Be sure a variety of communication methods are available. Posted written rules communicate only to individuals who can read them. Picture signage enhances understanding of written rules. In some cases, such as posting "no diving" areas, it is also important to clarify that serious injury or death can occur if participants do not obey the rule. Be prepared to explain your rules and the reasons for them. All staff must also be committed to rule enforcement. If staff members do this positively, participants will learn appropriate behaviors and minimize accidents.

Surveillance

Someone must have continual scanning of participants as their sole responsibility whenever the waterfront is in use. This continual scanning is called surveillance. Assign a minimum of two individuals to surveillance duty at all times. Responding to an emergency and securing the area require at least two people. To respond appropriately to waterfront emergencies individuals should be certified by a recognized national agency as possessing skills appropriate to the breadth of activities and situations on the particular waterfront area. Among the most commonly required skills are

- cardiopulmonary resuscitation (CPR), adult and infant or child (professional rescuer level),
- first aid (professional rescuer level),
- lifeguarding,
- rescue procedures appropriate to participant usage of small craft (if a part of the waterfront),
- rescue procedures appropriate to specific

natural conditions (surf rescue, for example), if appropriate, and

- rescue procedures appropriate to specialized activities taking place (scuba diving, for example), if appropriate.

In planning supervision and surveillance it is important that each area having a specific purpose should have separate surveillance staff. Swim area personnel, for example, should be responsible only for swim; rescue boat personnel assigned to cover sailing should cover just sailing and not sailing, canoeing, and waterskiing. Different activities require distinct surveillance and rescue skills. You may need to assign additional staff based on specifics of the tasks required. Small craft surveillance staff should include a rescue power craft driver and a separate individual or individuals on the boat to perform rescues. Assign staff accordingly. If appropriately certified individuals are not available, do not use the waterfront.

Often individuals responsible for surveillance also need to communicate information. When doing so, they should not interrupt their waterfront scanning. They should make their comments brief and to the point; if necessary, explain to the individual that they are listening but must continue to look at the waterfront. Refer an individual to a supervisor or nonscanning staff member if more detailed communication is necessary. Beyond friendly smiles and greetings, avoid social communication while on duty.

WATERFRONT EMERGENCY ACTION PLAN

Surveillance begins with an *emergency action plan*, a detailed written outline of what staff members should do in response to an emergency. Post this plan at the waterfront. All staff should participate in regularly scheduled practice drills using this plan. These drills should include situations in which surveillance staff do not know the emergency is a drill. When the drill is in progress, an appropriately credentialed individual should observe and evaluate it. After the drill,

Table 9.1
RULES GUIDING PARTICIPATING IN WATERFRONT ACTIVITIES*

CONSIDERATIONS	GUIDELINES
Who can participate?	☐ *Age:* Younger children require closer supervision than adults capable of mature judgment. Senior citizens may lack the physical dexterity to act swiftly.
	☐ *Demonstrated ability:* Beginning skill level participamts and individuals whose skill level is unknown require more supervision than advanced participants.
	☐ *Prior experience and prerequisites:* Individuals with no prior experience or who meet only minimim prerequisites require more supervision than experienced participants.
	☐ *Equipment available:* The greater the amount of equipment in use the closer the supervison must be.
	☐ *Size of area:* Small, crowded space needs additional supervison (to avoid collisions and mishaps), as do large, spread-out participation areas.
Where can participation take place?	☐ Designate areas for specialty activities, such as diving, and prohibit access to other activities, such as driving small crafts.
What equipment may participants use?	☐ Only children supervised by parents may use water toys.
	☐ Participants may use swim equipment only with permission of the lifeguard on duty.
	☐ Individuals wishing to use small craft equipment must comply with check-out procedures established by supervisors of the area, and safety checks must be performed routinely on all equipment.
	☐ Only individuals who have met set criterion may use springboards.
	☐ Only competitive swimmers supervised by their coaches may use starting blocks.
	☐ Allow no recreational use of safety and rescue equipment. Participants should wear PFDs at all times in those activities requiring them. Make equipment available only after weather warnings are cleared.
What behavior is appropriate to participate ?	☐ No horseplay.
	☐ No running.
	☐ No participation outside of set hours.
	☐ Gentle handling of equipment.
	☐ No drug or alcohol use during participation.

Table 9.1 (continued)

CONSIDERATIONS	GUIDELINES
What are the health or medical contraindications?	☐ Restrict individuals with uncontrolled tonic or clonic seizures from operating power craft. ☐ Participants with other medical problems should have medications well secured to their bodies in case of, for instance, a capsized boat. ☐ Participants should leave the water and use appropriate facilities for toilet needs. Dispose of garbage according to local regulations. ☐ Employ multiple means of emergency signaling to meet needs of the visual and hearing impaired.
What attire is appropriate to participation?	☐ Small craft and personal watercraft users, water skiers, and sailboarders must wear PFDs. ☐ Swimmers should wear bathing suits; although swimming in a T-shirt and shorts is possible, the additional weight is unsafe for the swimmer and cumbersome for the rescuer. ☐ Participants should always use helmets, harnesses (for sailboats), and wet suits if required.

*Note: Examples are for reference purposes. They are not meant to be all-inclusive. Individual waterfront circumstances will dictate rule specifics. Participants should strictly follow federal, state, and local ordinances and laws governing participation and means of participation.

discuss the results with everyone involved. If warranted, undertake remediation or procedural corrections immediately.

Initiating an emergency action plan begins with recognizing an emergency situation. The next step is alerting additional staff for assistance and initiating rescue efforts. In an emergency, additional staff may mean concession workers, maintenance personnel, supervisory people, surveillance staff on break, or workers from other areas of the camp or park. Where no additional employed staff are present, rely on bystanders to assist in an emergency. Figure 9.1 is a suggested emergency action plan for a small, two-surveillance-person waterfront. Whether to clear the area of participants is a decision that you must make case by case. If certified rescue personnel cannot supervise remaining participants you must clear the area. If surveillance can continue and participation will not impede rescue efforts, participation can continue.

Open-water rescue efforts rely on using equipment. Based on the size of the water

area under surveillance, water conditions, and the type of activity, each specific use area should have rescue craft fully equipped to handle any possible rescue: swim rescue equipment (rescue buoy, rescue tube, rescue board); land and dock extension rescue equipment (ring buoy, pole); spinal injury rescue equipment (backboard, cervical collars, straps, head immobilizer); body search equipment (masks, fins, snorkels); resuscitation equipment; first aid kit; blankets; bloodborne pathogen contagion reduction equipment; and communication device to contact the emergency medical services. In addition, grappling irons and a towboat should be available to the entire waterfront.

All staff must be thoroughly trained in rescue procedures and the use of available equipment before you open any waterfront for participants. In addition, staff should practice rescue drills during regularly scheduled emergency simulations through the season.

No rescue is complete until it has been documented. Regardless of circumstances,

Emergency Action Plan

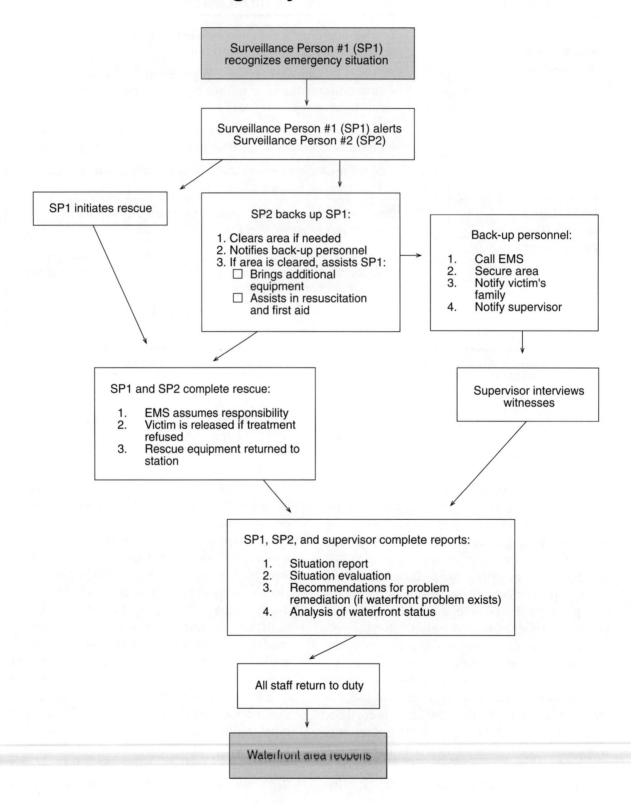

Figure 9.1   Emergency action plan.

you must report any rescue in writing. Individual waterfront facilities should have specific forms, similar to figure 9.2, ready for documenting water-rescue incidents and accidents requiring first aid. The emergency action plan not only stipulates who performs which tasks during a rescue but also includes who is responsible for completing paperwork and reporting to the waterfront chain of command.

SELECTION AND CONDUCT OF THE ACTIVITY

You must control the use of waterfront equipment. Establish criteria to ensure that equipment users are properly prepared and capable of safe use. When making this assessment, always consider the age of the users and their ability to pass a swim test and life jacket use

---

Incident Report Form

Date of accident _____ Time of accident _____

Name of victim _____

Address _____

Home phone _____ Business phone _____

Location of accident _____

Staff attending   _____   _____

                                           _____   _____

Witnesses (nonstaff)   _____   _____

                                           _____   _____

Details of accident _____

_____

_____

_____

Action taken by staff _____

_____

_____

_____

Staff reporting _____ Date_____

Department head's signature _____ Date_____

Figure 9.2 Standard incident report form.

Reprinted, by permission from Club Corporation of America. 1988. *Standards of design and construction of an athletic facility.* Club Corporation of America.

test to determine deep-water survival capability, a test to determine skill in handling specific types of small craft, and a knowledge test to determine if they can operate a craft correctly and within the law. Perform a credential check to determine prior instruction and attained skill level, and make an equipment check if participants will be using their own equipment. In circumstances where it is necessary, make sure participants make a financial bond or deposit.

Although you can expect users to assume a reasonable degree of responsibility for themselves, what level they consider reasonable is a function of age, skill, knowledge, and maturity. Aquatic sports often look easier than they are. Often a participant is not in a position to accurately judge skills needed in an aquatic situation. Combine this inaccuracy with overestimation of personal abilities and a dangerous situation is in the making. Waterfront us-

INSTRUCTIONAL PROGRAMS

Adding an instructional program to a waterfront operation greatly enhances safe usage. Participants who are taught skills and safety procedures specific to their waterfront activity will be less likely to cause or be involved in an accident. Maximum benefits of instruction will occur if instructors are credentialed by a recognized national organization. This might include the following:

- Swimming—Red Cross, YMCA, Ellis and Associates, Swim America

- Canoeing and kayaking—American Canoeing Association, Red Cross, American Alliance for Health, Physical Education, Recreation and Dance (AAHPERD) Aquatic Council

- Sailing—U.S. Sailing Association, U.S. Yacht Racing Union, Red Cross, AAHPERD Aquatic Council

- Powerboating—U.S. Power Squadron, U.S. Coast Guard

- Water exercise—Aquatic Exercise Association, U.S. Water Fitness, AAHPERD Aquatic Council

- Scuba—PADI (Professional Association of Dive Instructors)

Use an established curriculum, particularly to ensure that you leave no critical items out of instruction. Monitor class size to allow all participants maximum participation, which should include hands-on experience with all equipment and supervised practice time. When you use equipment for instruction, make sure that it is appropriate to the ability of the student. Make available printed materials for additional study, with future participation based on completing the instructional program or a screening test. Participation in specific camps for each activity would also improve ability.

In any instructional setting, a certified individual, in addition to the credentialed individual responsible for instruction, should be charged with surveillance of the class group. In this way the instructor can properly focus on teaching while another staff member focuses on safety surveillance. Safety on the waterfront begins with the example set by waterfront owners and operators. High safety standards set an expectation of safety for all participants. Instruction presented in this atmosphere will result in waterfront safety, not only on the instructional waterfront but also on any waterfront where the instructed individual participates.

age criterion must be clear, particularly regarding equipment.

ADMINISTRATION

Property owners and operators are ultimately liable for what occurs on their waterfront. Safety begins with these individuals.

Operations

No waterfront should open until it has undergone a complete safety inspection and all staff are trained and ready. Although closing a waterfront on a hot summer day isn't a popular thing to do, sometimes it is a necessity. You should close a waterfront for the following reasons:

Safety on the waterfront begins with the example set by waterfront owners and operators.

- Water is polluted.
- You cannot mark or remove a hazard (natural or manufactured) from participant access.
- Severe weather conditions exist:
    1. Electrical storm
    2. Dangerous current or tide
    3. High wind or waves
    4. Tornado warning
    5. Severe weather watch
- Properly certified individuals are not present for surveillance.
- All rescue equipment and craft are not in place and ready for use.
- A rescue is in process and other participants cannot be under surveillance of a rescue-certified individual.
- A drowning or death has occurred.

In general, reopening should not take place until the weather front has passed, the participant emergency is over and surveillance is reestablished, the hazard is removed or restricted, or an investigation regarding the incident has been completed.

Record Keeping

Written documentation of daily events serves several purposes. You can improve safety factors through analyzing accident situations, determining causes, and rectifying problems. Written records also provide factual information necessary to properly defend against lawsuits. Often cases go to court years after the fact. A written record remains when human memory fades. Waterfront owners and operators should keep thorough written records (see table 9.2).

Figure 9.3 is a suggested waterfront operations checklist. Expand it as necessary to meet the needs of specific waterfront organizational formats and activities. A well-run waterfront will be a safe waterfront. It is attention to details that creates an environment for safe aquatic activity.

BIBLIOGRAPHY

American Red Cross. 1988. *Basic water safety*. Washington, DC: American National Red Cross.

Rhulen, M. n.d. *Camp tips: Lake and river aquatic safety*. Glen Allen, VA: Markel Rhulen Underwriters & Brokers.

Table 9.2
DAILY, MONTHLY, AND ANNUAL RECORD-KEEPING ITEMS

Daily records	Monthly records	Seasonal records
☐ Air and water temperature	☐ Emergency training drills	☐ Hiring of staff
☐ Weather	☐ In-service training	☐ Staff credentials and certifications
☐ Patron participation	☐ Staff evaluations	☐ Preservice training
☐ Equipment use	☐ Operational expenses	☐ Equipment inventory
☐ Accidents		☐ Budget
☐ Unusual incidents		☐ Emergency action plans
☐ Maintenance		☐ Facility rules and operating procedures
☐ Staffing		☐ Program evaluations

Waterfront Operations Checklist

Date _____ Time _____   Staff_____

Water temperature _____   Air temperature _____

Weather _____

_____

Item	Status		
	OK	Problem	Problem resolved
Environment			
1. Water area			
☐ underwater hazards			
☐ currents/tides			
☐ lifelines			
☐ marker buoys			
☐ channel markers			
2. Beach cleanliness			
☐ no litter			
☐ trash receptacles			
☐ organic matter			
3. Pier safety			
☐ surface			
☐ ladders/stairs			
☐ safety markings			
☐ diving board(s)			
4. Dock moorings			
☐ anchors			
☐ lines			
☐ cleats			
5. Surveillance staff/guard stands			
☐ clean			
☐ equipment in place			
☐ shade coverings			
☐ drinking water available			

(continued)

Figure 9.3   Waterfront operations checklist.

	OK	Problem	Problem resolved
6. Safety and rescue equipment			
☐ telephone			
☐ communication flags/ walkie-talkies			
☐ small craft (rescue equipped)			
☐ backboard (spinal injury)/ straps			
☐ cervical collars (multiple sizes)			
☐ head immobilizer			
☐ first aid kit			
☐ blankets			
☐ stretcher			
☐ resuscitation equipment			
☐ contagion protection equipment			
☐ ring buoys — number/ location			
☐ rescue buoys — number/ location			
☐ buddy board/water in-out board			
☐ grappling irons			
7. Signage for rules			
☐ emergency contact process			
☐ beach use			
☐ dock use			
☐ pier use			
☐ water use			
Supervision/Surveillance			
1. Current credentials on file			
2. Preservice training documented			
3. Emergency Action Plan posted			
4. Chain of command posted			
5. Duty roster posted			
6. Emergency Action Plan drill evaluations on file			

Figure 9.3 *(continued)*

	OK	Problem	Problem resolved
7. Evaluation procedure on file			
8. Accident report forms on file			
9. State and local codes and ordinances on file			
10. Safety and rescue equipment			
Selection and Conduct of Activities			
1. Beach furniture			
☐ clean			
☐ good repair			
2. Row boats/oars — number available			
3. Canoes/paddles — number available			
4. Kayaks/paddles — number available			
5. Sail craft/rigging — number available			
6. Power craft/motors/oars — number/type available			
7. Fuel — storage and access security			
8. Personal flotation devices — number/type available			
9. Instructional swim equipment — number/type available			
Administration			
1. Use permits on file			
2. Security — locked areas secure (list)			
3. Vehicles			
☐ cars — license/key location/ parking			
☐ trucks — license/key location/parking			
☐ trailers — type and usage/ parking			

Ritz, C. 1989. *Waterfront management: A syllabus for the aquatic council course teacher of waterfront management*. Reston, VA: Aquatic Council, American Alliance for Health, Physical Education, Recreation and Dance.

Schirick, E. 1991. Risk management: Preparing your waterfront safety plan. *Camping Magazine*. April.

chapter 10

Sailing and Small Craft Safety

Susan Skaros

People today are turning to a variety of small craft for their recreational and leisure time activities. Small craft are 16 feet long or less and powered by motor (electric or fuel), wind (sailboards, sailboats), or human (rowboat, canoe, kayak). Whether sailing on a large bay, canoeing in the wilderness, powerboating on a lake, or rowing while casting for fish, there are rules and safety precautions common to all small craft. To prepare people for the pleasure of using small craft, we need to develop programs and guidelines to ensure safety, adequate preparation and training, proper equipment maintenance, prevention of accidents and injury, and emergency response. This chapter focuses on the concerns and specific problems associated with small craft programs and provides recommendations that will help these programs run smoothly and safely.

Most small craft accidents are caused by lack of preparation, inadequate equipment maintenance, insufficient training or supervision, lack of proper surveillance, or a combination. The key to risk management in small craft safety is *pay attention to detail!* A missing clip on a personal flotation device (PFD), a small leak in a gas hose, a quickly moving weather front, or mixing alcohol and boats can mean the difference between life and death. Taking time to develop a thorough, organized small craft program—one that addresses the 5 Ss of wise small craft use, safety, supervision, surveillance, selection, and support—will spell the difference between success and disaster. In addition, there must be familiarity with and acceptance of federal, state, and local regulations regarding small craft. Everyone running a small craft program or using small craft is responsible for knowing these regulations.

ENVIRONMENTAL CONDITIONS

Environmental conditions include site selection and facilities, maintenance, equipment, and tripping (off-site usage and transportation). Identify potential hazards, and either avoid or remove them. Take steps to ensure rapid accessibility to all participants in the event of an emergency. Backup resources must be readily available.

Site Selection and Facilities

Having the proper site for conducting small craft activities, especially for beginners, is necessary to having a safe, successful program. Table 10.1 contains the guidelines for choosing an appropriate site. This type of site will allow small craft participants to learn and practice with a minimum of outside risks.

Facilities include equipment storage, repair areas, and an off-the-water classroom area. The storage and repair area should have hangers, racks, or shelves for paddles and oars, masts and booms, rigging and lines, rudders, dagger boards, tillers, and sail bags. It needs an airy, sheltered space for drying sails and PFDs to prevent rotting and damage. If powerboats are used, keep motors, fuel containers, fuel, and lines in a well-ventilated, fireproof, *locked* area. In addition, a workbench for performing minor repairs and an area for painting or repairing craft and equipment make ongoing maintenance easier.

The classroom facility should be in a sheltered area and used during adverse weather conditions (fog, moderate to high winds, electrical storms) or when you are presenting didactic information. Although an indoor area with electrical access is ideal, it is not necessary unless you are using video materials.

All facilities should be in good repair, easily accessible for everyone, including participants with special needs, and as clean and free of debris and pollutants as possible. Keep hazardous materials such as fuel, paint, and varnish in a well-ventilated, flame-resistant, locked area according to state and local regulations.

Maintaining Facilities

Daily inspections of the small craft area are imperative for a safe program and preventing accidents. In addition, train every participant to continuously watch for signs of equipment wear or malfunction and for environmental hazards. Encourage them to report these findings immediately. Replace, repair, or remove the compromised equipment before continu-

Table 10.1

CHARACTERISTICS OF AN APPROPRIATE SITE FOR SMALL CRAFT ACTIVITIES

☐ Have a protected area such as a bay, inlet, or small lake.

☐ Be well away from strong currents.

☐ Be away from swimming areas.

☐ Be protected from excessive motor boat, commercial traffic, waterskiing, or personal watercraft use areas.

☐ Have clearly marked areas for small craft activites.

☐ Have designated traffic patterns to and from the docking area.

☐ Have an observation area, preferably elevated, for tracking crafts — this is particularly important for sailing.

☐ Be in a clean, pollutant-free area.

☐ Have adequate accessibility for participants with special needs.

☐ Be free of any submerged or large objects.

☐ Be free from overhead electrical and telephone wires to avoid entanglement by masts and rigging.

☐ Have an easy, smooth access to the water and craft for participant safety and to reduce risk of damage to the craft.

☐ Have a firm bottom in shallow areas.

☐ Be free of debris on the shore and in shallow areas.

☐ Have a designated area for each type of small craft when multiple types are in use.

☐ Have a designated dock, floating pier, or anchorage area. Docks and piers should be within 1 ft of water and at least 3 ft wide.

☐ Have available and rapidly staffed rescue and safety equipment appropriate for the type of small craft being used, area being covered, and water conditions.

ing the activity. Conditions change quickly, and what was, initially, a clean, hazard-free area or piece of equipment can rapidly become dangerous. Employ additional vigilance in areas with moving water, tides, and after storms. If you cannot physically remove a hazard from the small craft area, it must be clearly marked and avoided.

Lakes, rivers, shorelines, and coastlines are constantly changing. Add to that such activities as fishing, waterskiing, and personal watercraft use, and the potential for hazards becomes immeasurable. Therefore, maintaining the small craft area includes the following:

• Checking the area, including trees, bushes, shoreline, and mooring areas for fishing lines and lures

• Removing all litter, especially cans, bottles, pop-tops, and glass

• Removing and disposing of dead fish and animals, branches, weeds, and other residue that washes up on shore, as they cause health risks

• Cleaning and stocking toilet facilities at least daily

• Checking daily under and around docks, piers, rafts, moorings, and small craft for any objects that may have become snagged or trapped

• Inspecting all safety equipment and rescue gear, including craft, to ensure they are fully

© Mary Langenfeld

People today are turning to a variety of small craft for their recreation and leisure time activities.

stocked, in good repair, and in operating condition at the beginning and end of each day the facility is operating

- Inspecting shelters and storage facilities at least weekly to ensure they are sturdy, secure, and free of hazards
- Inspecting the overall area for stinging insect nests; loose tree limbs (widow makers); poisonous snakes (in indigenous areas); and erosion of paths, traffic areas, shorelines, and around buildings

By having specific areas assigned to staff, and by using a checklist, this can be accomplished quickly and efficiently.

Equipment

There are four focus areas you need to include in equipment management. The *selection* of equipment must be appropriate for the site, activity, type of program (instruction, racing, tripping), and age and type of participant (young child, adolescent, older adult, special

needs). Proper *maintenance* prevents accidents and ensures safety. Appropriate *storage* ensures ease of equipment maintenance and reduces repair costs. Correct *usage* of equipment reduces the likelihood of accidents and injuries.

Selecting Small Craft

Proper craft selection is vital to program safety and success. It is the singular most important aspect of the small craft program, aside from safety. Consider several factors before selecting equipment, including purpose, cost, facilities, storage, maintenance, program, and type of participants. Table 10.2 can help clarify the choices. Proper equipment selection will contribute to the success and enjoyment of participants, reduce accidents, limit repairs, and minimize costs.

Selecting Safety Equipment

The proper selection of safety equipment may mean the difference between success and disaster, life and death. The most impor-

Table 10.2
CONSIDERATIONS FOR CHOOSING A SMALL CRAFT

☐ What type of site is available?

☐ What are the main small craft interests in the area this program will be serving?

☐ What other aquatic activities will be occurring in the area at the same time as the small craft program?

☐ What age group and skill levels will this program serve?

☐ Will there be an instructional program, recreation use, or both?

☐ What special equipment and adaptation of small craft is required for individuals with special needs?

☐ Will there be tripping opportunites, and if so what type?

☐ Who will be instructing?

☐ What is the emergency rescue and assistance potential of the area? Poor assistance capabilites might speak against wide-ranging small craft activities like sailing.

☐ How many staff will be available, and what is their background and training? A well-staffed program with many certified individuals would lend itself to a more diverse and sophisticated program than would one that is sparsely staffed and minimally trained.

☐ What is the budget for small craft, equipment, and repairs?

☐ What type of storage and maintenance facilities are available (e.g., on-site versus storing and repairing in another area of facility)?

☐ What ancillary equipment do you need for each type of craft (masts, sails, booms, tillers, paddles, spray skirts, flotation bags, PFDs, helmets, etc.)?

☐ What are the prevailing weather conditions you will face (e.g., wind and wind shifts, fog, sudden storms, rip tides, etc.)?

☐ Will this be a seasonal or year-round program?

☐ What is the water depth of the area? Shallower water and sloping shoreline might speak against keeled sailboats; rocky shoreline and rivers would lend themselves to aluminum or durable plastic paddles.

tant piece of safety equipment is the personal flotation device or PFD. Everyone should wear a Coast Guard-approved PFD that is in good condition and appropriate for their size, weight, and activity whenever they are on board small craft. The PFD must be properly sized, secured, and clipped when in use. Advanced swim skills do *not* constitute an exception to this rule.

In addition to PFDs, there are other safety items you need to address. Kayakers and white-water canoers should wear helmets when practicing rolls and when shooting rapids or tripping. Spare oars or paddles should be onboard motor craft and sailboats in case of wind loss or motor failure. Sailors must use harnesses when *hiking out,* or trapezing. In addition to self-bailers, bailers are essential equipment for all open craft, especially in potentially rough or open water. Every craft on open water or when tripping should have a signaling device, such as an operational flashlight, metal mirror, or a signal flare. Each participant should have a whistle that can be heard for long distances firmly secured to their PFD. Larger craft and those used for tripping, distance sailing, or racing should carry a type IV PFD or heaving line for rescue purposes. Keep in mind that you must meet federal, state, Coast

PERSONAL FLOTATION DEVICES

PFDs come in four styles. Type I is bulky with flotation pockets front and back and the ability to support the head of an unconscious person faceup out of the water. You usually find this type on commercial craft. Type II is the vest with flotation pockets in the front and behind the neck. This type is also able to support the head of an unconscious person faceup in the water. This type is often used in general purpose boating, with poor swimmers, for boaters with special needs (seizure tendencies, spastic movements), and in camp programs. Type III is the sleeveless jacket PFD favored by canoers, kayakers, and sailors. It has more flexibility and warmth, and allows more arm movement. It will *not* support an unconscious person faceup in the water. Type IV is the seat cushion. You can use it as a throwing or swimming assist for a person who has fallen overboard or is in trouble. Type V, or Special Use Device, is for special activities such as barefooting, and water-ski jumping. These devices take the form of a full or partial body wet suit with floatation built in.

There are two types of fill (flotation substance) used in PFDs. Kapok, a dried plant material, has been used for years. It is placed inside plastic bags in the PFD, and as long as it stays dry, it floats nicely. Unfortunately, the challenges of sun, weather, misuse, and improper drying often cause the plastic to dry and crack. This allows the kapok to become wet, at which point it loses all its buoyancy. The PFD is then useless as a self-rescue device. Foam is the other type of fill used. This substance does not have the limitations of kapok; however, it is bulkier. Foam seems to be the preferred fill for PFDs, even if some maneuverability may be lost. Canoeing and kayaking type III PFDs retain their flexibility because they are made with narrow strips of foam rather than large pieces.

All PFDs must be Coast Guard approved and have a stamp or label so stating visible on the PFD. All participants must be sure that their PFD is appropriate for size and weight indicated on the label. Small children, individuals who are thin, those with special needs, and those who have muscle coordination impairment (e.g., multiple sclerosis, cerebral palsy, myasthenia gravis, or seizures) should have a PFD that will support the head out of the water, even when unconscious (type I or II) and a *crotch strap*, which, when secured, will keep them from falling out of the bottom of the PFD when they are in the water.

You can use type IV PFDs, the seat cushion, for throwing and swimming assists, but *only* if they are not used to sit on, because they are filled with kapok. The person you are assisting must be conscious and able to move easily and comfortably in the water to use the type IV PFD. This type PFD should not be the only type on board and you should *not* rely on it for personal safety. The federal government and many states have enacted legislation requiring a type I, II, or III PFD on board for each person. A type IV PFD would be in addition to these.

Guard, and local regulations for each craft. A list of safety equipment you should have onboard powerboats and larger sail craft includes the following:

- Throw bag or heaving line
- Coast Guard-approved type I, II, or III PFD in good condition for *every* person onboard
- Extra throwable safety equipment (type IV PFD, ring buoy, rescue tube)
- Audio signaling device (whistle, bell, horn)
- Extra oars or paddles in case of motor or wind failure and to extend to a tired swimmer
- Fire extinguisher for craft with combustible fuel power
- Extra line and rope

- Bailing device

In addition, craft you are using for tripping or day sailing should have a visual distress signaling device (flares or flags for daytime, flares, electrical lights, or flashlights for nighttime), running lights if the craft is likely to be out after dark, an anchor, a first aid kit with emergency phone numbers, a tool kit and spare parts, a compass and navigation charts (topographical maps for canoers and kayakers), a weather radio, and a cellular phone or two-way radio.

Although much of this equipment is not needed for day-to-day small craft instructional use, it is important for individuals and families who go out for an extended time or distance in their craft. Make participants aware of the need and function of this equipment as part of their training program.

Also necessary is surveillance and rescue equipment. We present considerations for selecting this equipment in table 10.3. Once you have taken these into account, equip the rescue craft and make them available and easily accessible *at all times*. If key rescue equipment is inoperative or unavailable, halt the program activities until you can make a replacement or repair.

Maintaining Equipment

Equipment maintenance is vital for safety and preventing accidents. In addition, proper care and maintenance can reduce costs. Establish a maintenance schedule and adhere to it to ensure nothing is overlooked. Consider length of program (seasonal versus year-round), weather conditions, craft usage, participants' skill, and needs. Minor repairs can be made, if appropriately trained and skilled persons are available, during the program season, but most major repairs must wait until the off-season. Should a major repair be required during the small craft season, it may mean a program change.

Preventing damage is the best way to minimize repairs. Some suggestions for accomplishing this include the following:

- Avoid dragging or scraping craft on the ground, especially when embarking or disembarking.
- Enter craft *only* when it is afloat.
- Exit craft before it touches the bottom.
- Ensure secure mooring or racking of craft when not in use.
- Securely tie down craft to avoid wind damage.

Table 10.3
GUIDELINES FOR SELECTING SURVEILLANCE AND RESCUE EQUIPMENT

☐ What type of small craft are participants using?

☐ What is the age and skill level of participants?

☐ Are there any participants with special needs?

☐ What size area do you need to cover?

☐ What type of waterfront area is involved (e.g., lake or river, isolated or populated, rocky shoreline or sandy beach, etc.)?

☐ What is the background and training level of the staff?

☐ Who is responsible for performing rescues?

☐ What surveillance facilities are available?

☐ Where is the closest accessible area for intervention by emergency medical services (EMS)?

- Use bumpers or old tires on docks and piers in case of collision or bumping while docking.

- Hang PFDs, spray skirts, and sails in a dry, well-ventilated area for adequate drying.

- Avoid using paddles and oars, especially wooden ones, for pushing off from shore or for leaning on—this causes the tip to crack and split.

Maintaining equipment covers several areas: craft maintenance and repair, maintenance for each type of craft (sails, ropes and lines, motors, gas lines, spray skirts, tillers and rudders, oars and paddles, portaging yokes, harnesses, etc.), maintenance of safety and rescue equipment (first aid kits, two-way radios, rescue tubes and ring buoys, backboards, etc.), and maintenance of ancillary equipment (docks and piers, mooring arms, course and hazard buoys, trailers, tripping gear, etc.). When possible and affordable, keep backup equipment available to avoid removing craft from service for an extended time. Keep parts that often need replacing or are easily lost (e.g., shear pins, nuts, bolts, rope, PFD clips, etc.) on hand in ample supply and variety.

Craft maintenance varies according to type and material. Aluminum craft seldom need repair and stand up to considerable wear and tear, but when damaged, you must send them to a professional for repair. Wooden and canvas craft often dry out during the off-season and need some initial time in the water to allow seams to seal. They are easily damaged, need continuous repair if great care is not taken, and often need annual painting or varnishing. You can do some repairs on-site, but major repairs require a professional and can be expensive. Fiberglass is durable, and you can usually do repairs on-site. Although these craft are heavy, they can withstand a great deal of punishment. This type of craft may be useful for a program that does not require moving craft in and out of the water. A good cleaning and waxing at the beginning and end of the season or several times a year may help preserve the finish. Plastics like Kevlar, Royalux, and newer materials are lightweight, forgiving,

and easy to repair. Unfortunately, the initial cost of these craft can be high.

Inspect small craft daily for damage. Sand down or repair splintered wood and fiberglass or sharp aluminum edges and rivets to prevent injury. Inspect seats, gunwales, oarlocks, turnbuckles, blocks, lines, masts, and so on daily, and replace or repair them immediately to avoid further damage. In short, each craft should be in the best possible condition whenever it is in use.

Maintaining equipment associated with small craft is essential for safety and function. Inspect PFDs, sails, spray skirts, kneeling pads, ropes, harnesses, and lines carefully at the beginning of each season for insect and rodent damage. Continue to check them before each use for signs of wear or damage. Check wooden paddles, oars, tillers, dagger boards, and rudders for splinters and cracks.

Annual sanding and varnishing with a good grade marine varnish or polyurethane will help prevent damage. Inspect all lines, painters, halyards, sheets, and mooring lines daily, and replace them if showing signs of wear. At a minimum, completely replace them at the beginning of the season or twice a year if a year-round program. To prolong their service life, keep them clean and neatly coiled when not in use. Keep any piece of equipment with moveable parts free of dirt and sand, and, if required, lubricate them regularly. Motors need an annual tune-up and change of spark plugs. Blow gas lines clean, and check rubber fittings, O-rings, bulbs, and hoses for cracks and leaks. Handle any piece of equipment that uses combustible fuel in a well-ventilated area, and replace it *immediately* if it is cracked, worn, or leaking. Dry sails daily after use, then fold and store them in their bags in a dry, well-ventilated area. Repair any rips or tears as soon as you notice them to prevent further damage.

Also, inspect safety and rescue equipment at the beginning of each day. Fully stock first aid kits, including report forms. Check radio or telephone communication lines at the beginning of each day, and replace batteries routinely *before* they wear out. Establish a backup communication system such as flags, whistles, or boat horn, and use it with the radio and telephone system if the primary system fails. This is especially important if the facility is large and the small craft are spread over a wide area. Inspect rescue boat equipment at the beginning of each day along with whatever means of power they use (motor, oars, etc.). Replace any faulty or nonfunctioning equipment immediately and repair it as soon as possible.

Ancillary equipment such as mooring arms, dock bumpers, canoe or kayak racks, and paddle and oar racks is used constantly. Check it daily, just as any other common use equipment. Repair damaged equipment as soon as possible to prevent injury to participants and damage to other equipment.

Other ancillary equipment such as portage yokes, boat and canoe trailers, and tripping gear may be used only at special times. Thoroughly inspect this equipment before use and, again, at the end of the trip or activity. Pull damaged equipment and repair it before making it available for use. Trailers must meet federal and state licensing and safety regulations. Use them to transport boats and gear only, *never people*.

Storage

Equipment storage covers both long- and short-term storage. Long-term storage is used at the end of the season, usually over the winter. Key concepts include the following:

- Storing securely or stacking small craft and equipment to prohibit falling, crushing, scraping, or damage
- Ensuring all PFDs, kneeling pads, sails, spray skirts, lines and ropes, and so on are clean and dry and stored in an insect- and rodent-free area
- Painting, varnishing, and thoroughly drying all equipment before placing it in storage
- Completely draining and storing all motors, gas cans, gas lines, and fuel-related equipment in a well-ventilated, locked, fireproof area
- Checking and inventorying all equipment before storage, sorting damaged items, and

repairing them before storing
- Making sure all craft and equipment are stored in an area sheltered from wind and weather
- Ensuring all storage areas are securely locked and equipment is not accessible

Equipment that is stored in good condition should be ready for use, with a minimum of preparation, when the new season opens.

Short-term storage is used during the day and at the close of each day's activities. Store all craft to prevent use during off hours or by unauthorized individuals. Restrict access to equipment and craft during program hours so staff can keep track of what is being used and by whom. Establish a check-in and check-out system to avoid random or inappropriate usage. Remove fuel cans, lines, and motors from craft at the close of each day and store them. At any time during the day, you should be able to account for every small craft and piece of equipment. Maintain an equipment condition log or chart indicating daily inspection, damaged equipment, equipment out for repair and by whom, use status, and staff responsible for the specific designation.

Equipment Usage

Monitor and supervise how, when, where, and by whom small craft and equipment are being used. Length, type, and style of small craft and age, size, and ability of participants will determine how many people can be aboard each craft at any time. At a minimum, the *freeboard* (amount of craft visible above the waterline) should be at least twice the *draft* (amount of craft below the waterline). Staffing and weather conditions also are factors to consider. Skill level of participants will determine if they can solo, go in pairs, or need instructors on board. It will also determine the type of craft they use—sailfish or sunfish are good for beginner sailors, and kayaks are appropriate for individuals with previous canoeing experience. Some programs may find a progressive method, training participants in rowboating followed by canoeing and sailing, is amenable to the site, number of craft, and staff qualifications as well as to skill level and numbers of people involved.

Establish and post definite guidelines and rules for small craft use. Hours of small craft waterfront operation should be during daylight, defined as one-half hour after sunrise and one-half hour before sunset. Small craft do not belong on the water after dark. Any craft designated for after-dark use *must* have running lights and signal devices. Reserve this for rescue craft only, and restrict use to individuals well trained in after-dark rescues. Also, small craft do not belong on the water under adverse weather conditions (e.g., brisk winds; electrical storms; fog; or in dangerous water conditions, such as high waves, rip tides, or strong currents). Even experienced boaters can have serious problems under these conditions. Should foul weather catch boaters by surprise, they should be trained to seek the closest safe harbor, notify the program facility of their location, and wait for pickup or clear weather.

There is great potential for inappropriate use of small craft. Establish specific regulations clearly stating that reckless behavior, use of small craft during unsupervised periods, or use while under the influence of alcohol or mind-altering substances will result in prohibition of use and possible dismissal from the program. Wanton abuse of small craft and equipment and reckless behavior while onboard should also result in prohibition of use.

Consider participant age and water readiness before assigning small craft. Young children and individuals with special needs might be better served with a flat-bottomed rowboat, which can safely hold three or four participants and an instructor. This is especially true if swimming skills are minimal. As comfort in the water and familiarity with small craft improve, it is possible to advance these participants to more complicated, less stable small craft, such as canoes, kayaks, and sailboards or sailboats. Individuals with special needs should *not* be restricted in their use of craft based on disability alone. Rather, encourage them to develop water-adjustment skills and alternative methods for using all types of small craft.

Secure all small craft during nonuse hours, and close off the small craft area itself. This may be no more than covering check-in and check-out boards and roping off the area. Overturn and chain down canoes, kayaks, small sailboats, and sailboards, and moor larger sailboats, rowboats, powerboats, and rescue craft. Remove motors from powerboats, if possible, and store them to prevent unauthorized use. In facilities that serve a nonresident clientele, establish a means of locking access to the small craft area. This may mean a chain-link fence and locked gate.

Develop a method of accounting for craft, equipment, and participants, both on the water and in the program area, during use times. Schedule a gatekeeper to assign craft and equipment use and identify who the users are. Many camps use a board with an identifying name or number tag placed on a diagram of the craft being used. Individuals check out with the gatekeeper when they are going onto the water and check in when they return. You can also account for equipment in this manner.

Tripping

One exciting activity for which you can use small craft is tripping. Whether the trip is a day sail down the coast or a 10-day wilderness canoe trip, certain basic safety concepts apply. Every trip must have a float plan. This plan identifies where the trip is going, potential campsites, put-in and pull-out sites, emergency resources, water and provisioning sites, who is going on the trip with names of all participants and staff, and check-in points. Experienced staff should check all waterways in advance. Note any private lands or docks, and obtain permission before the trip if there is a potential need for use. Test water sources for potability. This is done routinely in public use areas, and you can check with local government sources. Note hazardous areas and establish alternative passage, whether roping, walking down, or portaging around, before arrival. Set up contingency plans in case of an injury or illness, adverse weather conditions, or unforeseen emergencies or problems. Establish periodic check-in times with the main program facility before departing, with the understanding that failure to report within several hours of this time will result in an emergency response. To facilitate these check-ins, write the phone numbers in waterproof ink, laminate them, and place them securely in the first aid kit or other key piece of equipment. Take along two sets of these numbers and place them in different craft.

Although specifics of tripping are beyond the scope of this chapter and many resources are available that describe this activity, we do need to address a few points. In addition to the float plan, there are several other im-portant considerations. The type of small craft must be appropriate for the trip you are anticipating. Sunfish are not appropriate for day sailing down the coast of a large lake or the ocean, and wooden canoes will not tol-erate the challenges of white-water canoeing. Bring spare paddles, PFDs, line, and key equipment. Canoes, kayaks, and larger sail-boats should have a heaving line or type IV PFD for rescue purposes. All participants should have, at a minimum, a hat, sunblock,

© CLEO Photography

Whether the trip is a day sail down the coast or a 10-day wilderness canoe trip, every trip must have a float plan.

long-sleeved shirt, swimsuit, sunglasses, whistle or signaling device attached to themselves at all times, and swim socks or shoes they can get wet. Participants must wear PFDs whenever they are on the water.

SUPERVISION

Supervision implies a unilateral responsibility, but in reality, small craft use demands efforts by all staff and participants to operate safely. A risk-management philosophy that places responsibility for proper behavior on each individual will yield a stronger, safer program.

The first step in effective supervision begins with communicating what you expect of everyone who participates in the small craft program (i.e., the rules and regulations by which everyone must abide). By providing this information along with an explanation, participants can decide whether this program is appropriate for their needs. Encourage those who do not feel they can abide by the established rules to seek their small craft experiences elsewhere. See a comprehensive list of important points to address when forming rules in table 9.1, pp. 138-139.

The staff is ultimately responsible for communicating the rules to all participants *before* their small craft experience begins. Because of the diversity of ages, backgrounds, and language of individuals who may wish to participate, use a variety of communication techniques. Posted written rules may need to be multilingual. Picture signs are easy to understand as long as you keep them straightforward and simple. Post them at a level all participants can easily see—a small child will have difficulty seeing a sign posted at an adult level. Review shapes of marine warning signs and their meanings (e.g., no wake zones, swimming areas, scuba diver, hazards, channels, navigation buoys, etc.) before participants go out in their craft. In addition, review emergency procedures and signals and be sure participants understand them. You may need some additional rules if there are hazards in the area. Failure to address the seriousness of these hazards would be considered negligence on the part of program leaders and supervisory personnel.

It will not be unusual for participants to question staff about rules, and staff should be prepared to answer appropriately. In addition, they must be committed to enforcing all rules at all times even if participants are rude or unpleasant. Usually, if the staff present rules in a positive, pleasant manner with reasonable explanations, most participants are willing to cooperate and will benefit from a safe environment in which inappropriate behavior and accident risks are minimal.

Address a breach of any rule immediately, but politely, with a warning to refrain from further inappropriate behavior. The Q-1-2 technique taught in the YMCA Lifeguarding program is a quick, simple, nonthreatening, and easily enforced method of encouraging appropriate conduct. Emphasis is placed on acccident prevention, and the process works well with both children and adults. "Q" refers to the question which is raised when the potential for a dangerous action or rules violation presents itself. For example, an individual who is seen filling up a bucket with water and sneaking up on someone else might be asked, "Were you planning on pouring that over someone's head?" Often the question itself is sufficient for making the point and altering the inappropriate behavior. "1" is a verbal warning and explanation of why the observed behavior is inappropriate. "2" is a time-out. If inappropriate or dangerous behavior persists in spite of the first two steps, participants need to be removed from activity and given time to reevaluate their behavior (YMCA 1994). Individuals who persist in breaking rules may need to be completly removed from the setting until they can learn to correct and control their behavior. There can be no compromising of safety at any time! It is far better to employ stringent rule enforcement than to risk injury. All staff is responsible for enforcing the rules and regulations at all times.

Supervisory personnel should meet basic, minimal requirements. Organizations such as the American Camping Association, Girl Scouts of the USA, Boy Scouts of America, as well as state regulations, may have minimal requirements for facilities under their supervision. In addition, keep in mind the following recommendations:

• The individual ultimately responsible should be at least 21 years old and certified by a nationally recognized agency (American Red Cross, YMCA, AAHPERD, Ellis and Associates, Boy Scouts of America, U.S. Lifeguarding Association, American Heart Association, or an equivalent) as determined by state code in lifeguarding, some area of small craft instructing (sailing, canoeing, kayaking, powerboating), first aid, and cardiopulmonary resuscitation (CPR).

• Assistants should be at least 18 years old and certified as a lifeguard. Small craft instructing certification, especially in their area of responsibility, is preferred, but training and experience through a recognized program (American Red Cross, American Canoeing Association, Power Squadron, U.S. Sailing Association, U.S. Yacht Racing Union, AAHPERD) will suffice. They should also have training in first aid and CPR.

• Tripping staff should have experience and advanced training in the activity they are supervising. At least one person should be 21 years old, and all staff should meet CPR, first aid, and lifeguarding requirements.

• Aides should be at least 16 years old (where allowed by law) and have good swimming ability and familiarity with small craft, first aid, CPR, and basic nonswimming rescue skills.

Often, programs can develop some staff from in-house participants, supplementing with new staff from outside the program.

Staff-to-participant ratios vary according to age, ability, and activity. In this setting, staff refers to persons at least 18 years old with the responsibility, authority, and training to work with individuals involved in a small craft program. It does *not* include aides, staff in training, untrained (in small craft) program staff, or auxiliary staff who assist individuals with special needs. Sailing guidelines recommend 10 to 12 students for every instructor, with an additional instructor or assistant for every 10 participants in addition to that. This ratio would hold true

for surveillance staff also. Therefore, a sailing class with 16 participants should have two instructors *and* two surveillance staff. Other small craft such as rowboats, canoes, and kayaks do not usually spread as widely apart as sailboats. Table 10.4 gives recommended staff-to-participant ratios for these other craft.

Surveillance

Supervision relates to communicating information necessary for a safe small craft program. Surveillance, an integral part of supervision, refers to the overall, continuous observation of all participants once they become actively involved in small craft activities. The most important responsibility staff has is surveillance. This involves continuously scanning the area. Every staff member must be constantly vigilant. They look for potential problems, hazards, and inappropriate usage. There should be a minimum of two staff assigned solely to overall surveillance of the area and craft. This may require an observation point or tower, depending on the size of the area and the number of craft being used at any time. Large areas with a variety of craft in use should also have surveillance staff patrolling the water. All staff doing surveillance should be credentialed by a nationally recognized credentialing agency as having skills and training appropriate for the type of craft, waterway, activities, potential emergency situations, and participants in the program. Basic level credentials and skills required for this responsibility include the following:

• Professional rescuer level CPR with training for all age groups.

• Standard level first aid training; however, at least one first responder trained individual is advisable.

• Lifeguarding.

• Advanced training and ongoing practice in small craft rescues for every type of craft being used.

• Specific training for the type of waterfront area being used (surf, white water, current, rip tides, etc.).

Table 10.4
STAFF-TO-PARTICIPANT RATIOS FOR SMALL CRAFT ACTIVITIES (EXCLUSIVE OF LIFEGUARDS)

Participant age	Staff-to-participant ratio	Assistants and lifeguards onboard
4-5 years	1:5	Yes
6-8 years	1:6	Depends on swimming ability
9-14 years	1:8	Only if poor swimmers
15-18 years	1:10	Only if poor swimmers
19 and over	1:20	Only if poor swimmers
Special needs	Depends on age and type or extent of disability; may even be 1:1	Depends on age, swim ability, type of disability

If you are conducting more than one type of activity at a time, each activity must have its own surveillance staff. Beginner activities, those with young children, individuals with special needs or significant medical problems often need many more staff. This could possibly mean a one-on-one ratio.

No staff member should serve in more than one capacity at any time. Attempting to serve as both the instructor and the surveillance person at the same time is hazardous and unacceptable. In many areas it is even illegal. The designated lifeboat or rescue boat should have its own specific staff with a minimum of a driver and an observation person. If appropriately trained and certified staff are not available to provide adequate coverage, do not hold the activity. Surveillance staff involved with observing and scanning from a land-based observation area only need not be trained in the same manner as those manning safety or rescue boats. They should have some training in the previously mentioned areas, but do not need to be certified. They *must* have direct communication (two-way radio, telephone, signaling device) with staff in safety boats.

Surveillance staff have responsibilities both on and off the water, including the following:

- Educating staff and participants to minimize hazards and risks

- Ensuring that PFDs are worn appropriately at all times

- Providing at least one surveillance staff for every activity

- Establishing and enforcing a system of accounting for all staff and participants involved in an activity, including an ongoing participant count during the activity

- Instituting a "clear the water" recall system (flags, whistles, horns, two-way radios in safety boats) and ensuring *everyone* responds to it immediately

- Establishing a distress signal for participants (waving a paddle in a circular motion for canoers, waving arms up and down at the sides for sailors)

- Ensuring all participants and staff are appropriately attired for the weather and the activity
- Enforcing safety rules, proper behavior, and hours of operation
- Prohibiting throwing any debris or objects overboard other than rescue equipment
- Keeping interpersonal communication succinct
- Avoiding obstruction of the viewing area of responsibility *even for a second*
- Saving all social interactions for when off duty

To ensure surveillance personnel are able to maintain peak performance, institute a shift rotation schedule. No one should be in any area of responsibility for more than one hour—less under adverse weather and temperature conditions.

Small Craft Emergency Action Plan

Both chapters 3 and 9 clearly describe and define the emergency action plan (EAP). Specifically design an EAP for the small craft area, including open-water and tripping plans. All staff members must know their role when the EAP is initiated. We strongly recommend repeated practice using the EAP. At a minimum, staff and participants should be involved with monthly practice sessions. Clearly post the EAP in every building, by every telephone and two-way radio, and at every check-in and check-out site in the small craft area. Also include it in first aid kits. During an emergency, call all boaters off the water, but rescue efforts should proceed with staff involved. The rest of the staff can join in only *after* their participants are off the water and safe. At least two of the rescue staff should be trained in using scuba equipment and open-water diving.

Surveillance staff closest to the emergency should render assistance immediately, and if an individual has disappeared from sight, mark the point where last seen with a dye marker, boat, or anchored float as best as possible. In the event of a possible missing participant, account for all individuals and staff, *both on land and on the water*, using a check-in list or board. If a person is still missing, immediately obtain additional assistance from local search-and-rescue teams. Practice sessions should include underwater search around docks and mooring areas, as these are sites of potential slips, falls, and head and neck injuries. Assign one staff member to record all attempts at rescue—even during drills. Once the rescue attempt or drill has been terminated, all primary staff members involved should document the event. This documentation should occur for all emergency and first aid events, no matter how minor. In the event a real emergency occurs, debriefing for staff and participants by trained crisis intervention staff is essential.

SELECTION AND CONDUCT OF THE ACTIVITY

Appropriate selection of participants in a small craft program is necessary for safety and reduction of liability. Although many people use small craft without any training or swimming ability, this is *not* a situation with which responsible small craft program directors wish to be involved.

Selecting Participants

Most agencies sponsoring small craft instruction programs have swimming prerequisites for entry into their courses. These should be checked and met before participants begin an instructional program. Test all participants in the aquatic environment in which they will be boating, because passing a swim skill test in open water is often far more difficult than in a pool. Relegate nonswimmers to rowboats and stable craft in the company of a lifeguard. Some recommended swim tests for various craft are as follows.

For canoeing or kayaking, the participant should be able to do the following:

1. Jump into deep water (six feet or greater) while fully clothed and swim, tread water, float, bob, or otherwise stay afloat unaided for five minutes.

2. Properly put on a PFD that is thrown to him or her while in deep water, and swim at least 10 yards.

3. Preferably, the participant should have a certificate of successfully completing a beginner swim course from a nationally recognized program (American Red Cross, YMCA, Ellis and Associates, Swim America) in addition to completing the first two steps.

Sailing prerequisites include the following:

1. Completing a 25-yard unassisted swim.

2. Entering deep water (over the head) and staying afloat unassisted with face out of the water for five minutes while wearing normal sailing clothes (treading, survival float, back float, or combination).

3. Putting on PFD while in deep water and floating or swimming unassisted for three minutes.

Determine these skills before any further involvement in the small craft program or facility.

In addition to aquatic ability, there are other considerations for participation in a small craft program. Very young children and some special needs individuals may require assistance handling and propelling small craft. All participants should take a remedial skill test for the specific type of craft they will use to determine familiarity and ability; a knowledge test, written or oral depending on age, to determine awareness of facility rules; small craft safety and legal requirements; and a tip test (capsizing) to ensure participants are able to perform self-rescue techniques. A check of previously earned certifications or credentials to ascertain prior training is also necessary. If participants are using the facility but bringing their own equipment, check the equipment for proper function and repair status. Programs allowing participants to use small craft without participating in an instructional program may wish to require payment of a bond or deposit. Adults or parents and guardians should fill out a signed statement that they agree to abide by the established rules and regulations and acknowledge the authority of staff to terminate activities or remove participants from the water.

Instructional Program

An instructional program is key to developing a safe, ongoing small craft program. Participants who learn small craft skills and safety are less likely to have accidents and injuries. An instructional program should include the following:

- Use of an established, nationally recognized curriculum to avoid leaving out essential information.

- Class size appropriate for the number of craft, size of craft, size of area, and number of instructors to allow participants maximum opportunity for skills practice. Most recognized instructional programs have well-established recommendations for class size and instructor-to-student ratios.

- Participation that includes the opportunity to have hands-on experience and practice with all equipment and skills.

- Supervised practice time.

- Equipment appropriate for the age, size, and ability of the student, including adaptations for persons with special needs.

- Associated printed materials for additional information and study.

- Advancement to higher level activities based on successfully completing the instructional program or prerequisite screening skills test.

- Parental permission specific to the type of craft being used before a minor can participate. They should be informed of potential risks involved in participation.

ADMINISTRATION

Ultimately, all responsibility for what occurs in the small craft area lies with the owner or operator, with the designated director being charged with carrying out a safe program. Individual participants are responsible for their own behavior, but accountability for educating and guiding these individuals, as well as enforcing safety rules and regulations, lies with the administrative personnel. Staff are charged with enforcing a safe small craft program.

Operations

To conduct a safe small craft program, administrators must ensure that staff and facilities are ready to meet the challenges imposed by a diverse group of individuals, many of whom may be ignorant of and unskilled in small craft safety. A program is not ready for implementation and should not be opened if any of the following exist:

- An insufficient number of trained staff.

- The waterfront area is polluted or has overgrowth of aquatic plants (algae, weeds) that could hinder rescue attempts.

- A hazard in participation areas cannot be removed or marked.

- Severe weather or water conditions (severe weather warning, electrical storm, dangerous currents or tides, high winds or waves, fog).

- An inadequate number of properly certified individuals for surveillance.

- Safety and rescue equipment are not in good repair and available for use.

- The EAP has been implemented and a rescue procedure is underway.

- A critical event has occurred (near drowning, death) requiring crisis intervention and debriefing.

- An investigation of a critical event is currently underway.

Once these situations have been rectified, the program is ready to be initiated or resumed.

Record Keeping

Keep certain records to meet liability requirements, for insurance purposes, and to determine use. Written documentation is necessary for implementing insurance claims, analyzing safety implementation, achieving accreditation, documenting instructional and program completion, and litigation purposes. Record a current listing of staff credentials and certifications with expiration dates along with a copy of the EAP for each

A well-designed small craft program enables participants to enjoy the pleasure and excitement of boating in a safe and friendly environment.

area. Also, annually record the registration and serial numbers of all craft, motors, and trailers (this is necessary for obtaining state licenses for craft, aids in identifying stolen or missing craft, and facilitates recouping losses from insurance companies). Monthly, record all staff training and in-services, and document all participants in instructional programs and certificates issued. Record, daily, all first aid and emergency or rescue activities, no matter how minor, in case of investigation or future litigation; craft usage; disciplinary action; and small craft area closures with reasons for closing and actions taken before reopening. Annually record opening and closing inventories, documenting repairs and equipment replacement or disposal.

CONCLUSION

Conducting an organized, safe small craft program takes a great deal of preparation and training. A haphazard approach can only spell disaster. Although much of this information may, at first, appear overwhelming, properly instituted, the small craft program is well on its way to being safe and well run. Achieving this end will produce well-trained individuals who can learn to enjoy the pleasures of small craft usage in a safe and friendly environment.

BIBLIOGRAPHY

American Camping Association. 1993. *Camp boating: Program and curriculum guidelines.* Martinsville, IN: American Camping Association.

American Red Cross. 1964. *Basic outboard boating.* Washington, DC: American Red Cross.

———. 1981. *Canoeing and kayaking.* Washington, DC: American Red Cross.

———. 1995. *Community water safety.* Washington, DC: American Red Cross.

American Red Cross and United States Sailing Association. 1992. *Start sailing right!* St. Louis: Mosby Lifeline.

American Red Cross and United States Yacht Racing Union. 1991. *Basic sailing instructor's manual.* Washington, DC: American Red Cross.

Arthur, M., and S. Ackroyd-Stolarz. *A resource manual on canoeing for disabled people.* Hyde Park, ON: Canadian Recreational Canoeing Association.

Dougherty, N.J., IV, ed. 1987. *Principles of safety in physical education and sport.* Reston, VA: American Alliance for Health, Physical Education, Recreation and Dance.

Hannah, G., ed. 1986. *Safety oriented guidelines for outdoor education leadership and programming.* Canadian Association for Health, Physical Education, and Recreation.

YMCA. 1994. *On the guard II.* Champaign, IL: Human Kinetics.

chapter 11

Whitewater Activities

Michael Kinziger

Compared with other outdoor adventure activities, whitewater river sports are relatively new. Today's boom began in the 1960s, when new designs, technology, and materials made possible the canoes, kayaks, and inflatable rafts we now use. This, in turn, opened up new rivers and attracted all skill levels for exploration and recreation. As with other adventure sports, there were accidents and fatalities. River runners and kayakers soon earned a reputation as daredevils and risk takers. There certainly was a great deal of danger in those early days. Accidents are usually the result of ignorance, and most river fatalities each year involve unknowledgeable boaters. River runners and organizations that run river trips need to examine these accidents and reaffirm their commitment to safety in the sport.

The statistics from groups such as the ACA (American Canoe Association) and from agencies such as the U.S. Coast Guard have profiled accidents to determine the common ingredients in river fatalities. Five recurring problems have surfaced:

1. River runners are not wearing personal flotation devices. Life jackets are not worn, forgotten, or not capable of saving a person due to improper design.

2. Cold water or cold weather is present. Many accidents occur in spring, a season of high water levels and cold water. River runners are usually not dressed properly for the numbing effects of cold water. Drownings are often caused by hypothermia, in which exposure to cold water or cold weather inhibit ability for rescue.

3. Victims are often inexperienced. Most fatalities involve inexperienced river runners who have had little or no formal instruction or practice.

4. Alcohol or drugs are contributing factors. Alcohol and drugs affect the coordination and

Though kayakers have a reputation of being daredevils, most kayaking accidents are the result of ignorance.

judgment of river runners, who need to respond quickly and intelligently to hazards.

5. The victims are often nonswimmers. The ability to swim well increases a person's comfort level on the water, which usually increases the ability to perform well in stressful conditions.

In addition, ACA's River Safety Task Force has examined accidents since 1976 and has arrived at several conclusions:

1. Misrepresentation of ability can lead to river runners attempting rapids or river sections too difficult for their skills. River runners are attempting difficult rapids early in their development, when they are less able to comprehend what can go wrong on a river trip and how to respond to a new emergency situation.

2. The nature of a familiar run or rapid has been altered by changing environmental factors. Fluctuating water levels from rain, runoff, or dam release can drastically affect the character of a river. Complacency with an often-run section of water and hazards such as recently down trees can create unanticipated dangers.

3. Equipment affects a river runner's ability to perform safely. The new high-tech, high-performance equipment can hinder ability to run rivers safely if participants do not practice enough to develop adequate comfort levels. Conversely, using inadequate equipment in more challenging water can make recovery from a capsize difficult or impossible.

4. An inadequate support party can limit the effectiveness of rescue operations in an accident. We do not recommend running rivers alone or in parties of less than three. River running in groups with experienced leaders and sweep craft can offer security and efficient rescues.

From the beginning, it is the responsibility of leaders and individuals to analyze their abilities honestly and resist the external pressure to negotiate a section of river, a particular rapid, or a particular drop. The best course of action is based on safety. Encourage leaders and participants to err on the side of safety throughout their river running careers. Newcomers are more inclined to listen to safety guidelines, but it is equally important for experienced boaters and leaders to remember safety considerations.

ENVIRONMENTAL CONDITIONS

What is the magic that draws people of all ages and abilities to the river? Rivers have always been objects of power and reverence, inspiring symbol and myth and, alternately, love and fear. River running introduces the drama of being somewhere that a person manifestly doesn't belong. Maneuvering down a river is balancing on that razor's edge where a person is neither out of control nor ever really in control. It is playing with forces so much greater than your own that you develop a feeling of fighting the river, and when you stop fighting there is a moment when you feel part of it. One thing you quickly learn is that there are some places, some rapids, where the river takes the river runner, and you develop a commitment to run all the way through a stretch, rightside up or upside down, in your craft or out of it. Like the river itself, the passenger must be loose and flow. Much of the attraction of river running comes from its basic improbability: it seems strange that you can go down wild-looking rapids. All the qualities of pure sport, including subtle and powerful movements, an array of techniques to master, thinking, reacting, and split-second timing are present. Aesthetics are the final ingredient! The rock- and tree-filled landscape that ever so slowly passes by is magnified with the sound of water, sometimes quiet and other times roaring.

Water is lazy in that it flows downhill continuously until an obstacle forces it in another direction. Water generally seeks the easiest descent—the steepest, clearest route within the riverbed. There are four factors to consider when assessing the difficulty in navigating or selecting a portion of river to run.

Assessing River Difficulty

To most potential boaters, whitewater rivers are a primal source of fascination due to the sight, sound, and power of the rushing current. However, to the veteran river runner, each river has predictable, orderly, and reliable effects on the surface, which allow the boater to anticipate how currents and rapids will affect their craft.

Gradient or Elevation Loss

This is normally expressed in vertical feet per mile from a river's source to its mouth or within given sections. Averages can be deceptive because steepness is characterized by two conditions—rapids and pools. A *rapid* is a steep incline with fast current that is generally shallow. A *pool* is less steep, slower, and has deeper water. The higher the gradient, the faster the river flows. The head of a rapid is often slower than the middle or lower section. As the fast current meets slower current or the pool, it is abruptly slowed and often forms waves.

Volume of Flow or Discharge

This is the volume of water moving past a given cross section of river per unit of time. Flow is measured in cubic feet per second (cfs). The most practical method to determine discharge is to measure the stage of a river and use a conversion table that relates stage to discharge. Stage is the height (in feet) of the water level, higher than an arbitrary zero point. The limits of navigability are represented by rivers that combine high volume of water with extreme elevation loss.

River Width

The riverbed itself partly determines the difficulty of the run. Narrow riverbeds may have tight turns and constrictions and are more likely to be blocked by fallen trees and rocks. A decrease in river width funnels water into a constriction that can cause turbulence (see figure 11.1a). Water moves slower near the river bottom due to friction with the riverbed, moves faster near the surface, and sometimes will have turbulence near river edges due to friction with the banks. Water moves faster and deeper near the outside of a bend with deep channels that are often undercut. Inside bends are usually shallow, rocky, and slow (see figure 11.1b).

River Hazards and Obstacles

Hazards and obstacles on the river are facts of life. The following survey of different hazards will assist you in assessing the difficulty of navigating or selecting a portion of river to run.

Low-Head Dams. Low-head dams (weirs) deserve special mention, because they have caused several drownings. They are usually constructed by humans and appear as a uniform horizontal line across the river. They form an hydraulic that is difficult to identify and difficult to get out of without help (see figure 11.2).

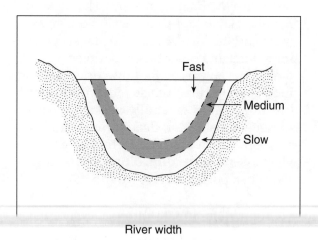

Figure 11.1a   River width affects river speed.

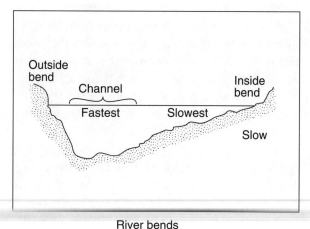

Figure 11.1b   With varying water speeds, river bends can be tricky to maneuver.

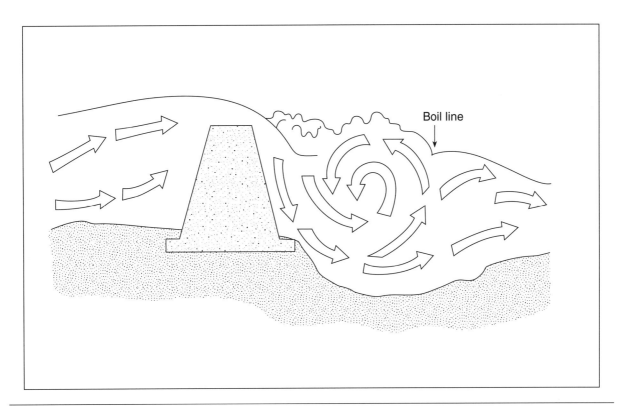

Figure 11.2 Low-head dam.

Hole or Hydraulic. A hole is similar in design and function to the reversal that forms below a low-head dam. It arises when water flows over a natural feature, like a rock or ledge, and falls swiftly: the surplus water is pulled back upstream creating a reversal current (see figure 11.3). The steepness of the drop, the width of the hole, and the distance from the drop to the bottom of the boil line (a point where the water rises and splits—some water reverses and some continues downriver) have bearing on the danger of the hole. You can run some holes easily, and experienced river runners often play them. Picking the wrong hole can be a major error because the hole can trap and hold objects in the turbulence.

Strainers. Strainers are downed trees or other obstacles that filter water over, under, and through, but may hold a larger object against the mass of logs and branches. A strong current will congest a person or river craft against this mesh, making rescue difficult. Strainers are especially hazardous on outside corners and during periods of high water or runoff.

Undercuts and Potholes. Undercuts are large rocks in the water that are narrower at the bottom than at the top. Potholes are smooth, eroded depressions in rocks. The danger of undercuts and potholes is that river craft can be pushed under or into them and become trapped by the force of the water.

Entrapment. One of the biggest dangers of a capsize in white water is entrapment, a term for getting any body extremity, usually a foot or leg, caught against the river bottom by the force of the water.

High and Low Water. Rivers change dramatically between high and low river levels. Low water usually means exposed rocks, obstacles, and shallow, impassable channels (see figure 11.4a). The primary goal in low water is to identify and maneuver through the deepest channels while avoiding becoming broached. There is also the possibility of abrasive damage to your river craft. High and continuous white water can be a hazard for river craft, as well as for a person who has fallen out of a boat or raft

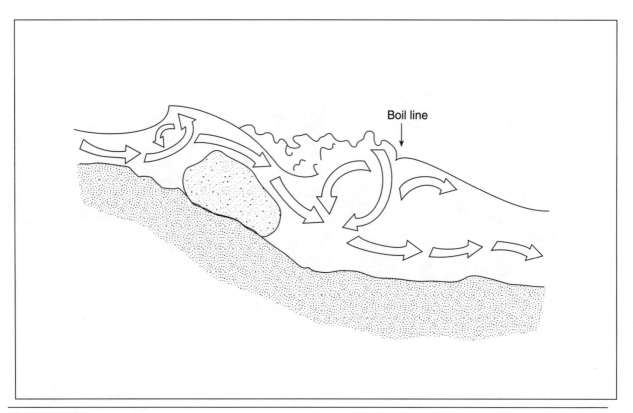

Boil line

Figure 11.3   Hole or hydraulic.

(see figure 11.4b). Breathing and rescue can be difficult.

Cold Water. Long, cold swims quickly bring on immersion hypothermia, a lowering of the body's core temperature.

The section titled River Terms on page 185 contains a list of terms necessary for effective communication in the whitewater environment.

Selecting River Craft

The type of craft you select to run whitewater river sections falls into one of three categories: (1) canoes, (2) kayaks, and (3) rafts. These craft have many similarities and differences. The river runner needs to consider many possibilities when making a craft decision. It is always best to rent or use a variety of equipment before making a final decision. Rafts are usually the easiest craft to start with and offer the opportunity of having an experienced leader in the raft for a river runner's initial experience. Rafts also afford more wild and challenging environments due to their greater stability in the water.

Canoes and kayaks require additional skill and practice before you can navigate more challenging river sections. When selecting a whitewater craft, consider the following elements: (1) size; (2) weight; (3) length; (4) design; (5) material; (6) occupancy (solo, tandem, four person, eight person, etc.); (7) flotation (open or closed); (8) skill level necessary to safely navigate; (9) transportation; (10) cost; and (11) others. Average river runners only own one or two whitewater craft in their lives. Therefore, making the best selection is difficult but important.

Classifying Rapids

The International Scale of River Difficulty classifies rapids on a scale from one to six, with class 1 being the easiest (see table 11.1). There are other rating systems, but this one is the most universal. Rating a rapid or a section of river is subjective. The class of rapid can change drastically with different water levels. River rapids will generally fall into one of the six listed classifications. However, if the water temperature is below 50 degrees Fahrenheit or you are on

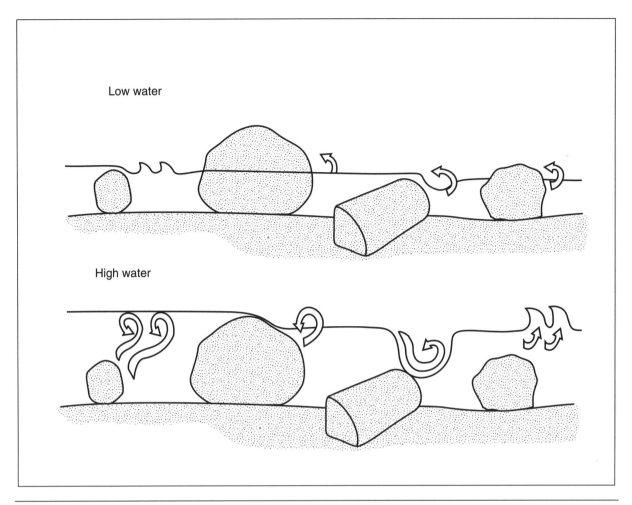

Low water

High water

Figure 11.4 a&b   Low water and high water

an extended trip in a wilderness or roadless area, consider the river one class more difficult.

SUPERVISION

An activity is only as good and safe as the practitioners who design, deliver, and debrief it. Qualifications for leaders or practitioners are arranged into two areas—hard and soft skills. Hard skills are easily trained and assessed and include (1) technical activity competence, (2) physical fitness and mental wellness, (3) first aid and CPR certification, (4) experience with safety and rescue, and (5) knowledge of environmental protection. Soft skills are related to working with people in the field and include (1) trip organization, (2) instructing the activity, (3) interpersonal communication, (4) problem-solving and decision-making ability, (5) sound judgment, (6) a code of ethics, and (7) personal qualities necessary to get along with people. Specific guidelines and responsibilities for staff leading river trips that involve canoes, kayaks, and rafts are provided in table 11.2.

Preventing Accidents

Good supervision can help prevent unnecessary accidents. Maintain constant supervision, especially on water. Listed here are specific suggestions that can improve the quality of supervision.

1. Leaders and organizations should be thoroughly familiar with the current standards in the whitewater activity and specific river sections they will run.

2. Establish and follow safety procedures.

Table 11.1
INTERNATIONAL SCALE OF RIVER DIFFICULTY

CLASS	RIVER AND RAPID DESCRIPTION	RIVER RUNNER OR PADDLER DESCRIPTION
I	*Easy:* small waves, riffles; correct course easy to find; minor obstacles.	*Beginner:* New paddler or someone unfamiliar with white water and strokes.
II	*Medium:* Continuous current, regular waves, and frequent rapids; course generally easy to recognize.	*Novice:* Familiar with elementary paddle strokes; has successfully paddled on class I water.
III	*Difficult:* High irregular waves, obstacles, and rapids require maneuvering; course not easily recognizable; swamps open canoes.	*Intermediate:* Has reasonable skill with all common maneuvers; has successfully paddled on class II water.
IV	*Very difficult:* Long and continuous rapids, powerful waves, boiling eddies, and holes that will keep a boat; scouting mandatory.	*Advanced:* Proficient in rescue from boat or shore; can roll in white water; has successfully paddled and led trips on class III water.
V	*Exceedingly difficult:* Long, violent rapids with difficult, irregular, unavoidable high waves and holes; extreme obstruction; rescue difficult.	*Expert:* Proven ability to negotiate any river in the area at reasonable water levels; has successfully paddled and led trips on class IV water.
VI	*Limit of navigability:* All difficulties increased to the limit; cannot be attempted without risk of life.	*Team of experts:* Must use every precaution available.

3. Prepare a written plan of each river experience. Include with this plan emergency procedures with emergency numbers in case of an accident.

4. Do not leave participants unsupervised, even when setting up the shuttle. This may require appointing a temporary leader.

5. Keep all participants and crafts in sight (of each other or by leaders). This requires each craft to be responsible for themselves and others.

6. Leaders need to anticipate hazards based on personal experience and river knowledge to promote the well-being of the participants.

7. Leaders should not be expected to super-vise or lead river sections beyond their ability or competency. Certain risks are a part of whitewater activity, but a leader should be involved only where the risks are reasonable.

8. Selecting the section of water to run is an important consideration. Determine participant age, skill, and size so you can gear the activity to the ability of the least skilled whenever possible.

9. Carefully examine the condition of equipment and facilities for hazards before and during river trips.

10. Leaders should never require a participant to perform an unreasonably dangerous task. They should also be aware of mismatched

Table 11.2
GUIDELINES AND RESPONSIBILITIES FOR WHITEWATER STAFF

GUIDELINE	EXPLANATION
Know the river.	☐ Be prepared to change plans to meet the existing conditions. We strongly recommend that leaders run rapids and river sections before leading groups on them.
Know who is new on the river.	☐ Be prepared to give instructions to the inexperienced on how to navigate the river.
	☐ Recommend that individuals *not* participate if it is beyond their ability. If in the leader's judgment an individual's ability or condition will jeopardize the group or individual's safety, the leader should recommend that individual not participate or portage around difficult river stretches.
Designate lead and sweep craft.	☐ The lead craft should know the river. The sweep craft should follow all other craft. Equip and train both for rescue.
Keep the river party compact.	☐ If the group is too big, divide it into independent teams with separate trip leaders, including lead and sweep craft.
Organize the shuttle.	☐ Determine how, where, and when the shuttle will run, and make plans for someone (or vehicles) to be at the take-out location for the return trip.
Teach and practice group- and self-rescue techniques.	☐ The leader should instruct participants how to rescue themselves. The leader must also explain organizational plans for group rescue if an emergency develops.
Know the current condition of weather, visibility, and water.	☐ The leader should inform the group of these conditions and make decisions based on related dangers.

partners or raft teams. Match partners by size, weight, and ability if possible.

11. Leaders should be well trained and certified in first aid and CPR.

12. We cannot overlook the importance of communication, because participants must be aware of the dangers in the activities. No person can assume the risk of dangers for which he or she is unaware and unable to appreciate.

Negligence is the basis of almost every charge against a leader in whitewater activity. Such a charge points to the failure of the leader or the leader's organization to do what was reasonable, prudent, or what normally would

have been done in a given situation. It is expected that leaders provide a standard of care based on the best practices and current techniques in the profession. River leaders may have to defend their actions by showing that they were reasonable and utilized good teaching methods. Certification is a benefit, because it shows that leaders have made an effort to become educated by obtaining knowledge and experience from experts. You can gain certification from organizations like the American Canoe Association, American Red Cross, and river rescue groups.

Staffing ratios are often the source of much disagreement, especially about defining a staff member (will an inexperienced parent suffice?) and how bound programs are by legislated ratios (particularly when school trips are involved). The ratios in table 11.3 for whitewater activity (*Safety Practices in Adventure Programming*, Priest and Dixon 1990) are merely suggestions. You should base the true ratio on the difficulty of the run, the experience of the participants, access to roads or emergency services, environmental conditions, and so on.

There should be no fewer than two staff for any activity, so in the event of an injury or illness to a participant or leader, the other staff member will be able to carry on with the activity or take necessary action.

River Rescue

Every river runner must be prepared to accept the consequences of an error in skill or judgment that leads to a swamped craft or a swim. If this happens, the participants and trip leaders must be able to rescue themselves and others. All paddlers must understand rescue priorities to avoid compounding the emergency situation. The first priority is the person in the water. All rescue is based on the participant's ability to self-rescue. The second priority is the swamped or pinned craft. Boats or rafts are rescued *only* after all participants are safe. The third priority is equipment. Equipment that has floated free of the craft will usually gather in eddies or along river bends.

Table 11.3

WHITEWATER STAFF-TO-PARTICIPANT RATIOS

ACTIVITY	STAFF	PARTICIPANTS
Canoeing	1	5
Kayaking	1	5
Rafting	1	8

Data from Priest, Simon, and Tim Dixon. 1990 *Safety practices in adventure programming.* Boulder, CO: Association for Experiential Education.

Rescues should be organized. River leaders should practice and keep updated with new techniques and equipment for effective river rescue. There are seven steps leaders need to be aware of at the moment of rescue:

1. Assess the predicament. What has happened? Where are the participants? How many are involved? Can the participants self-rescue? Can the situation get worse? Is time a factor?

2. Communicate the problem. Can you talk to the person or people that need to be rescued? Can you provide reassurance? Can you communicate with others in your river party or to passersby who may be able to help?

3. Determine the best possible means of rescue. Can you reach the person in trouble? Should you use a rope? Should you set up a rescue? Is it necessary to swim to the person? How many people will you need to set up and operate the rescue? Can you attempt more than one rescue at once?

Leaders have only a few seconds to decide all of the preceding.

4. Organize the rescue. Define tasks and delegate authority. Remember priorities! Stabilize rescued individuals. Prepare for first aid, CPR, and hypothermia treatment as necessary. If the situation warrants, send for help.

5. Consider alternative ways of rescue as the first rescue is proceeding.

6. Consider and organize a second attempt at a rescue if necessary.

7. Evaluate the rescue. This is a crucial and often-omitted step in rescue operations. What happened? What went right or wrong? How can the circumstances that led to the rescue be avoided or handled more effectively in the future? Complete a river rescue incident report form (see figure 11.5).

SELECTION AND CONDUCT OF THE ACTIVITY

Participation in whitewater activity carries with it many dangers. It is essential that participants possess rudimentary skills and follow criteria established relevant to the type

River Rescue Incident Report Form

Person completing report _____ Date_____ Time_____

Incident type: Rescue _____ Medical _____ Practice _____ Assist other group _____

Approximate air temp. _____ Approximate water temp. _____

Weather conditions _____
Incident location _____

_____

If applicable, reporting party's name _____

Address _____ City_____ State _____ Zip_____

Home phone (_____)_____ Work phone   (_____)_____

Time incident occured _____ Rescue initiated _____ Rescue secured _____

Personnel at scene:

     Names   Address   Time in   Time out

_____

_____

_____

_____

Incident leader   _____

Medic   _____

Primary rescuers _____

"Gofer" (recorder, personnel, equipment) _____

If applicable, complete below –

Name of victim _____ Age _____ Sex _____ DOB_____

Address _____ City_____ State _____ Zip_____

Employment _____ Phone (_____)_____

Activity participating in _____ Activity time lost _____

Is this a reinjury of an old condition? _____

Were there other contributing factors? If yes, what? _____

_____

(continued)

Figure 11.5   River rescue incident report form.

Did equipment contribute in any way to the accident? How? _____

_____

Has the injured party signed a release and is it available? _____

Has the injured party participated in this activity at this location before? _____

Is the injured party formerly or presently an employee? _____

Did the injured party contribute to the accident in any way? _____

Did the injured party state that he/she contributed to the accident in any way? _____

Did the injured party refuse first aid or evacuation? _____

Did another participant contribute to the injury? How? _____

_____

Were other peole injured in this accident? How? _____

_____

Medical type (Use as many as needed):   ___ Chest   ___ Spine   ___ Abdomen

___ Extremities   ___ Airway ___ Chest pain   ___ Blood sugar   ___ CVA   ___ Drowning

___ Drugs/Alcohol   ___ Shock   ___ Burns   ___ Smoke inhal. ___ Seizure ___ Resuscitation

___ DOA   ___ Head, ears, nose, throat ___ Unknown

Airway: ___ Clear   ___ Compromised   ___ Obstructed

Lung sounds: ___ Clear   ___ Wheezes   ___ "Wet"   ___ None

Pulses: ___ Full   ___ Thready   ___ Irregular   ___ None

Skin color: ___ Normal   ___ Flushed   ___ Pale   ___ Cyanotic (blue)

Skin condition: ___ Normal   ___ Cool, clammy   ___ Cool, dry   ___ Hot, moist ___ Hot, dry

Pupils: ___ Equal, reactive to light   ___ Unequal   ___ Sluggish   ___ Non-reactive

Vitals	Time	Blood pressure	Pulse	Respirations	Consciousness

Time of onset _____   Call rec'd _____   Enroute _____   At scene _____   From scene _____

Victim turned over to ambulance _____   Victim at hospital _____

Chief complaint

Treatment prior to arrival _____

_____

Figure 11.5   (continued)

Brief medical history, medicines, allergies, last time saw doctor, problems with heart, lungs, diabetes, epilepsy, asthma, emphysema, bronchitis: _____

_____

_____

Narrative — if medical include treatment, equipment used, physical survey. If rescue, include times, personnel, equipment, map if necessary. Photos?

_____

_____

_____

_____

Attach supplemental narrative if necessary.

Signature   Time   Date   Place

_____

Figure 11.5 *(continued)*

of boating (canoe, kayak, or raft) they will be doing and the type of environment (difficulty of river, water levels, water temperature, weather, etc.) they will experience to ensure safe and positive river trips. Guidelines for all river runners are provided in table 11.4.

While on the river, each participant should know group plans, hazards, which craft are designated as the lead and sweep, and the signals the group will be using. Each craft is also responsible for the craft behind it, so it is important to keep the parties compact and in close proximity. Although you can expect participants to assume a reasonable degree of responsibility for participation in whitewater activity, reasonable responsibility is a function of age, skill, knowledge, and maturity. Specific participant concerns differ greatly between rafting and canoeing or kayaking. These concerns include equipment, instruction, environment, and ethics.

Personal Equipment

All whitewater participants should be aware of personal equipment items they need to consider when running a river. You can use this list as a guideline. There will be much variance depending on water and weather conditions, time of year, experience, river difficulty, and so on.

- Clothing—synthetic wicking material next to the skin with breathable, warm, synthetic material for a second layer. You may wear a protective outer layer of nylon or laminated materials.

- Footwear—neoprene booties are best, but tennis shoes with wool or neoprene socks are an acceptable combination.

- Wet suits—provide protection from cold water and loss of body heat due to immersion or exposure to the elements.

- Dry suits—best protection of all (but most expensive) from water, wind, and wetness. They also help when floating.

- PFDs—Coast Guard-approved type I, II or III. It must provide a minimum of 15 1/2 pounds of flotation.

- Helmets—light, ventilated helmets with foam padding or suspension systems are preferred.

- Hats or hoods—either neoprene or some other type of pile cap that insulates when wet is indispensable in cold conditions.

- Gloves—a combination of neoprene and leather gloves provides the best blend of thermal protection and dexterity; leather will work.

- Knife—you can use a good, straight-blade knife for rescue.

- Whistle—a good whistle is necessary for communication and should work even when wet. It should be loud and attached to the PFD.

River Communication

The key to handling emergency situations is good, reliable communication. Leaders will find communicating at the scene of a river emergency difficult due to the inherent noise of the river. Therefore, the most basic method for communicating is using hand (or paddle) signals. You can use whistle signals to augment hand signals. The universal hand signals for whitewater rafting are on pages 182-184.

Table 11.4
GUIDELINES FOR ALL RIVER RUNNERS

GUIDELINE	EXPLANATION
Never boat alone.	The preferred minimum for canoeing, kayaking, and rafting is 3 craft (at minimum, experienced personnel should paddle 2 craft).
Always wear a personal flotation device (PFD).	PFDs should fit snugly and be type I, II, or III (U.S. Coast Guard Standards). These flotation aids are comfortable enough to wear for an extended time and are designed to provide a stable, faceup position for a wearer floating with the head tilted back. Type I PFDs are preferred.
Wear an approved helmet in class 3 water if kayaking or canoeing.	It could mean the difference between a bump or bruise and a broken skull.
Have a realistic knowledge of your boating ability.	Do not attempt rivers 2 or more class levels higher than what you have mastered.
Know and respect the river.	Some member of your party must know the river section you are paddling and understand the water classification.
Be practiced in rescue and self-rescue procedures.	At a minimum, a participant must know what to do in case of a capsize: A member of the river party must be competent with individual and river craft rescues.
Be aware of cold water and weather extremes.	Wear or have present proper clothing and equipment to combat weather and water extremes.
Learn to swim.	A person who can swim is more confident in moving water. If a participant cannot swim, the trip leader should be informed and make sure other boaters keep an eye out for that person.
Support and inform your leader.	Respect the leader's authority.

Figure 11.6a shows the signal for "emergency," "distress," or "need assistance." It is performed by extending the hand or paddle above the head and moving it steadily back and forth. You can also use three repeated blasts from a whistle to signal an emergency. Figure 11.6b is the signal for "stop." Extend the paddle horizontal to the body and perform a pumping or flying motion, or hold the paddle horizontally in front of body. The signal for "OK" or "all clear" is shown in figure 11.6c. Place the hands together to form an *O*, or place one hand on top of the head. Figures 11.6d and e show the signal for "move," "swim," or "move boat to the right or to the left." Extend two hands or a paddle above the head, then point left or right, depending on which direction the rafter wants to turn.

Canoeing and Kayaking Participant Concerns

Participants must be equipped with proper gear and should be in a craft they can safely maneuver down a stretch of river. Painters (ropes attached to canoe ends) and grab loops (cord loops attached to kayak ends) must be present on craft to aid rescue. In addition, kayaks and canoes must have flotation devices securely installed to displace as much water as possible in case of a capsize. Saddles, knee pads, and thigh straps can also be useful. It is imperative not to exceed weight capacity or recommended number of persons per craft.

Before paddling on white water, teach participants basic and advanced paddle strokes, allowing them to effectively maneuver and provide momentum to the craft. Dry land practice should precede water experience. Class II water (or more difficult) requires that participants can perform the following:

1. Eddy turns
2. Peel outs
3. Ferry maneuvers
4. Floating downriver if capsized
5. River safety signals
6. Wet exit (kayak)
7. Brace strokes (kayak)
8. Scouting techniques
9. Self-rescue techniques
10. Group-rescue techniques

Rafting Participant Concerns

Whitewater guidelines for canoes and kayaks generally apply to rafting. In addition, equip rafts with foot pumps in the event of deflation due to puncture, slow leak, or cold water. These inflatable craft should have multiple air chambers and should be test-inflated before starting a trip. Rafts should have taut perimeter guidelines threaded through the loops provided. The lead and sweep rafts should have throw bags and rescue material. Securely tie down equipment. Bring a repair kit capable of patching punctures. If rafts are not self-bailing, include containers to empty water.

Due to the potential to flip and overturn a raft, inform participants of their role in the event of a capsize or swim. Experienced rafters should be present in each raft. Teach team paddling and commands and practice them in quiet water before the dangerous rapids. Tell participants what to do if they are thrown into the water (i.e., float with head up to look downstream, place feet downstream to push off obstacles, remain upstream of the craft, do not attempt to stand up, and use hands and feet to maneuver yourself toward shore or an eddy). (These guidelines also apply when a swim happens while canoeing or kayaking.) Raft participants should know how to pull a swimmer back into a raft and how to be pulled back in themselves. The preferred method is to grab the swimmer by the shoulder sections of the PFD and firmly and quickly pull the person into the raft. Wear PFDs snugly at all times (so they will not come off when being rescued or during a swim), and have wet suits and helmets available if conditions warrant their use.

Paddle Strokes

Many similarities exist between the paddle strokes used for canoes, kayaks, and rafts. There are three types of strokes, which are based on the same principles of motion. *Power* strokes provide primarily forward or reverse momentum. *Turning* or *corrective* strokes turn the river craft so you can maneuver it from a

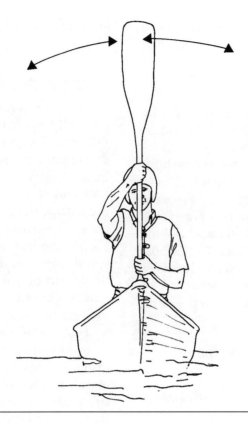

Figure 11.6a   Emergency.

Figure 11.6b   Stop.

Figure 11.6c   OK or all clear.

Figure 11.6d   Move left.

Figure 11.6e   Move right.

straight course or return it to straight course. *Braces* stabilize the craft and help with maneuvering.

The different strokes are often combined in a sequence to provide smooth, consistent movement of the craft. Although beginners usually practice strokes in a pure form, experienced paddlers use variations or combinations to achieve the desired effect. Strokes can be static or dynamic. A static stroke is a fixed position stroke requiring the craft to be moving faster than the current. A dynamic stroke is one in which you move the paddle blade against the current. There are two phases of each stroke. *Propulsion* is applying force on the paddle against the water that results in movement. *Recovery* is returning the blade to the starting position. Paddlers should strive to smoothly blend the phases of the stroke.

Although there are three basic strokes, there are many specific strokes in each category. The characteristics of the individuals, the class of water they are running, and the kind of craft they are using affect the type and number of strokes that river runners need to know to navigate safely down a river. Understanding how to execute efficient strokes should begin on dry land, move to slow water, then be used in whitewater activity.

ADMINISTRATION

Preventing accidents or injuries is essential in whitewater activity. From the beginning, river runners, leaders, and organizations should analyze their abilities and resist the pressure to make the river trip too challenging. Proper judgment is an issue we all need to address. River runners should accept a personal assumption of risk. They need to assume responsibility for their actions and their decision to participate in whitewater activity.

River runners should receive an orientation to basic safety practices. Appropriate clothing, equipment, group organization, and river running practices are a necessary part of the orientation. An orientation to self-rescue procedures is also necessary. Teach self-rescue techniques, and practice them before on-water experience, using a progression of activity and skills. Leaders should provide an adequate skill and competency base to meet the demands for all participants in a group so river runners receive a challenge that is not more than their ability. The class of water, weather, and temperature are important considerations for a safe and challenging river experience. These variables can change from trip to trip, requiring that leaders provide contingency plans for rescues and emergencies. All river groups should know rescue procedures and techniques.

Most of the contents of this chapter are intended as guidelines, *not* as hard and fast rules that you must always obey. You may need to break some rules, especially when going by the book might result in injury. In those situations, participants, leaders, and organizations must follow their best judgment and be prepared to defend the decisions they make based on that judgment.

RIVER TERMS

This is a list of whitewater rafting terms. You will need to know these terms before performing any whitewater activities.

Broaching—A craft that is pinned sideways to the current and usually out of the control of the paddlers.

Channel, chute or V—A supposedly navigable route through an obstruction.

Eddy—The water behind an obstruction in the current. Water may flow upstream.

Eddy line—The sharp boundary at the edge of an eddy, between two currents of different velocities or directions.

Ferry—Crossing the river in your craft from bank to bank with little downstream motion; mov-

In general, whitewater guidelines for canoeing and kayaking also apply to whitewater rafting.

© Cheyenne Rouse

ing sideways across the river facing upstream or downstream.

Flotation—A material used to keep a swamped boat afloat; can be Styrofoam, flotation bags, inner tubes, or any buoyant material.

Flow through obstruction—Obstruction in a river that water flows through, but not necessarily craft or participants.

Gradient—Number of feet per mile a river drops.

Hydraulic, hole, or keeper—General term for holes and back rollers, where there is a void in the river that water quickly fills.

Lead craft—First craft on a trip, consisting of knowledgeable paddlers with river knowledge and rescue experience.

Painter—A line attached to the bow or stern of a canoe. It is handy for tying a boat to the shore, and you can use it to facilitate rescuing an overturned craft.

Peel out—To leave an eddy, enter or leave the river.

Portage—To carry a river craft and its supplies around a river obstruction or overland between two waterways.

Rapid—A section of river characterized by steepening terrain, increased water speed, obstructions, and turbulence.

River left—Left side of the river when facing downstream.

River right—Right side of the river when facing downstream.

Scout—To look at a rapid from the shore to decide whether to run it, or to select a suitable route through the rapid.

Standing wave—Large, uniform waves at the base of a chute or other fast-flowing water as it enters still water.

Surfing—The technique of sitting on the upstream face of a wave or traveling back and forth across the wave when ferrying.

Sweep craft—The last craft down a stretch of river. Experienced leaders with rescue knowledge and equipment are in this craft.

BIBLIOGRAPHY

American Canoe Association. 1991. *Canoeing and kayaking.* Lorton, VA: American Canoe Association.

American Red Cross. 1981. *Canoeing and kayaking.* St. Louis: Mosby Lifeline.

Bechdel, Les, and Slim Ray. 1985. *River rescue.* Boston: Appalachian Mountain Club.

Bennett, Jeff. 1993. *Rafting.* Portland, OR: Swiftwater.

Department of Transportation, U.S. Coast Guard. *Annual boating statistics.* Washington, DC: Commandant, U.S. Coast Guard.

Jenkinson, Michael. 1981. *Wild rivers of North America.* New York: Elsevier-Dutton.

McClaran, Don, and Greg Moore. 1989. *Idaho whitewater: The complete river guide for canoeists, rafters and kayakers.* McCall, ID: Pacific Pipeline.

McNair, Robert E., L. Matty, and Paul A. Landry. 1985. *Basic river canoeing.* American Camping Association.

Palzer, Bob, and Jody Palzer. 1973. *Whitewater; Quitewater.* Madison, WI: Wisconsin Hoofers Outing Club.

Priest, Simon, and Tim Dixon. 1990. *Safety practices in adventure programming.* Boulder, CO: Association for Experiential Education.

Rugge, John, and James W. Davidson. 1983. *The complete wilderness paddler.* New York: Random House.

Schafer, Ann. 1978. *Canoeing western waterways: The mountain states.* New York: Harper & Row.

Tejada-Flores, Lito. 1978. *Wildwater: The Sierra Club guide to kayaking and whitewater boating.* San Francisco: Sierra Club Books.

Walbridge, Charles C. 1983 and 1986. *The best of the River Safety Task Force newsletter, Volumes I and II.* Lorton, VA: American Canoe Association.

chapter 12

Personal Watercraft Safety

Susan J. Grosse

The U.S. Coast Guard considers personal watercraft to be class A (less than 16 feet in length) inboard powerboats. The Personal Watercraft Industry Association further defines a personal watercraft as an inboard vessel less than 4 meters (13 feet) in length that uses an internal combustion engine powering a water-jet pump as its primary source of propulsion, and is designed with no open load-carrying area that would retain water. The vessel is designed to be operated by a person or persons positioned on, rather than within, the confines of the hull (Personal Watercraft Industry Association 1994).

Using personal watercraft is one of the fastest growing aquatic endeavors of this decade. The National Marine Manufacturers Association reported sales of more than 109,000 craft in 1993, a 30-percent increase over the previous year (Hallstrom 1994). From 1985 to 1990 personal watercraft sales more than doubled those of other boats (Kawasaki 1990). People are taking to the water not only to ride and race, but also to camp and vacation tour. Recognizing the versatility of personal watercraft, law enforcement and lifeguard agencies are increasing their patrol capabilities with personal watercraft. It is indeed the craft of the 21st century.

New, popular, and growing sports are not without problems, and using personal watercraft is no exception. Racing and stunt riding can be dangerous. Governmental regulation is a hot issue. Rider safety, aquatic participant user conflict, and environmental impact are all areas for concern. From use on small, inland lakes to ocean cruising, personal watercraft are controversial. This chapter will outline major factors to consider when deciding to use personal watercraft and purchasing equipment. We address principles of safe operation, legal issues, environmental concerns, and administration of aquatic programs including personal water-

The use of personal watercraft is one of the fastest growing aquatic endeavors in recent years.

craft. We caution readers that this is an emerging sport. As participation grows, new equipment is developed. As aquatic management organizations strive to meet needs of all users, it will be critically important to stay up-to-date on all areas presented.

ENVIRONMENTAL CONDITIONS

Many factors contribute to a safe environment for using personal watercraft. Small, single, stand-up rider models are popular for racing and pleasure riding. Larger, multirider, sit-down models can have a range of 60 to 80 miles (Splash Staff 1994), opening a variety of vacation, camping, and touring possibilities. Law enforcement and lifeguard agencies are finding more and varied uses for personal watercraft in patrol and rescue work. Everyone desires accident-free usage. Critical safety factors are selection of craft and site management.

Selecting Craft

Why take a personal watercraft instead of a regular powerboat? Powerboats have propellers, personal watercraft have a jet engine— no propeller to cause danger to persons in the water. Thrust and steering come from a jet stream of water. Hence the term *Jet Ski*, a Kawasaki trademark (Kawasaki 1990). Personal watercraft are also smaller, capable of travel where boats with deeper draft cannot go. There is no problem with anchorage; just pull up on shore. Personal watercraft are what Kawasaki calls *rider active*; the rider's entire body participates in craft operation. These powerboats (yes, they are by definition and by law powerboats) are fast, easy to operate, and economical to use. A jet stream engine uses less fuel, leaves a smaller wake, and causes less pollution. Then too, there is the overall appeal to the Harley rider in aquatic activity lovers! Safe use of personal watercraft begins with selecting appropriate craft. Table 12.1 is a list of things to consider when deciding what sort of personal watercraft to purchase.

Equipment Availability

There are several types of personal watercraft on the market. We can classify them according to ridership and rider position. The smallest, fastest craft are single-rider configured with the user standing during use. These are primarily for pleasure riding and racing. Constantly gaining in popularity are models in which the rider remains seated (according to Hallstrom 1994, accounting for 80 percent of new craft sales for 1993). You can use these models for solo, tandem, or three-person riding. You can configure seats with riders one behind the other or two persons side by side.

Select the size of craft and type of ridership appropriate to the interests of those who will be the primary users. Plan ahead of time. Do not use a craft for a purpose for which it was not intended. Overloading or not having a spotter when towing can result in a serious accident. Never exceed manufacturer's specifications for use of any craft.

Multiple-person, sit-down models have opened personal watercraft use to a whole spectrum of activities. Although pleasure riding is popular, other water activities are gaining participants. Most craft that can carry two people can tow. If towing a person, such as a person on a board or ski, the second person sits back-to-back with the driver and acts as a spotter for the towed participant. Multiple-rider craft have also opened activities for families. Now children can ride along with Mom and Dad. The extra storage capabilities of the larger craft and longer mileage ranges have made personal watercraft touring vacations increasingly popular.

Law enforcement agencies are turning to personal watercraft for patrol purposes. Lifeguard agencies responsible for large areas of open water are using multiple-passenger personal watercraft for patrol and rescue. During the 1993 floods, Kansas Department of Wildlife and Parks Conservation officers were recognized for using personal watercraft to rescue 11 victims (Currents 1994). In Hawaii personal watercraft are used for surf rescue where their speed and versatility make it possible to get to a victim, effect a rescue, and exit

Table 12.1
CONSIDERATIONS BEFORE BUYING A PERSONAL WATERCRAFT

WHAT TO ASK	WHAT TO CONSIDER
Who will be the primary user?	☐ Age (teen, adult, senior) ☐ Size and weight ☐ Previous watercraft operation experience
Will there be multiple users or riders?	☐ Single-rider craft ☐ Multiple-rider craft
What will be the primary activities of the users?	☐ Solo racing ☐ Solo riding ☐ Stunt riding ☐ Partner riding ☐ Towing other craft or objects ☐ Towing people on skis or objects ☐ Touring and camping ☐ Patrol and surveillance ☐ Rescue
What will be the use environment?	☐ Lake, river, or ocean ☐ Size of water area ☐ Type of shared usage ☐ Climate, year-round, or seasonal use ☐ Local regulations and ordinances
What cost factors will affect the purchase?	☐ Money for the craft itself ☐ Money for supplementary equipment ☐ Money for ongoing maintenance ☐ Rental subsidy

the high surf waves much more efficiently than a lifeguard with a rescue buoy (Kelly 1994).

Once you have selected the type of craft, some additional information is worth considering. Personal watercraft are designed for falling off; during capsize the craft will either shut off (safety lanyard detaches and shuts off throttle) or circle. Which system would you prefer? A longer, wider hull makes a craft easier to board and more stable. A deeper cut V makes a craft more comfortable. Center of gravity of the riders should be low on the craft. The smaller the amount of craft surface contacting the water the more agile the craft will be. Furthermore, different craft have different types of steering. Some steer by controlling a ski, some by controlling a jet nozzle, some by body weight shift of the driver.

Will the ride be a wet one or a dry one? Higher, more stable craft keep the rider dryer.

© Mary Langenfeld

As jet skiing has become recognized as a form of recreation as well as racing, tandem and threesome jet skiing has risen in popularity. However, even low-speed jet skiing has its risks.

Craft can ride on skis or on the hull itself. Try both, then decide. For a more stable, controlled ride passengers and driver should be able to maintain a neutral position on the seat during turns. Beginners may become better drivers if they start with a stand-up model to help them get a feel for craft balance. Also useful for beginners is an adjustable throttle stop (Splash Staff 1994).

How are personal watercraft evaluated? Johnson (1994) lists nine factors to consider in judging any craft:

1. Handling
2. Quickness, power, and speed
3. Stability
4. Ergonomics
5. Comfort
6. Noise and vibration
7. Appearance
8. Value
9. Fun

Only a test drive can tell. Because this is a *personal* craft, what works for one rider may not work well for another. Again, purpose of use is a main determining factor. Know the capabilities of the primary rider.

Safety Equipment

In addition to selecting appropriate craft, safety depends on having several necessary items: a safety lanyard for engine cutoff (attached to craft and rider), a correctly sized, Coast Guard-approved personal flotation device worn securely by all riders (class IV throwable devices may not substitute), an orange warning flag, a fire extinguisher, and eye protection (to ensure vision of driver during spray and against glare).

Although not required, additional equipment might include the following:

- Wet suits for all riders (hypothermia can set in quickly).
- Wet boots (for added traction on craft foot pads).

- Helmet, at least a biker helmet; one with a brim gives better protection but the brim could catch. A full-face helmet will save teeth as well as brain.

- Anchor (standard or pack sack to fill with rocks).

- Tow line (in case you need a tow).

- Tool kit (usually supplied with craft purchase).

- Craft manual in dry bag (for trouble shooting on the water).

- Gloves.

- Whistle.

- Trail snacks (for quick energy pickup).

- First aid kit.

- Signal flares.

- Beach caddie (for moving craft from car or storage to water).

- Water rack or platform (for storing craft when not in use and keeping it safe from beach waves that might push it into the bottom or shoreline).

Check all equipment frequently to be sure it is in good repair and working properly. Before taking to the water, run a safety checklist. Although a mental list might be all right for private, individual use, complete a formal, written checklist before any use in a rental or loan situation (see Administration).

Maintenance

A safe user keeps the craft well maintained and deposits use and maintenance refuse in proper receptacles. Oil and fuel require special care. Store fuels in a locked place. Use safe receptacles and dispose of expended items appropriately. The oil slick you leave on the water could be the same slick you fall into! Your owner's manual covers your particular model craft, but figure 12.1 contains a checklist of basic items to review.

Participation Site

Critical to safe craft operation is selecting appropriate participation areas. Any power craft you use on water has environmental impact. A safe user does not endanger the environment through pollution, overuse, or destruction of habitat. Rarely do we have the luxury of a private aquatic area—open-water space is a shared commodity. Safe personal watercraft use means sharing.

Before putting craft on any water, users must check with local authorities regarding aquatic areas that may be closed to power craft users. Personal watercraft are power craft. Users can destroy some natural habitats and endanger species if they to not respect environmental limits. Do not expect all areas to be posted on site. The Personal Watercraft Industry Association supports care for the environment and recommends that each personal watercraft participant be aware of endangered species in your riding area and protect them; do not operate craft in habitat-restricted areas. Be aware that boat noise can disturb nesting waterfowl, and stay clear of nesting areas and seasons. Wash your craft after use to avoid transporting exotic plants to other lakes and rivers. Do not harass wildlife!

Always ride at controlled speeds so you can see and maneuver around water mammals, and near shore, avoid high speeds that create wakes and destroy shorelines. Observe all posted wake signs. In water anchorage be careful not to damage underwater areas such as coral; avoid sea grass and kelp forest areas (Personal Watercraft Industry Association n.d.).

Be responsible. Share with other water-space users, including those on shore. Being a safe and considerate boat driver means following all boating customs and rules of the road. Be predictable—other boat drivers should be able to determine your activity and course. Erratic behavior causes accidents.

Keep appropriate space between your craft and other water-space users. Stay out of swim areas. Observe any posted area restrictions. Stay clear of craft towing skiers; their tow line can injure you also.

Cross wakes carefully and well aft of other crafts, and avoid leaving a heavy wake in marina areas and along shorelines. Give right-of-way to sail craft and larger craft; you can maneuver easily, so do so. Pass cautiously; you

Maintenance Checklist for Your Personal Watercraft

_____ Open the hood and ventilate the engine compartment.

_____ Loosen the fuel tank cap to relieve pressure; add fuel if necessary and secure the cap snugly. Be sure you have enough fuel along for your outing.

_____ Use a sponge to remove any water or fuel residue from inside engine compartment before launching.

_____ Check throttle for proper operation.

_____ Check steering for proper operation.

_____ Check battery for fluid level and charge condition.

_____ Make certain all latches are functioning and secure.

_____ Look for any oil or fuel leaks; check oil level.

_____ Look under and around hull for any cracks or damage.

_____ Check that there is no debris in intake or jet nozzle.

_____ Check operation of bilge pump (if your craft has one).

_____ Secure engine hood cover and seat cover latches.

_____ Make sure choke and fuel reserve switches are in working order.

_____ Stow the tow rope.

_____ Make sure engine shut-off lanyard is in position and in good repair.

_____ Make sure personal safety gear, including PFD, is in good repair.

_____ Store registration papers and owner's manual in dry bags onboard.

_____ Boat number is visible and placed correctly.

_____ Check all trailering equipment for function and condition.

Figure 12.1 Maintenance checklist for personal watercraft.

Data from Kawasaki. 1994. Personal watercraft rider's handbook. Winter Park, FL: Marketing Resources Group International and Personal Watercraft Industry Association. 1994. Fun and safety on your personal watercraft. Washington, DC: The Association.

cannot always be seen as you come around a wake or a larger craft. Watch the entire water area, and be prepared to change course or stop well ahead of any obstacle or hazard. Remember your craft does not have brakes, and momentum can cause a collision even with a motor off.

Ride in a wide, variable area. Confining riding to one small area increases environmental impact. Stay within sight of shore so in case of emergency you can be seen and assisted, but be aware that many people who live along water do so because they appreciate the quiet of the environment. Ride well away from residential shore property.

Monitor your fatigue as you ride, because overtired riders are more likely to fall and less likely to be able to take care of themselves in an emergency. Quit before cold and fatigue reduce your self-rescue capabilities. If you camp or picnic, observe all laws and rules of etiquette regarding using private property, cleaning up your garbage, and building and putting out fires. Promptly and accurately report all accidents.

SUPERVISION

Ultimate responsibility for safe use of personal watercraft lies with the user. Each person must know and observe federal, state, and local laws and ordinances regarding operating personal watercraft. Each person must know and practice safe ridership. It is the responsibility of the craft owner to be sure every rider complies.

Laws vary. For specific details of Coast Guard laws governing small power craft, contact your local Coast Guard Auxiliary. Because personal watercraft use is a fairly new sport, and a growing one, laws and ordinances are going to be in flux for some time. In many states, interested individuals are just beginning to address issues of personal watercraft use. Regulatory powers are in dispute. A 1994 ruling of the Wisconsin Department of Justice granted regulatory power over personal watercraft, in which issues of safety are concerned, to local municipalities. Similar situations exist in many states. Owners must do their homework on regulations affecting the area they will be using. Table 12.2 is a general listing for guideline purposes only.

Although not having the power of law, commonsense safety practices make for safe water experiences (Hansen 1994). Leave a float plan—where you are going and when you will be coming back—with friends or officials. Every rider should wear a properly secured personal flotation device at all times. Attach the warning flag high enough so it can be seen across the water. Be sure your riding area is free from obstructions, swimmers, and boat traffic. Warm up your craft outside the launch area and after you are out a reasonable distance into the water. Respect the rights of other water area users; avoiding conflict can go a long way in facilitating legal use for everyone rather than restrictions legislated due to inconsiderate actions of a few.

Every person riding a personal watercraft should know how to swim and swim well in deep water. Craft operation is not recommended for persons under 14 years of age (Personal Watercraft Industry Association 1994). Even for those 14 and older, never attempt any stunts beyond your skill level; ride with other experienced riders in case you need assistance. Always have a second rider, seated backward as a spotter when towing; a mirror is *not* an appropriate substitute. Do not exceed manufacturer's limits for craft loading or operation, and never operate craft while using alcohol or drugs. A safe watercraft experience is much more enjoyable. Even the stunt experts will tell you, "Be responsible—ride smart and ride safe!" (Hemmel 1994).

SELECTION AND CONDUCT OF THE ACTIVITY

Personal watercraft are not toys. They are powerboats. As such, mature individuals who are competent deep-water swimmers and have had instruction in safety and operational techniques should operate them. As a major manufacturer put it, personal watercraft "are not for kids" (Kawasaki 1990).

Being Prepared

Anyone considering use or purchase of personal watercraft should first know how to swim and *swim well* in *deep water*. Personal watercraft are designed to fall, dumping the rider into the water. Depending on speed, this could occur with some impact. Riders must be comfortable with sudden immersion, including immersion of face. Riders should be comfortable wearing a personal flotation device and be able to control their body in water while wearing one. The following water test items can assist in determining an individual's readiness for personal watercraft.

Wearing long pants, long-sleeved shirt, and tennis shoes, fall into deep water, surface, and tread water for five minutes. Perform 10 deep-water bobs (lift arms overhead and submerge, pull arms down to sides, kick, and return to the surface for a breath). Wearing your Coast Guard-approved personal flotation device, fall into deep water, swim 25 yards, and climb out onto a dock or pool edge. Also, fall into deep water, come up and roll onto your back, count to 10, roll onto your stomach, count to 10, roll onto your back, and swim to safety.

If you determine you are comfortable in deep water, the next step is a safe boating course. Personal watercraft, as powerboats, must observe all laws, customs, and courtesies common to any other power craft. Drivers of personal watercraft must be predictable in their craft operation. The best way to learn the ways of the water road are through boater education courses. Stressing the importance of boater

Table 12.2
REGULATIONS FOR PERSONAL WATERCRAFT SAFETY

☐ The craft must be registered.

☐ Registration numbers must be properly displayed on the craft.

☐ There must be a wearable (class I, II, or III) Coast Guard-approved personal flotation device onboard for each person.

☐ There must be a fire extinguisher onboard.

☐ No night riding is allowed.

☐ No one under age 12 may operate a motor vessel.

☐ All nautical rules of the road apply to personal watercraft; they are classified as powerboats:

1. Nonpower craft (sailboard, canoes, rowboats, kayaks) have right-of-way over power craft.

2. In narrow channels, boats under 65 ft. cannot hamper progress of larger boats unable to maneuver in the channel.

3. On intersect, the boat to the right has the right-of-way.

4. When overtaking, the slower boat has the right-of-way.

5. Head on, both boats should give way, to the right.

6. All posted speed limits, channel markers, and restricted area buoys must be observed.

7. Noise level emissions of engines manufactured after January 1, 1978, may not exceed 82 dBA, measured at a distance of 50 ft. (Knight 1994).

☐ Additional state and local ordinances might govern such things as the following:

1. Licensing

2. Age of operators

3. Hours of operation of any power craft

4. Hours of operation of power craft leaving a wake

5. Towing people or objects

6. Jumping the wake

7. Required boater education courses

8. Operation by persons under 21 years of age

9. Protection of endangered species and habitat areas

10. Number of riders

11. Age required for rental

12. Automobile towing regulations

13. Boat landing and launch restrictions

education, leading manufacturer Kawasaki offers a $25 gift certificate to Jet Ski owners completing a boating education course (Currents 1994). Contact your local Coast Guard or Power Squadron for further formation on what is offered in your area. The Personal Watercraft Industry Association has endorsed the Personal Watercraft Education Course developed and distributed by the Center for Recreational Communication; call 407-629-4941.

Step three in the learning process is direct experience with your personal watercraft. This sport is deceiving. It is easy to just hop on and ride. But riding and riding safely are two entirely different things. Being a safe rider means the following:

© Cheyenne Rouse

Only mature swimmers instructed in safety and operational techniques should ride jet skis.

- Being familiar with the equipment: names of parts, location of gauges, location and operation of switches, operational theory
- Being able to start and stop the craft appropriately
- Being able to fall off and get back on your particular model craft
- Being able to operate all controls while keeping complete alertness for other water traffic
- Being able to steer the craft in tight as well as open areas
- Being knowledgeable in all laws and courtesies of operation

The checklist in figure 12.2 will help determine the safety of the participant and the craft before they are on the water. Learn and practice under supervision of an experienced rider. Do not experiment on your own. Your craft and your life are important investments. Treat them as such!

Special Circumstances

Some personal watercraft activities require additional safety considerations. With the advent of larger craft, possibilities for towed activities have increased. Larger craft can tow skiers as well as riders of tubes, wake boards, and combo skis. When undertaking towed activities, always use a craft big enough not only for a spotter but also for a fatigued skier. Also, post the warning flag high to assure visibility when the craft is in between the wake. See chapter 13 for specific guidelines about safe towing activities.

Stunt riding is gaining popular appeal. However, even experienced riders will recommend that each participant always wears appropriate safety gear, especially a PFD; makes sure his or her riding area is free from obstructions, swimmers, and boat traffic; never attempts any stunts that are beyond his or her skill level; and is a responsible rider —ride smart and ride safe (Hemmel 1994)!

Ocean surf riding has special hazards and requires additional safety knowledge and precautions. Experienced ocean rider Melinda McLaughlin (1994) recommends that you adhere to the following guidelines:

- Ride with three riders minimum and watch out for each other.
- Because of problems inherent with waves, make sure one person is an experienced ocean rider.

Personal Watercraft Preride Checklist

All items on this list must be checked off before any craft may leave the dock. All safety equipment must be in satisfactory condition. Cite any existing damage.

Craft _____

Date _____ Time _____

	Satisfactory	Negative
General craft condition		
• hull/shell condition	_____	_____
• gas tank full	_____	_____
Safety equipment		
• personal flotation device(s)	_____	_____
• safety lanyard	_____	_____
• warning flag	_____	_____
• fire extinguisher	_____	_____
• first aid kit	_____	_____
Additional equipment		
• anchor	_____	_____
• signal flares	_____	_____
• wet suit	_____	_____
• wet boots	_____	_____

Destination information:

Taken out by: _____ Due back: _____

Staff completing check-out: _____

Acompanying this form should be any insurance papers, payment records, liability releases, or documents signed indicating the user has read, understands, and agrees to abide by the rules of use.

Figure 12.2 Personal watercraft preride checklist.

- Never haul a personal watercraft to a downed rider; waves could knock the craft into you disabling your craft also.
- Get away from your craft if you fall off in heavy wave sets; the boat can smash into you or crush you beneath it into the bottom. Let your friends rescue you.
- Know when to let go of your craft. Toss it away if you are jumping a wave and your boat goes straight up in the air; it can come down on top of you.
- Beware of wave depth; the bottom appears farther than it actually is.
- Learn to read waves and wave behavior. Do not copy surfers; personal watercraft are different.
- Locate near a bay for riding in and out; also, this is a good area for towing friends needing assistance.
- Learn from experienced ocean riders.

ADMINISTRATION

Administrative duties related to personal watercraft are largely determined by whether the craft use will be private or commercial. Private use means the craft is owned and operated by the same individual or operated by individuals who have permission of the owner. Operation is for recreational purposes for which no money has changed hands, no employment is involved, and no specific duty or liability is stated or implied. Commercial use may be by the owner, employees of the owner, individuals who pay the owner for privilege of use (rent, lease), or other individuals to which the owner has a liability duty. In either case it is the owner who is ultimately responsible for safe use of the craft.

Privately owned craft are like any other small boat. Owners must follow all small craft laws, maintain their own craft, control use, and provide storage. Commercial craft use must be more highly organized. Ridership, maintenance, insurance, and licensing are administrative issues the owner is responsible for. All policies and procedures regarding use of personal watercraft should be in writing. Do not rely on word of mouth. In case of accident, documentation may be required in court.

Ridership

Owners need to implement rules related to who is eligible to use the craft. These rules should refer, but not be limited to, statements regarding the following:

- Age of rider—personal watercraft are not recommended for individuals under 14 years of age.
- Size, height, and weight of rider—varies with individual craft; check owner's manual for manufacturer's specifications.
- Swimming ability of rider—should be a competent deep-water swimmer.
- Previous boat driver experience—should have certificate of successful completion of a safe boating course taught by a recognized national organization.
- Insurance coverage—whose insurance will cover the rider? Personal watercraft insurance is available, and the craft should be insured.
- Type of ridership activities suitable for the craft.
- Prohibited ridership activities—if wake jumping is prohibited, for example.
- Time limit of use—hours allowed for operation, as well as individual time of use.
- Required use of personal flotation device.
- All laws and regulations regarding use on specific body of water.
- Skills check-out establishing familiarity with the specific craft the participant will use.
- Who is responsible for any damage to craft or personal property?
- What areas are accessible for riding? Be sure riders know and follow all marina channel, speed, wake, and docking rules and procedures.
- Fuel use and charges.

Prohibit individuals who do not or cannot meet all criteria of ridership from craft operation.

Recording Maintenance for Your Personal Watercraft

Owners are responsible for ongoing maintenance of all craft available for use. Keep records of maintenance schedules and operational status checks done before each rider uses the craft. Although you should advise riders to report problems, some will do so and some will not. It is the owner's responsibility to be sure the craft is working perfectly before anyone uses it. You can use the same check sheet before a craft is taken out and again when the participant brings it back in. At any time, the owner should be able to determine when a craft had a full maintenance check, what its status was when it was last brought in from a ride, who checked it before the next ride, and who has it out now. Any problems noted should have correction measures cited, with date and time the correction was made and who was responsible.

Insurance

Personal watercraft equipment range in price from $5,000 to $11,500 (Pendergrass 1994). This is a sizable investment. Even more valuable are the lives of individual craft users. Although industry estimates only 20 percent of the personal watercraft in use are insured (Pendergrass 1994), that doesn't mean insurance isn't necessary. Quite the contrary. Many owners assume their motor vehicle, homeowner, or renter insurance covers their personal watercraft also. This is not the case. Sometimes coverage is only partial. A general policy could be put in danger of cancellation if too many recreational vehicle accidents are recorded. Policy limits may be insufficient for aquatic accidents. Owners and potential owners must carefully research their insurance needs before putting craft on water.

The most complete coverage is packaged to include liability, medical payments, comprehensive, fire and theft, and collision (Pendergrass 1994). Often companies give discounts to individuals who have taken safe boating courses or to individuals with accident-free records. Personal watercraft liability can be costly. Obtain insurance!

Licensing

As power craft, personal watercraft must be licensed. Keep registration papers with the craft and put the license number on the craft. We also recommend that craft have individual identifying numbers or marks if they are part of a fleet. Craft having special-purpose use, police or lifeguard, for example, should state this so they are easily identifiable to other aquatic participants.

CONCLUSION

Whether ownership is a private or commercial responsibility is crucial. Responsible owners are safety-conscious owners. Responsible owners also have a stake in keeping waterways open to personal watercraft. This means doing everything possible to protect and preserve the future of the sport. Jan Plessner (1994), Jet Ski Watercraft User Relations Coordinator for Kawasaki, recommends joining a local club. If there is no local club, start one. Stay abreast of local concerns about personal watercraft. Make sure your area dealer is aware of any local problems. Self-police motor riding areas. Many fellow riders may not realize they are annoying someone or breaking a rule. It only takes a minute to educate someone about negative consequences of a noisy exhaust system or reckless behavior. Practice proactivity. Meet with local boating police, lawmakers, and shorefront property owners. Let them know you are a knowledgeable and responsible personal watercraft enthusiast and are available to discuss any concerns they might have (Plessner 1994).

RESOURCES

Major manufacturers include the following:

Kawasaki Motors Corp., USA
9950 Jeronimo Rd.
Irvine, CA 82718-2016
714-770-0400

Yamaha Motor Corp., USA
6555 Katella Ave.
Cypress, CA 90630
714-761-7842

WetJet by MasterCraft
100 Cherokee Cove Dr.
Vonore, TN 37885
615-884-2221

SurfJet International Ltd.
504 S. Washington St.
Janesville, WI 53545-1125
608-752-7873

Arctco, Inc.
600 S. Brooks Ave.
Thief River Falls, MN 56701
218-681-8558

For additional information contact the following:

American Power Boat Association
17640 E. Nine Mile Rd.
Eastpoint, MI 48021
810-773-9700

Boating US Foundation
880 S. Pickett
Alexandria, VA 22304
800-336-BOAT

International Jet Sports Boating Association
1239 E. Warner Ave.
Santa Ana, CA 92705
714-751-4277

Personal Watercraft Industry Association
c/o National Marine Manufacture's Association
3050 K St. NW
Washington, DC 20007
202-944-4980

United States Coast Guard
Boating Safety Division
2100 2nd St. SW
Washington, DC 20314-0001
(Call your local Coast Guard Auxiliary.)

United States Power Squadron NHQ
1504 Blue Ridge Rd.
Raleigh, NC 27622
(Call your local Power Squadron.)

Hallstrom, R. 1994. An analytical report on industry happenings. *Splash,* 17 September, 9.

Hansen, G. 1994. Be nice to your friends, Be even nicer to your enemies. *Watercraft World,* September.

Hemmel, J. 1994. Rollin' those runabouts. *Watercraft World,* September.

Johnson, J. 1994. Just for the fun of it. *Watercraft World,* September.

Kawasaki. 1994. *Personal watercraft rider's handbook.* Winter Park, FL: Marketing Resources Group International.

Kelly, D. 1994. Hawaiian waterman. *Personal Watercraft Illustrated,* 8 September, 9.

Kelly, D., and J. Hain. 1994. Toys r us. *Personal Watercraft Illustrated,* 8 October, 10.

Klarich, T. 1994. Learn the ropes. *Personal Watercraft Illustrated,* 8 September, 9.

Knight, S.E. 1994. Keep your eyes on the road, Your hands upon the wheel. *Personal Watercraft Illustrated,* 8 July, 8.

McLaughlin, M. 1994. Commotion at the ocean. *Splash,* 7 September, 9.

Pendergrass, T. 1994. Insuring a safe summer on the water. *Personal Watercraft Illustrated,* 8 July, 8.

Personal Watercraft Industry Association. 1994. *Fun and safety on your personal watercraft.* Washington, DC: The Association.

————. n.d. *An environmental guide for personal watercraft operators.* Washington, DC: The Association.

Plessner, J. 1994. Personal watercraft—An endangered species? *Personal Watercraft Illustrated,* 8 September, 9.

Rider ed art used by U.S.C.G. 1993. *Personal Watercraft Industry News,* Fall, 2.

Splash Staff. 1994. Livin large. *Splash,* 7 September, 9.

Understanding personal watercraft. 1990. 12 min, color. Irvine, CA: Kawasaki Motors, Media Development. Video.

Your guide to serious fun: Jet Ski watercraft information video. 1993. 16 min, color. Irvine, CA: Kawasaki Motors. Video.

BIBLIOGRAPHY

Currents: News and events. 1994. *Personal Watercraft Illustrated,* 8 September, 9.

Safety in Towed Water Activities

Leon J. Larson

T owed water activities and sports have become increasingly popular in recent years, and the variety of these activities has dramatically increased. High-powered specialty towboats have made this possible. Not long ago towed water activities included primarily what the American Water Ski Association (AWSA) terms *traditional* activities. That is, slalom, tricks, and jumping performed on conventional skis designed specifically for each purpose. Today towed water activities have expanded to include traditional waterskiing, barefooting, knee boarding, speed skiing, show skiing, wake boarding, skurfing, tubing, parasailing, and kite flying. Each discipline has its unique characteristics and, therefore, can pose different safety concerns.

This chapter will cover those concerns, along with general safety concerns related to boat driving and the role of the observer during the performance of these activities. The approach will be biased to concerns of organizations, such as ski schools, camps, and resorts that provide these activities as part of ongoing aquatic programs. There are several organizations that provide training in various aspects of boat driving for towed water activities, and we refer to those throughout the chapter.

ENVIRONMENTAL CONDITIONS

Site safety is an issue that is often ignored or overlooked. We cannot overemphasize the importance of providing a safe and secure area for inshore operations for towed water activities.

Site Safety

Considerations about the waterfront have been covered in chapter 9; however, if you will use a waterfront for initiating towed water sports, we should address some other areas of site selection and safety.

Docks should be in good repair with no loose boards, protruding nails, or slippery surfaces. Is there a beach area, and what is it composed of? Avoid rocky shorelines, as they

may injure the skier and damage the boat. Takeoff and landing areas should be free of obstacles and debris. If you cannot remove obstacles, clearly mark them so participants can avoid them. If swimming areas are nearby, maintain a safe distance of 300 feet from those activities. Also, consider the list of issues in table 13.1. All these factors are important in selecting a safe ski site.

Equipment

You should make a careful preactivity check of all equipment routine. Some specific areas to look at are provided in this section.

Requirements

Equipment requirements for the different types of towed water activities can vary widely. Requirements for safety equipment can also vary from state to state (see figure 13.1). Although a skier's equipment is generally considered his or her responsibility, equipment supplied by another individual, a camp, a ski school, or a tournament sponsor is the responsibility of that individual or supplier. This section will discuss equipment safety and use requirements.

In the booklet *Federal Requirements for Recreational Boats* the U.S. Coast Guard has set forth the following standard:

A water skier, while being towed, is considered on board the vessel and a PFD (personal flotation device) is required for the purpose of compliance with PFD carriage requirements. Although not required by federal law it is advisable and recommended for a skier to wear a PFD designed and intended to withstand the impact of hitting the water at high speed as when a skier falls. "Impact Class" marking class refers to PFD strength, not personal protection. Some state laws require skiers to wear a PFD.

Check your state laws for applicable PFD requirements. Generally a type III PFD is recommended for most towed water sport activities, however, you may wear a type V or Special Use Device for special activities such as barefooting, and water-ski jumping. These devices take the form of a full or partial body

Table 13.1
EVALUATING A TOWED WATER ACTIVITY SITE

☐ What type of waterway are you using?

☐ Is it a lake, river, open bay, cove?

☐ Is there a current to deal with?

☐ How much other boat traffic can you anticipate?

☐ During operation, maintain a distance of 300 ft. from obstructions such as docks, pilings, sandbars, and other boat traffic.

☐ There should be a minimum depth of 5 ft. of water in all ski areas to help prevent bottom contact in a fall.

☐ Discourage shore takeoffs and landings.

☐ Follow all rules of the road.

☐ Do not ski where there is a strong current, in narrow channels, or where there may be excessive boat traffic.

☐ Are lifeguards on duty nearby?

☐ Is a backboard available in the event of serious injury?

☐ What is the availability of first aid facilities and equipment, telephone, and hospital or emergency facilities?

☐ Keep a first aid kit in the boat.

☐ If refueling facilities are on site, is the system grounded?

☐ Are no smoking signs posted?

☐ Is a proper fire extinguisher available nearby?

wet suit with flotation built in. In all cases, a flotation device must be capable of floating the skier. The devices listed previously are designed to float an individual in a head-up position.

Equipment Inspection

Before embarking, inspect all equipment for proper function and wear and tear. Following is a list of things to consider when checking equipment. Although not intended to be all-inclusive, this list should help identify many areas of concern. An abbreviated safety checklist that you can use for quick reference is also provided at the end of this section.

The Towboat. Before launch, do a thorough inspection of the craft. Check that the plug is in and the propeller and rudder are secure. If the boat is an outboard, check the transom mount,

along with the throttle, steering, and fuel linkages. Visually inspect towrope attachment points: they must be free of sharp edges that can fray the rope and must be firmly attached to the boat. Check throttle and steering response; it should have minimal slack and respond with little effort. Do a housekeeping check. Clean up clutter in the boat. Last, check that all necessary safety equipment required by your state is onboard, in working order, and properly stowed.

The Towrope. Common to all forms of towed water sports is the towrope. Many specialty ropes exist. Most common is the 75-foot standard towline used for most recreational waterskiing. This line itself is available in several strand thicknesses and tensile strengths, from recreational to tournament. It is often sold in 70-foot standard lengths with loops on both

Quick Reference Equipment Safety Checklist

Towboat

_____	plug	_____	PFD each passenger
_____	propeller	_____	horn or whistle
_____	rudder	_____	flares
_____	transom motor mount	_____	flashlight
_____	throttle linkage	_____	paddle
_____	steering linkage	_____	first aid kit
_____	fuel linkage	_____	anchor
_____	towrope attachment points	_____	state and federal required
_____	rearview mirror		safety equipment
_____	housekeeping		

Towrope

_____ fraying

_____ shock tube (slalom only)

_____ tow strap (trick ski or
      barefoot line only)

Flotation devices

_____ torn material

_____ broken or worn buckles

_____ broken or worn straps

_____ broken or worn zippers

Ski

_____	sharp edges	_____	attachment (loose or missing screws)
_____	cracks	_____	fin (straightness and tightness)
_____	delamination	_____	kneeboard straps
_____	worn or torn binders	_____	valve (tubing only)
_____	cracks in hardware	_____	attachment point (tubing only)

Figure 13.1   Towed water activity equipment safety checklist.

ends. These loops allow attachment to the boat pylon or attachment ring on one end and a 5-foot handle section on the other. This configuration allows the individual to use his or her own custom handle. These lines are also available with shortening loops for water-ski slalom competition. Other specialty lines include the barefoot line, generally 100 feet in length, and the trick line, which is much shorter and can be shortened to the skier's preference to wake proximity. This line is also fitted with a special handle arrangement that may incorporate a toe strap for executing toe tricks. Inspect for fraying. Take a frayed rope out of service as it may snap, causing injury to the skier and boat passengers.

Flotation Devices. When inspecting these devices, look for torn material, broken or worn straps, or any potential problems that could cause the device to malfunction or break up in a hard fall. The device should fit snugly so it doesn't ride up in a fall. In all cases it must float the skier, preferably in a head-up position.

The Ski. With the ski we include water skis, knee boards, wake boards, tubes, and so on. With the exception of tubes, check these devices for sharp edges, cracks, and delamina-tions. Binders should be in good shape with no tears in the binding material or cracks in the hardware. They must be securely attached to the ski or board. Check all screws for tightness, and replace any missing screws. They should fit the skier snugly to ensure an element of control, but not so tightly as to cause injury from a nonrelease. Check the fin for tightness and straightness. On knee boards ensure that all straps are firmly attached and that buckles are in working order. For tubes check all attachment points for integrity, and secure valves to ensure that they do not cause injury. A checklist for towed water activity equipment is contained in figure 13.1.

Towed water activities and sports have become increasingly popular.

© Doug Dusane

Specialty Devices. There are certain other specialty devices you can use and should check for proper condition. They may include helmets for water-ski jumping. These should fit snugly, be nonbucketing, and have a three-point chin strap suspension. Arm slings for jumping must be in good working order. When towing slalom skiers, use a shock tube to prevent the handle from entering the boat upon sudden release.

Kite flying and parasailing present many unique safety precautions and, along with water-ski jumping, should not be attempted without professional instruction. Be sure you understand and heed all manufacturers' warnings.

SUPERVISION

Supervising participants in a towed water sport activity requires properly trained, responsible people. Towed water sports such as waterskiing require high speeds and forceful dynamics capable of seriously injuring a participant. For this reason supervision by competent individuals is essential.

The Driver

The importance of the driver in this equation is paramount. Remember, the skier or person being towed is considered an *extension* of the boat, and the driver must think in those terms. The driver must be especially alert to other boat traffic in the area and should be thoroughly familiar with the waterway that is being traversed. The driver should be aware of any shallow areas, sandbars, and obstacles in the boat path and steer clear of them. We recommend that operations take place in a water depth of at least 5 feet, and that, where possible, you maintain a distance of at least 300 feet from shore and other obstacles.

Before leaving the dock the driver should thoroughly inspect the craft. We gave a detailed description of this check in the equipment section of this chapter. Establish a means of communication with the skier before leaving the dock. The traditional hand signals illustrated in figure 13.2, a through g

are easy to use and universally recognized. Agree on an initial speed. If the skier is not sure of his or her speed preference or is a novice, 22 to 26 miles per hour is a good beginning. Never do tubing at a slower speed than will allow the tuber a good level of control. Knee boarding, wake boarding, and trick skiing all take place at slow speeds, 12 to 20 miles per hour.

When pulling the skier out of the water, apply a steady, gradual increase in throttle. Never yank a skier out of the water. Observing the skier as he or she comes up and applying throttle accordingly can help a novice skier maintain control. When picking up a fallen skier, always approach with the skier on the driver's side of the boat and in view at all times.

Turn off the engine whenever a skier is boarding from the water. Never let anyone ride on the boarding platform, gunwale, or bow of the boat while underway. Passengers should be seated at all times.

Ideally all boat drivers should have some formal training before taking on the responsibility of towing someone behind a watercraft. Courses for such training are available through the U.S. Coast Guard, the U.S. Power Squadron, and other qualified state boating agencies. A Trained Driver course is available through the American Water Ski Association. A listing of state boating agencies is provided on pages 212-215.

The Observer

The role of the observer is a crucial one and we should not take it lightly. The observer is the vital communication link between the skier and the driver. The observer must do the following:

- Concentrate on observing the skier at all times.
- Keep the driver informed of the condition of the person being towed.
- Relay any signals the skier gives.
- Inform the driver immediately if a fall occurs and if the skier has given an OK signal.
- Take responsibility for handling and keeping track of the towrope.

- Alert the driver if there is an imminent danger of running over a trailing rope.
- Maintain good housekeeping in the boat by keeping loose equipment properly stowed.

It is also preferable for the observer to be familiar with operating the watercraft in case the driver should become incapacitated or if assistance in rescuing a fallen skier becomes necessary. A good driver and observer team is essential to safety in towed water sports and is a confidence builder to the person being towed.

SELECTION AND CONDUCT OF THE ACTIVITY

Communication is the key to a successful outing. Once an individual is being towed behind a vessel, communication is limited. This section will explain techniques for establishing communication once underway.

Before Getting Underway

Before leaving the beach or dock be sure that the skier and the observer understand the hand signals they will use (see figure 13.2, a-g). Inform the skier of the proposed boat pattern or path and when to expect turns. Establish his or her skill level. Is this person a novice or a seasoned skier? This will provide the driver with a sense of how to pull the person up and how sharp a turn the skier can negotiate. Agree on a speed before setting out, and alter it only upon a hand signal from the skier. If the skier is a novice, establish a speed that will allow the individual a comfortable level of control.

Getting Underway

Once you properly establish communication, the activity may begin. This section provides, in detail, techniques that you can use to ensure as safe an experience as possible for all involved.

Traditional Waterskiing

If the skier is getting into the water from the towboat, turn off the ignition until the skier indicates *clear*. Never board or enter the water from the boat with the ignition on or the engine running as the propeller will turn even

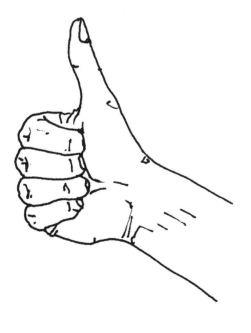

a

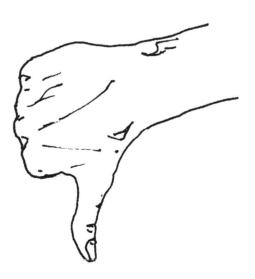

b

Figure 13.2a-b   Water-skier hand signals (a) speed up, (b) slow down.

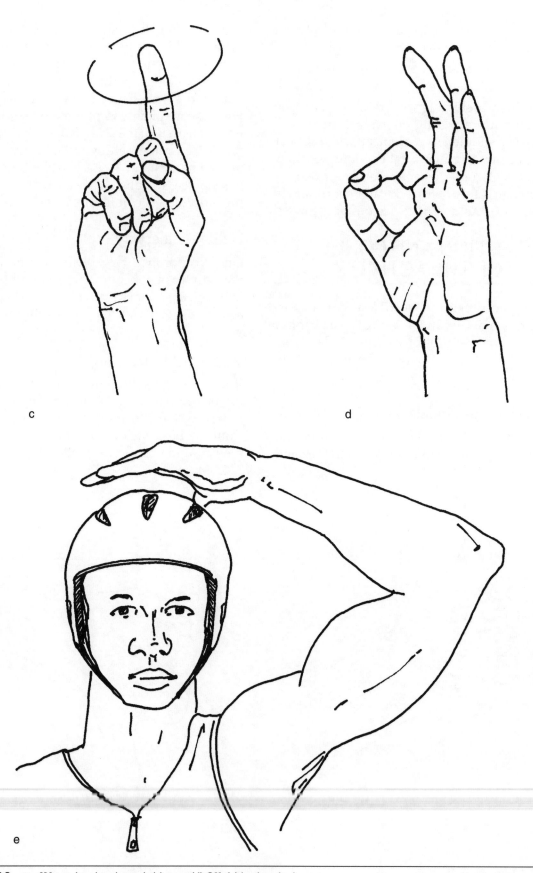

Figure 13.2c-e   Water-skier hand signals (c) turn, (d) OK, (e) back to dock.

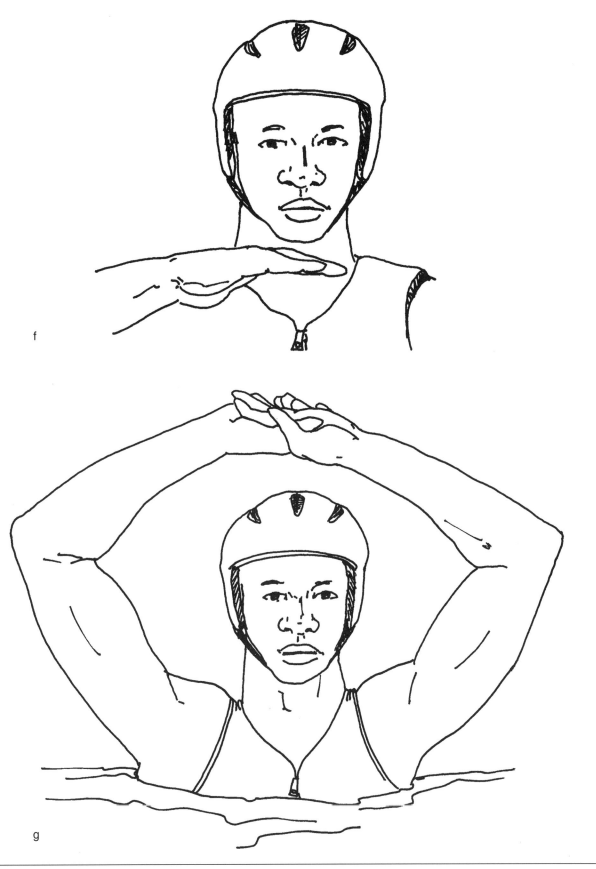

f

g

Figure 13.2f-g Water-skier hand signals (f) cut motor, (g)"I'm OK" after a fall.

when in neutral. At this point, the observer should be tending the needs of the skier, such as tossing the individual the handle if he or she did not take it already. When tossing the handle, always throw beyond the skier to avoid striking the individual. If the skier is ready to go, the observer can sit, preferably facing the rear to easily keep the person being towed in view; then instruct the driver to begin to take up the slack.

At that point, the driver may put the boat in gear and idle slowly until all the slack is out of the line. Check for boat traffic, and when clear look to the skier for the agreed upon start signal. "Hit it" is the most commonly used. When given the signal, apply throttle steadily, smoothly, and progressively, avoiding yanking the skier out of the water. Glance back frequently or use the rearview mirror to assess the skier's progress and level of control. Set a speed that the skier has predetermined, or set one that looks comfortable for the skier and have the observer watch for a hand signal indicating a faster or slower speed. Maintain a safe distance from shore and other obstructions. We recommend 300 feet. As you approach a turn, instruct the observer to give the appropriate signal or give it yourself. Leave enough time before the turn for the skier to acknowledge the signal. Make your turn progressively and as gradually as possible, allow-

ing the skier maximum control. When possible, apply enough throttle to maintain speed but not so much as to cause the skier to lose control.

If the skier should fall, be sure he or she gives a proper OK hand signal. If the skier does not give the signal, return to the skier with dispatch and have the observer ready to assist. If the skier is OK return at idle, approaching the skier from the driver's side when possible to keep the skier in view at all times. Keep a safe distance. Figure 13.3 illustrates two patterns that you can use to return the rope to the skier in anticipation of additional skiing. If the skier is finished skiing, turn off the ignition and have the observer assist the skier in shipping his or her equipment and boarding the boat. It is not recommended that skiers ski back to the dock or shore, because a mistimed landing can cause serious injury. When teaching a beginner it is advisable to reduce the boat speed allowing the skier to sink slowly into the water a safe distance from the shore or dock. Remember the skier is an extension of the boat and is the driver's responsibility to control.

Driving for Other Towed Water Activities

You can use similar methods for the other towed water activities with variations based

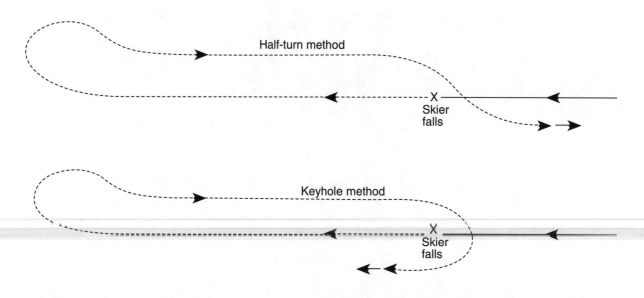

Figure 13.3 Picking up a fallen skier.

on the unique characteristics of that activity. For instance, barefooting speeds would be faster, typically in the 40-mile-per-hour range. You can use a boom device to assist beginners. These devices attach to the pylon and the gunwale of the boat and extend beyond the spray pattern created by the bow entry wave, thus creating a stable handhold for the barefooter. If the barefooter is dropping skis as a start method, remember where they were dropped and avoid running near them on a return pass. Take care to avoid dropping skis where they could become a hazard to other boat traffic. Deep-water starts for barefooting generally require more power than does traditional skiing as drag is greater; however, the driver must still avoid pulling the barefooter up abruptly.

Trick skiing, knee boarding, and skurfing take place at slow speeds, most often in the 12- to 20-mile-per-hour range. This does not mean, however, that you can use less vigilant observation. Severe injuries can happen even at these slow speeds. Trick skiers using a toe piece to practice toehold tricks should have their ropes attached to the boat using a quick-release device, with an alert release person on board to quickly release the skier if a fall is imminent. This will avoid dragging the skier through the water and help prevent knee and other serious injuries. When pulling a tuber, be cautious of extreme speed in turns. It is fun to whip around a turn, but it can also be dangerous.

Regardless of what type of skier you are towing, you should keep a steady speed, a straight course when possible, and follow all on-the-water rules of the road. Remember, it is the driver's responsibility to provide a safe environment for the skier.

Injuries

This chapter will not go into great detail on how to treat or care for injuries, but some basic first aid knowledge is appropriate for boat operators and observers. Those who will be towing skiers regularly as part of a camp or ski school operation should have first aid and CPR training through an accredited agency. The American Red Cross, the American Heart Association, your local affiliate of the National Safety Council, and local emergency medical services generally teach these programs. Keep a first aid kit onboard at all times.

Take special care when a skier is injured in a water-ski accident:

- The observer should immediately don a life vest if not already wearing one and get into the water to assist the skier.
- He or she should jump, not dive, to keep the skier in view at all times and avoid contacting the bottom should the fall have taken place in shallow water.
- The driver should never leave the boat. A drifting, driverless boat is useless and dangerous.
- The rescuer should evaluate based on sound first aid protocol, and make the victim as comfortable as possible.
- If no back or neck injury is apparent, help the skier, or if need be, lift the skier into the boat; do not drag the skier over the side.

Do this operation with the ignition turned off. Never transport a victim on a swim platform.

If a back or neck injury is apparent, carry out spinal immobilization. Obtain additional help, and bring a backboard with a cervical immobilization device (CID) to the scene. The swimmer should not attempt to provide immobilization unless trained to do so. Similarly, with a broken bone water provides buoyancy and will support sufficiently until help arrives. Bleeding in the water always looks worse than it is because the water will not allow a clot to form. Stop bleeding with direct pressure until help arrives. At no time should anyone apply first aid beyond their abilities as more damage can be done. The goal is to get the injured skier to shore without causing additional harm; then get professional help.

Towed water sports in America are becoming increasingly popular. They can be performed safely and provide a great source of fun and exercise for individuals and families alike.

ADMINISTRATION

Individuals, owners, managers, supervisors, counselors, and coaches all have a responsibility to provide a safe environment for those they are teaching or those using facilities under their control. Keep physical facilities in good repair and designed to provide a safe environment. Keep equipment in good working condition, and use it only according to manufacturer's specifications. Finally, train all personnel in the safe operation of the facility, and instill them with a good

sense of safe practices. Good administration will provide continuous oversight of these parameters; doing so will minimize accidents and circumstances that contribute to their cause.

STATE BOATING AGENCIES

Contact your state boating agency to make sure there are no other regulations or information that you need to know before you get out on the water (see figure 13.4).

State Boating Agencies

Alabama

Marine Police Division
Department Conservation & Natural Resources
Folsom Administration Building
64 N. Union St.
Montgomery, AL 36130
(205) 242-3673

Alaska

U.S. Coast Guard
Federal Building
P.O. Box 3-5000
Juneau, AK 99802-1217
(907) 586-7467

Arizona

Game and Fish Department
2222 W. Greenway Rd.
Phoenix, AZ 85023
(602) 942-3000

Arkansas

Game and Fish Commission
Boating Safety Section
2 Natural Resources Dr.
Little Rock, AR 72205
(501) 223-6400

California

Department of Boating and Waterways
1629 "S" St.
Sacramento, CA 95814
(916) 445-6281

Colorado

Division of Parks and Outdoor Recreation
13787 S. Hwy. 85
Littleton, CO 80125
(303) 795-6954

Connecticut

DEP Complex
Office of Parks & Recreation
Boating Safety Division
333 Ferry Rd., P.O. Box 280
Old Lyme, CT 06371
(203) 566-3781

Delaware

Division of Fish & Wildlife
89 Kings Highway
P.O. Box 1410
Dover, DE 19903
(302) 739-3440

District of Columbia

Metropolitan Police Department
Harbor Patrol
550 Water St. SW
Washington, DC 20024
(202) 727-4582

Florida

Department of Natural Resources
Florida Marine Patrol
3900 Commonwealth Blvd.
Tallahassee, FL 32399
(904) 487-3671

Figure 13.4   State boating agencies.

Georgia

Department of Natural Resources
Game and Fish Division
205 Butler St. S.E.
E. Tower, Ste. 1366
Atlanta, GA 30334
(404) 656-3534

Guam

Guam Police Department
287 W. O'Brien Dr.
Agana, Guam 96910
(671) 472-6363

Hawaii

Harbors Division
Department of Transportation
79 S. Nimitz Hwy.
Honolulu, HI 96813
(808) 548-2515

Idaho

Department of Parks & Recreation
Statehouse Mail
Boise, ID 83720
(208) 344-3810

Illinois

Department of Conservation
Division of Law Enforcement
524 S. Second St.
Springfield, IL 62701-1787
(217) 782-6431

Indiana

Law Enforcement Division
Department of Natural Resources
606 State Office Building
Indianapolis, IN 46204
(317) 232-4010

Iowa

State Conservation Commission
Fish & Wildlife Division
Wallace Building
E. Ninth & Grand Ave.
Des Moines, IA 50319-0034
(515) 281-2919

Kansas

Kansas Department of Wildlife & Parks
R.R. No. 2, Box 54A
Pratt, KS 67124
(316) 672-5911 ext. 108

Kentucky

Kentucky Water Patrol
107 Mero St.
Frankfort, KY 40601
(502) 564-3074

Louisiana

Louisiana Department of Wildlife & Fisheries
2000 Quail Drive
P.O. Box 98000
Baton Rouge, LA 70898-9000
(504) 765-2988

Maine

Department of Inland Fisheries & Wildlife
284 State St., Station 41
Augusta, ME 04333
(207) 289-5220

Maryland

Department of Natural Resources
Tawes Office Building
580 Taylor Ave.
Annapolis, MD 21401
(410) 974-3548

Massachusetts

Division of Law Enforcement
100 Nashua St.
Room 910
Boston, MA 02114
(617) 727-1614

Michigan

Department of Natural Resources
Mason Building
P.O. Box 30028
Lansing, MI 48909
(517) 373-1650

Minnesota

Department of Natural Resources
Boat and Water Safety Section
Box 46, 500 Lafayette Rd.
St. Paul, MN 55155-4046
(612) 296-4507

Mississippi

Department of Wildlife Conservation
P.O. Box 451
Jackson, MS 39205
(601) 961-5300

Figure 13.4   *(continued)*

Missouri

Department of Public Safety
Missouri State Water Patrol
P.O. Box 603
Jefferson City, MO 65102-0603
(314) 751-4509

Montana

Department of Fish, Wildlife & Parks
Boating Safety Division
1420 E. Sixth St.
Helena, MT 59620
(406) 444-4046

Nebraska

Nebraska Game and Parks Commission
2200 N. 33rd St.
P.O. Box 30370
Lincoln, NE 68505-0370
(402) 464-0641

Nevada

Department of Wildlife
Division of Law Enforcement
P.O. Box 10678
Reno, NV 89520-0022
(702) 789-0500

New Hampshire

Department of Safety, Marine Patrol
Hazen Dr.
Concord, NH 03305
(603) 271-3336

New Jersey

State Police
Marine Law Enforcement Bureau
P.O. Box 7068
W. Trenton, NJ 08628-0068
(609) 882-2000

New Mexico

Natural Resource Department
Parks and Recreation Division
Boating Safety Section
P.O. Box 1147
Santa Fe, NM 87504-1147
(505) 827-3986

New York

Office of Parks, Recreation & Historic
  Preservation

Bureau of Marine & Recreational Vehicles
Agency Building 1
Empire State Plaza
Albany, NY 12238
(518) 474-0445

North Carolina

Wildlife Resources Commission
Archdale Building
512 N. Salisbury St.
Raleigh, NC 27604-1188
(919) 733-7191

North Dakota

Game & Fish Department
100 N. Bismarck Expressway
Bismarck, ND 58501-5095
(701) 221-6300

Ohio

Department of Natural Resources
Division of Watercraft
1952 Belcher Dr.
Building C2
Columbus, OH 43224-1386
(614) 265-6480

Oklahoma

Department of Public Safety
P.O. Box 11415
3600 N. Martin Luther King
Oklahoma City, OK 73136-0415
(405) 424-4011

Oregon

State Marine Board
3000 Market St., NE #505
Salem, OR 97310
(503) 378-8501

Pennsylvania

Pennsylvania Fish Commission
3532 Walnut St.
P.O. Box 1673
Harrisburg, PA 17105-1673
(717) 657-4538

Puerto Rico

Department of Natural Resources
Commissioner of Navigation
P.O. Box 5887, Pta. Station
San Juan, PR 00906
(809) 724-2357

Figure 13.4 *(continued)*

Rhode Island

Department of Environmental Mgt.
Boat Registration Office
22 Hayes St.
Providence, RI 02908
(401) 277-6647

South Carolina

Wildlife & Marine Resources Department
Boating Division
217 Fort Johnson Rd.
P.O. Box 12559
Charleston, SC 29422-2559
(803) 795-6350

South Dakota

Division of Wildlife
523 E. Capitol Ave.
Pierre, SD 57501-5182
(605) 773-4506

Tennessee

Wildlife Resources Agency
P.O. Box 40747
Ellington Agricultural Center
Nashville, TN 37204
(615) 360-0500

Texas

Parks & Wildlife Department
4200 Smith School Rd.
Austin, TX 78744
(512) 389-4850

Utah

Division of Parks and Recreation
1636 W. North Temple
Salt Lake City, UT 84116
(801) 538-8321

Vermont

Vermont State Police Headquarters
Marine Division

103 S. Main St., Room 221
Waterbury, VT 05676
(802) 244-8778

Virgin Islands

Department of Planning and Natural Resouces
179 Altona & Wwlgunst
Charlotte Amalie
St. Thomas, Virgin Islands 00802
(809) 774-3320

Virginia

Commission of Game & Inland Fisheries
4010 W. Broad St.
P.O. Box 11104
Richmond, VA 23230-1104
(804) 367-1000

Washington

State Parks & Recreation Commission
7150 Cleanwater Ln., KY-11
Olympia, WA 98504
(206) 586-2165

West Virginia

Department of Natural Resources
Law Enforcement Division
1800 Washington St., E
Charleston, WV 25305
(304) 348-2783

Wisconsin

Bureau of Law Enforcement
Department of Natural Resources
P.O. Box 7921
Madison, WI 53707
(608) 266-2107

Wyoming

Game and Fish Department
5400 Bishop Blvd.
Cheyenne, WY 82006
(307) 777-7605

Figure 13.4   *(continued)*

RESOURCES

United States Coast Guard
Federal Requirements for Recreational Boats
Boating Safety Hotline
800-368-5647

American Water Ski Association Inc.
Safety Manual, Boat Drivers Manual
799 Overlook Dr.

Winter Haven, FL 33883
813-324-4341

American Camping Association Inc.
Camp Boating (Program and Curriculum
   Guidelines)
5000 State Rd. 67 North
Martinsville, IN 46151
317-342-8456

Safety in Skin and Scuba Diving

Ann Wieser

The underwater world invites exploration by those who seek adventure. When we venture underwater, we enter a living space that is totally different from our own. Once there we must respectfully share the space with the inhabitants of that world. In addition, we must understand the physical principles governing that environment as well as our body's response to it. The safety of ourselves and the people we supervise depends on our understanding and acceptance of these concepts.

Although skin and scuba diving are considered related sports, differences exist in the rules of the sport, the equipment used, and the level of training required. In skin diving or snorkeling, the participant swims along the surface of the water and performs breathhold dives to look at the underwater life. In scuba diving, the participant swims underwater and carries an air supply. Because the diver carries an air supply there are more activities in which to participate. These activities include wreck diving, photography, night diving, deep diving, salvage diving, drift diving, spear fishing, cave diving, decompression diving, and cold-water diving. Each activity requires special training and presents special concerns for the participants' safety. Other techniques in diving include using dry suits, Nitrox or other gas mixtures, and rebreathers. You must obtain specific training before attempting a dive using these techniques.

In general, safety concerns fall into three categories: environment, equipment, and participants. Skin and scuba diving can take place in quarries, lakes, ponds, rivers, springs, and oceans. Every location will have unique safety concerns. These concerns include water temperature, currents and tides, eddies, rapids or falls, water depth, pollution, entrance and exit points, and plant and animal life. Additional concerns include accessibility to transportation (for equipment unloading and loading and for

The supply of carried air makes scuba diving less limiting than skin diving and offers more activities to try.

emergency vehicles), communication equipment, and weather.

Skin and scuba diving both require equipment. Although scuba is more equipment intensive, if the equipment is not appropriate in either sport, the safety of the participants will be compromised. The concerns for safety include using the correct equipment for the activity, properly fitting the equipment, and appropriately maintaining the equipment. In addition, the participants must be trained in properly using the equipment before attempting the activity.

Participant safety concerns include anxiety and confidence levels, fitness levels, and training levels. Participants who are overly anxious can think themselves into a dangerous situation. Overconfident participants can push beyond their level of training or endurance and endanger themselves and others. Participants who have a low level of fitness will tire easily, not enjoy the activity, and not be able to keep up with the group. Finally, participants who have insufficient training, either on the equipment or with the specific diving conditions, are in obvious danger. By paying attention to basic safety concerns, participation in skin and scuba diving becomes enjoyable and safe.

ENVIRONMENTAL CONDITIONS

Factors that go into selecting a dive site include the usual trip concerns of food, lodging, transportation, and cost. In addition, consider the experience of the participants. The weather, currents, and tides are also a primary concern. It is not unusual for the dive site or the boat charter to require the participants to sign releases. If the participants are already certified divers, they may be required to show their C-cards and their logbooks. To a degree, the dive site or type of dive determines the equipment that you will require. Make sure you choose the correct equipment for the dive. For example, a night dive would require several lights for each diver, at least two shore lights, buddy lines, and so on, in addition to the regular scuba equipment. Check equipment for proper fit and

inspect it to see that it is in good working order. Pack spare parts (mask and fin straps, etc.), extra equipment (buoyancy compensator, regulator, weights, etc.), and a first aid kit. Once at the site, an environmental orientation to the area, the marine life, and the entry and exit points is necessary.

Location Considerations

There are many factors to consider when selecting a dive location. Weather, water conditions, and site characteristics are a few of these factors.

Site Selection

Each location presents different conditions that you must evaluate before beginning the activity. Evaluating the entry and exit points is a preliminary concern in site selection. Because both sports require equipment, convenient access to transportation and parking is important. In addition, access to communication equipment and access for emergency vehicles is imperative. Other considerations include a place to store and assemble gear, a walkway with a gentle slope to the water's edge, and an algae-free bottom.

Water Concerns

Because skin and scuba diving participants will be on or in the water for long periods, the water temperature becomes a prime concern. Long in-water exposure increases the danger for *hypothermia* (a decrease in the core temperature of the body). Wearing exposure suits (wet or dry suits) helps prevent hypothermia. Because exposure suits also protect against scrapes and stings, you should always wear them when diving.

The type of water will also affect the dive. Salt water has a greater density than fresh water; therefore, a diver in salt water will be more buoyant and require more weight. In addition, the density of water can vary with temperature. For example, fresh water is most dense at approximately 39 degrees Fahrenheit.

You need to anticipate thermoclines or abrupt changes of water temperature with increased depth. Even though surface water temperature may be warm, the water at depth may be quite cold and require additional exposure protection. Seasonal temperature changes, wind, and other weather conditions can intensify water stratification or create overturn, a process in which the deep water moves to the surface (and the surface water moves to the bottom). Generally, overturns decrease visibility and occur during the spring and fall.

Water depth is another factor to consider. The beauty of the underwater world is enticing and hypnotic. Often divers discover that they have gone deeper (or stayed longer) than originally planned. Skin divers who wish to extend their time and depth underwater often practice *hyperventilation*. Hyperventilation is a technique in which skin divers exhale several times sharply to lower their carbon dioxide levels. Lowering the carbon dioxide levels in the bloodstream inhibits the desire to take a breath, and the skin

diver can pass out underwater. When scuba divers slip below their planned depth, they encounter problems if they exceed the limits of the *dive profile*. Selecting a dive location in which the known depth is within the participant's training level and experience is one good way to avoid this problem. You determine the dive profile using either the dive tables (see figure 14.1) or the wheel, and it represents the possible depth and time combinations for the dive to be a no-decompression dive.

A brief review of the dive tables follows. This review only summarizes several basic rules of table or wheel use. Be sure you receive in-depth instruction in any dive planner you select.

All dive planners use depth and time combinations to determine safe parameters for a dive. Notice that the minimum depth is 30 feet (9 meters) and that the depth increases in 10-foot (3-meter) increments. Notice that the time

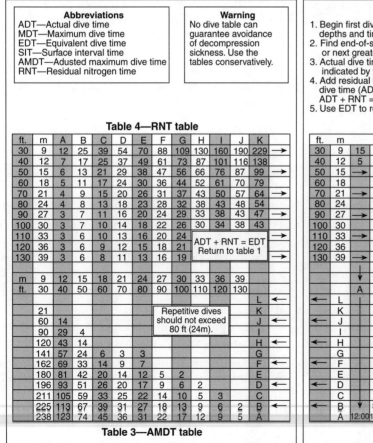

Figure 14.1 Dive tables.

Adapted from Graver. 1993. *Scuba Diving*. Champaign, IL: Human Kinetics for these tables is listed in 15-minute intervals. On any dive you do, do the deepest part of your dive first. That deepest depth becomes the depth you use when figuring your dive profile, even if you only spent a short time at that depth. If your dive is less than the minimum depth when planning your dive, use the minimum depth. If the deepest depth you reach in your dive is between two depths on the dive planner, use the next greatest depth on the dive profile. The rules for time are similar to those for depth. If the time of your dive falls between two times listed on the table, use the greater time to complete your dive profile. In addition to planning your dive, after you have completed a dive, refigure your dive profile to the actual depth and time of your dive; then log the dive in a logbook.

The simplest dive profile to plan is a nonrepetitive, no-decompression dive. If you plan to do multiple dives in one day, follow special rules and procedures. Be sure to review those rules when planning any repetitive diving. There are many different dive planners available in the form of tables, wheels, or computers. Select a dive planner that is easy for you to use, and get training in how it operates. Some divers use a dive computer as a backup to their dive profile while underwater. Although dive computers are accurate when recording the depth and time of the actual dive, never substitute their use underwater for dive planning.

Water movement can create problems for the diver if you do not consider it before the activity. Swiftly moving water can take you far from your dive site or beyond your exit point. Each dive location presents unique conditions to consider about moving water. Therefore, it is important to get an orientation to each site before starting the dive so you can plan the dive to take advantage of the water currents. Because fighting moving water can quickly lead to exhaustion, all divers must know what forms of moving water to expect and what to do when caught in that situation.

Pollution

Pollution is generally not a problem in locations that are specifically developed and promoted for diving. However, pollution can be-

come a problem in natural or unregulated sites. If you suspect that a dive site may be polluted, choose another site.

Underwater Environment

Consider marine life and underwater formations before a dive. It is important to know what is in the area and to encourage the divers to respect all plant and animal life. Knowing the underwater formations at the location is also necessary. Although some formations are rock, many are forms of marine life that grow slowly. Careless or wanton destruction of the formations ruins the dive location for others. Many formations create overhead environments that prevent direct access to the surface; novice divers should avoid these environments. In addition, many human-made structures that are now on the bottom have become dive sites. Many of these structures have deteriorated over the years, so they may have sharp edges or heavy metal parts that move in the currents. Inform all divers of the environmental conditions at each dive site so they can safely participate in the activity.

Equipment Concerns

Equipment is an important concern for both skin and scuba diving. All skin diving equipment—mask, fins, snorkels, an emergency buoyancy device, weights and weight belt, wet suits, and booties—must fit the individual. Before each dive, inspect your own and your buddy's equipment for broken straps and fasteners. Make sure everyone is familiar with all equipment they are using. After the dive, rinse and dry the equipment according to manufacturers' instructions.

Scuba diving is an equipment-intensive sport. In scuba diving the equipment becomes a life support system. For this reason, it is important that you give proper care to the equipment at all times. Safety of the equipment depends on a regular schedule of care and testing, as well as proper day-to-day maintenance and use of the equipment. In particular, have a certified equipment technician at a reputable dive center or facility service the tanks, regulator, and buoyancy compensator regularly. Check all equipment periodically for broken straps or fasteners; mend any cracks, scratches, tears, or holes before the next dive. Make sure that all equipment is cleaned, rinsed, and dried after each dive and before storage. With proper maintenance and servicing, your equipment should give good service for a long time. Before each dive each buddy in the team should inspect all equipment for proper functioning and for knowledge of operation.

Do not dive with unfamiliar equipment or equipment that is not in good condition; replace or repair any equipment that you do not feel is safe. If equipment does malfunction underwater, the buddy team should surface immediately (at the appropriate rate) and replace or repair the faulty equipment before attempting another dive.

Essential Safety Equipment

In addition to the basic equipment used in skin diving, table 14.1 lists the essential safety equipment to have available at every dive.

We strongly recommend an exposure suit for protection against the water temperature, scrapes, and stings. A flotation device or float with a dive flag either printed on it or flying from it may also be necessary in some open-water dive sites. In the water, we recommend a whistle or other signaling device. Additional pieces of safety equipment (such as a rescue bag or rescue tube) and a first aid kit should be available on land (see table 14.2).

Skin and scuba diving provide us with the chance to visit the unique underwater world. To fully enjoy that experience, we must plan that visit safely and carefully. Properly selecting the dive site, preparing equipment, and planning the time to spend underwater are important aspects of safe diving.

SUPERVISION

Anyone who intends to supervise participants in a skin diving or scuba diving activity must

Table 14.1
ESSENTIAL SAFETY EQUIPMENT FOR SCUBA DIVING

TYPE OF EQUIPMENT	PARTICULAR IMPLEMENTS
Group equipment	☐ Float or boat that is flying a dive flag ☐ Ascent and descent line ☐ Communications equipment ☐ Oxygen unit and backboard ☐ First aid kit and basic rescue equipment, including an extra buoyancy compensator, extra tanks, buoys, or markers ☐ Underwater compass, and a rescue bag or rescue tube
Personal equipment	☐ Buoyancy compensator ☐ Weight belt compass ☐ Watch ☐ Submersible pressure gauge and depth gauge, knife, which you should consider a tool and not a weapon to use against marine life

---

Table 14.2
NECESSARY CONTENTS OF A DIVING FIRST AID KIT

☐ A first aid manual, such as the *Underwater Diving Accident Manual* (Divers Alert Network [DAN] 1995)

☐ Money for phone, phone numbers for EMS and DAN

☐ Oxygen unit

☐ Pen and notebook

☐ Acetic acid solution

☐ Corticosteroid ointment

☐ Nonaspirin pain reliever

☐ Hot and cold packs

☐ Splints

☐ Clinging rolled bandages

☐ Single-edged razor blades

☐ Tweezers

☐ Waterproof adhesive tape

☐ Burn dressings

☐ Forms for accident reports (as in figure 9.2 on page 141)

☐ Pocket mask with case

☐ Rubber gloves

☐ Isopropyl alcohol

☐ Antibiotic ointment

☐ Cleansing soap

☐ Motion sickness medication

☐ Water

☐ Triangular bandages

☐ Gauze pads

☐ Utility scissors

☐ Small flashlight with extra batteries

☐ Band-Aids

☐ Emergency blanket

☐ Packets of sugar

---

have appropriate training and certification from one of the following nationally recognized, reputable regulatory agencies:

- International Diving Educators Association
- Multinational Diving Educators Association
- National Association of Scuba Diving Schools
- National Association of Underwater Instructors
- National YMCA SCUBA Program
- Professional Association of Diving Instructors
- Professional Diving Instructors Corporation
- SCUBA Schools International

Each agency specifies the credentials and qualifications needed to lead groups in skin diving and scuba diving. For example, one agency specifies a minimum of a Divemaster rating for some activities and a minimum of an Assistant Instructor rating for others. In all situations, current CPR and first aid certifica-

tions are necessary, and certification in using oxygen equipment is desired.

Buddy Teams

Supervision is enhanced by using buddy teams. Each person should have a buddy and should be instructed to look out for the welfare of his or her buddy. The members of a buddy team should swim side by side and within one arm's reach of each other. (The only exception to this precaution is in skin diving. The buddy teams in skin diving follow the "one up, one down buddy rule." When one diver goes underwater, the buddy stays on the surface and over the underwater swimmer.) In general, a group should consist of one supervisor and two buddy teams. Once underwater, the supervisor will be either in front of or between the buddy teams. An increase in the number of buddy teams requires more supervisors. With groups of three or more buddy teams, the supervisors should be located both in front of and behind the group.

The equipment check: buddies should inspect each other's equipment for completeness and proper functioning.

Lost Buddy Procedure

As a supervisor, it is important to keep all group members together. However, occasionally a group member or buddy team strays from the main group. At those times you will need to initiate either the lost buddy or missing diver procedures. The *lost buddy procedure* begins with doing a complete turn (360 degrees) in the spot where you are; look up and down for a color or shape that contrasts with the surroundings (fins, tank, etc.), and look for bubbles. Retrace your swim about 10 or 15 feet; do another 360-degree turn in one spot. Go up about 10 feet; do another turn. If you still haven't found your buddy after a five-minute search underwater, surface, inflate your buoyancy compensator, look for bubbles, and wait for your buddy to surface. Rejoin on the surface. If your buddy hasn't surfaced within five minutes of your surfacing, begin a missing diver procedure.

Missing Diver Procedure

The *missing diver procedure* begins with a recall and an accounting for all the divers in your group. Regroup on shore or on the boat. Post spotters along the shoreline or on the boat to look for bubbles. Notify other divers or boats in the area so they can help you search. If possible, check the shoreline, the cars, bath or locker facilities, and so on. Begin a systematic search pattern. If the diver has not been found after 20 minutes, notify the authorities for more assistance.

In the case of a scuba diving accident, specialized medical attention, including the administration of oxygen, is often needed. Mild symptoms of a diving injury include fatigue or unusual tiredness and itching. Place the diver in the lateral recumbent position (on his or her side with the head supported and the upper leg bent at the knee) and give oxygen. The oxygen treatment may relieve the symptoms or prevent them from getting worse. Continue the oxygen treatment for at least 30 minutes. Even if the symptoms have apparently subsided, they may reoccur if the oxygen is removed too soon. The victim should still seek medical help, even though the symptoms have subsided. If the symptoms continue after 30 minutes of treatment, treat as a serious injury and seek medical assistance immediately. Serious symptoms include pain, weakness, numbness, dizziness, nausea, or decreased consciousness. If a diver shows serious symptoms, place in the lateral recumbent position, administer oxygen, and transport to the nearest medical facility. In either situation, make sure that the EMS and hospital personnel know that the victim was breathing compressed air underwater. In addition, leave the victim's gear intact so the authorities can inspect it to determine the cause of the accident.

SELECTION AND CONDUCT OF THE ACTIVITY

Although skin and scuba diving are fun activities, they require intensive training. Skin and scuba divers need to be in good physical shape and comfortable in deep water. In addition, students must be able to complete the academic work and understand how the body reacts when under additional atmospheres of pressure.

Screening Participants

The age recommended for skin and scuba diving varies with the different certifying agencies. Some suggestions for minimum ages are given in table 14.3. Even though age is often the determining factor for participation, also consider maturity level.

Table 14.3
MINIMUM AGES FOR SKIN AND SCUBA DIVING

ACTIVITY	MINIMUM AGE
Skin diver	8 years
Junior scuba diver	12 years
Scuba diver	15 years

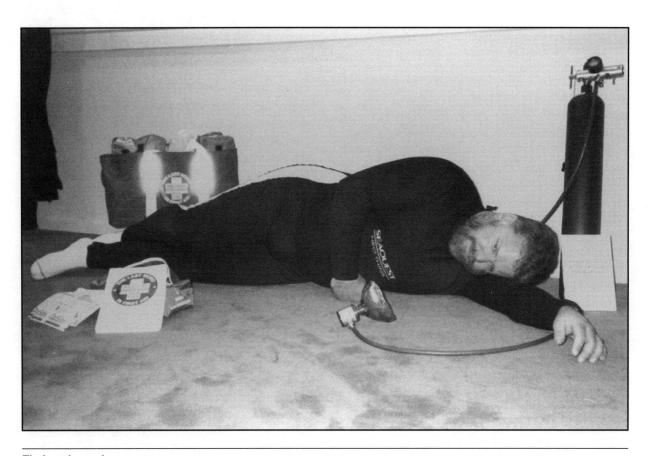

The lateral recumbent position.

Both skin and scuba diving are sports that emphasize relaxation; still, the activities are strenuous. It is important for the participants to be deep-water adjusted and have good swimming skills and fitness levels. Before starting any activity, the participants should pass a water test that evaluates their ability to complete a continuous distance swim (for example, be able to swim at least 400 yards), to remain afloat with ease for a time (for example, be able to do the survival float 10 minutes and tread water for 5 minutes), and to demonstrate various aquatic skills (for example, be able to surface dive and swim 4 body lengths underwater). Participants should also complete a medical form that evaluates at least the cardiovascular, pulmonary, otolaryngological (ear, sinus, and larynx), neurological, and gastrointestinal systems.

Instructional Concerns

An active-status instructor with current insurance should conduct any instruction in either skin or scuba diving. The material that needs to be covered includes academic information (for example, diving science, problem management, and environmental concerns) and skills. Basic skin diving skills include equipment inspections, buoyancy control (deflating and inflating the buoyancy compensator), airway control (mask and snorkel clearing), entries and exits, surface swimming, and surface dives. Basic scuba skills include proper use of equipment, buoyancy control (inflating and deflating the buoyancy compensator, hovering, and proper weighting), airway control (mask and snorkel clearing, regulator use, out-of-air techniques), entries and exits, descents, ascents and safety stops, and both surface and underwater swimming. In addition to the instructor, one person should do surveillance of the participants while the activity is in progress. The instructor can then focus on the learning situation, the students, and the material. The recommended class size will vary with the age and experience of the student, the activity, environmental conditions, and the certifying agency. You can accommodate more students in a controlled setting such as a classroom or pool. For skin diving in an open-water setting, one suggested maximum student-to-instructor ratio is 10 to 1. For scuba diving in an open-water setting, one suggested maximum student-to-instructor ratio is 8 to 1. These ratios would apply to favorable weather and water conditions only. Rough, murky, or cold water would require reduced student-to-instructor ratios.

Communication underwater is another essential skill. In both skin and scuba diving, communication is done using hand signals for a couple of reasons. First, it is difficult to speak distinctly with a snorkel or scuba regulator in your mouth. Second, words are garbled because of the difference in the speed of sound in the water compared with air.

Hand signals fall into three categories. Directional signs help you and your partner to stay together and agree on your direction of travel. Examples of directional signs are illustrated in figure 14.2, a through c.

General signs include tapping your watch to indicate time, showing your pressure or depth gauges to compare your air consumption or depth you have attained, or pointing out something you have found. Safety signs include the OK signs and the emergency signals illustrated in figure 14.2, d through h. Safety signs also include the signals illustrated in figure 14.3, a through c. Use these signs when you are low on air or need to share your buddy's air to get to the surface.

Proper monitoring of the submersible air pressure gauge makes the low-on-air or out-of-air situation a rare occurrence. However, the underwater world is so fascinating that it is easy to lose track of time, depth, or air consumption. The signs in figure 14.3 are universally used for out-of-air situations.

Communication with your buddy on a dive is important for safety, possible problem management, and for overall enjoyment. Therefore you should discuss and agree on your hand signals before you go into the water.

Safety Rules

Skin and scuba diving are safe activities as long as you follow the rules. Specific rules are

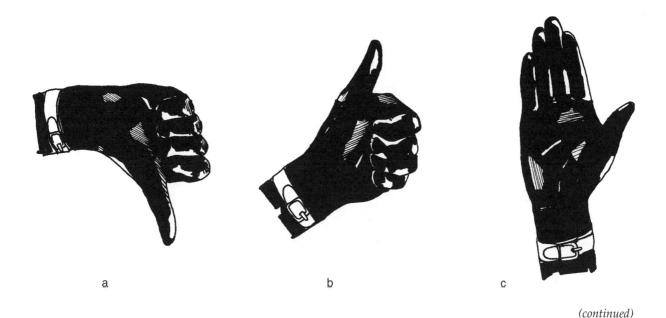

a   b   c

(continued)

Figure 14.2   Skin diving hand signals are (a) descend, (b) ascend, (c) stop.

Adapted from Graver. 1993. *Scuba Diving*. Champaign, IL: Human Kinetics.

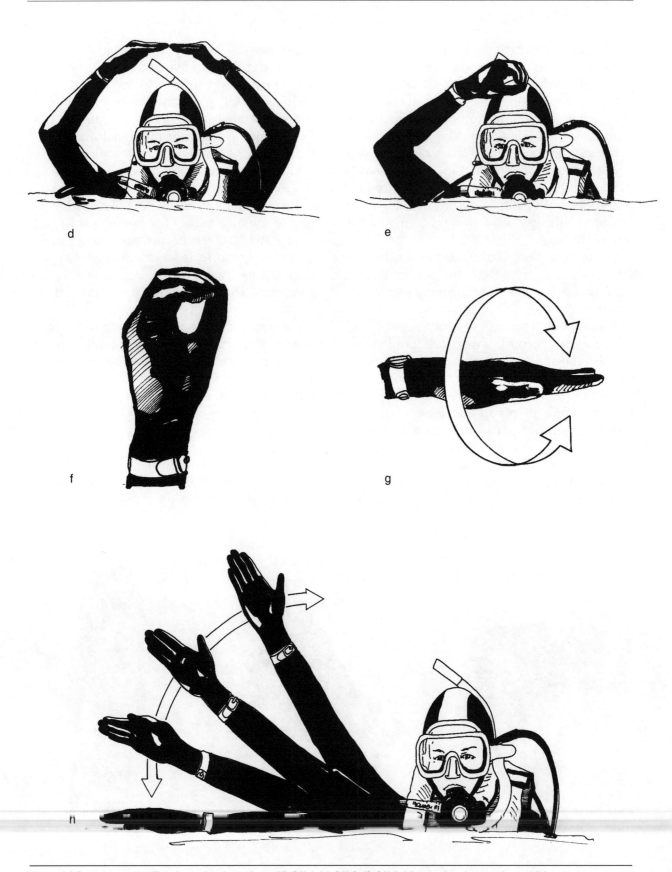

Figure 14.2 *(continued)*   Skin diving hand signals are (d) OK 1, (e) OK 2, (f) OK 3, (g) something's not right, and (h) emergency.

Adapted from Graver. 1993. *Scuba Diving*. Champaign, IL: Human Kinetics.

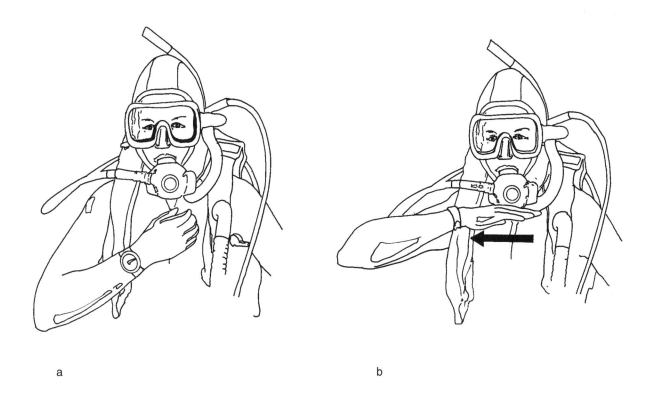

a   b

c

Figure 14.3 Scuba diving hand signals are (a) low on air, (b) out of air, and (c) give me air.

Adapted from Graver. 1993. *Scuba Diving*. Champaign, IL: Human Kinetics.

covered in the instructional phases of the activities. However, some safety tips for both skin and scuba diving include planning your dive, diving your plan, and following the dive objective. Stay with your buddy and the tour guide; do not wander away from the group. General safety tips for scuba diving include the following:

- Stay within your dive profile (depth and time).
- Always do a safety stop at the end of each dive.
- Always breathe; never hold your breath.
- Pay attention to your air consumption; plan the dive based on the person with the fastest air consumption.
- Follow the rule of thirds: use one-third of the air going out at the start of the dive so the remaining two-thirds is available on the return.
- Surface with 300 to 500 pounds per square inch (psi) in the tank; never let the tank get empty.

Providing appropriate training and following the rules for skin and scuba diving will continue to promote diving as a safe, enjoyable activity.

ADMINISTRATION

The organization of the diving activity often determines its safety and success. Even when other persons in the dive industry assist in planning the activity, the group supervisor remains the primary administrator. Also, although property owners and dive boat operators are ultimately liable for what occurs on their property, group supervisors shoulder the greatest responsibility.

Organization

For both skin and scuba diving, the supervisor must assume control of the group and encourage group members to follow safe sport practices. The group supervisors are responsible for the decisions about whether the dives will be made and who will make them. The group supervisor evaluates the conditions of the dive site upon arrival. Cancel the activity or change the site if the water is polluted, if other persons are fishing in the immediate area, or if severe weather conditions exist. Inclement weather conditions include the following:

- Chilling air or water temperature
- High winds or waves
- Rapid or dangerous currents or tides
- Electrical storms, hurricanes, or tornado warnings

Once you have made the decision to dive, the group supervisor organizes the group for the activity.

Organizational factors in both skin and scuba diving include establishing buddy teams, doing an equipment check and assembly, doing a predive safety check, and entering the water. Buddy teams for skin or scuba diving should review and agree on the objective for the dive, signals for communication, and emergency procedures before they enter the water. In addition, each diver should record the time he or she enters the water on a dive roster. In scuba, in addition to the entry time, the divers should record their air pressure at the beginning of the dive. At the end of the dive, both skin and scuba divers should record the time they exited the water on the dive roster. In addition to the time, scuba divers should record their ending air pressure and the depth of the dive.

Record Keeping

As in all activities, documentation in skin and scuba diving serves many purposes. You can use records of student progress to identify skills and knowledge areas in which students need more practice. You can use logbooks, journals, and accident reports to identify and record hazardous situations and make corrections or avoid those problems in the future. In addition, these records and reports can provide documentation in the event of a legal action. Finally, records provide a means of reviewing the effectiveness of the planning for an activity or trip. The documentation includes student medical information, liability releases, training records, tests and skill check sheets, copies of student C-cards or a record of the C-card number, dive rosters, logbooks, and accident report forms. For your own records, you should maintain copies of your C-card and certification information, passport, equipment list with model numbers, logbooks, insurance information, DAN membership, other agency and club memberships, and medical and immunization records in a safe place. You may also want to maintain files for trip organization information, including passport and immunization information, contacts for assistance with transportation reservations and hotel accommodations, previous itineraries, amount of luggage allowed per person, and a description and other information about the various dive sites.

CONCLUSION

Safe diving is an enjoyable and relaxing activity that opens a whole new world of exploration and adventure for the participants. Our safety and the safety of the people that we supervise depends on our understanding of that world. We can avoid many hazardous situations and ultimately enhance our enjoyment by becoming aware of the factors that can undermine that safety.

BIBLIOGRAPHY

Clinchy, R., and G. Egstrom, eds. 1993. *Jeppesen's advanced sport diver manual*. St. Louis: Mosby Yearbook.

Clinchy, R., G. Egstrom, and L. Fead, eds. 1992. *Jeppesen's open water sport diver manual*. St. Louis: Mosby Yearbook.

Divers Alert Network (DAN). 1995. *Underwater diving accident manual*. Durham, NC: Divers Alert Network.

Graver, D. 1993. *SCUBA diving*. Champaign, IL: Human Kinetics.

Griffiths, T., ed. 1991. *Sport scuba diving in depth*. Princeton, NJ: Princeton Book.

Pierce, A. 1985. *SCUBA lifesaving*. Champaign, IL: Leisure Press.

Professional Association of Diving Instructors. 1987. *Rescue diver manual*. Santa Ana, CA: Professional Association of Diving Instructors.

———. 1988a. *Encyclopedia of recreational diving*. Santa Ana, CA: Professional Association of Diving Instructors.

———. 1988b. *Open water diver manual*. Santa Ana, CA: Professional Association of Diving Instructors.

chapter 15

Mountain Biking and Bicycle Touring

Gary L. Wilson

Recreational biking for sightseeing, exercise, and challenge on off-road trails and smooth roadways best describes mountain biking and bicycle touring. Although mountain biking and bicycle touring are different, they have many risks in common, and we must address these so the activity is safe and enjoyable for the participants.

Bicycling is a safe activity, but accidents do occur when supervisory, participant, activity, and environmental factors are not adequately addressed. Attention to these factors is essential to risk management for those planning such activities in camps, recreation departments, and entrepreneurial endeavors. Before any planned bicycling activity occurs, thoroughly research, inspect, and evaluate each factor. Faulty brakes on a bicycle, an unsafe area, or an unprepared cyclist can each lead to problems with safety and risk management. The following discussions and checklists will provide the knowledge and guidance necessary to plan cycling activities that will be safe and enjoyable for all participants.

ENVIRONMENTAL CONDITIONS

The cycling environment and equipment cover many areas, and we must address each area specifically, taking nothing for granted. Keep in mind that there will be some risk in all activities, but reducing the risk to a minimum should be your goal. The following are areas that we cannot take for granted or overlook. To do so would invite serious problems and potential injury to participants. Your goal is to minimize that risk as much as possible.

As in all physical activities, there are risks in mountain biking—your goal is to minimize that risk as much as possible.

The Bicycle

Choose the proper bicycle for the type of riding you will do. Use touring bicycles on hard-surfaced roads designed for automobiles, and use mountain bikes with rugged wheels either on hard or natural surfaces. Using the touring bicycle for riding off road is dangerous and can lead to injury to the rider or damage to the bicycle.

For some organized rides (fund-raisers such as the Lung Association Bike Trek), the rider may be required to bring a previously distributed form completed by a bicycle shop indicating that the bicycle has been checked for safety and is capable of providing safe and reliable transportation throughout the event. Figure 15.1 shows the safety characteristics that you should look for when checking a bicycle. Camps and professional tour organizers should consider bicycle mechanical skills as an essential part of the job descriptions for those leading recreational bicycling events.

Also, make sure that the bicycle is properly sized (a bicycle that is too large or too small can cause personal injury to the rider or an accident); the seat is adjusted correctly for the rider; the tires are in good condition, fit properly, and are inflated appropriately; wheel attachments are tight; pedals are the proper type for the riding you will do; handlebars are the proper height; all gear is properly adjusted and arranged; and reflectors approved by the National Safety Council are in place.

Failure to pay close attention to each item can result in accidents and delays that you can easily prevent before the ride begins. Do a thorough check of the frame, because abuse of a bicycle can cause cracks or weak areas in the frame. Look for obvious cracks at the point where tubes join, and look for cracks in paint or ripples in the tube itself. Bicycle frames can fail. If this occurs at the wrong time, the rider can be seriously injured.

Basic Equipment

Many types of accessories are available and make bicycling safer and more enjoyable.

Some items in the following list should be required, and others can be optional. Base the decision about whether to require their use on safety considerations. Recent developments in saddles, clothing, suspension systems, and accessories all contribute to more comfortable and safer cycling. Encourage your group to take advantage of the latest developments in cycling technology. Figure 15.2 will be helpful in determining equipment needs.

There are many types of accessories; most enhance the cycling experience and others help prevent accidents. Encourage all riders to use the accessories they feel most comfortable with.

Touring Equipment

A sagged tour (in which a truck or automobile carries all heavy gear) takes care of all your equipment and eliminates the need for touring packs and racks. A day tour will eliminate the need to carry large amounts of equipment on the bicycle, but those on a self-contained tour should use the following list in addition to the basic accessories list. Using the equipment listed here in a loaded condition requires practice, and riders should test their skills with loaded bicycles (books can take the place of food, etc.) for several miles and days before the tour to develop the necessary riding skills with heavy loads.

- Helmet
- Gloves
- Riding glasses
- Two pairs of shorts (which prevent saddle sores and help promote comfort)
- Two riding jerseys with large rear pockets for food and small tools
- Small tool kit for basic repairs
- Cages for holding water bottles (carry as much water as possible)
- Large water bottles designed for your cages
- Handlebar bag with map case
- Extra tube and folding tire
- Small first aid kit
- Electronic speedometer for mileage checks

Bicycle Inspection Checklist

Trekker Name _____

Dear bicycle mechanic,

This is a checklist for a trekker participating in a bike tour. We appreciate your willingness to check this bicycle. The trekker is aware that they will be charged for any necessary repairs. Thank you for supporting our trek.

Frame ☐
Fork ☐
Brakes ☐

Check both brake levers to make sure they are tight to the handlebars. Check brake calipers to make sure they are centered.

Cable	Front ☐	Rear ☐
Shoes	Front ☐	Rear ☐
Brake adjusted	Front ☐	Rear ☐

Wheels

Check for proper spoke tension, tire pressure, and tire condition.

Trueness	Front ☐	Rear ☐
Rim condition	Front ☐	Rear ☐

Bearings

Check all bearings for side play.

Hub	Front ☐	Rear ☐
Bottom bracket ☐		
Headset ☐		

Derailleurs

Check derailleurs for lubrication and cable tension. Check controls for proper operation.

Cable	Front ☐	Rear ☐
Derailleur adjustment	Front ☐	Rear ☐

Nuts and Bolts

Check all nuts and bolts.

Crank arms and chain ring bolts ☐

Pedals ☐

Handlebars and stem ☐

Seat and seatpost ☐

Fenders, racks, and water bottle cages ☐

Items needing work have been corrected.

Bike shop stamp _____

Mechanic _____

Date _____

Neither bike shop nor mechanic assumes any responsibility or liability regarding this bicycle.

Figure 15.1 Bicycle inspection checklist.

What Do You Need to Bring on Your Trek?

What do you need to wear? What should you carry with you on your bike? How much can you put on the sag wagon? The three checklists below will give you guidelines to help you decide what to bring.

1.   What to Wear on the Trek

Even though we will probably have excellent weather, we will make recommendations for cooler, wet weather. When a bicyclist is prepared for bad weather, it is always easy to adapt to warmth. Layering your clothes is a good concept. It is then relatively easy to dress comfortably and adjust for your riding rate and changing weather conditions.

_____ *Helmet:* ANSI or SNELL approved. This is required equipment. A headband helps in cooler weather. A rearview mirror is also recommended.

_____ *Riding gloves:* Highly recommended for palm protection. A light polypropylene or wool glove will work well under them in bad weather.

_____ *Protective sunglasses:* 100% UVA and UVB protective.

_____ *Undershirt:* Polypropylene or wool undershirt is ideal. Cotton is okay in warm weather.

_____ *Outershirt:* Wool shirt or sweater if cool and/or windbreaker. Bike jersey is great.

_____ *Pants:* In warm weather, running shorts are okay. Cut-offs are questionable because they have a poor seam design for human seats on bicycle seats. Bicycle shorts are great even if they do look funny. For cool mornings or harsh weather, polypropylene or wool long underwear bottoms work well under shorts. Windpants can also be used. Sweats are fine for cool weather, but not for wet weather. To increase bun comfort some people use a seat cover of wool or similar synthetic material. Also, the Spenco Saddle Cover is receiving rave reviews.

_____ *Socks:* Wool or polypropylene in wet weather. Plastic bags over the socks in wet weather can help.

_____ *Shoes:* Bicycle shoes are ideal. However, stiffer sole running or tennis shoes work just fine. Try to avoid the type of sole that has bumpy or protruding surfaces that might prevent your shoe from slipping easily out of your toeclips. Although not necessary, toe clips and straps are recommended for safety, to help prevent your feet from slipping off the pedals, and efficiency, by improving your pedaling.

_____ *Raingear:* Loose fitting, two-piece waterproof nylon (not just water resistant) or waterproof, breathable fabric such as Helly-Tech or Gore-Tex is probably the best. Ponchos also work. Cheap plastic raingear is easily torn.

_____ *ID and money*

(continued)

Figure 15.2   Checklist for items to bring on your bike tour.

2.   What to Carry on Your Bike

Required items:

_____   Handlebar bag, seat bag or rear pannier

_____   Water bottle – in your bag or fixed with cages on your bike

_____   Tire patch kit and tire irons

_____   Raingear

_____   Trip-Tik (maps & directions)

_____   ID, money

_____   Reflective clothing

_____   Reflectors

Recommended items:

_____   Extra tube for your tire size

_____   Basic tool kit: screwdriver, adjustable wrench, pliers, etc.

_____   Tire pump

_____   Plastic bags for feet in wet weather

_____   Dry socks and shirt

_____   Bike lock

_____   Sunglasses, sun cream

_____   Toe clips and straps or clipless pedals

Optional:

_____   Camera (keep it well protected)

_____   Comfort kit for cruddy weather; 2 garbage bags

3.   What to Put in the Sag Wagon

Here's what you might consider putting into a well-marked bag for the sag wagon to carry. Keep your stuff confined to a bag about the size of an Army duffle bag. Be sure to mark your bags in huge letters for quick identification. It's also a good idea to mark individual pieces of gear and clothing.

Sleeping bag

Insulating ground pad

Duffle or other bag for gear:

_____ About 4 pairs of socks

_____ 2 changes of underwear and T-shirts

_____ Extra set of cycling clothes

_____ Casual clothes

Figure 15.2   *(continued)*

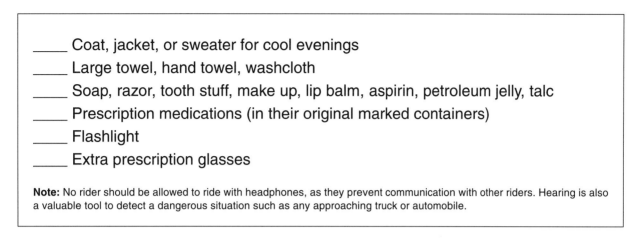

_____ Coat, jacket, or sweater for cool evenings

_____ Large towel, hand towel, washcloth

_____ Soap, razor, tooth stuff, make up, lip balm, aspirin, petroleum jelly, talc

_____ Prescription medications (in their original marked containers)

_____ Flashlight

_____ Extra prescription glasses

Note: No rider should be allowed to ride with headphones, as they prevent communication with other riders. Hearing is also a valuable tool to detect a dangerous situation such as any approaching truck or automobile.

Figure 15.2   *(continued)*

- Lightweight windbreakers or rain jacket for sudden showers and cool breezes
- High-pressure frame pump for inflating tires (try it before you buy it)
- Chain lubricant (try new lubricants beforehand)
- Pepper spray for aggressive dogs
- Small bell or horn for communication (many states require this)
- Racks designed for the front and rear for carrying camping equipment, cooking gear, and clothing
- Proper packs for these racks (sometimes called panniers) to carry the weight low on the bicycle to promote stability

Discourage riders from carrying any pack such as a hiking backpack or a day pack. The raised center of gravity, added weight to the shoulders, and the heat generated under the pack all contribute to fatigue, poor balance, and the increased chance for accidents. An example of an equipment checklist is on pages 237-239.

Mountain Biking Equipment

Mountain biking requires equipment and skills unique to the sport. Much equipment is similar to that used for touring, except for shoes and water-carrying systems. It is important to check the bicycle thoroughly so it is ready for the harsh treatment that occurs on trails. A list

of necessary mountain biking equipment follows:

- Helmet
- Riding glasses to block sun, tree limbs, and dust
- Gloves
- Proper shoes
- Riding shorts
- Riding jersey with large rear pockets
- Small tool pack
- Patch kit for tube repairs
- Extra tube and folding tire
- High-quality frame pump or inflation system
- Camelback water-carrying system (water bottles are difficult to use on rough trails)
- Small first aid kit
- Accurate trail map
- Chain lubricant (try the new lubricant ahead of time for best results)

Route Selection

Safe roadways for touring are difficult to find, so allow adequate time to do the necessary research. Keep a road description log so you can make route evaluations after you have researched the route. In the road description, make mile-by-mile log notations concerning the road surface, traffic flow,

© Cheyenne Rouse

When cycling, keep your pack on the cycle. The added weight of a backpack leads to earlier fatigue.

width of roadway, difficulty, and rest stops. An electronic bicycle cyclometer is necessary for this research in mountain biking, but you can use an automobile for touring or recreational road riding research.

Roadway Evaluation for Touring

In selecting roadways for touring, note the following factors.

- Traffic flow—some areas have high flow rates, which make touring dangerous.

- Adequate lane width for sharing the road with automobiles—automobiles should not have to move into oncoming traffic lanes when passing.

- Surface quality to prevent accidents and damage to wheels

- Terrain difficulty—the terrain should match the skill of the group.

- Clearance with local authorities—local police can often give safe alternatives and help with group management.

A check with local bicycle shops or clubs can save you time and give you valuable information about the local conditions. Often local riders will help you conduct the necessary research. Keep in mind that even though you do your job, automobile drivers are often at fault because they may fail to yield the right-of-way, either from poorly judging the biker's speed or simply because they do not understand that bicycles have a right to share the road. These automobile and bicycle accidents account for a small percent of the total bicycling incidents. Studies show that only about 12 percent of cycling accidents involve the automobile, and most of these occur when the cyclist is doing something unusual, such as riding on the left side of the road, failing to yield to crossing traffic, failing to yield when changing lanes, and sidewalk riding. The most common automobile and bicycle accidents involve the turning and crossing of one of the vehicles. With this information in hand, it becomes critical that all cyclists participating in an activity know the rules of the road and understand how to ride properly and safely.

Mountain Biking Area Evaluation

Mountain biking in natural settings creates a different set of risks and problems. Although automobiles and trucks are not problems as they are on highways, you now have to deal with terrain and the skills of your group. Another issue that you must address is sharing trails with hikers, horses, and motorized cycles. Trail sharing is a serious issue in many parts of the United States, and you must determine the status of bicycles on trails in the area you plan to use.

When selecting areas for use in mountain biking activities, note the following:

- Evaluate roadways if you will use them.

- Get approval from owners or managers of the area.

- Consult a trail-building guide for minimum environmental impact.

- Evaluate all portions of the route to be sure you can ride all parts. (Mark dangerous areas with flagging and arrows so riders will have time to dismount and walk if necessary.)

- Place flags and signs on the course to prevent riders from getting lost or off course.

You can find good trails for mountain biking in most national forests, but trails in national parks are off-limits for bicycles unless noted. The primary concern for trail choice should be safety and minimal environmental impact. The U.S. Forestry Service can help you locate trails, and consulting with the headquarters in the appropriate district can save time and energy in finding good trails for your group.

Most accidents in mountain biking involve falls rather than collisions with other vehicles. Most frequently these falls are caused either by attempting trails that are too difficult or by rider fatigue. Fatigue is a serious problem because the total body must be conditioned, and when the arms and hands are fatigued from braking and steering on rough terrain, the chances of an accident will increase. These falls are usually at low speed, but serious injuries can occur because the falls do not happen on smooth surfaces like a highway. Rocks, roots, and trees can do serious damage, and a ride leader must always be alert for a difficult area or rider fatigue. Few, if any, mountain bike riders can say they have never fallen, unless they have never ridden difficult trails. Ride leaders should be well prepared in first aid, because the chances are that they will use these skills often.

Weather

Weather can change while a ride is in progress, and the ride leader must make proper decisions to ensure the safety of all participants. Rain can make roadways and trails dangerous, and the ride leader should cancel or delay a ride until safe conditions exist. Floods can be a problem on some mountain biking courses. Groups should stay on high ground until the danger has passed. Lightning is a real danger during a biking event because of the metal used in bicycle construction. In a wilderness situation, riders should leave the bicycles in a safe place and proceed to a dense forest, safely away from tall trees, clumps of trees standing alone, rock outcroppings, ridges, and lakes. Locate shelter such as a large building or house during storms if possible. Stay away from trees, poles, and wires along the highway. Each year needless injuries occur because of dangerous weather conditions. Ride leaders must make quick decisions to protect their group from danger. Ride leaders should consider using cellular telephones for communication.

Although planning for any recreational event is time consuming, proper planning ensures that the event will be a success. To be sure of proper planning, establish a time line and place every task on it. The time line should include the task, contact persons, date, and the person responsible for doing the job. With a proper time line and a thorough inventory of jobs to accomplish, you can complete everything on time.

When you plan a cycling event, you are introducing participants to one of the healthiest forms of recreation known. The joy of pedaling up a mountain, crossing a stream, riding a quiet trail, or riding 100 miles a day is something participants will remember forever. Good planning will ensure that cycling activities will be safe and enjoyable for all participants.

SUPERVISION

Supervising cycling events begins with establishing procedures and rules regarding participant actions, so the event is fun yet safe. These rules should include the following.

Participant Control

The leader must make several important decisions determining the nature of a proposed cycling event. Among them are the following:
- Who can participate?
- What skills are necessary for participation?
- What type of activity can individuals participate in? There are many types of recreational cycling.
- Where can the activity take place?
- What type of rider behavior will you allow during the event?

For mountain biking, before taking riders onto trails, it is important that they practice riding techniques on easy to moderately difficult terrain. Participants should practice braking and cornering, climbing, and descending skills before taking to the woods. Even with much practice, it is important that the leader match the rider with the degree of trail difficulty and caution those riders who are not ready to try difficult areas. Encourage them to dismount and walk the difficult areas until they are ready to ride them. The leader should stress using the rear brake and using the front brake only slightly to avoid locking up the front wheel and falling. All riders should practice skills of lowering the body and moving the center of gravity back during descents and forward during climbs until they have mastered these skills.

Leader Responsibilities

Leaders in the field of recreational bicycling must have superior skills in many areas (see table 15.1). Training a cycling leader involves knowledge in many areas. With practice and time a person motivated to be a leader can become effective in conducting events that are as risk free as possible. We recommend that a potential leader use an internship with

---

Table 15.1

SKILLS REQUIRED FOR RECREATIONAL BICYCLING LEADERS

☐ Wilderness first aid, standard first aid, and CPR

☐ Knowledge of the rules of the road and the ability to communicate these rules to the group. We recommend thoroughly studying *Effective Cycling* by Forester (1994).

☐ Basic bicycle repair

☐ Fitness and health levels

☐ Cycling techniques

☐ Group communication skills

---

an experienced leader before leading a ride. A rider preparing to serve as a leader should also get involved with a local cycling club to learn about riding techniques and management.

Supervision during the event is a major part of risk management. Previous planning, bicycle inspections, and so on will mean little if event supervision is inadequate. Some things to consider when planning for supervising participants include grouping riders according to abilities and interests (groups of 10 riders or more should have 2 leaders), always having a leader in the front and end of each group, having each leader wear bright clothing to aid visibility, and making sure that there is constant surveillance to prevent problems.

SELECTION AND CONDUCT OF THE ACTIVITY

Most bicycle accidents occur because of mistakes the rider makes. Failing to yield to another vehicle, the inability to maintain balance, or attempting something that is too demanding can lead to accidents that riders can prevent through proper preparation. You can ascertain these factors using a pre-event questionnaire. We present an example of a pre-event questionnaire in figure 15.3. After the event begins, ride leaders should be constantly aware of potential problems so they can detect any difficulties before an accident occurs.

Human factors to address include the following:

- Age—encourage children to participate with adults.
- Rider experience—carefully note information on the rider survey so you don't place riders in dangerous situations.
- Rider skill—even though the rider has completed a questionnaire, the leader must observe ability in cycling.
- Rider fitness—you can determine fitness from the questionnaire, but always supervise closely in case the questionnaire was inaccurate.
- Rider health—require a recent physical.
- Rider knowledge—riders should understand the basic rules of the road before the event begins.

You can view some excellent videos, such as *Effective Cycling* available from Seidler Productions, or distribute pamphlets before the event that demonstrate the rules of the road for cyclists.

ADMINISTRATION

In recreational activities, planning must always include what to do in case of an emergency. Develop an emergency action plan before the event takes place so each person will know their task if an emergency occurs. The area in which the group is cycling will determine the type of action plan to use.

Rider Experience Resume

So that we can better plan your cycling experience with us, please complete the following resume as accurately as possible.

1. Name _____ Date _____

2. Age _____

3. Height _____

4. Weight _____

5. Sex _____

Please circle the appropriate answer for the last three months.

6. Approximate number of times per week you ride: 1 2 3 4 5 6 7

7. Your longest ride in miles during your weekly rides:
    1-10   11-20   21-30   31-up

8. Number of years you have been cycling: 1-5   6-10   11-15   16-up

9. Describe the terrain for your longest ride:
    flat   rolling   steep

10. Length of your longest ride in one day:
    1-10   11-20   21-30   31-40   41-up

11. Describe the trails you have ridden with a mountain bike:
    flat   rolling   steep   single track   double track   N/A

12. Describe the type of bicycle you have in terms of gears, type, model, and brand:

    _____

13. List cycling equipment you own such as helmet, panniers, etc:

    _____

14. Describe your idea of an ideal one-week biking holiday:

    _____

Figure 15.3   Rider experience resume.

Cycling in remote areas creates problems during emergencies that even the best planning and leadership will find challenging. Accident management in cycling events includes the following:

- Care of the injured
- Traffic control if necessary
- Group control
- Contact with rescue services
- Evacuating the injured
- Group leadership

The ride leader should carry pertinent information on each participant. A brief medical history noting drug allergies and anything else unusual should be part of this information, as well as emergency contact numbers, health and accident policy information, and release for treatment forms.

We should emphasize that planning must occur before you organize and conduct an event. Contact local authorities, rescue units, and volunteer services well ahead of the event so there is clear communication about how an emergency will be handled.

BIBLIOGRAPHY

Bull, A. 1992. *Learn mountain biking in a weekend*. New York: Knopf.

Chauner, E., and D. Coello. 1992. *Mountain bike techniques*. New York: Lyons and Burford

Effective cycling. 1994. Crawfordville, FL: Seidler Productions. Video.

Forester, J. 1994. *Effective cycling*. Cambridge, MA: MIT Press.

Henry, S., ed. 1994. *Bicycling magazine's complete guide to bicycle maintenance and repair*. Emmaus, PA: Rodale Press.

Matheny, F. 1989. *Bicycling magazine's complete guide to riding and racing techniques*. Emmaus, PA: Rodale Press.

Sloane, E. 1988. *The complete book of bicycling*. New York: Simon & Schuster.

van der Plas, R. 1993. *The bicycle touring manual*. San Francisco: Bicycle Books.

Fishing

Bruce E. Matthews

Most people envision fishing as a pretty innocuous activity. The thought of being in harm's way while fishing seems ludicrous. However, the fact is any fishing activity has the potential to snag the unwary or unsafe participant. Tiptoeing through the white water trying to cast to that little pocket just beyond reach; making just one last cast with that thunderstorm approaching; dealing with surf, waves, ice, freezing wind—anglers do get exposed to some marginal environmental conditions, not to mention problems with hooks, knives, and handling fish. This is not to suggest that fishing ranks up there with bungee jumping and shark wrestling in terms of a pure adrenaline rush, but plenty of hazards do exist for anglers.

To prevent accidents and injuries while fishing, as with other activities, the two essential ingredients are knowledge and good judgment. By understanding the hazards and how to avoid them, and practicing the appropriate skills, anglers can usually avoid exposure. By exercising good judgment, anglers can sidestep injury when they cannot avoid exposure.

This chapter will focus on identifying and reducing or eliminating hazards and exposures to those situations that may result in accident or injury while fishing. However, fishing often involves exposure to additional hazards less directly related to the activity, such as interactions with wildlife, boating hazards, weather, insects, and so on, and readers can find other chapters in this book that more specifically address them.

ENVIRONMENTAL CONDITIONS

Areas conducive to fishing are often breathtaking, but this does not necessarily make them safe. Making sure that a fishing trip doesn't turn sour is therefore important.

Site Selection

When choosing a site for fishing, consider safety factors along with the more obvious ones like the probability of catching a fish! Because fishing is practiced in a variety of environments, evaluate factors specific to safety in each environment.

Shorelines

Shoreline hazards may include the following:
- Quick drop-offs into deep water
- Slick rocks, muddy banks, and slippery stream and lake bottoms
- Litter, garbage, and junk that might cut, entangle, or otherwise harm participants

To minimize shoreline hazards, scout areas where you will be fishing. Identify hazardous areas, and post signs, rope off, or otherwise prevent access. Establish and stick to water safety rules designed to keep participants away from hazards. Where you must fish near hazards, establish and instruct participants in safety procedures, including using the buddy system and rescue techniques. Assure that proper supervision and rescue equipment are available, including reach poles, ring buoys, and throw lines. Pick up or eliminate the broken glass, discarded line, and other materials that might harm participants. Instruct participants about the hazards of the weather or tide changes. Know the tide tables from the area, and listen to National Weather Radio forecasts frequently.

Piers, Breakwalls, and Docks

Hazards typically found at piers, breakwalls, or docks may include the following:
- Slippery conditions, particularly due to ice, algae, or slime
- Rogue waves washing over
- Changes in the tide
- Heavy winds
- Uneven terrain, litter, or discarded line
- Absence of life-saving equipment
- Absence of ladders or other means of getting out of the water if someone falls in
- Absence of handrails, ropes, or wheelchair stops

Obviously many recommendations for shoreline fishing safety apply here as well. In addition to these, consider locating ladders or other places where participants can get out of

© Cheyenne Rouse

When choosing a site for fishing, consider more than just the probability of catching a fish—think about safety, too.

the water if they fall in. Also, carry long-handled nets or other fish-landing gear appropriate to the location. Discuss how to land fish safely from the pier, and stick to this procedure.

Wear footgear appropriate to the conditions. This may include felt soles, or caulks (golf spikes or Corkers) to minimize slippery conditions. If possible, establish handrails or ropes and wheelchair stops. In any case, know the limitations of angler groups, and match them to appropriate locations.

Streams (Wading)

When wading in streams, hazards may include the following:

- Fast currents
- Unexpectedly deep water
- Slippery rocks
- Deep holes
- Water levels rising unexpectedly (dam releases)
- Cold water

In addition to these recommendations, guidelines for minimizing stream wading hazards include instructing participants to recognize if a stream's current is safe for wading. Use a buddy system with two anglers wading together if necessary. Use a wading staff and shoes with caulks, felts, or other nonslip surfaces. When wearing waders, use suspenders *and* a wader belt, and wear a PFD. Exercise every caution and use good judgment when wading in cold water. Instruct participants on white-water safety.

If the current sweeps participants off their footing, instruct them to roll onto the back and swim feet first, using a backward sculling motion with hands until reaching calmer water. They should *not* try to put their feet down again until the water is shallow or calm. Wear polarized glasses to better see bottom hazards. Pay attention to water levels if dam-controlled waters are likely to rise unexpectedly. Find out the dam release schedule. Put a stake at the water's edge and mark the water level on it. Watch it carefully for changes, and listen for a signal indicating a release has begun.

Surf

Surf fishing, whether from an ocean beach or large inland lake, has its unique hazards. These include the following:

- Undertows, swift tides, and currents
- Large waves
- Slippery conditions
- Holes
- Sharks, jellyfish, skates
- Sharp coral, rocks, or broken glass

In addition to these recommendations for minimizing hazards, make sure to use care in high-wave conditions. Avoid areas and weather conditions where rogue waves are known to occur. Instruct participants in how to identify dangerous tidal currents, such as rips, undertows, and so on. Find out where the dangerous current areas are and stay away from them. Use the buddy system.

Wear wader belt and suspenders. Instruct participants that if caught in a rip or undertow, swim with the current and angle back to the shore. Know the tide tables, and use a watch to keep track of the time so you know when to start back into shallower water. Learn about sharks, skates, jellyfish, and other potentially harmful marine organisms. Do not enter the surf to fish where they are frequent. Do not wade barefoot or in shorts. In areas frequented by skates and rays, do the *stingray shuffle*, sliding feet along the bottom rather than picking them up and putting them down.

On the Water

Many people fish in boats on the water. Hazards may include the following:

- Weather
- Wave conditions (high or steep waves)
- Underwater obstructions, shoals, bars, and so on
- Deep water
- Inaccessibility if rescue needed
- Turbulence from tides (ocean), steep gradients (white water), or power plant outflows
- Currents

Small craft safety is a separate topic that we covered in chapter 10. Some additional recommendations are to arrange for participants to take a boating course from the Power Squadron or Coast Guard Auxiliary (contact 800-336-BOAT for course information in your area). Check for proper safety equipment, such as ring buoy, PFDs, signals, lights, radio, fire extinguishers, capacity plate, and so on. Don't go out if unsure of the safety conditions with the boat, boat operator, the weather, or water conditions. Go out with a U.S. Coast Guard-licensed captain on a vessel inspected by the appropriate authorities. Wear a PFD.

On the Ice

With the popularity of ice fishing in northern climes, consider hazards on the ice. These may include the following:

- Thin ice
- Weak spots and pressure ridges
- Cold weather and hypothermia
- Whiteouts and getting lost
- Ice floes breaking off and drifting out with anglers on them

Recommendations for minimizing ice fishing hazards include finding out where the dangerous areas are and staying away from them. Most ice anglers mark hazardous areas with evergreen or other branches. Use particular care in areas where the ice abuts open water. An offshore wind can break off ice floes and blow them out with anglers on them. Avoid areas where current enters the lake or springs bubble up from the bottom. Avoid pressure ridges.

Three inches of solid black ice is a minimum for one or two anglers on foot. Check ice depth frequently. Carry a rope, ice creepers, and ice grippers (one-inch-by-six-inch doweling into which you have set a thick nail, screw, or bevel-edged metal bar, sharp end protruding). If another angler goes through, lie spread-eagle on the ice, as far away as possible, while reaching a line, pole, sled, or other item to the dunked angler. Pull him or her out and roll to safe ice. Instruct participants that if they go through, they should catch themselves by leaning forward or backward to prevent complete submersion. Kick legs so they come to the surface, and attempt to swim onto the ice, rolling to-

ward safe ice. The ice grippers are literally lifesavers in this situation as they enable the stricken angler to pull him or herself out in a hand-over-hand manner.

Watch the weather, and pull fishing lines at the first sign of trouble. Carry a transistor National Weather Service radio, and check the forecast frequently. Also, carry a windbreak or tent and a compass. Take a bearing on destination while heading out onto the ice. Follow it. *Write it down.* Upon arrival, immediately take a bearing back to your starting point. *Write that down.* If your starting point is not visible, subtract 180 (if original bearing was 180 or more) or add 180 (if original was less than 180) to get your return heading. *Believe your compass.* If caught in a whiteout with no compass, stay put. Instruct participants on proper dressing techniques for the winter outdoors.

Weather

Weather is always a factor on a fishing outing. Anglers should be aware of the weather, if for no other reason than to blame it for no fish! Weather hazards faced by anglers include the following:

- Lightning storms
- Sudden changes, including wind shifts, microbursts, tornadoes, and similar phenomenon
- Hypothermia
- Heatstroke or heat exhaustion

To avoid weather hazards, set up a weather committee composed of individuals interested in learning more about the weather, or rotate weather forecasting responsibilities. Establish a weather officer position. Use the need to know more about the weather to provide incentives for participants to learn how to forecast.

Instruct participants on how to read the weather and recognize the signals for approaching hazardous conditions. Develop a safety policy for getting caught out in bad weather. In lightning storms, get off the water at the first hint of thunder or lightning, and stay away from tall trees or structures. Lay fishing rods, radio antennae, and other high objects down. Avoid being or standing near a taller target. Instruct participants in avoiding hypothermia, heatstroke, and heat exhaustion. Cover the symptoms and first aid procedures for all. Carry a National Weather Service radio and listen to the forecasts frequently.

Staying dry, warm, and protected from the elements is a prerequisite for fishing fun. Anglers should be remembering more than how cold they got or the wicked sunburn they acquired! Here are some factors to consider and a discussion guide for dressing properly for the weather.

Dealing With the Cold

To help people understand proper dressing for the cold, start with how a body loses heat. When a body loses heat faster than it can replace it, two things can result. Frostbite occurs if skin layers begin to freeze. Hypothermia, or the lowering of the body core temperature, occurs when the metabolism can no longer burn calories fast enough to keep vital organs at 98.6 degrees F. (First aid manuals and cold-weather survival publications describe these, as well as appropriate first aid, in great detail. The Adirondack Mountain Club, Box 867, Lake Placid, NY 12946, 518-523-3441 also has several good resources.) Either condition can be serious, and fatal, if left untreated. Human bodies lose heat in four ways (see table 16.1). To conserve body heat, understand and prevent each of these ways (see chapters 5 and 6 for more information).

Dealing With the Heat and Sun

A body deals with the heat by sweating. Wearing light, cotton clothing in hot and humid conditions may be an excellent strategy, because cotton's slow-drying, high water-absorption properties help keep you cool. However, in marginal situations, even with the temperature in the 60s, a cotton strategy can contribute to the onset of hypothermia. A better choice for hot conditions would be light, quick-drying clothing made of materials such as supplex, nylon, or polyester. These materials allow air to pass through to cool the skin, but dry quickly, thereby minimizing unwanted heat loss as conditions change.

Of course, sun protection is essential. We recommend long-sleeved shirts and long pants. Hats with wide brims and long bills are important. Sunglasses should be standard equipment. Sunscreen with a high ultraviolet protection rating is critical.

The Layer System

Today's outdoorsperson has many choices for outdoor wear. Although the type of clothing and material may vary, the smart angler chooses the layer system to dress for the weather and the activity. The layer system calls for a series of thin layers of clothing, starting with long underwear, and progressing outward to include water and wind protection as the fourth or fifth layer.

The layer system has the dual advantage of allowing for a wide array of activities, from strenuous to passive, and making maximum use of the excellent insulating properties of the dead air trapped between garments. If the angler heats up while hiking in, he or she can remove an outer layer, or ventilate through removing hat, gloves, or opening shirts at the sleeves and collar. If he or she gets cold, the strategy calls for putting on a hat, buttoning up, or adding another layer to match the condition.

Frequently in winter, folks will bundle up in heavy, one-piece snowsuits. These may be fine for sitting on snow machines, but they offer few alternatives for the angler who breaks a sweat while hiking a mile out onto the ice dragging a heavy sled, drilling a few ice holes, then sitting in the wind waiting for a bite, wondering why he or she is chilling down so fast.

Insects and Wildlife

Though a secondary consideration for most anglers, be aware of critters that sting, bite, or otherwise pose difficulties, particularly when the possibility exists of anaphylactic shock. Insect and wildlife hazards faced by anglers may include the following:

- Biting insects such as mosquitoes, blackflies, no-see-ums, punkies, and so on

- Ticks, especially deer ticks, which carry Lyme disease

Table 16.1
THE FOUR WAYS TO LOSE BODY HEAT

METHOD OF HEAT LOSS	EXPLANATION
Conduction	When a warmer body contacts a colder object such as a boat seat, rod handle, rock, water, and so on, heat will pass from that body to the object. To counter conduction, use insulation.
Convection	Often viewed in terms of windchill, convection occurs when moving air passes over exposed skin, blowing body heat away faster than it would normally be lost. To counter convection, use wind protection.
Radiation	Warm air likes to heat cooler air. Heat producers, such as the sun or a fire, warm air through radiation. In the same way a human body, as a heat producer, warms the air around it. The thin layer of warm air around a body, if unprotected, will move away from the skin to heat the cooler air. To prevent radiation, cover up and insulate. The outdoorsperson's adage, "If your feet are cold, put on a hat," is an example of an effective strategy. An uncovered head is heating the atmosphere. The body is ignoring your feet because it figures the brain is more important.
Evaporation*	Wet skin loses heat faster than dry skin, because water conducts heat better than air. This is why it is so important to stay dry in cold weather. Avoid sweating if possible, and protect yourself from rain and melting snow. Wear clothing made of fabric such as wool or polypropylene that resists wetting and retains some insulating value even when wet.

*Note: With another form of evaporation, *respiration*, the body breathes in cool air and breathes out warm, moist air. This likewise causes heat loss. You can't stop breathing, but in some cases it may help to cover the mouth and nose to preheat incoming air and minimize heat loss.

- Stinging insects such as wasps and bees
- Venomous insects and reptiles
- Rabid animals
- Poison ivy and oak
- Stinging nettles

To minimize hazards from insects and wildlife, use appropriate insect protection measures, including dressing properly and using repellents. Certain insects are likely to be a problem in particular regions at specific times of the year and day. For example, to avoid blackflies, don't go to the Adirondacks in late May. Find out when and where the bugs are at their worst and avoid them. Certain weather conditions make bug problems more likely. Hot, still, overcast, and humid days are going to be buggier than cool, windy, sunny, and bright days. Evenings and mornings are buggier times than midday.

In tick areas, stay in the center of paths, and avoid brushy areas. Do frequent tick checks. Dress to cover exposed skin and to foil a tick or blackfly attempting to access your skin. Tuck pants into socks or boots. Put a rubber band around pant legs and sleeves. Wear a hat and use a head net. Stay away from blue clothing, as insects seem attracted to it. Light-colored clothing is preferred by some people.

Avoid using colognes, perfumes, or other strong-smelling stuff. You might love the way Fruit Bowl shampoo makes your hair smell, but so will the bugs. Use repellents. Those containing DEET are popular and effective against all insects, including ticks. However, there are some serious questions about DEET's effects on human health, particularly with youngsters. The most concentrated formula we recommend using is 35 percent DEET, and even then you should use it sparingly, making special efforts to avoid contact with the eyes and mouth, or breathing it. DEET also does a wonderful job eating anything plastic, so keep it away from fly lines, tackle boxes, raincoats, and so on. A good strategy is to spread it on with the *back* of your hand. Other repellents contain oil of citronella, which is effective for many. Oil of pennyroyal is another alternative, as is Avon Skin So Soft lotion. Some swear by the effectiveness of swallowing lots of vitamin B or E a few days before the outing or a steady diet of *lots* of garlic.

Be sure any participant allergic to insect bites or stings carries an ANA kit with them, and be sure all instructors know how to use it. Medical permission forms should ask about insect allergies. Avoid areas where you know venomous insects, reptiles, rabid animals, and problem plants are common. Instruct participants on how to recognize and avoid them. Reactions to insect bites or stings range from mild itching to severe allergic reaction, even death. Review first aid procedures for insect situations every time an outing goes to an area where you find bugs. Be sure all leaders understand first aid procedures.

SUPERVISION

As with most outdoor recreation activities, the amount of supervision and level of credentialing required for fishing depends on the age and skill level of the participants, and the degree of risk in the environment where

Particular care is needed when fly fishing from a boat to avoid hooking your partner or yourself.

you are fishing. As a rule, the instructor-to-student ratio for fishing instructors actually fishing (not casting or doing dryland activities) with novice youngsters up to age 8 is 1:4. This is less for safety reasons than to ensure participants' success. As the developmental level and experience increase, the ratio can increase as well, but probably should never exceed 1:8.

Fishing instructors currently have no national credentialing body such as the American Red Cross. Many states offer aquatic education programs that train and certify fishing instructors. Most programs are based out of the state natural resource management agency (conservation department, fish and game department, department of natural resources, etc.). Also, in some states the 4-H Youth Development program trains and certifies fishing instructors. Contact the state land grant university, where each state's 4-H administration is located, for information. In several states there is a licensed outdoor guide program, which may require a certain level of competency in outdoor skills including fishing. The National Outdoor Leadership School (NOLS) certifies outdoor leaders, some of whom have had fishing as part of their training experience. Aside from these, we strongly recommend current certification in first aid and basic water safety from the American Red Cross.

SELECTION AND CONDUCT OF THE ACTIVITY

In general, the best course is to follow appropriate water safety guidelines while fishing. Using a buddy system, assuring appropriate supervision, making sure of current lifesaving and first aid certification, assuring that adequate lifesaving gear is available and in good condition, knowing the swimming ability of participants and proceeding accordingly, and establishing and enforcing behavioral ground rules regarding safety are all essential elements in conducting a safe fishing program.

Casting Safety

Casting with fishing rods, whether cane poles, spin casting, bait casting, spinning, or fly

USING PFDS WHEN FISHING

Insofar as personal flotation devices (life vests) are concerned, we *strongly* urge their required use by all participants whenever they are in or near moving water or water that is more than 12 inches deep. In some states regulations require that all children 12 and younger wear a PFD while in a boat. PFDs should be required. Instructors should always be setting the example by wearing their own.

rodding, involves a significant risk from flying hooks and weights. To avoid hooking others or yourself, or having your casts wind up in unwanted locations, follow these guidelines:

- Always look behind before every cast.
- Use dummy plugs when practicing. Save the hooks for actual fishing.
- Use short casts until you develop the ability to make longer ones.
- Watch the wind, especially while fly casting. Try to position so the wind is less likely to pile up back casts around caster's head.
- Don't fish or cast around power lines. If lure gets tangled in one, cut it off and leave it.
- Wear hats, sun or safety glasses, and long-sleeved shirts for protection from flying hooks.
- Instruct participants in safe practices when a lure gets caught in the rocks or trees.

Safety Around Hooks

Although hooks are generally necessary when fishing, minimize their use until you need them to catch fish. Use dummy plugs for casting practice and eye bolts for knot tying. Use single barbless hooks whenever possible. Whether barbless hooks are more efficient or humane for fish is an open question. What is not debatable is the difference between barbed and barbless hooks stuck in humans. Barbless hooks come right out as they went in. Barbed hooks sunk past the barb mean a trip to the hospital.

In wilderness settings with no medical help available, if an angler is impaled with a barbed hook anywhere except near the eye, you can remove the hook in two ways. The first is to continue to push the hook all the way through the flesh so the point and barb emerge. Using a pair of wire cutters, clip off the point and barb and back the hook through. Use lots of disinfectant, and don't let anyone else watch. This method is not for those with weak stomachs!

The other method is more controversial. It involves looping a heavy line around the hook bend, depressing the shank near the hook eye, and pulling the line backward to guide the barb back through the same wound channel it entered. This method is best practiced on an orange before attempting it on humans. Please note that once the barb is into the skin, we recommend no method of removal except by a doctor.

Barbless hooks are now available from many sporting goods outlets and catalog companies. However, if you cannot locate barbless hooks you can suitably modify a hook with a barb using a good pair of needlenose pliers. Simply press the barb all the way back down to the hook wire. If the hook is too large, a small file will suffice to take down the barb. We provide additional hook safety recommendations in table 16.2.

Safety Around Fishing Knives

Knife safety is another important consideration. Knives have a certain mystique for many youngsters, and their possession is sometimes viewed as a mark of maturity. Because of this, knives offer fishing instructors a unique opportunity to have motivated youngsters learn and demonstrate responsibility. Knife carrying should be a privilege, earned by demonstrating competence and responsibility. Consider using a *totin' chip* policy as is often used in scouting. After safety instruction, issue the scouts their totin' chip, or license to carry a knife. If observed doing anything unsafe, a corner is cut off the chip. If the scouts lose four

corners, they can no longer carry or use a knife for a period of time.

Generally, tools other than knives work best for most fishing situations. Wire or nail clippers can cut most fishing lines more safely than knives. The most likely use for a knife is in cleaning fish. Keep knives sharp, and cover the blade when not in use. Fixed-blade or lock-blade knives are far safer than other types of knives. Keep knives out only when in legitimate use, and never leave them lying around.

Handling Fish

Fish handling is an important safety consideration. Certain species of fish can impart painful injuries, and you should handle them all carefully to minimize the danger of the hook getting entangled with the angler. When teaching someone to handle fish, use dead fish to model proper technique. Keep a few in a freezer, and thaw them out for the demonstration.

Teach each angler how to identify hazardous areas, such as teeth, gill covers, sharp fins, and spines. Most fish species have teeth, though not all are hazardous. Some species, such as the members of the pike family, bluefish, and barracuda, sport dental equipment that is obvious even to the novice. Others, such as walleye and salmon, are not so obvious. It is an excellent idea not to practice lip-landing (a practice you often see with bass anglers on TV shows in which the angler grips the bass's lower jaw between thumb and forefinger and lifts it from the water) until you know the youngsters can differentiate between black bass and all other species.

Other fish have stiff spines. The members of the catfish family possess spines capable of causing painful puncture wounds. These spines are located on their dorsal and pectoral fins and can cause an allergic reaction in some. Many fish have sharp rays on their dorsal fins, and others have sharp gill covers. Perch and walleye are among the prime offenders in this category. Understanding these safety factors can sometimes motivate youngsters in developing their fish identification skills.

Other considerations include quickly killing and preserving the flesh of the fish you wish

Table 16.2
HOOK SAFETY RECOMMENDATIONS

- ☐ Establish and enforce firm rules for behavior around hooks. Horseplay around hooks should have serious consequences.
- ☐ Use safety glasses at all times when casting.
- ☐ Discourage any action that could result in hooks being tossed (for example, untangling lures).
- ☐ Develop incentives for not leaving hooks laying around.
- ☐ Remove hooks from rods except when fishing.
- ☐ Wear hats and long-sleeved clothing when casting.
- ☐ Demonstrate hook-sharpening techniques. Sharp hooks are safer than dull ones.
- ☐ Demonstrate and practice fish handling in a safe manner to avoid getting hooked while unhooking a fish.

to eat. Demonstrate proper killing techniques. Discuss catch and release techniques from both a biological and ecological and an ethical standpoint. Demonstrate the most humane practices for assuring optimal chances of survival by the released fish.

ADMINISTRATION

As with any outdoor recreation activity, administering it involves appropriate record keeping. Activity plans, participants attending, leaders assisting, dates, times, and notable occurrences should all be part of a standard log for the activity. Of course, if the fishing instructor wants to keep a record of fish caught, successful lures, and, best of all, fishing hot spots, the activity supervisor can't be blamed for wanting to see the log regularly!

BIBLIOGRAPHY

Matthews, B.E. 1993. *NY sportfishing and aquatic resources education program leaders manual*. Ithaca, NY: Cornell University, Department of Natural Resources.

National 4-H Council. 1997. *National 4-H sport fishing project curriculum*. Washington, DC: National 4-H Council.

Schmidt, Bob. 1989. *Sportfishing and aquatic resources handbook*. Washington, DC: Future Fisherman Foundation.

Hunting and Shooting

Dwaine Marten

Every good hunter is uneasy in the depths of his conscience when faced with the death he is about to inflict.

Jose Ortega y Gasset, *Meditations on Hunting*

Hunting and shooting are as old as humans. As recently as 10,000 years ago, humans lived exclusively by hunting and gathering. Primitive hunters, as archeological and ethnological evidence overwhelmingly indicates, regarded game animals as fully equal players in life's drama. Hunting was more than an economic activity and more than sport; it was a religious sacrament, a holy occupation. The game animals hunted were not just respected, they were revered. The best hunters knew that they succeeded not only because of their skill, but also because of the game animal's willingness to give itself. This happened because the hunter venerated the animal and had a special relationship with it, which he carefully cultivated (Callicott 1981). In many cultures, the hunters gave thanks to the great spirit and the spirit of the animal they were about to consume, commenting on how good the meat tasted. We can argue that hunting is a part of our culture, handed down from generation to generation. As in past civilizations, some groups choose to domesticate animals and become planters, some continue to hunt, and others choose some combination. If today we hunt because our ancestors hunted, it is fair and appropriate that we emulate the spirit in which they hunted. That spirit was not egotistic and competitive. Above all, it was a state of mind that deeply appreciated the interdependency of humans and their animal relatives—bound together not only by external economic relations but also in spiritual communion.

Therefore, the sport of hunting, like all other sports, must have a philosophical, ethical, and spiritual base. For the sport to be respected, it must abide by its inherent values, beliefs, and rules. Those who participate must respect the environmental and ecological consequences of hunting on the biotic community. The hunter must also respect the rights of other citizens to use the same resource areas safely.

For you to become a safe, responsible participant in the sport of hunting and shooting, you need to develop knowledge, correct attitudes, and skills in the following areas: firearms safety, choice of hunting and shooting companions, map and compass reading, basic survival skills, basic first aid, target identification, and selection of clothing and equipment. For an in-depth presentation of each skill, you will need to contact other resources.

ENVIRONMENTAL CONDITIONS

Although you may enjoy the environment you are hunting and shooting in, if you do not follow proper safety guidelines it can quickly turn deadly. Don't wait until an accident occurs to learn proper safety techniques.

Selecting a Campsite

Selecting a safe campsite is an important consideration. Finding the right campsite in the fall is easier than during the summer tourist season. Setting up camp in the immediate area you plan to hunt can contaminate the spot and interfere with the game's travel patterns. Maintain a half-mile buffer zone so game won't be disturbed by a chugging generator, snarling chain saw, practice rounds from rifles, or other noise. Quiet backpackers can get by with a shorter transition zone, but don't make the mistake of pitching a tent too close to a game trail. A herd of rutting elk may run over your campsite in the middle of the night.

Pitch the tent on ground that is level or slightly higher on one end to allow water drainage if it rains and to help sleepers elevate their heads slightly higher than their feet. Take advantage of natural windbreaks such as hills and

THE FOUR *A*'S OF HUNTING

For you to become a true hunter and sportsperson, you must internalize the Four *A*s, Awareness, Attitude, Action, and Achievement (involvement + education = the responsible hunter).

Awareness is knowing that you can become a victim of high emotion when you spot game. It is natural to become excited, but you must be aware of your emotions. As a hunter you must know the limits of your ability to control your emotions. Be aware of your responsibilities to the landowners, the environment, wildlife, other hunters, other outdoor users, and nonhunting citizens. Know your personal limitations as well as your abilities, hunting skills, and physical endurance. Be aware of the limits of your firearms and other hunting equipment.

Correct **attitude** is hunting for the sake of hunting, not simply bagging game. Concentrate on developing attitudes of courtesy, safety, and responsible behavior. The reward of hunting is far more than simply killing game. View hunting as a learning endeavor, a sharing experience, and an ecological-awareness undertaking, with bagged game a bonus. Courtesy will be rewarded with friendliness and concern. Safety consciousness will prevent mishaps and tragedy. Sharing will guarantee more hunting opportunities and lasting relationships. A law-abiding attitude is essential to personal pride.

Emotional awareness plus proper attitude puts you on the track toward positive **action**. Restrain the urge to shoot before you're sure.

- Assume every sound and movement in the woods is another human being until you positively identify it as wild game.

- Check for other hunters and a safe backstop before you raise your firearm.

- Double-check to make sure the game is legal before you shoot.

- Have safe shooting zones in mind at all times and stick to them.

- Control your emotions to control your firearm.

By taking these positive steps, hunting will become a satisfying experience. Hunters must study and learn all they can about wildlife, both in books and in the field. Always ask permission to hunt. Everybody likes invited guests, but few like uninvited ones. Always plan, organize, and prepare equipment, firearms, vehicles, and clothing before the hunt. It satisfies anticipated nervousness and fulfills the urge to be afield. The hunter needs to sharpen observation and target-shooting skills during the off-season. Share game with landowners, friends, and family.

Realistic expectations lead to feelings of greater **achievement** and personal satisfaction. Unrealistic ones result in frustration and disappointment. They also cause overanxiousness to kill game and can result in a tragic hunting accident. Concentrate on safety and accident prevention. When you achieve safe, responsible behavior, you have taken a major step toward assuring your future enjoyment and safe hunting.

woods, and avoid flood-prone low spots, open areas where lightning could be a threat, and nearby dead trees that might come crashing down in a storm.

Camp Rules

Select someone to be the huntmaster. It is the responsibility of the huntmaster to assign camp chores and enforce the camp rules. Usual camp rules include no loaded firearms in camp; unload firearms before entering camp; store firearms in a safe, dry place that you can secure; and no alcohol in camp. If you decided that you will allow alcohol in camp, be sure that all drink in moderation only. Hunting camps are poor places to party. The risks of serious injuries are just too great. If the camp becomes an unsafe place to enjoy the hunt, excuse yourself and leave.

Camp Equipment

Having proper camp equipment makes your hunting trip more enjoyable, and it ensures that you have all you need to survive and remain uninjured. Table 17.1 provides a basic list of camping equipment you will need.

Clothing

Humans are warm-weather animals, and hunting is usually a cool-weather sport. When humans venture into colder regions, they must carry their tropical environment with them or risk discomfort, serious disability, or even death from hypothermia. There are four major factors that accentuate the problems of dealing with cold weather, all of which may plague the unprepared sportsperson:

1. Temperature
2. Wetness
3. Wind
4. Altitude

Hunters must select clothes that protect the body from all four conditions. In addition, they must understand how the body produces heat and how the body loses heat.

Heat production by the body is a metabolic function. The heat is generated by burning food with oxygen within each cell. The quan-

tity of heat the body produces by this method can be extremely variable, depending on how much work the muscles must do and the availability of fuel. The key to this puzzle is activity, availability of food, and conserving body heat.

The body loses heat by direct radiation, conduction, convection, and evaporation. The function of clothing is to protect the body from their effects. Well-chosen hunting clothes will maintain the body at a reasonable temperature, whatever the weather. You achieve insulation by trapping air at body temperature in layers of porous clothing and stopping the wind from blowing it away.

Ideally your clothes should insulate from heat as well as cold, but in practice this is difficult to achieve. We clothe the body by starting with the skin and layering to the outside. The layer that goes closest to the skin should provide warmth and be able to draw moisture away from the skin. Some of the best materials for this are synthetic, such as polypropylene, Capilene, and Thermax. The middle layer continues drawing moisture away from the body and out toward the surface. Wool or fleece garments work best for this layer, and they are comfortable and not constricting. The outer layer is the final protection against the environment. This layer protects us from wind, rain, and other outside elements. The outer layer should be large enough to fit over the first two layers without restricting movement. An excellent material for the outer layer is Gore-Tex. Gore-Tex allows the moisture on the inside to evaporate away from the inner layers while keeping outside moisture such as rain out.

Having selected the type of material for your clothing, you always need to consider the choice of color. It may be necessary for the clothing to blend into the background of the terrain or for you to be visible to other hunters. For visibility, we recommend that your outer layer of clothing display approximately 400 cubic inches of blaze orange.

Selecting a quality pair of boots is your next decision. If your feet have stopped growing, spend every dime you can scrape together on a high-quality pair of boots. There are dozens

Table 17.1
CAMP EQUIPMENT

☐ Ammunition	☐ Foam sleeping pad	☐ Portable radio	☐ Air mattress
☐ Ax	☐ Fuel	☐ Propane	☐ Playing cards
☐ Flashlight	☐ Generator	☐ Rain gear	☐ Winch or comealong
☐ Backpack	☐ Gloves	☐ Reading material	☐ Water purification tablets
☐ Batteries	☐ Grill	☐ Shovel	☐ Rope
☐ Binoculars	☐ Portable folding table	☐ Space blanket	☐ Wash basin
☐ Bedding	☐ Knives	☐ Cot	☐ Towels
☐ Boots and extra laces	☐ Snow tire chains	☐ Cleaning kit	☐ Toilet paper
☐ Bungee cords	☐ Hand warmer	☐ Snow shovel	☐ Sponges
☐ Plastic tarp	☐ Hatchet	☐ Toiletries	☐ Duct tape
☐ Masking tape	☐ Heater	☐ Themos bottle	☐ CB radio or walkie-talkie
☐ Camp permit	☐ Handgun and holster	☐ Headlamp	☐ Camera and accessories
☐ Camping stools	☐ Hot pads	☐ Cooler	☐ Hand tools
☐ Candles	☐ Tow chain	☐ Plates	☐ Water jugs
☐ Canteen	☐ Hydraulic jack	☐ Stakes	☐ First aid kit
☐ Chain saw and fuel	☐ Maps	☐ Splitting maul	☐ Nails
☐ Clothing	☐ Registration	☐ Sunglasses	☐ Electrician's tape
☐ Coffee pot	☐ Jumper cables	☐ 10-quart pails	☐ Hunting licenses and tags
☐ Compass	☐ Keys (extra)	☐ Tent	
☐ Calker	☐ Fanny pack	☐ Poles	☐ Lantern
☐ Cookstove	☐ Portable toilet	☐ Cooker and propane	
☐ Fire starter & extinguisher	☐ Chemicals for toilet	☐ Matches	
☐ Food			

of reputable makes of boots, each offering something special. Whatever you buy, it must have a strong formed toe and thick, heavily cleated soles with a lace system that is strong and secure.

The next decision is whether you want an insulated waterproof boot. This decision will depend on the application you have in mind. When fitting a boot, follow these guidelines to ensure a proper fit.

- Wear the type of sock you will be wearing on the hunt.

- With the boot unlaced and the foot pushed well forward, it should be possible to slip a finger down the back of the heel inside the boot.

- When the laces are firmly fastened, this slackness should be taken up.

- Tap the toe of the boot gently against a wall or on the floor; your foot should scarcely move inside.

- Stand on your tiptoes, keeping your back straight. If the boot won't let you do this at all, it is too stiff, but make some allowance for the fact that the leather will soften with use.

- When in this position, check for any pinching over the top of your foot or any sagging at the side of the boot.

- Finally, you are ready to break in your new boots. Never go to the field with a new pair of boots. If feet, socks, and boots are properly matched and maintained, blisters rarely happen and your feet will be happy campers.

The Day Pack

A day pack is a must for every hunter, and the hunter should never leave the vehicle or camp without it. This pack can be the key to your survival, because you will never know when it may be necessary for you to spend the night in the woods. Table 17.2 is a list of items you may wish to include in your day pack, on your belt, or in your pockets, depending on your geographical area.

SUPERVISION

Selecting a competent supervisor for a shooting sports program is necessary for a successful program. The department chair or administrator of a public school should consider the following criteria: (Note: Not all successful hunters or shooters make good supervisors.)

- Education—a person with an education degree that provides training in high-risk activities and group management in physical activity is preferred.

- Organizational skill—has successfully demonstrated his or her organizational skills in high-risk activities or other shooting sports programs; has a working knowledge of group dynamics, group design and pairings, appropriate geographical location of each active pair or group, and, most important, the proper location of the instructor(s) in relation to the activity.

- Background check—conduct a complete background check, including recommen-

dations (letters, phone interview, etc.), past work performance, driving records, police records, and so on. Good citizenship is a requirement.

- Certification—the person should hold an NRA instructor rating or similar certification.

- Technical competency—the supervisor must have a working knowledge of guns, ammunition, target shooting, and field and range safety procedures to guide the program.

Supervisory Procedures

The supervisor must have total control of the program within the administrative guidelines of the organization. The supervisor should solicit the input of others, use a committee structure where appropriate, seriously consider all suggestions, then generate a decision. In the final analysis, the supervisor must be held accountable for what happens in the program. Therefore, the supervisor must have the power to dismiss an instructor or a student from the program immediately for safety reasons. The administration should review each reported dismissal to see that the safety guidelines were violated and administrative guidelines were followed. Instructors in the program should have essentially the same qualification as the supervisor except depth of experience.

The key to a safe program is strict adherence to the safety procedures discussed in this chapter. Violating these procedures cannot be tolerated. Once all the participants in the program understand the importance of the safety rules and the necessity of their strict enforcement, you should not experience any difficult situations. Therefore, all participants must have a clear understanding of the consequences for failing to comply with the rules. Cover all safety procedures, as well as the program content, in the classroom. Each student should achieve a perfect score on all safety procedures before going to the field or the range. Post all safety procedures in the classroom, on the range, and in other appropriate areas.

Successful shooting sports programs are personnel intensive. We recommend that you

Table 17.2
THINGS TO INCLUDE IN A DAY PACK

☐ Compass	☐ Pink toilet tissue	☐ Knife	☐ Sunglasses
☐ Whistle	☐ Canteen	☐ Space blanket	☐ Sharpening steel
☐ Binoculars	☐ Candle	☐ Butane lighter	☐ Garbage bags
☐ Ax	☐ Fire-starter material	☐ Band-Aids	☐ Flint and steel
☐ Matches	☐ First aid kit	☐ Handiwipes	☐ 50 ft of fishing line
☐ Steel wool	☐ Gauze bandage	☐ Triangular bandages	☐ Wound compressess
☐ Extra socks	☐ Petroleum jelly	☐ Safety pins	☐ Nylon fluorescent ribbon
☐ Elastic bandage	☐ Cold medication	☐ Belt	☐ Antidiarrheal medication
☐ Moleskin	☐ Adhesive tape	☐ Handkerchief	☐ Nylon rope
☐ Anti-inflammatory	☐ Flashlight	☐ Antibiotic cream	
☐ Iodine	☐ Medical card	☐ High-energy food pack	
☐ Topographic map(s)			
☐ Signal mirror			

use a ratio of one adult instructor to six students when conducting range exercises. Organize the students into pairs. One student should assist the partner, by kneeling or standing behind the shooter and critiquing his or her partner's performance in a positive manner. The adult should supervise the group, checking for adherence to proper shooting technique and safety procedures. The lead instructor or supervisor controls all activities on the range by command.

Adult Supervision in the Field

The students' field experience can become a high-risk activity if not properly supervised. Therefore, we recommend that one adult supervises two students in the field. Conduct the first experience in the field with unloaded guns, and expose students to an obstacle course that will provide the typical safety problems encountered during a hunt. Keep accurate records of the students' progress, correct errors in behavior, and conduct a postsession evaluation of student progress.

Parental Involvement and Orientation

Require the parent(s) of each student to attend the first session with their child or children. Make the parent(s) aware of the program requirements, basic safety procedures, risk assumptions, and their responsibilities for the student's success. They need to understand that, on completing the program, the student is not ready to go to the field unsupervised. Parental supervision in the field is one of the most important links for safe field experiences. Students must continue to practice and refine their safety and hunting skills. The parent should make the final decision as to when their child is ready to go to the field unsupervised by an adult. On completing the orientation session, the parent(s) and student(s) should receive a form that describes the risks involved in the program and outlines the parent and student responsibilities. The student and the parent(s) should acknowledge in writing that they have listened to the orientation session, read the material on the form, and understand its content. Figure 17.1 on page 268 is a generic informed consent form that you can use as a model.

The key to safe and enjoyable hunting is strict adherence to reasonable safety procedures.

SELECTION AND CONDUCT OF THE ACTIVITY

Developing and assessing readiness is a difficult area because there are no known test instruments that will tell an instructor which student is safety conscious and which one is not. Driver education instructors have been working on this problem for years with little or no success. Age is not a reliable indicator of responsibility, although it is generally accepted that students who are old enough to have a hunting license (usually 14 years of age) are old enough to participate in a shooting sports program. In many states, the law requires that all beginning hunters of any age complete a hunter education program before receiving a hunting license. We recommend that all students in elementary and secondary school receive basic gun safety instruction appropriate for their age group. Initiating such programs at the elementary level could prevent many tragedies.

The best assessment tool is a carefully planned program that assesses a student's competence at each level of instruction. Careful assessment of knowledge, range drills, safety procedure, shooting skills, handling skills, and field skills will provide the primary insight to each student's readiness. Dismiss students or ask them to repeat the program if they fail to meet the minimal standards. The instructor, therefore, must set up skill-building activities in each activity area, monitor, and record student progress. However, the final test will be how the student performs under the excitement and stress of the hunt. This is an unknown factor that the instructor cannot account for in a controlled activity situation. The supervisor or instructor cannot promise that a student will always behave safely after successfully completing the program. The instructor must, however, be able to state that the student has successfully met all program requirements.

Safety Rules of Participation

Follow the guidelines prescribed here. They will make your hunting trip much safer and more enjoyable.

Choice of Hunting Companion(s)

Your choice of a hunting partner(s) is the most important single element of a successful hunt. Hunting is for fun, and fun is impossible with a selfish, boorish, or dangerous hunting companion. Choose your hunting partner with great care, and rate yourself by the same measures. A hunting companion should be a close friend whose natural virtues you know and whom you know to be durable under stress.

Gun sense is vital in a hunting partner. You can hand a gun to a person and evaluate his or her total experience in a few minutes. The real hunter handles a gun with assurance, ease, and respect. She or he knows guns. You owe it to yourself and your family to side with such a person, and you owe it to your partner to return in kind.

A shoot may be a grim trial to be endured together or a dream hunt to remember. In either case, it is a mutual enterprise to share without selfishness—sharing shooting opportunities, hunting techniques, food, equipment, water, and something of each other. It must never be seriously competitive, greedy, and I oriented (How Do You Rate as a Hunting Partner 1972).

Firearm Handling in the Home and Field

Approximately two-thirds of all gun-related accidental deaths occur in the home, and more than 700 persons lose their lives each year in hunting accidents that could have been prevented. It is usually not the first-time hunters nor the experienced ones who have accidents. The problem seems to be in the 15- to 24-age group who has at least three years of experience, is momentarily careless, and fails to follow the rules of hunting safety. Therefore, it is imperative that hunters be skilled in the safe handling of firearms. These rules are not difficult to learn, but consistently applying them is challenging. The responsible person lessens the chance of an accident by following some basic rules of firearm safety (NRA 1989a).

Before Going Into the Field

Before going to the field, a hunter needs to develop his or her firearms skills. You must understand how a gun works and know when a

Informed Consent Agreement

Thank you for choosing to use the facilities, services, or programs of _____. We request your understanding and cooperation in maintaining both your and our safety and health by reading and signing the following informed consent agreement.

I, _____, declare that I intend to use some or all of the activities, facilities, programs, and services offered by _____ and I understand that each person (myself included), has a different capacity for participating in such activities, facilities, programs, and services. I am aware that all activities, services, and programs offered are either educational, recreational, or self-directed in nature. I assume full responsibility, during and after my participation, for my choices to use or apply, at my own risk, any portion of the information or instruction I receive.

I understand that part of the risk involved in undertaking any activity or program is relative to my own state of fitness or health (physical, mental, or emotional) and to the awareness, care, and skill with which I conduct myself in that activity or program. I acknowledge that my choice to participate in any activity, service, and program of _____ brings with it my assumption of those risks or results stemming from this choice and the fitness, health, awareness, care, and skill that I possess and use.

I further understand that the activities, programs, and services offered by _____ are sometimes conducted by personnel who may not be licensed, certified, or registered instructors or professionals. I accept the fact that the skills and competencies of some employees and/or volunteers will vary according to their training and experience and that no claim is made to offer assessment or treatment of any mental or physical disease or condition by those who are not duly licensed, certified, or registered and herein employed to provide such professional services.

I recognize that by participating in the activities, facilities, programs, and services offered by _____, I may experience potential health risks such as transient lightheadedness, fainting, abnormal blood pressure, chest discomfort, leg cramps, and nausea and that I assume willfully those risks. I acknowledge my obligation to immediately inform the nearest supervising employee of any pain, discomfort, fatigue, or any other symptoms that I may suffer during and immediately after my participation. I understand that I may stop or delay my participation in any activity or procedure if I so desire and that I may also be requested to stop and rest by a supervising employee who observes any symptoms of distress or abnormal response.

I understand that I may ask any questions or request further explanation or information about the activities, facilities, programs, and services offered by _____ at any time before, during, or after my participation.

I declare that I have read, understood, and agree to the contents of this informed consent agreement in its entirety.

Signature _____

Date of signing _____

Witness _____

Figure 17.1   Standard informed consent agreement.

Reprinted from ACSM. 1992. *Health/Fitness facility standards and guidelines.* Champaign, IL: Human Kinetics.

PRIMARY RULES FOR HANDLING A FIREARM

Treat every firearm as if it were loaded, at all times.

Always keep the muzzle of the firearm pointed in a safe direction.

Be sure of your target and beyond.

gun is unloaded and safe. When a person hands you a gun, always assume that it is loaded until you have personally checked to see that it is unloaded. To perform this task, you must be familiar with the different types of guns.

There are two basic firearms classes, long and short guns. In the long gun class there are rifles and shotguns (see figure 17.2). In the short gun class there are revolvers (single action and double action) and semiautomatics. You need to cock or pull the hammer back on a single-action revolver, whereas you need only to pull the trigger on a double-action revolver.

The single- and double-action revolvers have a cylinder that serves as the magazine (a holder in or on a gun for cartridges to be fed into the gun chamber) and a hammer for the firing mechanism (see figure 17.3a). The semiautomatic, as in figure 17.3b, has a slide action that automatically activates when the gun is fired and the recoil reloads the chamber.

In addition, the future hunter needs to become familiar with the different types of action on long guns. There are bolt action, lever action, pump action, semiautomatic, hinge action, and muzzle loaders (see figure 17.4 a-f).

When checking to see if a gun is loaded, keep your fingers and hand away from the trigger and trigger guard. Unload each firearm as follows:

- Muzzle loading firearms—due to the nature of the muzzle loader, it is not easy to tell if a gun is loaded. If you suspect that a muzzle loading firearm may be loaded, do not try to unload it yourself. Have a qualified individual make sure that the gun is unloaded.

- Bolt action—open the action by lifting the bolt handle and pulling it to the rear, and visually check the chamber and magazine to make sure that both are empty.

- Lever action gun—open the action by pushing the cocking lever down and forward. It closes by pulling the lever toward the stock. With the action open, visually check the

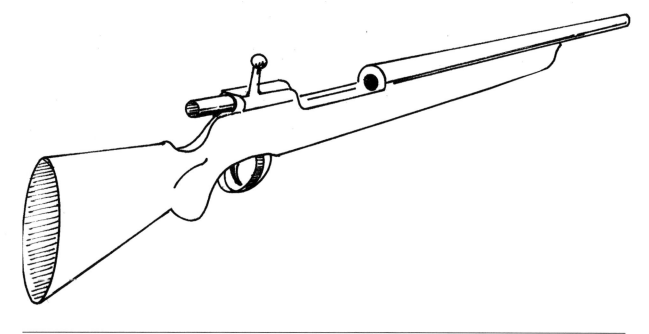

Figure 17.2   Long gun.

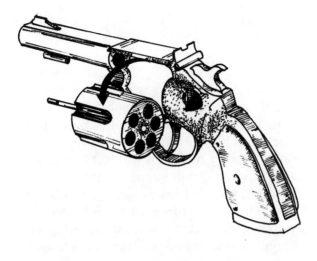

Figure 17.3a   Revolver.

Figure 17.3b   Semiautomatic.

chamber and magazine to be sure that the gun is completely unloaded.

- Pump or slide action gun—open the action by depressing the action release and pulling forearm to the rear. With the action open, visually check the chamber and magazine to be sure that the gun is unloaded.

- Hinge action (over-under, single, and double barrel)—push the release lever to one side and the barrel(s) will swing downward. Then remove the cartridges and inspect the chamber(s).

- Semiautomatic—open the action by pulling the bolt handle back and locking it open. This ejects the cartridge from the chamber. With the action open, check the chamber and magazine to be sure it is unloaded.

A responsible hunter develops his or her firearms handling and shooting skills before going to the field. Regular practice of the safety rules with target practice improves the hunter's ability to shoot accurately. When you practice the range and field safety rules regularly, they become a part of your lifestyle. For example, when a friend asks to inspect your gun, you will automatically open the chamber, inspect it, and hand an empty gun to him or her, who in turn should inspect the chamber. Violating the basic field and range safety rules may inadvertently lead to tragedy or near tragedy.

Safe and secure storage of the guns in your home requires that untrained individuals (especially children) be denied access to the guns. Keep guns in storage unloaded and separate from ammunition. It is advisable to insert a commercial lock mechanism over the trigger as an additional precaution (NRA n.d.). Nearly two-thirds of all gun-related accidents occur in the home. Never assume that people know or follow safety rules simply because they claim to have knowledge of firearm safety. Table 17.3 is a list of important rules to know before you go out into the field (NRA 1989a).

Planning the Hunt

Once you have mastered the skills of shooting and gun handling and have completed a hunter education program, the next step is to develop a plan for your trip to the woods or field. Planning for a safe hunt is the key to a successful and enjoyable experience in the field. How you organize the hunt and what items you include in your plan will depend on the type of hunt (big game or small game), length of the hunt, terrain, potential weather conditions, altitude of the terrain, choice of companion(s), and your mental and physical condition.

The most important factor in the plan is the hunter's mental and physical condition. The hunter should have a complete physical several months before the scheduled hunt.

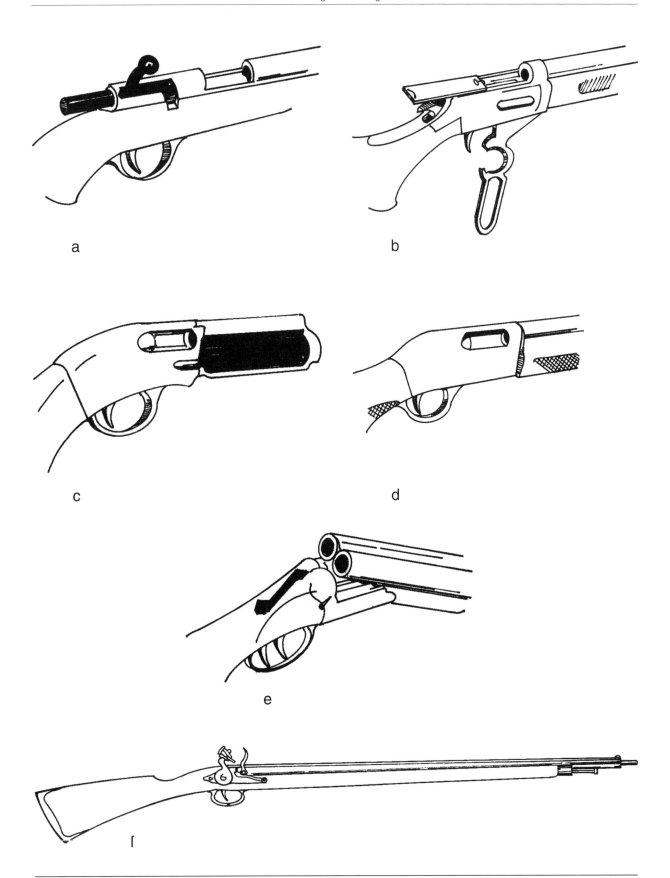

Figure 17.4a-f Long guns are loaded in several ways: (a) bolt action, (b) lever action, (c) pump action, (d) semiautomatic, (e) hinge action, and (f) muzzle loader.

Table 17.3
FIELD SAFETY RULES

RULE	EXPLANATION
Be positive of your target's identity before shooting.	Take the time to fire a safe shot. When you wonder whether you should shoot, pass up the shot. Bagging the game is not worth the risk. Excitement or greed are the cause of many hunting tragedies.
Use the right ammunition for your firearm.	Carry only one type of ammunition to be sure you do not mix different calibers.
If you fall, try to control where the muzzle points.	After a fall, check your unloaded gun for dirt and damage, and make sure the barrel is free of obstructions.
Unload your gun before climbing a steep bank or crossing slippery ground.	Slipping or falling could cause unintentional discharge of the firearm or could cause it to be damaged or clogged with dirt.
Crossing a fence can cause unexpected danger if not done properly.	When you cross a fence alone, unload your gun and place it under the fence with the muzzle pointed away from where you are crossing. When hunting with a companion, unload the gun and keep the action open. Have your companion hold the gun while you cross. Then retrieve both unloaded guns from your companion.
Never use a scope sight as a substitute for binoculars.	It is not only dangerous, but it is a felony to point a gun at another hunter.
Alcohol, drugs, and hunting do not mix.	Drugs and alcohol may impair your judgment, and keen judgment is essential to a safe hunt.
Be aware of fatigue and what it does to impair good judgment.	Fatigue could influence you to become careless and clumsy, which may cause an accident. Fatigue can also cause you to see things that are not there.
When you have finished hunting, unload your gun before returning to your vehicle or camp.	This will again prevent an unintentional discharge thus making your walk out of the hunting area as pleasant as your walk in.

The hunter needs to know if there are any preexisting medical conditions to plan for before the hunt. Once the physical exam has been completed, the hunter needs to prepare his or her body physically for the hunt. Fatigue will reduce peripheral vision, mental alertness, coordination, and mobility, resulting in increased vulnerability to accidents.

Fitness and Exercise

Physical fitness is many things to many people, yet all fit individuals have one thing in common—a continuing ability to function comfortably and effectively in their environment. Regular, vigorous exercise enhances the quality of life by increasing the physical capability for work. A hunter must have the physical capabilities to withstand the activity the hunt requires. It does not make much difference what exercise regimen you chose, as long as you follow these four criteria: it provides stamina and endurance, you can schedule it regularly, you can perform it year-round, and you enjoy doing it.

Eye Care

An eye examination is necessary for good eye care. Excellent visual acuity is essential for clear target identification. Eyes use a surprisingly large amount of physical energy, and nearly everything that leads to physical fatigue can lead to eye fatigue. A special hazard to the eyes is bright snow, especially at high altitudes, which can result in snow blindness. You can prevent this condition by using protective sunglasses or goggles.

Ears and Hearing Care

The average hunter may not realize that time on the firing range affects his or her hearing. However, studies have shown a significant hearing loss in people whose sole exposure to noise has been small arms qualification courses. This is completely preventable by wearing one of the many insert or muff hearing protection devices while practicing firing.

Foot Care

Your feet are your primary mode of transportation on a hunt. If your feet are not in good condition, you will seriously impair your ability to safely travel over rough terrain. Inspect your feet carefully, looking for bumps, corns, sore spots, calluses, length of nails, and skin condition. Keep nails and skin spotlessly clean, because clogged pores lead to chafing, blisters, and, sometimes, infection.

Selecting the appropriate socks is essential. There are two possibilities: a single pair of thick, high quality woolen or synthetic socks, preferably with a loop pile for softness, or a thin pair of fine wool socks next to the skin with a pair of coarser socks over the top. Unlike manufactured fibers, wool can absorb up to 37 percent of its own weight in water without feeling wet. If you choose a synthetic sock, make sure it is equal to or superior to wool socks in water-carrying and wicking ability.

Map, Compass, and Trip Plan

Humans have no innate sense of direction. Sooner or later, a hunter who spends time outdoors will become lost. Left without any exterior cues, such as sun, wind, lay of the land, landmarks, and stars, a person will become temporarily disoriented and travel in a large circle. The only safe way for a hunter to travel by foot through new or old terrain or inclement weather is with the aid of a good map and a compass. In the pretrip planning phase, you and your companion(s) should purchase a good topographical map of the area you intend to hunt. Carefully study the map, locating all roads in the area, stream-flow directions and drainage, major land formations and landmarks (ridges, peaks, hills), type of terrain, known distances from one location to the next, and the general features of the land. Once you have developed a good understanding of the area, it will be easy for you to travel through new or old territory without becoming lost.

Going to the Field

When transporting a gun in any vehicle or boat, follow this set of rules (NRA 1989a):

- Be sure the gun is unloaded.
- Place it in a protective case.
- Position the firearm securely so it will not move about during travel.
- To transport a gun on a public vehicle, check first with the carrier's agent concerning regulations.

Handling a Gun in the Field

There are approximately six accepted ways to carry a gun safely while having it ready for quick use. The position in which you carry the gun will always depend on the position of your hunting companion(s) and the type of terrain

S.T.O.P.

If you should become lost, use the acronym S.T.O.P. *Sit down.* If near nightfall, build a fire for emotional and physical comfort. The fire can serve as a signal, and it gives you something to do while you take mental inventory of your situation. *Think* about your situation. Does anybody know where you are and when you are supposed to return? Are your partner(s) or other hunters likely to be nearby? *Observe*—look for landmarks, and check your compass and map. Locate your present position if possible. Check the weather to see if you need to plan for a shelter. Is there anything in your immediate area that could be dangerous to you (slides, flash floods, lightning, etc.)? *Plan*—after sitting down, thinking, and observing, plan what to do. Should you try to walk out? You should rarely try to walk out of the woods in the dark. The risks of injury are just too great. If the day is fading fast, carefully select a place to camp; don't let the time of day pick the campsite for you. If you are not seriously injured, you have your day pack, a good campsite, shelter, and a fire. You may experience some discomfort, but you will survive in good shape. In the morning, once you have located known landmarks, you can more easily and safely walk out to a road or to your camp.

If you cannot find your way, or if you cannot move an injured partner, prepare to stay in one place and wait for help. Be ready to signal rescuers. The international call for help is three signals of any kind (three blasts from a whistle or three spaced rifle shots). Three spaced shots or three blasts from a whistle will usually attract attention from members of your hunting party, other hunters, or other recreation users in the area. The whistle is a better choice for signaling than firing shots because it is distinct, loud, carries well, and is not ammunition driven. You can use a fire, smoke, a signal stamped out in the snow, pink toilet tissue laid out, small logs, or a mirror to attract the attention of rescuers. Always leave a trip plan of the area you plan to hunt with a responsible person, family member, park ranger, or companions, and do not leave that area without notifying some responsible party.

The best survival tool you have is your head. Stay cool, think, plan, and put the plan into action. If you can avoid hypothermia, you can live three weeks or longer without food and three days without water. So don't panic; you will live to hunt another day.

---

you are traversing. The following rules apply to all carries (NRA 1989a):

- Keep the muzzle under control, pointed in a safe direction at all times.
- Keep the safety on until ready to fire.
- Keep the finger outside the trigger guard until ready to fire.

Ready or Two-Handed Carry. This type of carry gives the best control of the gun and muzzle, allowing you to raise your gun quickly for a shot. The barrel should parallel a line midpoint between the ear and the point of the off shoulder (see figure 17.5). This is the best and safest carry when hunters are lined up abreast.

Cradle Carry. This is a safe carry if there is no one walking or standing in the direction the muzzle is pointing. If you have a companion walking beside you, do not use this method (see figure 17.6).

Elbow Carry. This is a safe carry in open terrain if there is no one walking in front of you. If you encounter brushy terrain, switch to the two-handed carry to avoid entangling the barrel in the branches (see figure 17.7).

Shoulder Carry. The shoulder carry is safe when walking beside or behind someone. Take special care to keep the muzzle pointed upward. Do not use this carry when others are behind you (see figure 17.8).

Figure 17.5 Ready or two-handed carry.

Figure 17.6 Cradle carry.

Figure 17.7 Elbow carry.

Trail Carry. The trail carry is when you hold the gun by one hand at the point of balance. Do not use this carry when someone is ahead of you (see figure 17.9).

Sling Carry. The sling carry is a safe way for a hunter to travel a long distance without fatiguing the arms or hands. It leaves both hands free. This carry does not work well in dense woods or brush because the barrel could become entangled and the gun may be pulled off the hunter's shoulder (see figure 17.10).

Firing Zones

When hunting with others, establish zones of fire so no hunter will endanger others (see fig-

Figure 17.8   Shoulder carry.

Figure 17.9   Trail carry.

ure 17.11). If three hunters in pursuit of game birds were walking across an open field, the middle hunter's zone of fire would be birds flying in the center of the field. The zone of fire for the hunter on the right would be birds flying in the area to the right side. The third hunter's zone of fire would be birds flying in the area to the left. The same zones of fire apply when hunters are walking abreast in pursuit of small or big game. Each hunter must fire only in his or her zone of fire; to do otherwise would endanger your companions. The same rules apply to hunting in a blind or boat.

ADMINISTRATION

Before initiating a shooting sports program, the organizing entity should conduct an internal audit of their potential program assets. Answer the following questions:

- What type of program do we want—BB gun, pellet gun, shotgun, small bore, or large bore?

- Who will be responsible for supervising the program?

- What is the availability of affordable insurance?

- How will we finance the program?

- Are there facilities available in the community that will meet the requirements of the desired program?

- What is the availability and cost of equipment (i.e., guns, targets, range equipment, trained instructors, etc.)?

- What support can we expect from the

Figure 17.10 Sling carry.

gun and ammunition companies, National Rifle Association, local sporting goods companies, the state's Division of Natural Resources, parents, and the local rod and gun clubs?

If you can satisfactorily answer these questions, the organization could begin to establish a shooting sports program. Community cooperation will be a key factor to the success of the program. By their nature, shooting sports programs usually require facilities and personnel from outside resources. For example, few public schools will have an indoor rifle range, skeet range, trap range, sporting clays range, or a large bore range. In fact, many communities will not have these facilities available. The availability of facilities will primarily determine the breadth and scope of the program.

CONCLUSION

Hunting is a sport that all age groups can enjoy. The key to safe hunting is responsibly handling all firearms and applying the Four *As*—Awareness, Attitude, Action, and Achievement. Guns do not kill people: people kill other people with a gun because they do not think before they act. You are in control of your state of mind. Be a hunter true to the spirit of hunting and the spirit of our ancestors. Remember,

A peculiar virtue in wildlife ethics is that the hunter ordinarily has no gallery to applaud or disapprove of his conduct. Whatever his acts, they are dictated by his own conscience, rather than by a mob or onlooker. It is difficult to exaggerate the importance of this fact. (Leopold 1966)

BIBLIOGRAPHY

Bauer, E.A., ed. *Hunter's digest.* Northfield, IL: Digest Book.

Berglund, B. 1972. *Wilderness survival.* New York: Scribner.

Bever, D.L. 1992. *Safety: A personal focus.* St. Louis: Mosby Yearbook.

Callicott, J.B. 1981. *A non-hunter talks about hunting. Involvement + Education: The responsible hunter.* Madison, WI: Wisconsin Department of Natural Resources.

Cuerdon, D. 1992. Get out. *Men's Health,* October, 76.

Elman, R., and J. Peper., eds. 1975. *Hunting America's game, animals and birds.* New York: Winchester Press.

Geer, G. 1993. Geer on gear for '93. *Soldier of Fortune* 18 October, 30.

Harlow, W.M. 1979. *Ways of the woods: A guide to the skills and spirit of the woodland experience.* Washington, DC: The American Forestry Association.

How do you rate as a hunting partner? 1972. *Grouse Cover,* October-December.

Kjellstron, B. 1976. *Map and compass: The complete "orienteering" handbook.* New York: Scribner.

Kodet, E.R., and A. Bradford. 1968. *Being your own wilderness doctor.* Harrisburg, PA: Stackpole Books.

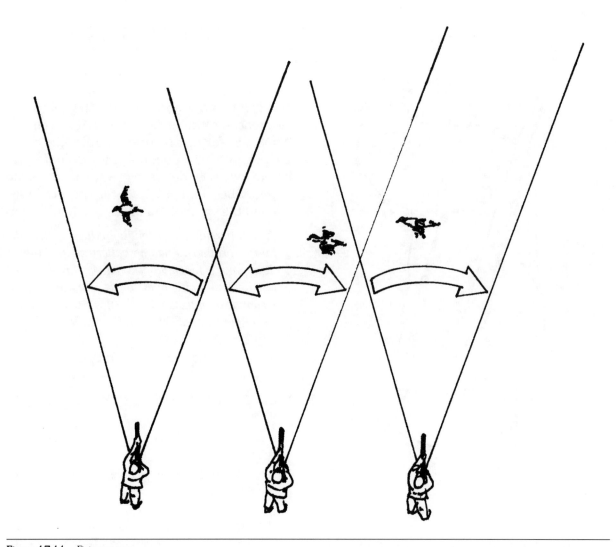

Figure 17.11   Firing zones.

Leopold, A. 1966. *A sand country almanac.* New York: Oxford University Press.

National Rifle Association of America (NRA). 1962. *NRA home firearms responsibility: Student manual.* Washington, DC: National Rifle Association of America.

———. 1989a. *Firearms safety in the field.* Washington, DC: National Rifle Association of America. (H3N0099 pamphlet)

———. 1989b. *Safe gun handling: It's as easy as one, two, three.* Washington, DC: National Rifle Association of America. (ES3N0010 pamphlet)

———. 1990a. *Hunting and outdoor skills: Student manual.* Washington, DC: National Rifle Association of America.

———. 1990b. *A parent's guide to gun safety.* Washington, DC: National Rifle Association of America. (200M pamphlet)

———. 1990c. *Responsible hunting.* Washington, DC: National Rifle Association of America. (HE3N0024 pamphlet)

———. 1991a. *A guide to firearms operation.* Washington, DC: National Rifle Association of America. (ES3N0136 pamphlet)

———. 1991b. *Gun safety rules.* Washington, DC: National Rifle Association of America. (EF3N0016 pamphlet)

———. n.d. *At home with guns.* Washington, DC: National Rifle Association of America. (ES3N0136 pamphlet)

———. n.d. *National Rifle Association safety rules.* Washington, DC. National Rifle Association of America. (EF3N0016 pamphlet)

Nature's notebook: The 10 commandments of gun safety. 1989. *Kentucky Happy Hunting Ground,* November.

Ortega y Gasset, J. 1985. *Meditations on hunting*. New York: Scribner.

Platten, D. 1979. *The outdoor survival handbook*. David and Charles, 160.

Puretz, S.L. 1982. First aid supplies for backpacking. *British Journal of Sports Medicine* 16 (1): 48.

Scharff, R. 1963. *The hunter's game, gun, and dog guide*. New York: Collier Books.

Slahor, S. 1992. Just-in-case kit/safety. *Lapidary Journal* 45 (10): 67.

Varani, A. 1993. Winter backpacking. *Trail and Timberline* 890 (February): 31.

chapter 18

In-Line Skating

Daniel E. Della-Giustina

Beth A. Loy

According to the Sporting Goods Manufacturers Association, about 19 million persons ages six and older in-line skated at least once during 1994, compared with 13 million in 1993. In-line skating, savored as a way to combine exercise, recreation, and enjoyment, has become one of the most popular recreational activities during the past decade. According to the National Safety Council, there were 33,500,000 roller and in-line skaters in 1996. With popularity, however, has come controversy. With the thrill of being able to attain speeds of up to 50 miles per hour and to travel on almost any paved surface, we must consider the chance of injury. As in-line skates become more popular, the number of injuries seems to be following close behind, increasing from an estimated 37,000 injuries in 1993 to almost 76,000 injuries in 1996. On one weekend, New York City's Lenox Hill Hospital treated 17 in-line skaters for injuries. On the West Coast, about a dozen in-line skaters show up at the Santa Monica hospital emergency room every weekend, and in San Francisco, David Miles, who coordinates Golden Gate Park's patrol, says that up to 15 skaters are hurt each day (Mitchell 1991). Falling is commonplace in the sport of in-line skating, and head injuries can be deadly. In 1993 there were 2,000 in-line skating head injuries reported.

There are important financial considerations as well. The Consumer Product Safety Commission estimates that in-line skating injuries cost society $180 million in 1993, with an average injury cost of about $5,000. These costs included hospital bills, physician bills, and missed workdays.

Safety has become a serious issue where skating is concerned. Given that there has been no relationship between skating ability and the type of injury incurred (Perlick et al. 1982), safety problems are not limited to beginners. All participants and supervisors must be made aware of safety issues. The proper way to prevent injuries begins with attention to environmental conditions, through supervision and adequate conduct of the activity.

ENVIRONMENTAL CONDITIONS

In-line skating is a fun and exciting activity. However, this enjoyment does not come without risks. The in-line skating environment, especially outdoors, can be dangerous. Don't get caught unprepared.

Skating in the Outdoor Environment

Skating outdoors is different than roller-skating in a controlled environment such as an indoor rink. Parents must take precautionary measures with youngsters, discussing basic safety requirements and where to skate.

To avoid falling and to stay in control, the in-line skater should know where to skate. The skater should carry out proper in-line skating techniques to be able to concentrate on skating conditions of sidewalks, playgrounds, and other areas. This will assure proper control in case of challenging conditions or emergencies (i.e., cracks in sidewalk, etc.). Skaters should skate on smooth, paved surfaces without too much traffic and avoid skating on streets with surfaces having water, sand, gravel, or dirt. Skaters should not skate at night because others cannot see them, and the skaters will have problems identifying obstacles.

In addition to directly observing and analyzing data that show accident patterns, we should extend to all in-line skaters the knowledge, skills, and attitudes necessary for a safe and healthy environment.

The following guidelines are important to keep in mind each time you skate:

1. Because uneven surfaces can cause severe injuries, skaters must skate on uniform, dry, and paved surfaces clear of debris.

2. A skating surface should not be common to any other pedestrian or vehicle traffic.

3. Never skate at night, and always wear bright clothes containing reflective gear.

4. Skaters should never wear anything that could possibly restrict hearing or obstruct vision.

REGULATING IN-LINE SKATING

Larger cities are beginning to regulate in-line skating, because in more populated areas people use it as transportation due to massive traffic congestion. According to Mike Dingman, marketing coordinator for Toronto-based Rollerblade Canada (a subsidiary of Minnesota-based Rollerblade, Inc., which controls more than 70 percent of the in-line skate market), Guelph and Georgetown are two Ontario municipalities that have already enacted bylaws prohibiting in-line skating on city sidewalks (Menzies 1992). As many cities are proving in court, even though no traffic laws pinpoint in-line skating, in-line skaters are subject to traffic laws. If a skater neglects to obey all traffic laws, including traffic lights, stop signs, and speed limits, he or she may be fined.

Manhattan has instituted speed limits for in-line skaters in Central Park, and Huntington Beach, California, has banned them from business districts (Mitchell 1991). Laws are also attempting to stifle the popular *hitching*. This occurs when an in-line skater hooks onto a vehicle's back and attempts to hold on while skating behind a moving vehicle. Even though it is considered a fad in some cities, police are beginning to crack down on the craze by fining both the skater and the vehicle driver.

Equipment

Skaters wearing approved knee pads, elbow pads, and hockey gloves specifically designed for skating or skateboarding are maintaining safe and healthy environmental conditions. Even though bicycle helmets are the most popular protection for a skater's head, the new type of helmet developed by Bell Sports Image Pro is now being recommended, because the back of the helmet is elongated to protect against spinal cord and neck injuries. Also necessary are specialized splint-type wrist guards that protect against the wrist injuries common when skaters fall on an outstretched arm (Nesbitt 1993).

More injuries occur to the wrist than to any other part of the body, says the Consumer Product Safety Commission. More than one-third of all injuries were fractures, and one-third of these involved the wrist (Perlick et al. 1982). In addition, wrist injuries result in fractures more often than sprains or strains. Dr. Ullis, a specialist in sports medicine at the UCLA Student Health Service, recommends a quarter-inch thick acrylic resin brace, which guards about four inches of the wrist and lower arm, curving to absorb energy as the skater falls (Health on Wheels 1980).

Athletic shorts and pants with padding will help protect against severe muscle and bone damage, and skaters should wear socks to prevent slippage, making sure the skate boots fit properly. Because of the increasing popularity of roller-blading among women, Canstar, makers of the popular Bauer skates, responded with specific gear and padding called the Women's Pelvic Protection.

To protect against teeth and jaw fractures, Dr. Edwin Joy of the American Association of Oral and Maxillofacial Surgeons (personal communication) recommends mouth guards specially designed by a dentist for an individual fit. Also, skaters need approved helmets and chin guards to safeguard against serious head disfigurement.

Maintaining Equipment

Maintaining skates will also prevent injuries. Basic start-up precautions that will reduce the risk of skating injuries are practicing in an isolated place before attempting anything difficult, avoiding uneven and wet surfaces, and wearing properly fitting skates. Also important

© Cheyenne Rouse

Choose smooth, paved surfaces with little traffic.

are inspecting your skates, cleaning wheels frequently, and examining toe stops for a secure fit. Tighten loose bolts and plates with a standard wrench, screwdriver, or special skate wrench.

One side of the skate will usually wear faster than the other side, causing an unsafe skate. Rotate wheels and wheel bearings regularly, and replace them when worn, usually about every two years. Also, axles and wheels should be tight and bearings sound, making sure wheels do not play from side to side. Monitor brake pads, shoe strings, and liners and replace them when necessary.

A necessary part of in-line skating is properly adjusting wheel configuration. Adjustments are necessary when the type of skating changes. For regular skating, keep wheels level. For trick skating, figure skating, or hockey, the wheels should be *rockered*, which is the front and back wheels are ad-

justed higher than interior wheels. Adjustments for the skater's particular activity will help make an easier and safer skate.

SUPERVISION

Supervision centers on high-risk groups and how to proactively educate and concurrently supervise in-line skating as a recreational activity. In-line skating produces the most injuries among children age 10 to 14, with 73 percent of all in-line skating injuries occurring among this age group. You can handle some hazards associated with these activities by direct planning and learning activities with boys and girls at school (Della-Giuntina and Yost 1991). To prevent serious injuries from in-line skating, include related safety skills and attitudes in safety classes.

Safety education has been defined as the area of experience in which boys and girls learn to make wise choices when possible injury to self or others, or property damage, may be involved (Della-Giustina and Yost 1991). Teachers are at the heart of safety education, because many parents may lack the resources and training to give supervision on safe practices. Common activities involving in-line skating present special hazards, and teachers must be aware of the activities involved with building safety awareness. Instructing in-line skating should be incorporated into the classroom the same as bicycle safety, stressing the use of helmets with both recreational activities.

Insufficient knowledge or skill is a major contributor to high injury rates among in-line skaters; effective teachers will discover the best way to help their students be successful. Methods available for successfully teaching in-line skating include the following (Della-Giustina and Yost 1991):

1. The experiential method or learning by doing—by practicing in-line skating activities, even in a physical education class, the students will be able to develop skills that will enhance their abilities to skate safely.

2. The program and project method—projects may include surveying and reporting on neighborhood regulations and programs that will improve the students' knowledge about the recreational activities they participate in, particularly in-line skating.

3. Dramatization or make believe—videotapes and television can make an especially forceful impact on children age 10 to 14. Most importantly, dramatizations of how in-line skating accidents occur, their results, and their aftereffects can make an everlasting impression on young adults.

4. Visual instruction with verbalization—visual instruction is highlighted by visual aids, including films, slides, computers, photographs, charts, and transparencies. Verbalization includes discussion with students about in-line skating activities, not giving overbearing instructions. Visualization and verbalization left alone are not enough; however, combining the two will allow children to retain information more rapidly, because they can see as well as read and hear.

If children learn the consequences of their unsafe acts before they result in a deadly incident, injuries will not only be less severe but also less frequent.

SELECTION AND CONDUCT OF THE ACTIVITY

The skater can avoid serious injuries by conducting in-line skating appropriately, while selecting the most adequate responses to potentially hazardous situations. This begins with falling and stopping appropriately.

One result of the high injury rates for in-line skaters has been Skate Smart Month. Bauer, First Team Sports Inc., Rollerblade, and Roller Derby Skate Corporation named June the designated month to stress in-line skating safety. In conjunction with this annual program, the In-Line Skate Association (ILSA) publicized and circulated the Top Ten Advisories (Menzies 1992), listed in table 18.1.

Falling

Learning how to both stop and fall is also an important means to avoid injury. Dr. Stephen Weinberg, assistant clinical professor of sports medicine at the Illinois College of Podiatry, recommends practicing falls on a soft lawn or on a gym mat before getting out on skates for the first time (Southwood 1979). Typically, skaters try to break their fall in ways that increase the likelihood of injury. For example, when skaters lose their balance, they attempt to break their fall by plummeting forward onto outstretched arms. The more appropriate way to fall would be in a relaxed manner rather than a stiffened posture. When first making contact, the skater should roll with the momentum, preventing skin abrasions. Skaters want to land on flesh or muscle rather than on bones or joints, sitting down while keeping knees bent and back curved.

In-line skating is safer and more relaxing when you allow yourself plenty of open space—it's more fun, too!

Table 18.1
ILSA TOP TEN ADVISORIES

1. Wear protective gear, including a helmet, knee and elbow pads, gloves, and wrist guards.

2. Achieve a basic skating level before taking to the road.

3. Stay alert and be courteous at all times.

4. Always skate under control.

5. Skate on the right side of paths and trails.

6. Overtake pedestrians, cyclists, and other skaters on the left.

7. Stay away from water, oil, or debris on the trail and uneven or broken pavement.

8. Observe all traffic regulations.

9. Avoid areas with heavy automobile traffic.

10. Always yield to pedestrians.

Reprinted from Canada Safety Council. 1992. In-Line Skating. *Living Safety*, Spring, 16-19.

Stopping

When novice skaters first take to skating, they must realize that stopping does not come easily. Skating out of control on asphalt or cement can be hazardous (Nesbitt 1993). Skaters must begin on slightly rolling hills, moving to more sloping hills only after they have mastered stopping. The skater should wear protective gear to absorb the impact.

In a study by Dr. Peter Sharkey (1997), an orthopedic surgeon, one of his findings supported the fact that during high-speed falls onto outstretched hands, wrist guards are not always enough to protect in-line skaters from fractures. In addition to wearing wrist guards, all in-line skaters should practice falling on their side and not on their outstretched hands.

Don't skate on crowded walkways or weave in and out of lanes. The important element to learn is how to stop. It is important that the skater learn several forms of controlling stops particular to in-line skates:

• The skater may use the rubber bumper located at the back of the skate's heel. When the skater wishes to stop, raise one foot while pressing the heel down and dragging the rubber bumper on the ground. Balance is important for this type of stop, so the skater should attempt to lower speed before depressing the heel.

• A second type of stop is called the *S-stop*, which resembles downhill skiing. The skater moves from side to side, slowing down as each turn becomes more parallel to the other.

• Many skaters prefer the *T-stop* because it is easier to control at high speeds. To T-stop, drag the braking leg in back, perpendicular to the supporting leg, allowing more contact with the pavement and resulting in a quicker stop.

• The *bail out* is a fourth type of stop associated with in-line skating, usually occurring in a time of panic. When skaters realize their speed is too extreme, they aim their skates toward some grass and begin running once the skates hit the grass.

ADMINISTRATION

From 1993 to 1995 the U.S. Consumer Product Safety Commission (CPSC) noted a 184-percent increase in the number of injuries involving in-line skaters. This is the reason CPSC believes accurate data is important to properly administer this popular activity.

In-line skating is primarily an individual sport, but this is not always the case. For providers of in-line skating products and services, there are some issues to consider. When buying or renting, require skaters to read and sign off on safety procedures and techniques before you allow them to proceed. This will help protect the provider from claims of liability. Keep extensive records on all cases of injury. Many dealers will offer low-cost group classes and information on local clubs to get beginners started. If you offer such classes, it would be a good idea to look into liability insurance as well. Skaters must be aware of the health risks (importance of medical insurance).

CONCLUSION

Without a doubt, in-line skating can be a dangerous pastime, and the chance of injury is an important consideration. Extensive research on the design of in-line skates is necessary to help prevent serious injuries as a result of the skates themselves. Education, however, is at the heart of injury prevention, because in-line skating has inherent risks that are not eliminated by expertise. All in-line skaters should receive instruction in skating and safety techniques.

BIBLIOGRAPHY

Del Balzo, Denise. 1993. Safer in-line skating. *Glamour*, September, 130.

Della-Giustina, Daniel E., and Charles Peter Yost. 1991. *Teaching safety in the elementary school*. Reston, VA: American Alliance for Health, Physical Education, Recreation and Dance.

Fishbein, Marriann Meister. 1992. In-line, in motion. *Current Health 2*, March, 10-11.

Health on wheels: Skating safety. 1980. *School Safety World*, 6.

Menzies, David. 1992. It's the wheel thing. *Living Safety*, Spring, 16-19.

Mitchell, Emily. 1991. Whiz! Zoom! Crash! Ouch! *Time*, 75.

National Safety Council. 1996. *Accident facts*. Itasca, IL: National Safety Council.

Nesbitt, L. 1993. The in-line skating experience. *The Physician and Sportsmedicine* August: 81-82.

Osborne, Terry. 1986. Ice and roller skating. *Current Health 2*, December, 11-13.

O'Shea, Michael. 1994. Parade's guide to better fitness. *Parade Magazine*, 27.

Perlik, Paul C. et al. 1982. Roller-skating injuries. *The Physician and Sportsmedicine* April: 76-80.

Rappelfield, Joel. 1992. *The complete blader*. New York: St. Martin's Press.

Sharkey, Peter. 1997. High speed falls. *Family Safety and Health*, Summer. Itasca, IL: National Safety Council.

Southwood, Art. 1979. If you fall for roller skating. *Family Safety*, Fall, 17-19.

U.S. Consumer Product Safety Commission. 1994. *News from CPSC Office of Information and Public Affairs*. Washington, DC: U.S. Consumer Product Safety Commission, 9 June. (Release #94-091.11)

Welborn, Elizabeth. 1980. *Roller skating without risk*. July, 43.

Wheel appeal. 1988. *National Geographic World*, September, 26-31.

Wishon, Phillip M., and Marcia L. Oreskovich. 1986. Bicycles, roller skaters and skateboards: Safety promotion and accident prevention. *Children Today*, May-June, 11-15.

Ice Skating

Gary R. Gray

The recreational sport of ice skating is a safe activity as long as you follow certain guidelines. It is a vigorous physical activity that you can perform anaerobically to gain the benefits of short, intense physical activity, or you can enjoy it aerobically if you wish to gain the cardiovascular benefits of vigorous, sustained activity. Ice skating is an exhilarating winter activity that allows many enthusiasts to enjoy the great outdoors.

In addition to protecting against problems or injuries related to exercising in cold weather, you must pay particular attention to preventing injuries from falls and even falling through thin ice. Although the physical movements of ice skating outdoors are the same as skating in an indoor arena, you must be more careful in preventing injuries while skating outdoors due to a more inconsistent environment. The most noticeable difference between the indoor environment and the outdoor environment is often the quality and smoothness of the ice.

ENVIRONMENTAL CONDITIONS

As with any physical activity enjoyed outdoors, participants must be alert to environmental factors. This section will discuss various environmental conditions, including quality of the ice, falling through the ice, treatment after falling through the ice, winter weather concerns, and equipment.

Quality of the Ice

Perhaps the most significant factor in determining the enjoyment of the outdoor skating experience is the quality of the ice. Unlike a climate-controlled indoor arena in which the ice is skillfully made and groomed with sophisticated equipment, ice surfaces outdoors are either those constructed by manual labor or those that occur naturally in the environment, such as ponds and lakes. Due to the potential of wide variability in outdoor ice skating surfaces, or even variability among different portions of the same surface, you must guard against falls from items such as, but not necessarily limited to, the following:

- Bumps and rough ice caused by the wind or uneven freezing
- Cracks; refrozen, cracked surfaces; or thin ice with air pockets beneath
- Exposed rocks, dirt, grass, leaves, or tree branches either on the ice or frozen into the ice

Falling Through the Ice

Probably the most serious mishap that can occur to a recreational ice-skater is a drowning due to falling through the ice. Exercise extreme caution when skating over deep water and while skating on ice of unknown thickness. Be careful to check the thickness of the ice whenever in doubt. Even when you do this, remember that the thickness of the ice at one location might vary significantly from another location at the same site. The Minnesota Department of Natural Resources (cited in *Billings Gazette* 1995) recommends that you stay off ice less than 2 inches thick. They recommend at least 4 inches of ice for ice fishing, 5 inches for snowmobiling, 8 to 12 inches to support the weight of an automobile, and 12 to 15 inches to support the weight of a pickup truck. Certainly it is not unreasonable to expect the ice to be *at least* 4 to 6 inches thick to support the weight and vigorous movement of an ice-skater.

If a skater falls through thin ice, take quick action so that drowning or death by hypothermia does not occur. An individual could fall through a hole in the ice and not be able to resurface at the same location, thus making drowning almost certain. If you are able to grasp the edge of the ice while falling through or otherwise remain partially above the surface of the ice, there are several things that could increase your chance of survival. The Minnesota Department of Natural Resources (cited in *Billings Gazette* 1995) recommends that the skater do the following things:

- Remain calm to conserve energy, and think clearly about getting out of the ice
- The victim should not attempt to remove winter clothing. This clothing might provide some buoyancy and can help to keep the victim warm.

- It is best to return to the area where the fall occurred because the ice in that area is more likely to be able to support you in getting out of the water. Ice near open water, however, is slippery and difficult to grasp.
- To get out of the water, kick as hard as possible with the legs to push yourself up and onto the ice.
- Certainly the victim's chances of survival are increased if a partner or supervisor can pull the victim to safety by using a rope or other item, such as a hockey stick, extended from a safe distance.

See chapter 16 for more information.

Treatment After Falling Through the Ice

After falling through the ice and getting back to safety successfully, the skater must work quickly to avoid or overcome the potentially devastating effects of hypothermia. The exact steps the skater takes will depend on the specific circumstances related to his or her situation, such as the following:

- Whether your entire body was immersed in the frigid water or only a certain portion, such as both feet up to the knees
- Whether you were immersed in the water for a short or a long time, and what effects the immersion had on body core temperature
- Whether you were immersed in a remote area or near immediate assistance, and how long it will take to obtain assistance, including medical assistance if necessary
- Whether you are alone or not, and the amount of additional, dry clothing and shelter that is available

Regardless of the specific details surrounding the fall through the ice and the desired response to this event, the principles for recovering from such an experience are the following:

- Get to safety as soon as possible.
- Help any other skaters who might also have fallen through the ice.

- Seek shelter and dry clothing.
- Maintain or regain normal body temperature.
- Obtain medical assistance if there is any question concerning possible injuries, such as broken limbs, head injuries, or hypothermia.

Winter Weather Concerns

The outdoor ice-skater must be concerned about winter weather, as would any outdoor enthusiast pursuing his or her sport during this time of year. Weather conditions can change rapidly; therefore, the skater must be prepared for a variety of conditions while skating. In addition to the potential for rapidly changing weather during a day of ice skating, a skater must be prepared for changes in body temperature from periods of heavy sweating, followed by periods of rapid cooling if he or she stops skating for a time. Therefore, to maintain a comfortable body temperature and control the effects of sweating followed by rapid cooling, the skater should dress in layers. By dressing in layers of clothing, the skater can take off or put on layers as the conditions demand. Especially important to the concept of dressing in layers is to have an outer shell that will break the wind. You can obtain expert advice on new and constantly changing winter clothing fabrics at any reputable winter sports store.

Skaters should always be aware of current and forecast weather conditions. In addition to being aware of and dressing for low temperatures while skating during the winter months, you must be equally concerned about dangerous windchill conditions. Dressing appropriately for extremely low windchills and properly rehydrating the body due to potentially heavy sweating caused by vigorous skating are important factors for every ice-skater. You must also be concerned with the effects the weather can have on ice, especially during the beginning and ending phases of winter when ice conditions can change rapidly from significant fluctuations in the weather, such as air temperature and rain. As always, exercise extreme caution when you are uncertain of ice conditions, particularly the thickness of ice over deep water.

Equipment

As with many recreational activities, the equipment you use in ice skating can be an important factor in having an enjoyable experience and preventing injuries. Skaters should always wear good quality ice skates that are regularly sharpened. Sharp skates allow you to turn, stop, and maneuver safely and properly. Lace skates firmly to provide adequate ankle stability but not so tightly that you diminish necessary blood circulation to the feet and ankles. Double-tie or replace exceptionally long laces with laces of the proper length so that long, loose ends do not end up under a blade and cause the skater to fall. In addition to wearing good quality, appropriately maintained skates, skaters should also wear other important equipment as needed.

Novice skaters, and often even more experienced skaters, should anticipate falling and, because of this virtual certainty, they should wear appropriate equipment to guard against injury from these falls:

- We strongly recommend *helmets*, such as ice hockey helmets or cycling helmets, for beginning skaters. Falling skaters typically strike the back of their heads on the ice; therefore, they need protection to prevent serious injury.

- Wear *gloves or mittens* to protect the hands while falling, because skaters commonly extend their hands toward the ice instinctively. Hockey gloves are beneficial because they are padded and provide additional protection.

- Skaters should *dress appropriately in layers* to prevent becoming chilled or, in even more serious situations, experiencing hypothermia. Properly cover exposed body parts, such as the face and head, in extremely cold and windy situations to prevent unnecessary heat loss and frostbite.

Other important equipment for an outdoor ice-skater, as with enthusiasts of virtually all outdoor activities, is a well-stocked first aid kit.

Appropriate items to include in the first aid kit are Band-Aids; bandages; and supplies for cuts, contusions, abrasions, sprains, strains, and even broken bones.

SUPERVISION

Someone who is able to assist in preventing injuries and to help if injuries do occur should supervise novice skaters. If a skater falls to the ice and strikes his or her head, for example, it is important that another person is there to assist appropriately. If a more serious emergency occurs, such as a skater falling through thin ice, it could be a matter of life and death that a supervisor respond immediately and appropriately.

A supervisor should try to prevent injuries by cautioning skaters to avoid collisions with other skaters and with objects, such as bushes, trees, rocks, and so on, that might be present on or near the skating surface. Generally, you should not skate alone, particularly if the ice surface is new to the skater, the ice is over deep water, or the ice thickness is unknown or greatly variable. Although it is not advisable, experienced, adult skaters will sometimes elect to skate alone if the ice surface is several inches thick, frozen evenly to a consistent thickness, and the water depth below is shallow. If these ideal conditions exist, the experienced, adult skater should be careful to inform someone exactly where he or she will be skating and when he or she expects to return. Children and inexperienced ice-skaters should never skate alone.

The supervisor should diligently inspect the ice before anyone skates on it. This inspection should ensure that the ice is thick enough for all skaters to skate on safely. It should also ensure that dangerous cracks, open holes, and other dangerous conditions do not exist. This inspection must be done thoroughly and carefully, particularly if the supervisor is not familiar with the specific piece of ice being used. The individuals in charge should supervise actively by interacting with the participants, watching for the signs and sounds of cracking ice, keeping an eye on the weather conditions, watching for potentially reckless activities, and so on.

The supervisor should also determine that the area of ice is large enough for the number of skaters to move about safely, as well as determine that the number of supervisors is adequate for the number of skaters, given the specific nature of the skaters' ages, skill, experience, familiarity with the skating surface, and so on. It is also helpful if the supervisors are certified in first aid, CPR, and basic water safety in the event that an emergency situation develops.

SELECTION AND CONDUCT OF THE ACTIVITY

Ice skating is an activity that virtually anyone should be able to learn and perform safely. Essentially, ice skating is nothing more than shifting the body's weight while the rear foot pushes off the ice to propel the skater across the ice. The critical element in synchronizing this movement is balance. Therefore, individuals who find balancing activities troublesome might expect to find ice skating challenging. However, with proper instruction and adequate practice, including feedback from a knowledgeable supervisor or instructor, most people can become successful skaters and avoid injury. In fact, practicing correct ice skating technique can prevent most potential injuries.

Basic Skating Instruction

Seaton et al. (1983) have provided clear, basic instruction to the beginning ice-skater. They indicate that proper body position in the prestarting phase of forward skating consists of the following:

- Flexed knees, with the tip of the knee just ahead of the skate.
- The feet placed slightly wider than shoulder-width apart.
- The body leaning slightly from the hips, which remain in line with the center of the skates for balance.
- Head nearly erect.

- The eyes focused on the direction of movement, but peripheral vision allowing the skater to be aware of other skaters, nearby obstacles, and so on. It is important to be completely aware of your surroundings to prevent inadvertent collisions.

In the starting action, the rear skate turns out at a 45-degree angle, as the lead skate moves slightly ahead. The rear foot then pushes against the ice with the entire blade surface, as the leg extends and the body weight shifts to the lead skate. The skater is now gliding. The shifting of the weight forward continues into the proper, forward lean (for rapid starts the lean is exaggerated toward the side of the lead foot). The arm action synchronizes with the leg movement to provide a rapid thrust of the lead arm forward and the trail arm backward. Skaters should not lean so far forward that they lose their balance, causing a fall to the ice.

The lead skate remains pointed straight toward the intended direction. It completes a short glide before the inside edge pushes hard against the ice, and the foot turns outward at a 45-degree angle for maximum thrust, as described for the rear skate in the initial phase. Forceful arm action is essential for optimum speed; control; and facility in turning, stopping, and starting. By taking short strides, skaters can avoid straightening the upper torso too rapidly in the starting action, thus impairing forward momentum and reducing speed. Short strides enable the skater to maintain control, facilitating stopping and changing directions quickly to avoid collisions.

Carefully analyze the action of the rear, or thrust, skate, because the rear skate provides the force for accelerated speed. Following the thrust, move it forward quickly and as close to the ice as possible, with a straight blade and a flexed knee. The rapid shifting of the weight of the body forward, the extension of the rear leg after the push, and the arm action provide the power for increased movement. The length of the stride and glide varies according to the speed and action desired. Shorten it in the starting phase and in turning or changing direction, and lengthen it in acquiring high speed. The synchronized lifting of the arms with each stride and redistributing weight aid both stride and glide.

© CLEO Photography

Many children love to skate, but note the loose skate laces of the girl on the right which could result in a fall.

Falling

Be careful when falling to use the fall to absorb the body's weight and momentum. Especially when falling backward, be careful not to lock the elbows. With locked elbows, you might increase the likelihood of causing compression injuries to the elbows and shoulders. In addition, when you lock the elbows, you reduce the potential absorbing action of the arms.

Stopping

Use a double-leg stop to change direction and come rapidly to a stationary position. The upper and lower torso, in conjunction with the skates, execute a rapid quarter-turn parallel to the newly desired direction. With the skates close together and the knees flexed but rigid, shift the body weight to the inside skate, permitting movement in that direction with little loss of speed if you properly execute the maneuver. Straightening the knees as you transfer the body weight backward and exert force on the inside of the skates provides the resistance to stop. We do not recommend this stop for beginners because maintaining proper balance during this rapid deceleration is vital. Further, the stopping action is produced by cutting the inside edges of the skates into the ice. Take great care when learning this skill; learn this stop first from slow speeds.

A single-leg stop is similar to a double-leg stop except that you lift the outside skate from the ice as the inside leg and skate make the stop. A quick crossover in the new direction is then permitted. The single-leg stop is safer and easier than the double-leg stop for beginners to learn. The rear leg, or drag leg, actually helps the body to balance rather than doing much stopping action.

Changing Direction

You perform a change of direction, or turning to the right or left, by rotating the upper body over the glide skate before executing a crossover step with the opposite leg. Rotate the hips and transfer the body weight to the flexed knee of the glide skate. The glide skate now thrusts forcefully off the inside edge, as the body lean increases to aid in acceleration. Again, a lifting action by the shoulders and arms increases turning proficiency and reduces ice friction.

Reversing, or transferring forward movement into a backward skating position, represents a pivot maneuver at the start of a stroke. The body executes a full turn, pivoting on either leg, as the free leg swings around in front of the body with a snap of the hips and arms. Use extreme care when learning this maneuver because the skater's balance can be hindered during this pivoting action.

Proper Skating Behavior

Skaters, like participants in most other physical activities, should avoid rowdy behavior to minimize the likelihood of causing injury to themselves and others. An unsuspecting skater could be startled and caused to fall if another skater unexpectedly bumps, pushes, or collides with him or her. Never come up behind another skater without the other person's knowledge of your presence.

As with other activities that involve the risk of collision, both individuals in a potential collision have a shared responsibility, if moving, to avoid the collision by changing directions or stopping. If only one person is moving and the other person is stationary, then the moving person should either change direction or stop to avoid a collision that could injure either party. Generally, you can reduce the potential for collisions if adequate space is available for the number of skaters participating. This is particularly important with novice skaters who might not have developed consistent body control, the ability to change direction quickly, and the ability to stop suddenly. Table 19.1 contains some basic rules to follow.

ADMINISTRATION

As with all other physical activities, you can enhance participant safety in outdoor ice skating with some basic administrative procedures.

Areas to consider include but are not limited to the following:

- Providing skaters with a safe ice skating surface that is free of hazards such as rocks, trees and limbs, and so on
- Keeping the ice as smooth as possible and plowed clear of snow
- Checking the ice surface for adequate ice thickness and ensuring skaters are not exposed to cracks and weak spots
- Providing assistance as skaters need it, such as appropriate skating instruction, adequate supervision, and so on
- Providing or obtaining necessary first aid as needed for injuries and other emergencies
- Documenting accidents to facilitate appropriate follow-up
- Keeping other records that might be required to enhance program quality, such as parental permission for minors to participate, written physical activity warnings, and so on

BIBLIOGRAPHY

Anchorage (Alaska) School District. 1987. *Elementary physical education supplemental materials, ice skating*. Anchorage, AK: Anchorage (Alaska) School District.

Minnesota Department of Natural Resources, cited in *Billings Gazette*, 12 January 1995, C1.

Seaton, D.C. 1983. *Physical education handbook*. Englewood Cliffs, NJ: Prentice Hall.

Table 19.1
GUIDELINES FOR SAFE SKATING

- ☐ Each skater should carefully watch where he or she is going.
- ☐ Get up quickly after a fall.
- ☐ Keep your hands close to your body with the fingers curled under the hands when getting up from a fall, particularly if there are other skaters in the vicinity.
- ☐ Sit down when a backward fall occurs; this keeps the head up by contracting the abdominal muscle and falling onto the buttocks.
- ☐ Always skate under control, and give beginners the right-of-way because they are not as skilled in body control.

Data from Anchorage (Alaska) School District. 1987. *Elementary physical education supplemental materials, ice skating*. Anchorage, AK: Anchorage (Alaska) School District.

Index

About the Editor

Neil J. Dougherty IV, is a professor in the Department of Exercise Science and Sport Studies at Rutgers University. A nationally recognized speaker and author on the topic of safety and liability in physical activity and sport, Dougherty has written or edited seven textbooks, including *Sport, Physical Activity, and the Law* (Human Kinetics, 1994). He also has written more than 25 journal articles and has made more than 80 national and regional presentations.

Dougherty has served as president of the School and Community Safety Society of America (SCSSA) since 1996 and has received two SCSSA awards—the Charles Peter Yost Professional Service Award (1997) and the Scholar Award (1994). He has extensive teaching experience in risk management as well as consulting experience on matters pertaining to tort liability in recreational activities.

Dougherty holds an EdD from Temple University. He and his wife, Margaret, live in Point Pleasant, New Jersey. In his spare time, he enjoys fishing, golf, and water sports.

About the Contributors

Kenneth S. "Casey" Clarke, PhD, has a long distinguished career in health and safety issues facing sports and recreational participants and program providers. In the 1960s he oversaw the American Medical Association's pioneering application of sports medicine to organized and recreational sport. In the 1970s he chaired the NCAA Committee on Competitive Safeguards and Medical Aspects of Sports and served as AAHPERD's last vice president for safety education before its reorganization. In the 1980s he helped the U.S. Olympic Committee create its sports medicine, sports science, and drug control programs. In the 1990s he joined SLE Worldwide as senior vice president of risk analysis and currently serves on the CDC/ NIH advisory body on athletic injury surveillance. He has received numerous awards for his professional contributions.

Daniel E. Della-Giustina, PhD, is a professor in the Department of Safety and Environmental Management at West Virginia University. He received his PhD in Safety, Health, and Higher Education from Michigan State University. At the American Society of Safety Engineer's Professional Development Conference in June 1995, he was presented with the Divisions' Safety Professional of the Year Award. He is also the recipient of both a Scholar Award and a Presidential Citation from the American School of Community Safety Association. He has published numerous papers, books, and periodicals on safety practices and programs, including coauthoring *Fire Safety Management Handbook, Planning for School Emergencies*, and *Teaching Safety in the Elementary School*.

Norman L. "Buddy" Gilchrest, professor of Health, Human Performance, and Recreation at Baylor University, has a passion for adventure and wilderness. He teaches adventure activities, leads workshops, and guides groups in mountaineering, backpacking, skiing, scuba diving, and bicycling. He is a frequent speaker, consultant, and author on adventure topics. He has received numerous awards, including Honor Awards from AAHPERD and AALR, and the Honor Award and David K. Brace Award from the Texas Association for Health, Physical Education, Recreation, and Dance.

Gary R. Gray, EdD, is professor and chair of the Department of Health and Physical Education, the athletic director, and director of the Employee Wellness Program at Montana State University-Billings. After teaching and coaching three years at MSU-Billings, he directed the Sport Management Program at Iowa State University from 1987 to 1994. He served as the Insurance and Risk Management chair for the National Congress of State Games for seven years and developed the risk management plan still used by the NCSG. He is former president of the Society for the Study of Legal Aspects of Sport and former editor of the *Journal of Legal Aspects of Sport*.

Susan J. Grosse is the 1997-1999 president of the American Association for Active Lifestyles and Fitness (AAALF) and the past chair of the AAALF Aquatic Council. She is currently the chair of the physical education department at the Milwaukee High School of the Arts and serves as the editor of *Aqua Notes*. She has published numerous articles and several books, including material on instructional swim, adapted aquatics, small craft water exercise, and lifeguarding.

Michael Kinziger, PhD, is an assistant professor at the University of Idaho. He has taught in the recreation program for five years and currently serves as the director of the Outdoor Recreation Leadership minor. He teaches classes covering whitewater canoeing, whitewater rafting, cross-country skiing, and backpacking. He previously taught for 11 years in the recreation program at the University of Wisconsin-LaCrosse. He and a partner have established four long-distance open boat records: St. Croix River (190 miles), Wisconsin River (445 miles), Palouse River (162 miles), and the Yellowstone River (600 miles).

Leon J. Larson, CSS/WSO, is chairman of the Safety Committee for the American Water Ski Association (AWSA). As the AWSA Waterways Education Committee chairman and AWSA Risk Management Committee member, he has worked extensively on the development of the safety program for AWSA. He also helped develop the water ski safety program for the American Camping Association. In addition to being a senior judge, senior scorer, senior driver, and a 30-year veteran competitor, he is a certified safety specialist with the World Safety Organization, and is an affiliate member of the American Society of Safety Engineers. He has authored numerous magazine articles.

Beth A. Loy, MS, is a Human Factors Consultant with the Job Accommodation Network at West Virginia University, where she specializes in providing accommodation suggestions for individuals with cumulative trauma disorders, back impairments, and other occupational injuries and disabilities. She holds an MS in Industrial and Labor Relations and is currently pursuing a doctorate in Resource Economics. She previously worked as an Engineering Technician for the National Institute for Occupational Safety and Health, and has been a speaker and presenter for various national and state organizations.

Dwaine Marten received his doctorate in Health and Safety from Indiana University, his master's degree from Southern Illinois University, and his bachelor's degree from Bemidji State University in Minnesota. He coached and taught at these universities, as well as MacMurray College, before retiring from the University of Idaho. He was the coordinator of health and safety for over 30 years, as well as a consultant on school safety and other safety issues in South America and the United States. His interests include hunting, reading, fishing, and woodworking.

Bruce E. Matthews is chief of the Information and Education Office at the Michigan Department of Natural Resources. He previously was a faculty member at the Cornell University Department of Natural Resources, where he served as director of the New York Sportfishing and Aquatic Resources Education Program. He has been a U.S. Coast Guard-licensed charter fishing boat captain and a N.Y.-licensed guide. His articles and photographs have appeared in numerous outdoor magazines.

Raymond J. Ochs is an associate professor and coordinator at the Traffic Safety Institute at Eastern Kentucky University, where he also serves as the project director for the Kentucky Motorcycle Program. He is a chief instructor-trainer for the Specialty Vehicle Institute of America's All-Terrain-Vehicle Safety Institute, and a chief instructor for the Motorcycle Safety Foundation. He has assisted these organizations in professional development and curriculum development projects and activities.

Susan Skaros is a physician assistant at Sinai Samaritan Medical Center in Milwaukee, Wisconsin. She is also an instructor-trainer in small craft safety, emergency response, and lifeguard training for the American Red Cross. She has participated in numerous wilderness canoeing and camping adventures. She has written several articles on contagion risks for activity and aquatics personnel.

Betty van der Smissen, JD, is a professor at Michigan State University and is admitted to the Michigan State Bar. She teaches both an undergraduate and a graduate course in legal aspects and is the author of a three-volume reference work titled *Legal Liability and Risk Management for Public and Private Entities*. She speaks nationwide and conducts workshops on risk management and legal liability in the fields of physical education and sport, camping and adventure activities, and parks and recreation.

Joel M. Stager, PhD, is an associate professor of Kinesiology at Indiana University. He maintains an active graduate research program in exercise physiology and is the director of the Indiana University Human Performance Laboratories. His professional interests are in the exploration of design limitations of the cardiopulmonary system during exercise. He has authored papers on the physiological effects of hypoxia, the use of acetazolamide as a ventilatory stimulant, ventilation during hypoxic exercise, and others pertaining to early physical training and growth and development.

Jeff Steffen, PhD, is currently the director of the graduate Physical Education program at the University of Wisconsin-LaCrosse. He received his doctorate from the University of Iowa and is a previous director of the outdoor physical education program at the University of Northern Colorado. He has been leading outdoor trips for 17 years for public school students and college students in adventure pursuits.

Jim Stiehl, PhD, is the director of the school of Kinesiology and Physical Education at the University of Northern Colorado. He received his doctorate in Education and his master's degree in Physical Education from UCLA, and is the recipient of a Scholar Award and a Research Writing Award from AAHPERD. Mountaineering and outdoor education are his primary interests and passions, and he has authored books and journal articles on various outdoor education topics.

David A. Tanner, MS, is completing a doctorate in Human Performance with an emphasis in pulmonary physiology at Indiana University. His master's thesis investigated high-altitude nutrition during a mountaineering expedition to Mt. McKinley, Alaska. He applied the principles discussed in this book to design the diet for the members of the expedition. He is also an experienced ultra-endurance athlete, having completed the Race Across America bike race, the Western States 100-Mile Endurance Run, the Swim Around Manhattan, and the Hawaii Ironman Triathlon.

Ann Wieser, PhD, has been the Coordinator of Aquatics Instruction at the University of North Carolina-Greensboro since 1988. She received her doctorate in Education and her master's degree in Exercise and Sport Science from UNC-Greensboro. She serves on the Aquatics Council with AAHPERD from which she received a Service Award, is a member of the National Swimming Pool Foundation, and was honored as a Red Cross Volunteer of the Year by her local chapter. Her research interests include aquatic therapy, development of aquatics professionals, and fitness aquatics.

Gary L. Wilson, EdD, received his doctorate and master's degrees in Health and Physical Education from the University of Tennessee-Knoxville. His positions and honors have included chair at The Citadel in the department of Biomechanics, Health, and Outdoor Education; vice president of the Recreation Section of AAHPERD (Southern District); Executive Board of The Cooper River Bridge Road Race; South Carolina Health Educator of the Year; and South Carolina State President of the American Lung Association. He is a PADI scuba instructor, South Carolina State Champion Bicycle Road Racer, and a veteran mountain bike racer.

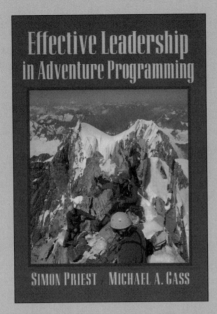
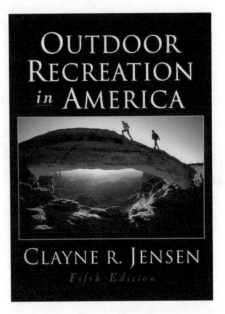